THE DEADLY CAESAR

A NOVEL OF THE LATE ROMAN EMPIRE

EMBERS OF EMPIRE VOL. V

Q. V. HUNTER

Eyes and Ears Editions
130 E. 63rd St., Suite 6F
New York, New York,
USA 10065-7334

Copyright © 2015 Q. V. Hunter

*

All rights reserved
No part of this publication may be reproduced, stored in a retrieval system, or transmitted in any form, or by any means, electronic, mechanical, photocopying, recording or otherwise, without the prior permission of the Publishers.

ISBN 978-2-9700889-8-1

This novel is entirely a work of fiction. The names, characters and incidents portrayed in it, while at times based on historical figures, are the work of the author's imagination.

Q. V. Hunter has asserted the right under the Copyright, Design and Patents Act, 1988, to be identified as the author of this work.
eyesandears.editions@gmail.com

1. Hunter, Q. V. 2. Julian the Apostate 4. Late Roman Empire 5. Historical Fiction 6. Rome 7. Late Roman Empire 8. War 9. Espionage 10. Action & Adventure 11. Historical Thriller 12. 4TH Century

TO P, 'OUR ROCK'

ALSO BY Q. V. HUNTER

The Veiled Assassin, Embers of Empire, Vol. I
Usurpers, Embers of Empire, Vol. II
The Back Gate to Hell, Embers of Empire, Vol. III
The Wolves of Ambition, Embers of Empire, Vol. IV
The Burning Stakes, Embers of Empire, Vol. VI

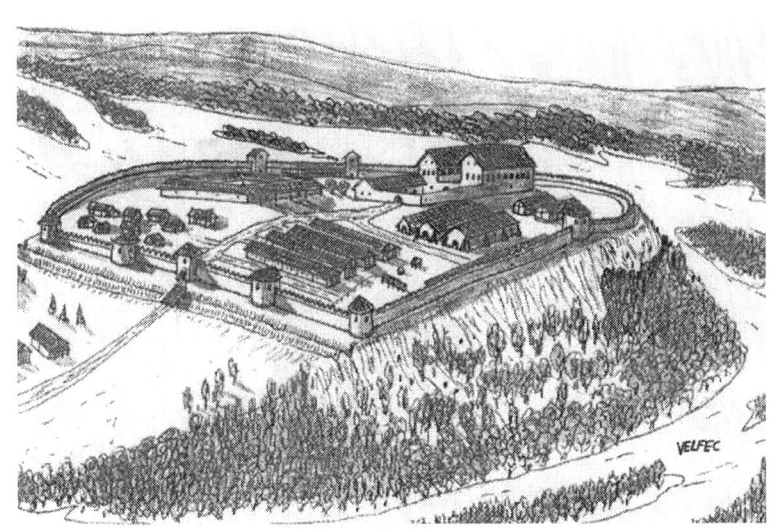

Mons Brisiacus

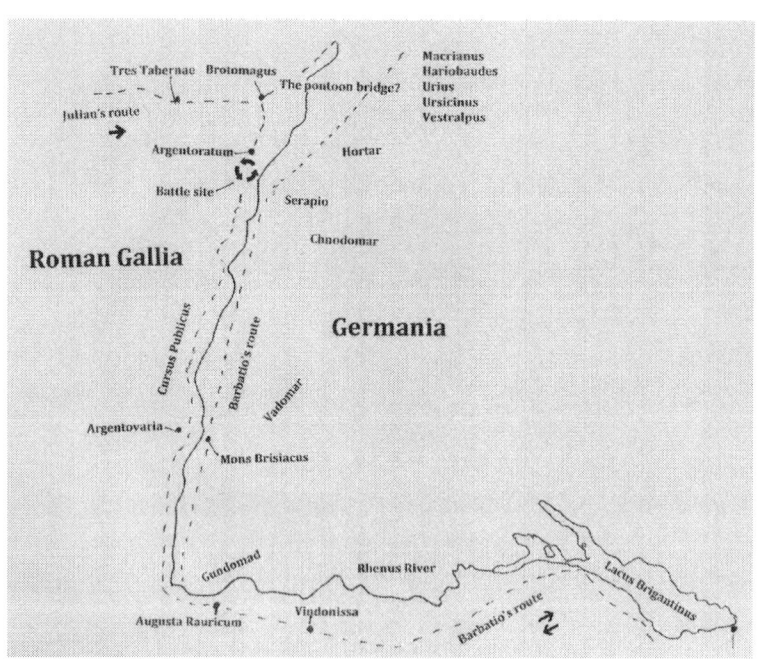

Map of the 357 Campaign

Table of Contents

Chapter 1, You All Live in Camps 1
Chapter 2, Alemanni for Beginners 13
Chapter 3, Barbarian Courage 29
Chapter 4, The Eternal Dwarfs Eternity 45
Chapter 5, An Unjust Miscarriage 57
Chapter 6, Victory Takes Wing 67
Chapter 7, Gunda's Song 83
Chapter 8, Losses at Lugdunum 99
Chapter 9, One Commander Too Many 115
Chapter 10, Gunda Makes a Choice 129
Chapter 11, The Death of a Dynasty 145
Chapter 12, The Goat of Glory 159
Chapter 13, The Search for Gunda 175
Chapter 14, Gunda's Lament 193
Chapter 15, Disaster on the Bridge 207
Chapter 16, Burning Boats 221
Chapter 17, The Broken Lyre 239
Chapter 18, Unexpected Brothers 249
Chapter 19, Blood on the Altar 263
Chapter 20, Deadly Odds 279
Chapter 21, More Than A King 295
Chapter 22, The Glint of a Blade 313
Chapter 23, *Agentes in Periculum* 327
Chapter 24, A Secret Throne 341
Historical Notes 355
Places and Glossary 361
Acknowledgements 367
About the Author 371

Chapter 1, You All Live in Camps

—Roma, April 6, 357—

'Were any of you in Senonae? Anyone captured in Senonae?'

I'd been shouting at mute prisoners all morning. My hoarse refrain produced not one single volunteer.

Hundreds of idle faces avoided our scrutiny. Ahenobarbus and I had worked our way halfway through an acre of human flotsam. We still had another half-acre to go.

'Let's give up. The sun's going down,' my fellow *agens* said through the linen muffling his nose against the stench. He took off his wool hat and wiped dusty sweat off his brow. The heat trapped by the camp's makeshift awnings and narrow granite lanes mingled with the fetid refuse under our boots. Around us hundreds of internees bickered and bartered over a rope to hang laundry, a bucket for water, or a shady spot out of the sun.

'Those women's baths need repairing,' I said.

'Some of their toilets caved in too.'

Hundreds of years ago, our Roman forefathers had built this camp outside the capital's walls as a transit point for valuable war captives. These low-roofed stone huts had received the misery of our conquering Empire in waves of different races and tongues. Caesar's prisoners, Pompey's human booty, and Aurelian's future slaves—our conquered peoples had landed here for sale or recruitment.

The camp had been built to house some two thousand detainees but I reckoned there were fewer than one thousand now. Still, it felt overcrowded and neglected. The centuries old 'facilities' were more ruins than anything else. Stone huts six feet in diameter were lined up, back-to-back, along narrow alleys. It might have been twenty years since anyone cleared the alleys of refuse or mud. Collapsed roofs and tumbling walls sat where they fell.

A woman sent up a piercing wail. I left Ahenobarbus to finish searching for a witness on that alley and trotted to a stone hut ahead and peered in. A prisoner was in the grip of childbirth, lying there in rags on a threadbare blanket laid over the broken flagstones. Half a dozen angry Alemanni women glared up at me out of the darkness and shooed me off.

Call me a soul too filled with images from old books, but this camp summoned up the Underworld of my childhood imagination. It was far too unsanitary and unsavory for the modern suburbs of Mediolanum, so maybe it suited old Roma. The new capitals enjoyed triumph and riches, but waved the human trophies of war down the road and farther south to us, to the careworn old City of Eternity that had lost so many other official privileges decades ago.

I heard Ahenobarbus' baritone echoing down the next alley, 'Anyone captured at Senonae?'

This season our imperial 'guests' were the Alpine Alemanni tribes infesting the plains of Gallia. Low walls bore baneful graffiti chiseled by despairing Gauls, Celts, Dacians, Syrians, Persians, Illyrians, Germani, Armenians—all headed for slave markets near and far. I couldn't decipher most of their exotic words or hate-filled symbols. But the fading images of lost landscapes and loved ones etched into the granite were saddening enough.

Some forlorn soul was plucking at a *lyra* but the riot of shouting men, crying infants, and scolding women snatched the fleeting melody away. Some Romans said the Alemanni could be talented musicians, but I knew of only four Alemanni worth mentioning—all army officers—Agilo, Scudilo, Hariobaudes, and Gomorarius.

These tribal people looked wilder, prouder, wilier and especially, angrier than the Franks who had produced the elegant and ambitious brethren of Silvanus, Malarichus, Bainobaudes, Laniogaisus and all the many other Franco-Roman nobles I'd known.

—THE DEADLY CAESAR—

The Alemanni seemed different somehow. They swarmed over Gallic farms and forests, but avoided our cities. It was as if they saw our protective gates and sturdy town walls as no more than coffins wrapped in nets—places that would trap their wild spirits.

'They're of no use to us.' Ahenobarbus said, rounding the last corner. 'They all claim they were seized at Brotomagus.'

'That battle was nearly a year ago.'

Ahenobarbus shrugged. 'Anyone captured before Senonae can't tell us the truth.'

For we were hunting for truth—*veritas*. We needed a witness. What had really happened during the siege of Senonae?

We knew this much:

Barbarian depredations had ravaged Gallic food supplies. Roman troops could only eat if they were dispersed across the disputed territory.

A Roman deserter had leaked to the Alemanni that Caesar Julian was wintering over in Senonae without the protection of essential troops—his *Scutarii* targeteers or the crack *Gentiles* made up of Goths, Franks, and Scythians trained into solid Roman cavalrymen.

But this was what we didn't know:

Once the barbarians had learned of Julian's vulnerability, how great was the danger? Had the *Magister Equitum*, General Marcellus, left our young Caesar to die at the hands of vicious hordes? Or was the bookish Julian inflating a minor skirmish to discredit the resented authority of his veteran commander?

General Marcellus would soon testify before the Emperor Constantius II's court that Julian was a boastful upstart of a slanderer. And the Emperor trusted the word of his fellow Pannonian.

On the other hand, the respected eunuch chamberlain Eutherius had been summoned by Constantius to report from Julian's headquarters where he kept an eye on the young Caesar. And Eutherius was an honest exception among a breed of men known more for avarice and intrigue than integrity.

In the end, Constantius trusted no one—not even his *agentes in rebus*. But he always used our *schola*, because he knew we were the only men around him not trying to usurp his power.

We *agentes* managed the vast imperial postal system and the thousands of miles of Roman road network. Less officially, the *agentes* were hated and trusted in one breath as men who controlled not only the Empire's communications but its information—intelligent information, hidden information—the knowledge that powerful men hid or twisted as it suited them.

What had happened indeed at the Siege of Senonae? Imperial family honor competed with imperial military reputation.

Careers and dynasty were at stake.

Faint lyre music popped up again, even more plaintive. The alleys closed in on me, as if I were sinking into a half-remembered dream of confusion and grief.

'Anybody taken in Senonae? I called out and felt warm spit hit my cheek as a pair of fleeting bare heels disappeared around a corner.

Ahenobarbus was right. This was no place to find ourselves—two lightly-armed *agentes*—once the dusky gloom blanketed this Hades of hopeless foreigners. Roman citizens might see us *agentes* as troublemaking busybodies and whisper behind our backs the slur *curiosi* or 'snoops' when we tried to carry out our inspections of road licenses, customs fees and provincial accounting books.

But in this place we were hate as if we were the very Romans who shunned us. Spit was nothing. In the dark, blades came out.

We should turn back for the far palisade where the army guards held informal court, chatting to the slave traders and trinket vendors who profited off these doomed people.

'Was anyone in Senonae?' I yelled one last time. There was a strange hum of murmurs competing with my shout.

'Any of you in Sen—hey—stop that!'

Near the broken stone wall of a trickling fountain, we spotted a scuffle breaking out. Jeers filled the air above a tangle of jostling rags and waving fists. Someone smashed a glass bottle.

'Leave them to it,' Ahenobarbus said, placing a restraining hand on my chest. 'Their quarrels have nothing to do with us. We're not the guards here. I'm moving on while that passage is freed up.'

He walked in the other direction, heading down an alley abandoned by gawkers drawn like flies to the fountain.

—THE DEADLY CAESAR—

I shoved myself through a wall of shoulders and stumbled into the open. A broken stone bench and the fountain perimeter made a crude gathering place. Two Alemanni fighters—their red-dyed hair coming loose in their scramble—pinned a squirming youth against the waist-high wall of the great basin. The taller attacker held the razor-sharp edges of his broken bottle under the boy's horrified nose.

I pressed the point of my *spatha* under his right armpit.

'You move, you lose the arm,' I said.

He might not understand Latin, but he understood the firm pressure of my weapon.

The victim seized his moment, jerked away, and melted into the crowd, but not before I noticed his perfect features—a long face with high cheekbones, eyes of a whitish blue, and gold hair that would never require the Alemannic warrior's clumsy dye.

The ruffian let the bottleneck shatter on the stones at our feet. From under a curtain of unwashed hair, he gauged my age, height, and strength. He glanced around the circle and saw no other Roman—only fellow prisoners as desperate as himself. He pulled back from the point of my *spatha* and signaled with his left hand. Someone from the crowd tossed him a cooking knife—short but sharp. He hunkered down now and keeping his eyes on my sword, readied himself for a duel, making circles in the air with his short blade.

Scowls from all sides had registered downright disappointment not to witness the handsome boy being disfigured or blinded. But it seemed the show wasn't over. A Roman might be murdered in the anonymity of their crowd.

The thug held only his humble knife and with my short *pugio* in my left hand and ready *spatha* in my right, I had a huge advantage. But if I weren't careful, his kitchen tool would do me in as well as any other weapon.

Alemanni fighters were full of agility but notorious for quitting a fight that didn't go their way early on. I knew he'd lose patience and lunge at me soon.

After all, he had an audience to please. I didn't.

We paced around each other for long minutes. His admirers grew restless. Growls of frustration told me my delaying tactic might pay off. I gave him the benefit of a few polite feints of my sword to bait him to go for me.

His eyes were unfocused from drink. I weaved from side to side to dizzy him. He lurched forward, his left hand fumbling for my right shoulder to pin me down for a thrust to my innards. He had a powerful grip but I twisted free and rounding behind him, got in a good stab at his middle.

Clutching his side, he tumbled back against the fountain rim and cursed. I hadn't sliced deep. He'd be fine, if any of his miserable fellows cared to clean him up.

I circled the fountain barking at the onlookers, 'Who was at Senonae? Come on, who was there?' They fled from me without a word—each greasy tunic, fur-trimmed cloak, or leather-clad leg slipping away from the dismal basin in fear.

Dispirited, I trudged off after Ahenobarbus. It wasn't like me to fail such a simple mission and I had little reason to hasten home to the Manlius townhouse on the Esquiline Hill. Our best rooms had been commandeered by the Mediolanum court to house officials on 'advance.' They came preparing for the Emperor's first-ever visit to the Eternal City in a few weeks' time.

Normally, their self-important presences would not have kept me from the comfort of a jug of wine shared with our elderly custodian Verus. Truth be told, it was something more personal that made me shun the house for the rough shelter of our *agentes* headquarters up on the Caelian Hill. My son Leo and his mother Kahina were about to decamp for the summer to holiday in the port of Ostia. Leo's Manlius inheritance provided an airy apartment, dockside offices, and a thriving warehouse business. Kahina claimed unconvincingly that the opening of the sailing and trade season demanded her supervision of our very capable managers.

For months I had hoped that Kahina and I would reunite as the lovers we'd been for a short and frantic week many years ago. That had happened long before I realized she was promised to the Commander Atticus Manlius Gregorius, my unyielding father.

Now Gregorius was dead, the civil war was over, and miraculously, some of her wits had recovered from the trauma of wartime slavery.

—THE DEADLY CAESAR—

Then a new barrier had arisen between us. I did not see how we could overcome this new obstacle.

In short, Kahina attributed her slow restoration not to the tireless nursing by Leo's nanny Lavinia, the patient good humor of Leo's teacher, or the simple healing powers of time and peace.

No, she believed that her return to modest health was a gift from Christ, her 'savior' worshipped as both god and man by our state religion, Christianity.

Worse, Kahina took it for granted we would educate nine-year-old Leo as a Christian. I respected Kahina's Numidian-born Catholic devotion. However to a Manlius like myself—even a bastard product of a Manlius officer and his Numidian seamstress slave—the idea of the heir to one of Roma's great senatorial aristocratic families kneeling to a carpenter god-man was appalling.

A girl might perhaps be raised in the state cult to hedge the family's social bets in these disputatious times, yes. But my only son, though he was never acknowledged as such, would *never* be raised a Christian.

We would raise Leo to worship the gods of his ancestors, to keep the house shrine of the protective *lares* tended, and to offer thanks for his life's successes in Roman temples—as my grandfather, the great Senator Manlius would have expected.

Leo was to be raised reading the same classics I had intoned as an obedient slave child to the blind Senator until the child knew them as well as I had. I wanted no son of mine putting "mercy" or "charity" above the rigors of bravery, duty, and discipline that built the greatest empire in the world.

If I left it to Kahina, our Leo would end up as one of those property-hoarding church sycophants clogging the *Cursus Publicus* to get to yet another vapid theological conference.

Or worse—Leo might become a penniless fool like that 'saint' Anthony who'd died in the desert only a year ago. If Kahina had her way, Leo might already be promising the Church acres of Manlius vineyards and oyster beds carefully built up by centuries of family prudence and investment. As his legal trustee, I would prevent such nonsense.

Kahina and I had parted on a sour note, so very far from the warmth I longed for. My hopes of marriage and even more children seemed like the mocking taunts of gods short of amusement up on Olympus.

I spied Ahenobarbus near the camp perimeter buying a glug of bad liquor from a needy old woman, as much from pity as thirst. Before I reached him, someone grabbed my tunic sleeve. It was the vacant-looking Apollo I'd saved from an ugly future.

He gave the flip of hand, as if to identify me for someone looking on.

'I can't help you any more. Just stay away from those men.' I made a sign that they'd slit his throat if he showed up back at the fountain, but my hand froze at my neck.

Just behind him was his mirror image in the figure of a woman around eighteen. She had the same eerie eyes tinged with frost and long tangled hair, like pale straw caked with grime. Her jaw was rounder and her nose a bit smaller. She was more mature than the boy, to judge by the drape of an unkempt *palla* pinned over a faded brown bodice of coarse cloth belted over an indigo skirt.

She clasped a lyre against her chest. Her defensive pose reminded me of soldier adjusting his breastplate. The instrument's tortoiseshell fingerboard was chipped in a few places and it was missing one of its seven strings. Her ivory *plectrum* dangled around her elbow from a frayed ribbon.

I met her narrowed gaze. I could scowl as well as she.

'Take care of this boy.' I pushed him into her sturdy figure to make my warning clear and strode away from them. Ahenobarbus hailed me to hurry with him to the camp gates for fresh air and a hot meal.

The girl ran after me, pushing other prisoners out of her way. She grasped my tunic so hard, I feared the seam would rip.

I jerked myself free. 'No money.'

Straightening her shoulders, she came nearly to my own respectable height. 'I know what happened in Senonae. Why do you ask? Will you pay me?' Her Latin was good.

'Possibly. We have a lot of questions. How many of your men laid siege? What delayed General Marcellus from relieving the town? Was it just a little skirmish? Did your side ever have a chance to capture the Caesar?'

She hesitated. Did my torrent of questions exceed her Latin skills?

I began again, more slowly. She laughed in my face. Her teeth were straight and white. Her cheeks flushed underneath the grit of camp life.

'You take me for a fool, Roman!'

'No, you might be a clever girl who can tell me what happened in Senonae. Estimate the numbers as best you can. Describe the siege carefully. I will know if you are telling the truth. Was the Caesar in danger from your brave warriors? Was he really so alone?'

'And where was General Marcellus? Who needs to know?'

'The emperor of the known world, Constantius II.'

'Ha! I know a world that isn't Roman. Let the emperor of the Roman world ask me himself.'

It had been a long day. I lost patience. 'State your price and give me answers. What were your numbers? How many days did your brothers lay siege?'

I picked out just enough coins to pay for a new *palla*. 'Here, buy a proper bath and a better covering. I'll tell the guards to release you in my custody for as long as that takes.'

'I'm not a prisoner.'

She laughed again and lolled against the wall of a hut too broken down to house anyone human.

'But you're in this camp.'

'So what is your great Eternal City but one enormous, stinking camp? One million beggars in streets full of ox shit and rubbish?'

I glanced around us at the dozens of miserable prisoners sleeping, crawling, and crouching in this abyss.

'And I suppose you are free?'

'As free as you. Maybe freer. Freedom is hard to come by.'

She flicked an insolent finger on the *biarchus* insignia attached to my tunic. 'I get in and out of here with a few bribes to the guards. I look after my brother and cousin. Hermund and Urius were captured and I followed them here. Urius caught a sickness. He needs medicine.'

'Use my coins. Now give me answers.'

'Oh, no. My price is nothing less than freedom for them and safe conduct for all three of us back to the Agri Decumantes. Hermund is in danger. Those louts were trying to disfigure him for a reason.'

'Why?'

'To "save" him,' she said with a snort. 'In their drunken goodwill, to rescue Hermund from sale to a slaver. His beauty attracts the wrong kind of buyer—or that's what our warriors back there say.'

'I can't guarantee the boys' freedom.'

'Then I won't tell you what happened in Senonae.'

She plucked at her lyre strings and hummed some song. Ahenobarbus caught up with us. I told him Gunda's offer.

'Don't believe her, Numidianus,' he said.

'I suppose she's just trying to get them out of here.'

'You can't blame her. Who wants to be stuck tending family in this dump?'

I wasn't as suspicious as Ahenobarbus, but desperation made people resort to any lie. My sympathy might blind me to her tricks.

He looked her over. 'I doubt she knows anything.'

I muttered out of her earshot. 'She insists on telling the Emperor in person.'

'A likely scene!' The *ducenarius* burst out laughing. Cheap liquor and heat had worn us down but the image of this savage girl testifying before the fastidious court of Mediolanum was comic refreshment.

We headed for the southwest gate facing the city.

'Wait,' he said, stopping short. My heart sank as I saw my superior officer rethink her offer.

Then he muttered, 'No, forget it.'

We showed our *agentes* insignia to the guards on duty and passed back out into the fresh air. We recovered our horses and rode along the Via Nomentana toward the beckoning northeast gates of Roma some miles away.

I reined in my horse. 'Wait, Ahenobarbus.'

'What is it, Numidianus? I'm hungry.'

'Before you joined me, the girl said, "And where was General Marcellus?".'

'So?'

'All I'd asked was, who was at Senonae and how many laid siege?'

'You never mentioned Marcellus?'

'Never. She raised his name.'

We turned our horses around and hurried back toward the fuggy prison camp.

'But we don't let the brother or cousin out until we've used her,' Ahenobarbus said.

'In any case, Constantius will never rate a wild Alemanna's testimony above the word of General Marcellus or the Chamberlain Eutherius.'

'No, Numidianus,' Ahenobarbus answered, 'but *Magister* Apodemius surely will.'

Chapter 2, Alemanni for Beginners

—THE PORTA COLLINA, ROMA—

Allowing only that her name was Gunda, our informer marched ahead of our plodding horses by many paces on the busy highway to the northern gates of the city. She acted keen to be seen as a free woman and not some downtrodden prisoner under the humiliating custody of two Roman *agentes*. Since escort was one of our *schola*'s regular duties, anyone might assume she was under arrest.

As the center of the known universe, the city had seen every kind of human being under the sun. Even so, other travelers gave the ragged-haired girl and her lyre poking out of its sack a wide berth. The only thing this high-stepping barbarian risked tripping over was her own astonishing *hubris*.

Ahenobarbus was too tired to argue with her, but once or twice I nudged her elbow with my boot to subdue her independent gait. With a toss of her silvery-gold mane of dirty hair, she shook me off with a sneer.

'Don't discipline me. I'm not helping *you*. I'm helping Hermund and Urius. Maybe I give you too much credit. Maybe you saved Hermund for the wrong reason. Maybe you want him for yourself.'

She kept her eyes fixed on the distant horizon where sentries passed flames from torch to torch in preparation for the night watch to come. We wanted to reach Roma before the main gates closed for the night but she refused to ride with one of us.

'Don't insult me,' I said. 'I just don't like bullies. We don't need more trouble in the holding camps. The guards already have to deal with your disease and filth.'

'It's the disease and filth you hand us. Look at that city ahead of us, your great Roma—an enormous camp of disease and filth. In the forests, by the lakes, on the high peaks, we lead a bracing, healthy life.'

She spit on my boots. They were only worn-out *calcei* with high floppy cuffs and stretched out leather laces, but it was hardly polite.

'So stay in your caves and shepherd huts. Why steal Gallia out from under honest farmers?'

'We like to eat as much as Romans. We need fields, not mountains. The Emperor gave us your fertile land. Why shouldn't we use it?'

I wouldn't argue ownership of disputed territory. 'What do you know about General Marcellus?'

'I know what I know. I will only talk to the highest officers of your empire. You are a low-ranked nobody—a softhearted *nullus* who likes little boys.'

This was rough ingratitude to someone who'd risked a knife thrust for her brother, but the cut went deeper. I was still, to my frustration, ranked only *biarchus*, upper class. Soon *Ducenarius* Ahenobarbus would be eligible to join the *principes officii*, the chiefs of staff overseeing operations and legal administration of provinces across the Empire.

Now around thirty, (an ex-slave has to guess his birth date) I felt trapped—without trust, appreciation, or any prospect of making it even to *centenarius*. I was materially comfortable as a member and trustee of the Manlius household—but I craved more from my career. Any Roman man craved glory.

And the harder I strived, the more I fell into controversy and disaster.

Gunda saw her goading had hit home. 'I suppose you rescued Hermund out of duty.'

'You'll have to talk to our *magister*. If you hold back, we'll toss you out on the streets again.'

'I will need clothes and money for the baths.'

—THE DEADLY CAESAR—

We'd promised her that much, although looking at her calloused heels in her worn-out shoes, the fraying hem of her bunchy skirt, that hand-me-down *palla*, and the clanking bag of rubbish slung across her back, I doubted any mere scrubdown would transform her into an admired asset of intelligence gathering.

While we waited for clearance at the gates—the presence of all *agentes* had to be registered under Roman law—Ahenobarbus tried his luck with Gunda. She told him she had polished her Latin during domestic service to a bishop in Augustobona Tricassium. That was a point in her favor. As a former slave in the Manlius household, I knew sharp ears and quick eyes could pick up a lot. On the other hand, I wouldn't trust any dish this girl served me without a taster at my side. Her loyalties seemed firmly attached to the snowy heights of her people.

We shouldered our way through teeming streets. Busy *tabernae* spilled their customers right into the street with the deafening cacophony of early evening. We wandered from one bathhouse to the next—Gunda between us—searching for an establishment holding women's hours.

Junia's Baths looked cheap and decent. Gunda pouted under the peeling sign painted with a sponge and *strigilis*.

'I need tip money for the attendant, Roman, or my things might be stolen. Don't think I don't know how to get decent service. I'm not one of those barefoot girls from across the river.'

I expected the Junia proprietors hadn't changed their pool water for at least a week and the scum of body oils—or worse—coated the benches and floors. Yet Gunda hesitated on the threshold of that mean establishment as if we'd dropped her stark naked on the doorstep of Trajan's Baths.

She handed me her lyre for safekeeping. The strings gave a dissonant hum as I slung it across my own back by its leather strap.

While Gunda did her ablutions, Ahenobarbus and I found a *taberna* with enough customers to attract favor but not so many we'd end up eating standing up. We rested our weary legs under a low table behind an L-shaped bar.

'How long will she take?'

Ahenobarbus scanned the day's offerings chalked up on a board. He joked, 'Judging by the dirt caked behind her ears, we have time to take the *Ad Ovo Usque Ad Mala* menu.' He ordered the All You Eat Special from the egg starter to the apple dessert and every kind of roasted meal, fish or meatball in between.

There were many things a couple of *agentes* might talk about over a jug of watered wine or refreshing *posca*, but the topic of the season was a crackdown on abuses by some of our more 'enterprising' fellow agents.

'. . . The *Magister* couldn't overlook it. Gaius Turellius had to go. In exchange for passing on the accounts, he pocketed twenty-five percent of the grain revenue taxes.'

'I thought five percent was our maximum cut.'

Ahenobarbus shook his head. 'The maximum is twelve in peaceful times. But even fifteen is outright corruption if half of northern Gallia can only farm inside their city walls for fear of raids. There's too little to go around. Turellius lost his sense of proportion. There are other ways to pad your retirement fund. Putting the whole *schola* into disrepute isn't helping any of us.'

'What will happen to him?'

'A quiet dismissal. We don't want to draw attention to our own rotten fruit. As long as Constantius finds us useful, the service is safe.'

'Let's hope this Gunda wins us some valuable points with information on Senonae.'

'It might buy a little time from *consistorium* enemies like General Arbetio and Chamberlain Eusebius. There are too many who listen to those two.'

'But a man must set aside something. What about your retirement fund?'

Ahenobarbus expected my question. 'Numidianus, I have discovered an irreproachable method of stamping coin out of thin air and straight into my little bag here.'

He patted the purse hanging off a strut of his wide belt.

'It's like minting your own money, my friend. I write references for spoiled brats applying to our training school. Rich families can be very grateful when they see their precious Romulus or Remus heading up the Caelian to enter the Castra's junior class.'

'No one's ever asked me to write a reference.'

I gulped down some wine. Other *agentes* got ahead on more than the modest tips I'd accepted throughout my ten years of service.

'Writing fancy letters for pimply puppies is easy. The problem is, the more lucrative our career is thought to be, the less attractive the types who seek enrollment.'

'I was recruited to serve the Empire, not my retirement savings.'

'Come on, you landed on both boots, didn't you? Appointed *tutor legitimus*, managing a great fortune for that rich little squib?'

It must remain a secret that the rich little squib was my own unacknowledged son, so I mopped up anchovy sauce with a piece of bread before answering: 'I wish you'd stay in the service, Ahenobarbus. The *Magister* won't live forever. You're the obvious man to take over. You were the senior *agens* in the Arelate court. Constantius trusts you. You have the service's interests at heart.'

'Not everyone would agree with you.'

'The last man to head the service is *Ducenarius* Gaudentius. He shows no respect for procedure and will step on anyone's shoulders to please the Emperor.'

'Careful, Numidianus. Gaudentius has requested transfer to the staff of the Praetorian Prefect Florentius to keep an eye on that young whelp, Julian. Paulus Catena made a mess of that assignment already. Now he's investigating some pagan oracle scandal in Alexandria.'

'Good riddance to them both.'

'Constantius hasn't made up his mind to let Gaudentius succeed Catena at Julian's headquarters.'

Ahenobarbus said no more. It was that kind of discretion that made him my candidate to succeed Apodemius at the Castra Peregrina.

We were dipping into a delicious peppered octopus stew when an over-perfumed customer tried to elbow her way past our table. Under her light brown cloak, she wore a beige wool dress woven through with soft rabbit hair yarn in a square pattern. A fortune in glass and silver beads covered the slope of her bosom. She grabbed the stool next to Ahenobarbus and, glancing with ill-disguised haughtiness at the juices dribbling down his chin, shoved him aside to grab our salt saucer.

Ahenobarbus shoved the bitch back. Only when her fingers dipped a piece of bread straight into our stew did we realize this stunning lady, her forehead festooned with curls half-hidden by a fold in her *palla* was—yes indeed—our scruffy Gunda.

'Make room for me. I'm hungry,' she said.

We two *agentes* stared at each other and then at Gunda's startling transformation. The metallic clanking in her private reticule had turned out to be a collection of gold bracelets of fine twisted bronze wire holding small blue stones. Large earrings of looped gold wire dangling glass beads set in filigreed gold hung from her earlobes.

She shifted her *palla* off her forehead to reveal rouged cheeks and lips. Discreet lines of black rendered her pale blue eyes all the more startling. Over her dress and necklace, she had fastened her cloak to both shoulders Germanic fashion with twin *fibulae* of gold bear heads connected by a triple gold chain.

'You look . . . clean,' Ahenobarbus said.

'I look like a goddess.'

She gave me a tightlipped smirk of satisfaction and swallowed a meatball whole. She pulled out a small, sharp knife with a deer horn handle to cut up an apple.

'Do you know how long this hairdo took?' She turned right and left to display an astonishing tower of golden lacquered curls and braids held in place with tiny bronze pins. The centerpiece on her crown was a gold fox pin with garnet eyes.

'Finish up,' I said, handing back her lyre. 'We have a meeting with a very powerful old man who seeks the truth. He has no interest in fancy hairdressing and doesn't like waiting.'

Gunda looked like a society whore out of Suetonius' *Lives of Famous Prostitutes*, but I had to admit—noticing all eyes were fixed on her as we made our way out of the eating-house—a gorgeous society whore.

※※※

—THE DEADLY CAESAR—

Magister Apodemius had suffered ill health for as long as I'd known him. On the very day he talent-spotted me in the study of a wealthy North African olive oil producer. I'd noticed his knobby arthritic feet cushioned in special boots. His hidden knife and wary gaze told me he was more than another aged friend borrowing books from his neighbor's library.

Like some house god whose shrine shelters the entire civilized world, Apodemius kept a flame burning in his study through the night hours. From his window, you heard the market vendors calling out their wares every morning. You saw the torches carried by the *aediles* as they patrolled the streets at dusk. On those rare occasions I'd seen Apodemius in stark daylight—like that day he rescued me from the fury of the Caesar Gallus' murderous minions—he was almost always in disguise.

I would not have staked even one day's pay on naming his exact age.

Tonight we three waited in his outer office while his deaf masseur finished kneading those swollen joints. The slave emerged at last, carrying the usual tray of half-eaten snacks that kept Apodemius' featherweight frame alive.

We ushered Gunda, bracelets tinkling away, into the familiar sanctuary. Apodemius rose from behind his desk with difficulty to greet us.

It had been many months since my duties required me to report directly to the *Magister*. His gaunt appearance shocked me. The fluffy strands of white hair that usually floated in an aureole around his high brow were matted down by unhealthy perspiration. His breath was short. He sat down as soon as possible in his favorite chair with the goatskin cushion bursting its stuffing.

Gunda startled me by passing around the long desk and taking the old man's hand in hers.

'I am honored to meet you, *Magister*.'

'Why are you here, my child?' he said.

I shot Ahenobarbus a glance before he made his excuses and left to duties elsewhere.

'Your *agentes* came to the camp where my brother Hermund and cousin Urius are held prisoner,' she stated. 'This man said they want informers. I will not tell you anything without a guarantee that both Hermund and Urius be freed in exchange for my cooperation.'

Apodemius offered Gunda a plate of forgotten custard tarts. She shook her overdressed head. 'I've been fed, thank you.'

'Who are you?'

'I am Gunda. I worked in the household of the bishop of Augustobona Tricassium.'

'Why?'

'Why?'

'Yes, why? Why were you not betrothed five or six years ago? Why are you not busy with babes at your breast? Were you taken prisoner? Sold into slavery? Were you a hostage? What brought such a proud beauty across the wide Rhenus to wait on some minor bishop?'

Gunda was silent.

'Is my Latin too fast for you, child?'

'No, *Magister*.'

Apodemius could wait the girl out. I used the awkward pause to scrutinize the huge map pinned to the cork lining the wall behind his desk. The eastern half of Gallia bristled with orange-tipped pins and encircled towns as far as thirty miles west of the Rhenus.

A single gold pin was stuck not far from Colonia Claudia Ara Agrippinensium. Caesar Julian was that gold pin. Those silver pins around the gold were the forces that answered to General Marcellus.

Gunda took a deep breath. 'I did not come here to explain myself. This man came through the camp asking about Senonae.'

'And what do you know about Senonae?'

'General Marcellus dined with the bishop during the winter quartering of your troops. I was in the room when officers told the general that the Caesar was under siege. I saw Marcellus' reaction.'

'Which was what?'

'That is for the Emperor's ears only.'

'Do you intend to accuse the *Magister Equitum* of dereliction of duty or to commend him for sound military judgment?'

—THE DEADLY CAESAR—

Gunda stiffened. 'I know which is which. I cannot trust anyone else to deliver my message to Emperor Constantius as well as myself. I do not trust any Romans.'

She shot me a look dripping with disdain.

'You are right, Gunda. And your noble birth entitles you to speak for yourself.'

Gunda drew a sharp breath.

Apodemius smiled with satisfaction. '*Biarchus* Numidianus, allow me to congratulate you on bringing me the daughter of the Alemannic high king Gundomadus and niece of the equally powerful king, his brother Vadomarius.'

Apodemius pulled himself to his feet and turned to his map.

'It is your family that commands the Agri Decumantes, here.'

He swept his hand across a triangle of territory cutting like a bent knee into the east bank of the Rhenus. This was land the Flavian emperors had conquered and Aurelian had fought to retain a hundred years ago, but Roma had finally abandoned it to Gunda's people with a series of uneasy forays and agreements.

'How did you know?'

Apodemius nodded with a shade too much satisfaction. 'My guesses are rarely wrong, my child.'

He turned to me: 'Numidianus, for all your famed powers of observation, could you not spot that a female so ready to speak her mind to Romans of any station, speaking excellent Latin, and wearing a vulgar fortune in Alemannic jewelry could not be a common Alpine goat-girl?'

Gunda bristled. 'My father Gundomad believes himself a valued ally of your Emperor. We hold a treaty signed by Constantius II himself. At his invitation, our warriors crossed the border to defeat your Usurper Magnentius.'

'And now we turn on your people to drive them back from fertile land—'

'We are betrayed by your hallowed Julian. The Franks raid Agrippina, yet you allowed the Franks to settle Toxandria. You make them soldiers—even tribunes and generals. What about us? We have no *curiales*, no governors, no scribes or *quaestores*. We have no interest in cities or towns. We do not even agree among ourselves on anything. We could not rule your Gallia from councils or churches if we tried.'

'No, you could not.' I could not resist shooting a dart back at her.

'So you treat us like dogs. From the far northwest the Burgundian tribes press in on us. Your own map up there shows it. Constantius used our people for his purposes, to break Magnentius, and now he rules unchallenged because of our help. Without honor or apology, he breaks our treaty.'

'He has broken no treaty, child.'

'Then why does he send his cousin to drive us from fields we earned in good faith?'

'Do you intend to tell Constantius of your bitterness?'

'I intend to restore his goodwill for our people with my information. The Alemanni can be just like your Frankish commanders—federates, not enemies.'

Slipping off a sandal, Apodemius began rubbing his right sole with a smelly liniment.

'It's a poor season to emulate the Franks, Gunda. Of course there are longstanding Franco-Roman families. But the Franks that leveled Agrippina to smoking ruins made a rather poor impression. They destroyed everything between that capital and Augustodunum before they were repelled by our young Julian.'

He gave her a less than benign glare. 'No, Gunda, I would not mention the Franks to the Emperor.'

'I will have my interview and your guarantee that my information will free my brother and cousin. Unlike Romans, I keep my side of a bargain.'

Apodemius took up a *stilus*, scribbled down a short message, and handed the wax tablet across his desk to me.

'I will recommend an audience for you. Let the consequences be on your well-coiffured head. Now leave us. My assistant outside will understand this message. Give it to him. He will find you a private room here in our barracks until your departure for Mediolanum. You are not to return to the prisoners' camp tonight. You are not to communicate any of our conversation to anyone.'

Gunda looked displeased. 'Urius needs medicines and they both survive on the food I smuggle in.'

'We'll see they are cared for during your absence.'

—THE DEADLY CAESAR—

Gunda didn't move. She could not summon up the words that would pin Apodemius down to a firm promise Hermund and Urius would be released. I took the tablet with one hand and her arm with the other and all but forced her into the care of the clerk working at a desk outside.

'Numidianus, stay behind for a moment.'

Not for the first time, I found myself closing the door and standing in silence, waiting for Apodemius to speak. He buried his head in his hands and for many minutes it seemed he'd forgotten I was still there. Then he gave a long sigh, broken by the cry of *aediles* outside marking the small hour of the night.

'That girl has shown remarkable courage. She could have let you two pass through the camp and out the other end.'

'I don't know what exactly what she overheard about Marcellus, but her angry comportment will warp her credibility as a witness.'

'It is anger mixed with pride. Look at the map,' he said. 'Her people have had more than three years to move westward from the Rhenus as far as here and encroach on all the great estates of Gallia, seizing and starving more than forty towns and taking their mayors and bishops captive.'

He snapped his gnarled fingers at the center of Gallia.

'As for how they've observed their side of Constantius' so-called treaty—' he shook his bony head. 'They've terrorized or destroyed the cities of Argentoratum, Brotomagus, Tabernae, Saliso, Nemetae, Vangiones, and Moguntiacum. They got as far as Augustodunum last June. When Julian's troops relieved Tricassae during the last campaign season, the poor inhabitants refused at first to open the gates to him. They were so paralyzed by Alemanni attacks, they couldn't believe the Caesar's tiny contingent was even Roman.'

'But Julian is waging war on these settlers without permission?'

'Someone has to reassert control. What else could the Emperor do? He is obsessed with Persia, but he couldn't let Alemanni ravage all the cropland in Gallia three hundred *stades* west of our border in the meantime.'

I detected an admission.

'So Constantius *did* break his treaty with them.'

'Constantius might not have done it Julian's way. He would have negotiated these settlers off Roman territory, reset the treaty terms, or bought them off. But our young Julian has taken it upon himself to cleanse the entire territory with his sword. He is filling our prison camps with Alemanni as fast as he fills his tent with volumes of Marcus Aurelius and Julius Caesar.'

'*Magister*,' I cleared my throat, 'You let that girl see your map, your papers, your entire center of operations.'

'From her travels and contacts, she could probably draw an even better map. And what is so secret about my office in the center of an imperial compound used by our service, not to mention the *frumentarii* service before us? We must forge a useful relationship with anyone offering honest information. Our fragile position is no secret to those who inquire. Every blue-faced Pict must know by now we're the least favored department in government.'

'So why did you dismiss her just now?'

'We don't wash all imperial laundry in front of strangers.'

'You mean, why is there such a command vacuum for the energetic Julian to fill?'

Apodemius heaved a sigh.

'Exactly. Where is our hero General Ursicinus? What has he been doing up there in the Lower Rhenus, letting towns and garrisons drop into barbarian hands like rotting fruit? We're not talking about challenging disciplined imperial troops here! We're talking about pushing back rivalrous little kings, warring tribes, petty raiders, rear guard ambushers, amateurish skirmishers, cattle thieves, roughnecks, and brigands—no more than that. Ursicinus should be able to roll back this wave of mayhem—treaty or no treaty.'

'Ursicinus made his name burning rebels alive in the East. Perhaps he counts the days until he returns to the command on the Persian front. And he owns valuable property in the East, property that the Lord Chamberlain Eusebius has been trying to get his hands on for years.'

'Ursicinus has weathered more than one season of sabotage from Eusebius,' said Apodemius.

'Yes, I saw his blustering defense two years ago, but you know when it comes to property, Eusebius's avarice never dies,

—THE DEADLY CAESAR—

Magister. I'm more curious as to this General Marcellus. Surely he wants to succeed.'

'Your Gunda may carry the key. I suspect that Ursicinus and Marcellus have resented Caesar Julian from the start, but whether because Julian exaggerates his minor victories at the expense of our Alemanni enemies, or because he's doing Roma's job for his superiors—that's what I can't tell.'

'For someone with no field experience, Julian's first year in the field was impressive.'

'With such bloodshed? If we can negotiate with these people tribe by tribe, we can win. But Julian's schoolboy war might provoke them to bury their rivalries and unite against us for the first time. Constantius will regret that.'

He ran his knotty fingers up bronze pins lining the eastern bank of the Rhenus.

'Here is the base, the so-called *herrschaftszentrum*, of Gundomadus, and here, that of his brother Vadomarius.

'Who are these pins?' I pointed to the bank between our garrisons in Noviomagus and Borbetomagus.

'Two more *reges*, Hortarius and Suomarius. Farther north again, ready to move across to Moguntiacum stand these kings: Urius, their own Ursicinus, Vestralpus, and finally Macrianus and Hariobaudes up here. Strung out like you see here, it's easy for our fortifications to keep them at bay.'

'Is Gunda's father a man to unite them against us?'

'No. Gundomadus sticks to his word and keeps his fighters on their side of the river. But I have worrying reports that some of the other kings are less cooperative, especially Gigas, a sort of *rex maximus*.'

'Is Gigas his real name?'

'No, it's what the Romans up there nicknamed him. His true name is Chnodomarius. He operates in the very middle of these tribes, here, facing Argentoratum. Just north, downriver, is old Mederichus and his son Serapio.'

'Serapio? Hardly a barbarian name.'

Apodemius smiled, 'Mederichus spent his youth as a Roman hostage and was greatly impressed by the cult of Serapis. Under him are more petty *reguli* ruling the *pagi* that were once Roma's, along here on the right bank. Underneath their regal class are their noblemen *optimates*, followed by warrior *armati*.'

'We are lucky Gunda's father sticks with Constantius.'

Apodemius gazed up at the forest of pins. 'I wonder what she heard at that bishop's table.'

'Well, I look forward to reading the report of her testimony,' I said with a chuckle. 'As soon as you're satisfied, I'll release her brother and cousin from the camp myself.'

I made to leave and get in a little sleep before resuming my regular duties. I was glad not to have to return to that festering camp at sunrise.

Apodemius gave that laugh I'd come to distrust.

'You're going to escort our proud Gunda to the Emperor yourself and report to me as soon as Marcellus' trial is finished.'

'But the Mediolanum court is Gaudentius' turf! You saw how he resented my actions in Agrippina while he was held in detention. You know he blames me for our failure to bring General Silvanus back alive. Shouldn't we leave Marcellus' hearing to him?'

Apodemius' voice tightened. 'She will go with you, Numidianus. Surely you noticed how our Alemanni princess insulted and dismissed you out of hand?'

'Yes, I did. Not that I care, but I'm happy to see the back of her.'

'Don't take her barbs so seriously. She'll cooperate best if you continue as her escort. She offers us a unique window into barbarian politics. It's not every day an Alemanna noblewoman walks into my study. There's much you must learn from her—why was she sent to a bishop, of all things? What are the relationships between these ruling families? How does this Chnodomarius stand among them since he led his men in victory against the Usurper's brother Decentius during the civil war? How firm is her father's alliance with us?'

'Please, *Magister*. Let Gaudentius take over. He has such a forceful personality.'

'You've demonstrated quick reflexes when something goes wrong. A fresh set of eyes may detect things in court that Gaudentius has come to take for granted.'

'Is Julian still sending his eunuch chamberlain as defender?'

'Well, yes, but as Constantius appointed Eutherius as watchdog over Julian in the first place, Eutherius is still Constantius' man.'

'Surely the Emperor can distinguish for himself between the word of a senior general and that of a mere chamberlain?'

'Not necessarily. But thanks to you, we will offer an objective witness—an Alemanna who despises us all.'

'Surely we can't trust Gunda?'

'Of course I don't trust her, Numidianus! I don't trust anyone. I just use everyone to hold this blasted empire in one piece.'

He fumbled around on his desk for fresh reports to read. It was a signal I'd come to recognize, as was the dismissive wave. 'I see the Marcellus hearing is the Ides of April. Leave by first light.'

There was nothing more for it, but to collect my travel things and hope it would all be over soon enough. I could have slipped back up the Esquiline Hill to snatch a comforting drink with Verus but I was in no mood to see our house filled with pompous time-servers sprawled around the main rooms.

I made my way to the front gates of the ancient Castra's walls, but my purpose was thwarted. The tall front door of the old Temple of Jupiter Redux stood bolted and padlocked. According to Emperor Constantius' edict of February the previous year, all pagan temples had been shuttered. The death penalty had been laid down for offering sacrifices to our gods or cultivating their images.

Of course, our Castra custodians had held out for as long as they could, just as the entire city's old families clung to Roma's traditional beliefs. But even our *schola* had capitulated at last. Finding the doors locked, I remembered why. The Emperor was arriving in Roma at the end of April. Even in our great city where the old families lit their shrines to the house gods of ancient times, we must welcome the arrival of the leader of the imperial Catholic Church.

Behind those heavy doors, I knew, stood an empty marble hall, its walls lined with plaques mounted by soldiers praying to return to their distant homes someday, or grateful for a safe return to loving arms in the Eternal City itself. The temple's floor was stained, the altar dusty, and the ashy lamps long left unlit. But during my ten years as an *agens*, I'd come here many a time to pray for those I loved. The temple's ancient echoes comforted me.

Here I'd offered my prayers for recognition that Commander Gregorius would acknowledge at last that I was his natural son. At that altar, I'd prayed for promotion from circuit rider. Prostrate on the stone, I'd begged in tears for the safe return of Kahina from brutal enslavement. Inside I'd offered fervent thanks to the gods for saving Leo from a horrendous mutilation in Antiochus. In this temple I'd prayed for friends far away and family long dead.

And the gods had answered every one of my prayers.

Was I to pray no longer as my fathers and grandfathers had? Would I never bring Leo here to offer thanks for our family's good fortune? Was he to find himself kneeling like the slave I once was to an eastern desert 'savior,' impossibly both man and god, hanging dead off a wooden cross?

I banged on the temple doors just to hear the echo inside. Of course no one opened them. I went back to the simple cell I knew so well from trainee days and this time I prayed, not to the gods, but for them.

Chapter 3, Barbarian Courage

—TO THE IMPERIAL PALACE OF MEDIOLANUM—

I faced a 'Scylla and Charybdis' dilemma—to choose one woman's insulting tongue or another's religious sermonizing. Though the sailing season had reopened and there was ready transport up to Genua, passing through Ostia risked bitter argument from Kahina in front of our boy.

Call me a coward when the future of my son was at stake. I could be bolder in any swordfight than in the delicate contest over Leo's mind and soul. Kahina's blind gratitude to her Christ stood between us like a solid stretch of Aurelian wall blocking all compromise.

The true gods had been good to us after so many bitter trials—not least in returning Kahina to home and freedom. Perhaps the Fates meant for us to be a family, perhaps not. But first Kahina had to recognize their powers. She had to abandon this misguided attempt to turn our boy into a sanctimonious priest.

I chose Gunda's barbed condescension. But the inland route north was slower. Even a fast carriage with an official *evectio* to use the *Cursus Publicus* would get us to Mediolanum in no less than week. I was relieved when she announced she could ride a horse and that her sense of urgency was even greater than mine. She worried her cousin Urius would succumb to his malady, despite many reassurances that Apodemius' man would check on them with medicines and food for both boys.

Desperate to earn their release from the foul camp, she rode off with me through the city gates wearing respectable travel dress under a solid cloak. She had combed that ridiculous hairdo into a practical style. Her gaudy jewelry was back in her rumpled sack. Her lyre lay strapped against her back in its coarse covering.

Riding at full pelt would cut our travel time down to four or five days. I would not have enjoyed the tedious journey from Roma to Mediolanum at half the speed and twice the banter. As it was, Gunda seemed disinclined to say anything at all. When I suggested we stop over at a busy *mansio* to rest for the night, she shrugged from her saddle, as if to insist that it was I who needed rest and food—certainly not the daughter of Gundomadus.

'When exactly did your father sign his treaty with the Emperor?' I asked her over our lentils and cups of *posca*.

'After our battle against Constantius in Augustodunum.'

'But you lost! The terms could not have been much to your advantage.'

'Lost the battle? Is that what the Emperor tells you Romans? Even when the terms of settlement favor us?'

She peeled away the tough end of a fig with her little deer-horn knife and sucked out the fruit's juicy flesh with relish.

'Tell me about Gigas,' I said. 'We hear he is a great leader and that we Romans should respect him.'

Perhaps such idiotic flattery might loosen her tongue.

She looked at me as if I were a gullible fool. 'Chnodomar is a bully, thanks to his height and strength. I have nothing good to say about Chnodomar.'

'I see. All the Alemanni do not bow to him as overlord?'

'After he defeated the Usurper's brother Decentius, Chnodomar placed himself above the kings of our other tribes. But not everyone approved his self-elevation. My father's people decide their own fate. We intend to live in peace with Roma.'

'How long were you in the household of the Bishop of Augustobona Tricassium?

'Almost a year.'

'Did General Marcellus visit often?'

'Yes. Why not? Winter quartering is dull for a veteran officer. The bishop offered generous fare, conversation above the local gossip, and other attractions.'

'Of which you were one?'

She shrugged, accepting the compliment as her due.

—THE DEADLY CAESAR—

'That complicates our task. General Marcellus might recognize you at the hearing. That will weaken your usefulness as a surprise witness.'

'You can expect General Marcellus to act surprised that I was so attentive to anything he said back in Tricassium.'

'Why did you live in the household of a religious politician? Surely such a situation was beneath your station?'

She tossed her head with a little too much defiance.

'My father wanted an education for me—to learn your Latin, your religion, your politics, and your music. The Franks learned long ago that success inside your borders means knowing your ways. We Alemanni will do the same.'

'You must have learned Latin very fast.'

She played with a salt dish on the table and avoided my scrutiny.

'So someday your father will marry you off to a high Roman official or military officer?'

'Why not?' She gave a slight, bemused smile.

'Why not indeed? Many Alemannic and Franco-Roman officers marry Roman women. Why not the reverse? The daughter of Gundomadus might be a credit to a Roman bridegroom.'

'You think so?' She gripped her little knife hard, turning her knuckles white. 'You don't find me too barbarian?'

'*Romanitas* comes quickly to clever outsiders.'

'And abandoned with regret by Romans who find themselves trapped on the wrong side of the border.'

'I suppose you've seen Roman prisoners in your father's stronghold?'

'Yes,' she said, scooping up the last her lentils, 'and I would prefer to live as a Roman.'

'I wish you good luck and great happiness.'

'Thank you.'

She scraped her bowl clean and tore off more bread to wipe up the last drops of *garum* seasoning. 'When you discover I am the wife of an important man, perhaps I'll put in a word for you—if all goes well for my brother and cousin, that is.'

I laughed out loud at her haughty presumption. She tried to pay for her food. Her purse was bulging with small coins. Had she sold some rich trinkets to cover this journey?

'The *schola* covers our travel costs,' I said, gently pushing back her palm offering *folles*.

'Make sure you list my costs to the very last coin,' she said. 'I won't be part of any petty thievery. I intend to deal honestly with the Emperor.'

Constantius II hardly had time to check my travel chits. Gunda's insinuation I was a petty expense account fiddler rankled. I watched her swinging hips as she sashayed toward the exit leading to the bedrooms above the dining room. In a sudden temper, I caught up with her.

'If you think so little of us Romans, why would you marry one?' I said. 'Because none of your own heroes could stomach your lip?'

She stopped with one boot on the first stair and turned a pale face to me. Without warning, she slapped me hard in front of the lingering diners behind us. I felt a trickle of blood where one of her filigreed rings had broken the skin of my stubbled cheek.

I checked an impulse to return the blow. Gunda was an official state witness. I was her escort. The *schola* had rules about abusing witnesses under escort.

But somehow that last jibe had hit a very raw nerve. I returned to the *mansio* public bar and ordered a beaker of wine. I fought off an urge to head up the stairs right after her and...? I emptied my cup and refilled it to the brim.

⚜⚜⚜

We arrived at the doors of the Mediolanum *consistorium* a few minutes after Marcellus' defense began. I would be less conspicuous that way, slipping in ahead of Gunda to lurk behind notaries and *domestici* delivering extra writing tools, cool beakers of *posca*, and cushions for the elderly members.

Only *Ducenarius* Gaudentius spotted me. His raised eyebrow said he was no happier to see me than I him. I retreated a few steps deeper into the crowd of hangers-on.

—THE DEADLY CAESAR—

Happily for me, over a hundred officials attended the audience. The eyes of my particular enemies—especially the powerful eunuch Lord Chamberlain Eusebius—focused on General Marcellus haranguing the Emperor from the center of the marble hall.

Still wearing his insignia of *Magister Equitum*, the command of the Gallic cavalries from which he was now so publicly cashiered, General Marcellus was in a floundering rage. His powerful voice, accustomed to decades of shouting orders across the battlefield, echoed hard around the marble chamber. Signals and frowns from his allies among the *consistoriani* did nothing to quiet his protest. His bellowing could be heard in the antechamber outside where Gunda sat carefully veiled in a shadowy alcove. I am sorry to say, the fancy coiffure was back.

'There was no danger to the Caesar, *Imperator*, as I have explained already twice!'

Constantius had dressed for a working day in a gold-embossed tunic shirt over deer suede leather trousers. One shoulder was swathed with a purple ceremonial cloak embroidered with golden *orbiculi* and lavish trim along the edges. He raised an eyebrow to prompt the court interrogator to prosecute harder.

'We measure the Caesar's days inside the walls of Senonae as more than thirty. If you are right and there was no danger, General, why did Caesar Julianus not repel the attackers himself?'

The quaestor's quavering, halting style aggravated the bullish military veteran into greater indignation.

'Ask the Caesar, not me!' Marcellus' great belly shook with fury.

'Was he not pressed to his limits repairing the city walls with his few troops in a race against time?'

'Exaggerations and excuses!' Marcellus shouted. 'The Senonae walls were old, yes, but they were secure.'

'Yet we read reports of our Caesar side by side with his soldiers, rebuilding ramparts with his own hands and searching the horizon night and day for the arrival of relief troops.'

'And we wonder who dictated that touching, poetic account,' the General growled.

'He sent more than one appeal for reinforcement?'

'I didn't count. Look, our Caesar is new to warfare. I knew the Alemanni besiegers were insignificant brigands. Why else did they melt away like snow after a mere month? Should I drag good soldiers from one garrisoned town through disputed territory just to comfort perfectly good troops sequestered safely inside another?'

He pulled off his dress cap of expensive felted wool and patted down coarse, thinning strands of black hair. The heft of his drooping stomach fought his wide, strutted *cingulum*. He gripped the pommel of his *spatha* to settle his temper. In his choleric state, he was more than capable of making a fateful misstep fueled by military pride and contempt for soft eunuchs and frail senators.

And misstep he did: '*Imperator*, it is my unhappy duty to inform you that your cousin Flavius Claudius Julianus aspires to nothing less than that very *cathedra* upon which you now sit. Oh, he's ready to fly high, that boy. I accuse him not only of inflating his string of little scuffles into fantastic myths of bravery. He is cheating his superiors—*Magister Peditum* General Ursicinus, myself and even you, *Imperator*, of due credit for Gallic ground regained.'

'General!' One of the *quaestores* present could not contain his shock at the accusation. 'You accuse our sovereign's cousin of treason?'

'No, no, don't put words in my mouth. Of rank amateurism. We professional soldiers have too long tolerated this "scholar's" maverick campaigns. His so-called tactics are based on nothing more than reading outdated volumes of Julius Caesar and Marcus Aurelius but I—'

The general broke off, choking on his own anger. A *domesticus* poured him a glass of watered wine, but the general flung out his arm, sending the ornate goblet of priceless blue glass shattering against the floor not far from where I sheltered behind the scribes.

'All right! Sack me. Dismiss me. Fire me. But I will have my say first. I accuse this goatish bookworm of insolence, of disobedience to your command, of—of—unfettered ambition, of disloyalty. Yes disloyalty! Disloyalty to your divine image which you placed in his care and even of treasonous plots... plots and . . . and . . . conspiracies that go undetected, against your own imperial person!'

It was a miserable, misguided gambit.

If Marcellus, Pannonian-born like the Emperor, had only held on to his decorum and kept the dignity of the court in mind, he might have recovered Constantius' trust and gotten Julian sacked from command instead. But his performance had slipped too far into Greek melodrama marred by his purple face, quivering figure, and unregulated temper.

Worse, Constantius II was very fond of his imported glassware.

Still, accusing Julian of treason might even work. General Marcellus knew as well as anyone that Constantius began and ended every day beset with a terror of treason. He'd fought a costly civil war against the 'barbarian usurper' Magnentius. He'd outfoxed the old military claimant Vetranio. He'd let thuggish rivals behead another challenger—his second cousin Netropius. He'd executed his first cousin Gallus at the first hint of independent rule. And two years ago, he'd sent General Ursicinus to Agrippina to assassinate the 'Thirty-day Emperor,' the tragically loyal Franco-Roman General Claudius Silvanus.

Was this not ample proof that teamwork was not exactly our emperor's forte?

Julian had many enemies among the *consistoriani*. At Marcellus' inflammatory blast against the Caesar, they tossed questioning glances at the Lord Chamberlain. Eusebius held more sway than any man alive over the Emperor. Already armed with vast properties and powerful contacts in the Eastern Empire, Eusebius was busy expanding his Western web of influence by befriending the rising men of the Church, synod by synod.

Some courtiers whispered with a vicious, sarcastic smirk that poor Constantius II enjoyed only 'some influence' over his rotund *praepositus cubiculi*.

We all knew the round-shouldered boy-philosopher Julian had been dispatched off to Gallia under a token escort as a mere placeholder. If he survived the Gallic wilderness, he was to be nothing more than an image-bearer, a raw youngster trailing behind senior commanders like Marcellus and Ursicinus with his cousin's purple robe draped across his arms like an acolyte at a Christian Mass.

I scrutinized the Emperor's familiar features for a clue. As usual, I could read nothing in those cow-eyes, heavy jaw, rigid posture, and granite expression.

Not a muscle in his face moved for some time. Only, by the slanting rays of midmorning I noticed how the Emperor picked nervously at some loose stitching just underneath a fold in his ornate cloak.

'We will hear any witness in the Caesar's defense,' he said.

'The Caesar was in no danger whatsoever,' the general shouted, unable to relinquish the floor.

Heavyset *domestici* moved in. General Marcellus was forced to the sidelines. There he fumed, desperate to see his career restored.

We all waited an excruciating five minutes in dead silence.

'Lord Chamberlain,' the Emperor asked at last, 'Has your brother eunuch been detained?'

'He should be here now,' Eusebius answered, repressing a twitch of his round, sweating face. He patted the soft fawn hair on his scalp as if there was nothing more he could do—though Eutherius answered to the Eusebius' *schola*.

During an interrogation of the bewildered Julian in 355 as to his relations with his doomed half-brother Caesar Gallus, I'd registered how much the head eunuch hated Julian—or rather, hated the *idea* of any Constantine who might inherit true power.

Eusebius might fear any honest man who bolstered Julian's reputation. He was as capable of political intrigue and outright crime as this eunuch Eutherius, an Armenian gelded as a boy captive, was renowned for his incorruptibility. If Julian's chamberlain had been waylaid on his way from Gallia to testify, I would bet a month's pay that the Lord Chamberlain had had a pudgy hand in it.

'We may be forced to retire the hearing for now, *Magister Memoriae*,' our teenage consul Flavius Hypatius said in a hesitant whisper to the Master of the Rolls. Aedesius, who supervised all admissions and the conduct of such hearings, nodded in agreement with the Emperor's Macedonian squirt of a brother-in-law.

—THE DEADLY CAESAR—

But just then, with a simple bow to the guards at the door, Eutherius rushed between the spectators crowding the entrance. He prostrated himself at full length before the Emperor's lambskin boots and knelt to give his account. He was a very tall, elongated, smooth-faced figure. Even below the imperial dais, he looked the seated Constantius straight in the eyes.

I had seen Eutherius only once before, when he'd served in the court in Treverorum as chamberlain to the dissolute Constans, the doomed younger brother of the Emperor.

How long ago the events of 351 seemed now! Had the predatory and irresponsible Constans listened to half of Eutherius' wise counsel, he would not have ended up cornered and desperate in a barren corner of Hispania, lunging at the back of my cohort commander Gaiso and running into my loyal blade instead.

Lurking in obscurity behind the scribes, I expected Eutherius would not recognize in my weathered face that eager Numidian cadet rider of Treverorum with his newly issued *petanus*. Considering the guilty taint that stuck to me in Treverorum after Constans' ugly death, I was grateful for today's obscurity. Eutherius might not have approved of his dissolute master, but he was always an obedient servant of the Constantine family.

'You attended Caesar Flavius Claudius Julianus in Senonae?' our second consul asked. This was Flavius Eusebius, the Emperor's other brother-in-law.

'Yes. I accompanied the Caesar from his investiture here to his rendezvous with the main army and throughout his subsequent campaigns. Following his successful drive against the Alemanni last summer, I attended the Caesar on his northern initiative to drive the Frankish invaders out of Agrippina and back across the Rhenus.'

'And what happened at the end of last summer?'

'Barbarian depredations had reduced the countryside so near to famine, the Caesar was compelled to disperse his troops to various towns that could feed them over the winter.'

'Even the Scutarii and Gentiles? The Caesar dismissed his crack Palatine troops from his personal bodyguard? That was his decision and no other commander's?'

'Yes. So they would not starve, Consul. The Caesar retained only a skeleton force with him in Senonae but did not advertise this fact.'

'Yet the Alemanni knew his Palatine troops had left him in an undefended town behind walls of rubble. How?' the consul asked.

'A Roman deserter, *Domine*—as we learned later from the barbarians captured in retreat.'

'And how would you describe the siege itself, *Praepositus* Eutherius? Was it a trivial standoff? A cheap show of force? A mere test of wills? Or did the siege pose a deadly threat to the life of your Caesar?'

'It was no trivial matter,' Eutherius stated in a ringing voice. 'As the numbers of Alemanni grew outside the walls, the Caesar slept only a few hours a night, constantly manning the ramparts, directing, rebuilding the fortifications night and day, eating the scraps on which every man and woman in Senonae subsisted, drinking the foulest dregs with the rest of us, and letting no soldier falter in his vigilance.'

'Empty panegyrics!' General Marcellus yelled from his corner.

The consul went on, 'How many barbarians were there?'

'Who can numerate such a rabble of fiends, Consul? I am sure their superior forces would have overrun and destroyed Senonae were it not for the determined action of the Caesar. The situation was desperate. The citizens were panicked. We sent word to the next cantonment where we understood General Marcellus was encamped, but no relief ever came.'

'Because no relief was needed, I tell you!' Marcellus exploded. 'This so-called man is lying on behalf of that arrogant upstart who is bulking up his staff and battle record to win the soldiers to his pennant for the day he takes over your throne, *Imperator!*'

Two guards now grabbed General Marcellus by both his burly arms. He saw with dismay that the poised, articulate eunuch was more persuasive. For all Marcellus' disruption, Eutherius never raised his voice or deigned to glance in the angry veteran's direction.

—THE DEADLY CAESAR—

'*Imperator*, I say before all observers here that I stake my post and my life on the loyalty of the Caesar to this throne.'

Yes, Eutherius was a Constantine man to the last.

The tightlipped Emperor sat weighing the straightforward testimony of a mere eunuch against that of a decorated commander.

'One more witness is listed, *Imperator*,' Aedesius murmured. 'A barbarian who can testify to the comportment of General Marcellus during the siege.'

'A barbarian? Who registered such a person?'

'The *Schola* of the *Agentes in Rebus, Imperator*, but I think we have no time for this person.'

'You are right, *Magister*. We have heard enough. We must deliberate.'

I was sorry to see Constantius write off Gunda so easily. It meant her brother and cousin stayed in detention, if they even survived. But the Emperor had heard enough. That was that. Every Roman knew better than to interfere with the rigid Eastern protocol of a Constantinian court.

'You must hear me, Romans. Your general is lying.'

Every Roman knew not to interfere—but then Gunda was no Roman.

She spoke from just inside the great doors. Shoving her way past the guards, she strode right up to the dais. She kissed the imperial hem and only then sank to her knees, arranging her *palla* hem around herself.

'I am your last witness, Flavius Julius Constantius Augustus, and once you have heard me, you need deliberate no longer.'

The *domestici* were already pulling her away, but Constantius stilled them with a raised palm.

'I am Gunda, *Imperator*. I attended the table of the Bishop of Augustobona Tricassium where I resided under the direction of my Alemannus father, King Gundomad. I speak of that same valiant Gundomad, brother of Vadomar, whom you fought three years ago outside Augustodunum and with whom you settled a treaty of peace.'

The tip of a smile almost broke on Constantius' lips. Perhaps he recognized something of the formidable father in this bold barbarian in a preposterous hairdo.

'We are listening.'

'General Marcellus was the bishop's guest many times, including the night he received the first summons to rescue Senonae.'

Constantius lifted on eyebrow to signal his attention.

'Do you recognize the General today?'

Gunda rose to her feet. Gathering her cloak around her with theatrical gravity, she toured the great hall in slow paces, stretching the suspense until she reached the scowling Marcellus.

'This is the man, of course,' she said. 'The Caesar's message was read out loud by one of his adjutants. The General listened to it. Then he laughed. He continued to eat his second course. The Bishop asked him how soon he needed to depart for Senonae.'

'What was General Marcellus' answer?' Consul Flavius Eusebius asked.

'He shook with amusement. He told the Bishop, "I may leave for Senonae, but only when it's obviously too late".'

'A foul barbarian lie!' Marcellus broke free from constraint and made for the girl. She foiled his anger by prostrating herself again, only inches from Constantius' spotless boots.

I could not believe what I saw next. From deep in the folds of her cloak, Gunda was drawing out her clever, sharp knife. Amid general laughter at Marcellus' thwarted outburst, I had only seconds to react.

I flung myself across the empty marble space to prostrate myself on top of her. The audience assumed I was protecting a state witness from harm. But I was protecting Constantius. I was pressing down and holding her treacherous right hand grasping the weapon before anyone—especially the Emperor—had detected the threat.

Marcellus reared back in frustration. Turning on his heels, he stormed out of the chamber.

Gunda had come to assassinate Constantius! All her testimony, her deal with Apodemius, her show of loyalty—it was all a means to wreak revenge for the broken guarantees on which her father staked his reputation.

Lying full on her panting torso, I was twisting her wrist inward until the point of her knife pressed into her own groin.

—THE DEADLY CAESAR—

'*Biarchus* Numidianus, we take it you are the escort responsible for the welfare of this witness?'

'Indeed, *Imperator*,' I answered, forcing Gunda's fingers to drop the knife back into the heavy cloth.

'We thank your *schola*, once again, for your initiative and intelligent service,' he said. He rose to his feet, trailing the *consistoriani* after him out the great doors. Dozens of notaries and scribes emptied the echoing chamber.

I gave Gunda's wrist one last merciless wrench and lifted her to her feet.

I gave a collegial nod to the departing Gaudentius. As Gunda wrestled to free herself from my grasp, I informed him I would be returning her to Roma without delay.

'Please pass on my congratulations to the *Magister*, Numidianus,' Gaudentius said. 'His witness provided the court with quite a surprise.'

I accepted his grudging compliment.

'Didn't she,' I answered, secreting her knife inside my tunic. 'Didn't she indeed.'

⚵⚵⚵

I returned Gunda bound in ropes back to the Castra. She took her new status as a genuine prisoner with perverse delight and pride, though this time her bed was far less comfortable and her freedom of movement curtailed.

Once my prisoner was installed, I raced to report to Apodemius how our *schola* has come within a blade's width of political annihilation for escorting an assassin straight to the Emperor's dais.

I found Apodemius in the middle of a conference. Some dozen men stood or sat crushed into his modest office. Some wore the insignia of *ducenarii* while others were dressed incognito, with so sign of belonging to our *schola* whatsoever. I recognized a few faces, graven and careworn.

These were some of the most senior *agentes* of our Empire whom mid-ranked *agentes* saw very little of in the normal course of duty. Their various styles of dress, complexions of all colors and seasons, and matted northern furs or ornate Eastern finery—these clues said that an important discussion had sped them here.

I had to be brief, even when reporting an assassin.

'. . . So Marcellus stays in disgrace and Caesar Julian won. But what do I do with her now? To prosecute her is to leak to our enemies how close the Emperor came to lying in a pool of his own blood—thanks to us.'

The *Magister* sighed. 'The Emperor is making his first visit to our Eternal city, the heart of the Empire, the soul of our great civilization, and the epicenter of power and peace. Our Alemanna hostage will have to cool off in her cell at the back of the Castra.'

'But was everything she said a lie?'

'No, Numidianus, I don't think so.'

He shot an apologetic glance at his patient audience. 'The daughter of Gundomadus *Rex* entertained a bold plan. The rival Alemanni tribes accuse Gundomadus of toadying too low to the Empire. She has tried to kill Constantius to win her father more respect. I warned you to be on the alert, Numidianus. And so you were. Well done.'

Dumbstruck, I stared at Apodemius. Surely he was not going to leave it at that?

'You can go now, Numidianus. No harm done.'

'No harm—?'

'Numidianus, perhaps your North African bloodline, as Romanized as it is, blinds you to the harsh fact that the lovely Gunda is nothing more than a *barbarian female*—uneducated, emotional, violent, and uncivilized. A wild, futile gesture should be no surprise. It lies in her nature.'

'Agreed, but—'

'—That said, there might be more to this Gunda than appears. We must discover all her hidden talents. But please, not now, not now.'

These senior officers had more pressing decisions to deliberate. Even I belonged to an intelligence and surveillance team preparing for the Emperor's arrival. Thanks to the race to Mediolanum and back, I'd missed one or two deadlines already.

Back in my own small work corner, I lit a pair of oil lamps and buried myself in routine reports until, exhausted and sandy-eyed, I surrendered to a nap on my narrow bed.

—THE DEADLY CAESAR—

The nights were growing warmer. I dozed badly and dreamt I heard faint strumming on a lyre filtering through the night hum of the massive city surrounding the Caelian Hill.

Dawn broke over the eastern walls too soon. The worn paved courtyard of the Castra lay dead silent, except for a mewling cat and the Castra slaves preparing the usual light breakfast.

I pushed the clinging lyre melody out of my foggy mind and headed across the courtyard for some curd cheese and honey.

At least I'd finished with that Senonae mission and the Hadean inhabitants of the prisoners' camp. I'd found a witness as ordered, but had had enough of Senonae, General Marcellus, and insolent Alemanni. If anyone was going to unearth more of Gunda's 'hidden talents,' from this point on, they could count me out.

Chapter 4, The Eternal Dwarfs

Eternity

—ROMA, MAY, 357—

If the historian Herodian once quipped, 'Roma is wherever the Emperor is,' my grandfather certainly disagreed. As far as Senator Manlius was concerned, the Empire's heart was in Roma, nowhere else, and a heart never budges from where the gods put it. The Emperor's big visit was a bid to reconcile his Christian regime with Roma's proud pagan aristocracy. Two hearts as one, as it were.

The great city's feelings were still raw at losing its position as the pinnacle of the world. By the time Diocletian came to our city to celebrate twenty years as emperor, Mediolanum was the main capital of the West.

Diocletian's tour was hardly a success. He complained that the Romans acted too 'familiar.' We didn't treat him like a monarch—just a ruler. He fled town thirteen days before he was due to appear before the Senate, where my grandfather waited to oversee the Emperor's consular ceremony with all the pomp and protocol handed down since Augustus.

As a young slave and unacknowledged bastard of the Numidian seamstress in the Manlius' servants' quarters, I'd often heard the blind and ailing Senator Manlius disgorge his anger at his treatment by Diocletian. The Senator had been a renowned speaker. All his life he'd prepared for the day when his soaring rhetoric would fill the ears of a seated sovereign facing him on the benches.

Instead, no emperor ever heard his eloquence. Snubbing Roman political society was bad enough. Snubbing my grandfather was far, far, worse.

Because it wasn't just a question of geography, it was a matter of tyranny over the elected voices of the Empire's representatives, he argued. To move imperial rule to Mediolanum, Treverorum, Antiochia, Nicomedia, or any other modern city meant you could flaunt indifference to Roman Senate approval and just lay down laws 'drawn up by a club of your cronies and sycophants.'

The more I saw of the *consistorium* advising Constantius, the more I recognized the truth of the Senator's outrage.

The dear old man ended up murdered in his study on the Esquiline Hill while defending his beloved Plutarch and Cicero from thugs and felons in a rampage against 'the old guard.'

Now Constantius II had deigned to cast a glance at the old crib of Republican values. The occasion of his visit was the Vicennalia celebrating his twenty years in office, timed a week after the city's official birthday.

Like some North African society lady or Eastern bishop armed with the latest guidebook, Constantius had requested a tour of all the sights. In a too-obvious dynastic display, the Emperor's wife Eusebia and his sister, the *Augusta* Helena would come too. His entire court, hundreds of ladies' maids, eunuch and attendants, notaries, and scribes would be hustling behind on his heels, recording each compliment or request and driving our city fathers mad with imperial whims.

The Vicennalia posed an unprecedented security nightmare for our *schola*, responsible for all roads and official escort duties. Roma was home to all peoples, nations, races, faiths, and political views, a volatile brew of opinions and passions coursing up and down our narrow streets from the slums of the Subura to the palatial homes on the garden hillsides—*all unpoliced.*

To hear it from Roma's Urban Prefect, Orfitus, a vast network of enemies skulked behind every column and peered over every rooftop on Constantius' proposed route. Apodemius had worked tirelessly with the *aediles* and the imperial advance party from Mediolanum to design an itinerary that would protect the Emperor from incident . . . or any more Gundas.

—THE DEADLY CAESAR—

Thus, *ducenarii* from across the Empire had been summoned to a late night meeting to pinpoint potential personalities, factions, or tribes that might use the Emperor's visit to their own fevered ends. If our officers also seized the opportunity to discuss rising corruption among our ranks or mounting political opposition to our *schola*'s powers, it would surprise no man there.

A few days later, I attended the first general Vicennalia briefing.

The gymnasium exercise floor was lined with stools. Our long-retired Escort Trainer, Publius, had been seconded from his comfy suburban villa to brief the younger ranks of *agentes* on the Emperor's *adventus* and to assign our various details.

Long before my day, Castra cadets had nicknamed Publius 'the Pompous Pigeon.' The finicky officer loved arrest protocol the way other men loved fine wines, rare orchids, or clever mosaic work. As a junior rider, I'd nearly flunked his labyrinthine course in Arrest, Charge, Detention, and Escort-into-Exile Procedures:

'... *Never forget to use the correct address, Clarissimus or Spectabilus, Matrona, or Domina—whatever the case may require, when relieving your charge of his or her stolen goods, incriminating documents, poisons or concealed weapons. Cause no injury while attaching shackles or ropes ... Ladies in particular appreciate discretion during examination of their reticulae. ... One doesn't simply dump their intimate items and cosmetics onto the floor. No, no, no. Search their private things out of sight of detainees but make sure the lady is well-bound or chained while you are distracted...*'

This morning an enormous painted illustration of the streets of Roma hung on a rod suspended from the glass dome. Constantius' destinations of special security concern were circled in bright purple paint. Publius armed himself with a pointer at the end of which he'd secured a clay figure of the 'Lord of the World and Our Eternity.'

Wiggling his emperor-on-a-stick, the retired Escort Master traced Constantius' progression starting forty miles from the city walls along the Aemilian Way and then along the Flaminian Way toward our gates.

I closed my eyes. This promised to be a very tedious morning.

I woke up from a doze right about when our clay sovereign reached the waiting Roman delegation. He would board an open vehicle stuck with gold and gems and streaming banners of silk *dracones*.

'... consisting of the first carriage for the Emperor, *draco* and spear carriers, personal bodyguards, followed by the second carriage for his immediate family members, guarded by masked ceremonial *clibinarii*, then a half dozen carriages for his *consistorium*, then the carriages carrying the heads of the palace and notary departments. So we insert our Roman municipal high officers here—can you there see from the back? Oh, lovely...'

Someone elbowed me to stop snoring. I straightened up as the clay puppet reached the Rostra to address the Senate, (how Senator Manlius would have relished that!) and then totted off to the equestrian games...

'At which point, *agentes*, your security headaches will ease, given the direct passage from the Palace to the imperial box... just remember, nothing must go wrong.'

Publius wiped off his sweating brow with a soft towel.

I'd seen far too much of our short, rigid-faced, suspicious Emperor to share Publius' excitement.

Constantius had favored me during his wavering deliberations with sensitive missions under the direction of Apodemius, but by now he'd earned my private contempt. The Emperor surrounded himself with intrigants, bottom-lickers, and played-out seat warmers. In any given week such 'advisers' took Constantius' authority lightly and instead cast glances at Lord Chamberlain Eusebius to one side or General Arbetio for their instruction.

Constantius was no coward. Nor was he dissolute, self-absorbed, or downright stupid. But he was better at waging civil war than defending us against the Persians. While he would be basking in our Roman spring, listening to the roar of the crowd and bestowing his unsmiling attention on a jaded city, our military reports promised that the Suebi would be raiding Raetia and the Quadi Valeria. A vicious wave of Sarmatians was laying waste to Roman holdings in Upper Moesia and Lower Pannonia. The Franks were consolidating their hold around Agrippina yet again.

—THE DEADLY CAESAR—

Yes, the Empire still held but the *Imperator* took more credit than he deserved.

Nevertheless, for one month, he would be Roma's guest. Just as Publius promised, the imperturbable, stocky sovereign passed along our designated route over the heads of thousands screaming, '*Auguste, Auguste!*' He acted the part of an imperturbable god. He never nodded or jerked, even when the wheel of his vehicle jolted or swerved. He never spit or wiped his face in the dust.

He never once moved his hands.

The only time he budged during that tedious *adventus* procession was for vanity, not acclaim. When his carriage trundled in its glittery state under a lofty arch, he bent down as if he were far taller than he was.

Prefect Orfitus managed the crowds well. Not under his watch was the population of Roma going to embarrass itself with vulgarity or over-familiarity as they had with Diocletian. During those first equestrian games, I was impressed to see Constantius didn't cut them off once he'd had enough. He let the contests go on and on until the revels were genuinely over.

'Perhaps Roma and the Constantines will make friends after all,' I said to Ahenobarbus at the end of the first week.

※※※

It was only on the third week of Constantius' visit that things went very wrong—but wrong where the poor old Pompous Pigeon's planners could never have guessed.

To my private glee, 'Our Eternity' declared himself overwhelmed by the scale and beauty of my beloved city. All the sights I'd long taken for granted as a little boy running errands up and down the Esquiline Hill for the Manlius household dazzled his lackluster eyes. Constantius could not remain expressionless when his father's own triumphal arch was pointed out to him as he surveyed Roma from the heights of the various seven hills.

He toured the Pantheon and gazed up at the glass 'eye' shining its rays down from the rotunda roof. As the sun moved across the heavens, the ray rested in turn on blue and yellow rectangular alcoves set in its curving walls, each recess housing a statue of a Roman hero. The Prefect Orbitus had built special scaffolding so the Emperor could mount, from one platform to the next, the side of its vaulted roof.

He viewed the marble faces of his illustrious predecessors, nose-to-stony-nose.

Constantius didn't flag a jot. The imperial cortege led military officers and palatine officials from the gigantic Temple of Venus and Roma to the Forum of Peace, then the Theatre of Pompey and the Odeum. He gasped at Vespasian's enormous amphitheater buttressed by gargantuan Tiburtine stone, and finally, at the Stadium of Domitian.

His party staggered on to Trajan's public baths south of the Oppian Hill. Circling the baths' gardens, Constantius declared there was no hope he could ever dream of creating something as wonderful.

Under my breath I agreed. I happened to be within earshot because, in rotation with two well-favored wrestling champions, I served to pad out the *Imperatrix*'s entourage of useless eunuchs and powdered ladies.

Constantius said he would limit himself to replicating the marble horse on which the statue of Trajan rode above our heads. His royal Persian lackey, the exiled Prince Ormisda, scoffed at even that. But then no one confused the insults of the laconic Ormisda with treasonous *lèse-majesté*.

'But it is all marvelous, Prince. We had no idea, did we? Here in Roma we could live in repose, peace, and safety.'

The Emperor turned to Eusebia. 'Fame usual exaggerates things. For once, Fame has proven herself inept—or spiteful. In describing Roma, Fame has been too stingy.'

Even discounted as political flattery, the Emperor's quip sent the Pompous Pigeon into a near-swoon of gratification.

With Augustan professionalism, Eusebia's caramel-brown Macedonian eyes caressed Constantius for his childlike delight at so much excessive fanfare and protocol. Her husband so rarely expressed . . . anything.

I admired Eusebia's steady grace through each day of touring and dining followed by another and yet another. The Empress was used to luxurious privacy unknown to ordinary mortals. This tour promised her nothing but site after site peopled by unfamiliar sycophants, with no hope of relief or retreat.

Yet the Empress' charm never faltered. She soothed her husband's tensions with her honeyed calm. Still childless and therefore hardly more secure in her marital bed than Constantius was on his throne, Eusebia hid her insecurities well.

We crisscrossed the city in carefully orchestrated groups of guests, guards, and worst of all, gaggles of Roman officials angling for a minute or two with 'Our Eternity.'

At one point, I found myself walking next to the Persian claimant before he boarded his vehicle.

'May I ask what you think of our city, Prince Ormidsa?'

The exiled Persian glanced at me with quick black eyes. 'I take comfort in this fact alone, *Agens*—that I've had learned in one week that even in Roma, men are mortal.'

Indeed, this endless display of prostration and submission, not to mention the expense and waste, sickened any honest Roman.

It must have been around the tenth day of these 'festivities' that the day-tripping concluded with a laborious climb up the insalubrious *Rupes Tarpeia* or 'Hundred Steps Stairs.' This was a sharp promontory jutting off the southern summit of the Capitoline Hill overlooking the Forum.

An octogenarian historian droned out the story of the cliff to hundreds of us positioned along the edge some eighty feet high. Everyone was groaning for lunch, but there was still a great deal of history to come. Sadly, none of it was appetizing.

Our Republican fathers had used this dangerous precipice as an execution site. Murderers, traitors, perjurers, and larcenous slaves—if convicted by the *quaestores parricidii*—were flung from this cliff to their deaths.

Severely disabled citizens suffered the same fate. Our ancestors had thought such unfortunates cursed by the gods. In this respect, I suppose, Christian compassion marked an improvement in our Roman traditions—but perhaps it was just my years as a slave that distorted my sympathies unduly.

Eusebia's usual smile faded. Her eyes, dilated with Egyptian kohl, widened even more than usual. She stared over the

Emperor's gilded shoulder armor at something just behind my right shoulder.

I moved back two paces and turned in time to look in the same direction, but saw no immediate threat. I saw only *Augusta* Helena turning fish-belly pale under her floating azure silk veil.

The Caesar's wife had always struck me as a wilting branch of the Constantine family tree. Cheated of her family's more ruthless fiber, she steeped herself in suffocating Christian devotion and whimpered no complaints at forced marriage to her bookworm cousin Julian.

A greenish cluster of sweat beads broke out on her unlined forehead, even though a cooling breeze swept over the summit.

All these tales of pitiless death were upsetting delicate Helena. She swayed and then, righting herself on an attendant's arm, gathered up her thin spring cloak and layers of skirts. She murmured some excuse and backed into the shaded porticoes of the Temple of Jupiter Optimus Maximus.

I glanced back a minute later. She'd gone, vanished down the rear of the hill with her own ladies—all summoned south with her from the Caesar's headquarters in northern Gallia. Moments later, her string of curtained litters headed back toward the imperial palace.

The holiday mood vanished. Many had remarked that under her excessive, drifting garments, the Caesar's wife might be pregnant. Was it not tactless to drag Helena up these heights to listen to tales of deformed newborns dashed to their deaths below?

For the first time in the tour, the Empress herself now begged fatigue.

Constantius looked more annoyed at missing out on further acclamation than worried about his sister's fainting spell. But he allowed that it was time for the next official lunch. He was looking forward to an afternoon tour of the Aqua Claudia with an engineer's briefing on the vast urban water delivery system.

Ducenarius Gaudentius appeared at my elbow, his rough features under that shaven head shining with self-importance.

'Follow the Empress back to her quarters. When you're relieved from duty, report to the Castra for further instructions.'

—THE DEADLY CAESAR—

He dashed after the Emperor and *consistoriani* for lunch and the aqueduct show.

For the first time in the Vicennalia, I found myself the senior *agens* responsible for a part of the imperial delegation.

It took me some fifteen minutes to catch up with the two imperial women and their train of ladies. Their passage through the teeming city had been cut clear for them by heralds and guards but I could only resort to the myriad shortcuts I'd known since childhood, trotting around clogged markets, fountains, and crowded watering holes, sprinting along back alleys and neighborhood gardens to arrive, breathless, at the grand walled edifice overlooking the Circus Maximus.

My insignia got me through the sprawling government compound and as far as the inner gardens approaching the residential perimeter. I could not help but notice as I passed along the walkways and fountains that large parts of the Palace were going to seed.

No wonder the Constantines preferred their modern capitals.

I presented my credentials to the imperial *domestici* guarding the imperial bedroom suites. I wasn't intending to hang around—just to ascertain exactly what or whom the ladies needed before Constantius returned from his sewage class and the imperial delegations were reunited.

'You can't go farther than this corridor, *Biarchus*,' a *protector domestici* told me. 'The household has summoned a doctor.'

'The air on the cliff was fresh. Surely the *Augusta* wasn't that sickened? Was there some incident on the ride back?'

'Nothing I heard.' He shrugged. The whims and frailties of any woman—even an *augusta*—were of little importance to him.

'Anyway, where was the doctor? Wasn't he on duty?'

'They don't want the palace doctor.'

'Who do they want?'

'Some Roman in town who studied medicine with a quack named Theopolis.'

'You mean Theophilus, the Ethiopian.'

'Do I?' The guard's stomach growled. He, too, was waiting for lunch.

The Ethiopian philosopher's high standing with the Empress as a healer and religious man was well known to our *schola*. But

Theophilus was far away, sent by the Emperor himself on a mission to Arabia.

'Let me through. I have to report back to the Emperor's party by mid-afternoon.'

It was a bluff but I gave him my full name, stressing the Manlius, which carried echoes of authority, and pointed to my insignia again. With exaggerated reluctance blended with equal parts suspicion and peckishness, he stood aside.

'If you're not back in ten minutes, I'll send someone to arrest you,' he called.

I raced along the echoing corridor because the sharp shrieks of women matched by low moans and wails of horror bounced off the polished surface leading to the women's quarters.

Two sinuous eunuchs hurried toward me. The beardless officials scuttled along, hunched over a crimson linen bundle.

'Stop!'

As their gilt-trimmed slippers skimmed the shining marble, they dodged my scrutiny.

I drew my *spatha*. They halted, their strange burden only inches from my gleaming blade. The taller one clenched his package tighter to his midriff and avoided my eyes.

Through the aroma of sticky, sweet bath oil, a warm animal smell wafted past my nostrils. I had stumbled on some unspeakable slaughter.

'What in Hades is going on in there?' I brandished my insignia and pressed my weapon against the breast of the shorter one. They both recoiled.

'Well?'

Their tongues froze to the roof of their mouths. Their feet stood rooted. You would think I was the Gorgon's head turning them to stone. The taller of the two turned the color of bad wine. I reached out my left hand to unwrap his foul-smelling package, but his companion's wild eyes warned me away from some gruesome omen.

'There's some illegal pagan ritual going on here, some sacrifice proscribed by law, isn't there? Speak up. You're secreting a slaughtered animal out of here.'

Hidden pagan sacrifice was a dark secret among Roma's old families who clung to traditional beliefs in the face of the state

Christian cult. Still, an animal sacrifice was hardly likely to be performed inside the Imperial Palace—not in the bosom of the Empire's leading Arian Christian family.

Surely I'd trapped the two courtiers in some foul and dangerous secret because they dropped to their robed knees and began to weep in a disgusting, furtive way. At that, my gorge rose. I respected our ancient gods, but I wasn't superstitious.

The metallic odor of bluish blood oozing between their trembling white fingers mixed with nervous sweat. The gold-hemmed linen had once been bleached ivory, judging from patches unstained by its sinister contents.

'Are you hiding a pagan priest in the residential wing? Speak up. You know what's legal and illegal. Who's responsible for this ritual?'

At that, the shorter one wailed in a high-pitched voice even creepier than women's sobs coming out from behind the closed, heavy doors beyond.

I lost all patience with this caterwauling. Twisting open the sodden linen I stared down at a thing both grotesque and animal, but almost human. Its miniscule fingers curled into tiny fists scarcely bigger than two olives. It had a heavy, swollen head like a bloody fruit, but a body that looked like a fish without scales.

It was a horror. I threw the linen covering back over it and, fighting down convulsions, I waved them on their miserable task.

It did not do to vomit at the sight of a dead thing like that, especially knowing that—had its luck held—it would have ruled the entire known world.

Chapter 5, An Unjust Miscarriage

—THE CASTRA PEREGRINA, MAY, 357—

What had *Augusta* Helena eaten? What had she drunk? Had she fallen, stumbled, tripped, or slipped?

How hot were her baths? How cold?

While the imperial family grieved, *Ducenarius* Gaudentius and his inquisitors wended their way through the bowels of the Imperial Palace. As the long evening turned into the first hour of the morning, they interrogated dozens of witnesses, from the bewildered palace doctor and the weeping ladies of Helena's suite, to cooks, servers, and even slaves with barely one name to their credit.

The Caesar's wife was bathed, medicated, and removed to a place of absolute quiet and privacy, a secret chamber even more sequestered than the women's quarters. Helena would be attending no more rich banquets or tedious lectures during this state visit.

We heard that Gaudentius would return to the Castra at dawn to file his report. In the meantime, I joined the other *agentes* working imperial tour duty in Apodemius' office for a briefing on possible changes to the Emperor's schedule.

'Gaudentius will learn nothing, nothing at all,' Apodemius said.

'Do you know something more, *Magister*?' Ahenobarbus looked worried that Apodemius was about to explain the mysteries of female miscarriage to his audience of somber-faced men.

'No. I know far, far too little,' Apodemius said.

He turned his back on us and fed morsels of flatbread to a cage full of cherished mice standing on a small table in the corner of his office. These *apodemi* were his private mascots, a conceit owing to the similarity between his name and theirs. From his secluded desk, they skittered and squeaked their accompaniment to each day's survey of the tragedies of empire.

The *Magister* also employed these rodents as 'tasters.' At least once in my presence, poisoned fruit intended for him killed the beloved doyenne of the cage, Clarissa. Tonight the survivors of such trials scampered around his fingers for crumbs.

I was junior to most of the men there, but I had been an eyewitness to Helena's misfortune.

'The Tarpeian Cliff was the last place I would take a pregnant visitor hoping to deliver a normal child. The stories of freakish births and infanticide must have upset the *Augusta*. Or she has suffered an accident of Fate.'

Apodemius didn't look up from his mice. 'Numidianus, the *Augusta* is a mature woman of education, commonsense, and placid temperament. As a devout and unimaginative Christian, she's immune to the whims of pagan gods punishing innocent newborns and their mothers.'

'But I saw her face, *Magister*, her expression was unsettled—'

'And whether the old gods are toying with the *Augusta* or not, our *schola* must leave such religious questions at the door of our shuttered temple,' Apodemius said. He turned back to face us all across his desk.

'No, my fellow *agentes*, we should suspect a foul and *human* deed. That's our job.'

'Who would want to harm her *fetus*?' Ahenobarbus asked for all of us. 'If anything, our imperial family is fatally short of heirs.'

He earned a rueful chuckle from some of the younger men at the back of the claustrophobic room. Our Emperor's first wife, the daughter of his half-uncle Julius Constantius and therefore a half-sister of Caesar Julian, had died in 352. The beautiful Empress Eusebia was still barren. According to Gaudentius, she experimented with one risky fertility treatment after another to consolidate her position as the Emperor's consort.

Having murdered most of his male relatives to secure the Empire for his brothers and himself, Constantius now faced an irony worthy of ancient Greek tragedies. The imperial family needed an heir as soon as possible.

—THE DEADLY CAESAR—

Apodemius tapped a crippled forefinger on some vellum documents. 'I had the palace doctor's scribe send me a copy of Helena's medical notes this afternoon.'

'A slim dossier,' observed Eino, seconded from the teaching staff for the imperial visit. He was a wise and gentle teacher, our resident expert on eunuchs—their society, variety, and history. I had taken his course before a mission to Antiochia, an Eastern capital utterly ruled by the Lord Chamberlain Eusebius' castrated minions. Eino was here tonight in case Gaudentius' questioning pointed to any eunuch mischief down in the sprawling palace.

'That is our problem.' Apodemius scanned our weary faces. 'There is nothing to know about the spotless Helena. She has no vices, few friends, and fewer enemies. She has no history of ill health or even common female complaints. With wide hips, an exemplary diet, and virtuous character, why should she not bear a healthy child?'

'It happened to my Dorinda for no good reason,' said a deeply tanned and prosperous-looking customs inspector. He'd recently transferred up from Hispania where vast estates manned by thousands of slaves produced food for the Roman markets. Surely like so many *agentes* auditing customs fees, he greased the wheels for himself as well as the producers. 'This *biarchus* fellow is right. If this wasn't due to something said on the cliff, it must be simple bad luck. It can happen to any woman once. Dorinda has given me three strapping boys since.'

'Except that it isn't the first such loss for our poor *Augusta*,' Apodemius murmured.

A respectful stillness masked our general surprise.

The *Magister* continued:

'What I am about to confide, fellow *agentes*, you will treat as of the utmost secrecy, not even to be discussed among yourselves outside this room. Many months ago, a senior guard at the Caesar's quarters in northern Gallia sent this. He has long been an asset to our flow of information. Forgive me if I do not reveal his name.'

Apodemius reached for a ragged-looking document and ran his finger along the lines.

'The pertinent paragraph is . . . *in addition, I take this opportunity to blah blah blah,* here it is, *the Augusta Helena was a* week ago delivered of a healthy baby son. But before the joyous announcement could be made or the imperial heir even swaddled, the infant began to fail. Before one circle of the sun was completed, he perished. My wife made discreet inquires over the following day among all the Augusta's ladies in attendance. They were suspiciously and uniformly silent.

I suspected that the child had been born defective in some way. Such bad luck would cast an ominous judgment over the new Caesar's victories in the field and endanger his reputation among the more susceptible troops. Only yesterday, I found a slave who dared to confide the following explanation. Nota bene, I have been unable to find any responsible citizen to corroborate her tale.

This slave told me the newborn was not defective. Knowing the slave was hardly old enough to bear a child herself and too young to have seen many births, I questioned her on this very thoroughly. The boy was perfect in facial appearance, lusty in voice, clear-eyed, and able-limbed. He bled to death because his umbilical cord had been severed fatally close to his entrails.'

Apodemius turned the page over and took a breath before continuing:

'After the birth, the attending surgeon left an experienced Gallo-Roman midwife in attendance. She struggled to close the newborn's gaping aperture with bandaging, but to no avail. The hemorrhaging was unstoppable. This young slave assisted in the midwife's tireless efforts by providing swabs and boiling water, hour upon hour, but—'

Apodemius laid the document aside and rubbed his bleary eyes.

'My fellows, the rest is just unnecessary female anatomical detail and the disposal of the imperial newborn's corpse. The most useful point remaining is that the midwife was blamed, of course, as within hours of the delivery, the incompetent surgeon had vanished.'

'It's not surprising he fled. The fury of Constantius can be terrible,' Ahenobarbus said. 'How could they have been forced, even in wartime Gallia, to call in such a quack?'

'Why does no one know any of this?' I asked.

'The Empire has waited too long for Constantius to produce an heir. The Emperor thought it wisest to say nothing. The

—THE DEADLY CAESAR—

Empress Eusebia sent packages of restorative medicines, recipes for poultices, copies of prayers, *et cetera, et cetera*. Eusebia's concern was palpable in every report I received.'

Apodemius paused. 'Call me a hardened cynic, but I began to wonder if Eusebia's attention wasn't a shade *excessive*.'

A few members in the audience leaned back on their stools as if a cold shadow passed over us. It might have been only a gust of moist, night air rising off the flowing Tiberis, climbing up our walls and in through Apodemius' open window.

'That was kind of the Empress,' one *centenarius* said at last. 'She has always had the interests of Julian at heart, more than anyone else in that family.'

'Certainly she has promoted Julian's interests above the interests of all others competing for the Emperor's favor,' Apodemius said, 'excepting of course, her own.'

On that unsettling note, we adjourned to our duties. In my case, it was with eyes and heart weighed down by a strange doubt that the world was, at least in certain ways, not at all as I had understood it only hours before.

☧☧☧

In the flurry of the Vicennalia celebrations, I'd forgotten our promise to look after Gunda's relatives. I requested a change in my Vicennalia shift and borrowed a state mount for the ride back to the prison camp to check on Hermund and Urius.

I had suffered one strange and fleeting sense of having been in that camp before. In the concentration of our search for a witness, I'd brushed it aside. Now as I came closer and closer to those crumbling walls, I knew I *had* been there before.

With my mother.

I recalled the day we were to be delivered to the central Roman slave market behind the Basilica Julica. My mother had combed her hair and wore a wide smile, as if we were attending a village festival in our native Numidian hills. No doubt she had been told to bathe and arrange her clothing as best she could. She was now a slave, property to be traded with or without her little boy.

That day had risen warm and clear, like this early summer day. We'd hurried out those same camp gates behind the trader. He'd driven us in a wooden cart to the city gates and then we continued on foot through the crowds and mounted the steps up on to the slave vendor's stand. Our feet were whitened with chalk and small placards hung around our necks.

She held me so tightly by the hand that morning that my arm lost all feeling. I had started to cry, not only because she was hurting me, but because she'd forced me to leave behind a little boat I'd fashioned from a piece of leather. She had scolded me for fighting with a playmate who had grabbed my craft as it floated in a wooden pail right next to that now-derelict central fountain.

'Stop crying. You'll have many fine toys from now on,' she said. She must have known somehow we were to be sold to her long-lost lover, my father, Commander Atticus Manlius Gregorius. A second later, she spotted him. That was when I caught my first sight of the tall and hardened soldier, a handsome man willing to pay anything the flesh monger demanded. I looked up into the sun through the thin palla shading my mother's eyes brimming over with tears of joy.

I had no idea who this man was or why he let the slaver drive such a swift, hard bargain. He wore a Pannonian cap over thick medium-brown hair. His military tunic was of spotless ivory wool, decorated with thick gold and silver orbiculi around its knee-length hem. He carried only a smart, decorative dagger to make his way through the streets followed by a sprightly *dispensator* named Verus on his heels, soon with his two human purchases in tow.

Those were my mother's last minutes of pure happiness. Within hours her soaring hopes had crashed as hard as Icarus on his melting wax wings. She found herself relegated to the back rooms of the Manlius townhouse on the Esquiline Hill, no longer the Commander's North African mistress, but a forgotten slave mending the rich clothing of his beloved, ailing wife, the Lady Laetitia.

But I was not forgotten at all.

I was worked hard, educated, tested and occasionally indulged.

After all, I was his Numidian bastard.

—THE DEADLY CAESAR—

I arrived at those same southern-facing gates, gained entry, and got directions. Apodemius had ordered the two Alemannic boys transferred to a quiet corner out of the central maze of alleys and huts at the northeast corner of the camp, close to the rear gates. They were safer here from tribal bullies—well-meaning or otherwise. But when I bent low to enter their stinking stone hut, the sight of Urius' white face shocked me.

'He's worse?' I asked my sweating escort.

'A fever, bad chills. Maybe the summer pest's coming early,' said the swarthy guard with the Greek-tinged accent of Sicilia.

This rotting camp was no more than a holding center for war's debris, including those too wretched to be nursed.

'You can't afford a breakout of fever here. These people may look like cast-offs but they're valuable state property.'

'I reckon,' said the guard, indifferent to others' profits. 'Some *tiro* from your outfit brought him honeysuckle medicine and a tonic for his headaches.'

I ducked back inside the hut and almost gagged on the acrid aroma of vomit and diarrhea. Hermund was laying wet rags on his cousin's forehead.

'You speak Latin like your sister?'

Hermund panicked at the sight of my Vicennalia trappings, more suitable for trailing around imperial tourists than tending outcasts.

'Of course. Back off,' he said. If he'd been allowed a weapon, it would have been pointed straight at me. Seeing me feeling my way through the squalid darkness, he tossed one arm over his cousin's chest to protect him. He primed one leg to kick me away just in case, but not because he feared I might catch the fever, too. He thought I'd come to toss the dying boy into the Tiberis.

Urius fought for every shallow breath. He would never leave this hut alive. It was a matter of hours.

I knew little about diseases, but years of serving as a *volo* slave attached the Commander Gregorius had given me ample time to learn the precautions of proper army encampments. A source of fresh water, clean air flow, and sewage trenches a safe distance from the tents—everything this hellhole lacked—came before the palisade was even staked in.

'Here, I've brought you food and drink.'

I dropped my package of dried fruits, ham, and cheese on the ground and tossed him a small corked wine beaker slung on a string. I kicked it closer to where they huddled in the sick man's foulness.

'And here's a potion. Kills the joint aches and headaches.'

He recognized the food, but distrusted the tonic. It was too tiny a dose to be of much use, but the Castra clinic eked vials out to *agentes* for free only as needed.

Hermund nodded. Perhaps he now recognized me as the man who had rescued him in the brawl. He grabbed at the food before anyone else in the camp could rob them.

The guard shone a faint torch into the darkness. 'You all right back there, *Biarchus*? I wouldn't stay one minute longer than I had to.'

His flame lit up Hermund's eyes, bright with the possible beginnings of fever.

I went back outside. 'I'll be back in a day or two to check on them. We're holding his sister up at the Castra. As soon as the other one dies, send me a message. We'll have to protect the survivor once he's alone. If he's got fever, he'll be better off up on the hill.'

'He'll be sold or sent to fight the Persians, either way,' the Sicilian said.

'Not yet. He's a state hostage. He might just find himself heading back home, if he's lucky.'

I pushed my way through begging prisoners and petty thieves ducking and dodging to get a grab at my *pugio* or coin purse. As I rounded into the main open area around the derelict fountain, I didn't like what I saw; a slave trader bickering with an army recruiter over three young men hardly older than Hermund. The handsomest of the boys—though it was hard to tell under the sweat stains and long filthy hair—was pushed into the trader's happy possession. The other two were shunted back into the sullen horde.

The slave trader leered with satisfaction. He passed the captive over to an ugly giant—Armenian by the look of his fancy-trimmed barbarian dress—who roped the boy's wrists together and started off toward the front entrance of the camp. Armenians were castrators, beyond the interference of Roman law once they got slaves beyond imperial borders.

The trader hadn't finished his day's shopping. He headed toward the back of the camp and the rear entrance where, if the odor of fever and refuse didn't deter him, he might get tipped off to poor Hermund.

I ran ahead of the trader, straight back into the polluted hut.

'You're coming with me,' I said, leaning through the doorframe. Hermund saw that I had indeed come for someone—but not Urius.

He pulled back against the wall, ready to fight me off. The hut's other 'residents' had fled long ago. I had at least the space to draw my sword. I pressed it against the boy's throat covered in golden-reddish down. He tried to fight me off by kicking, and rolling out of reach. I pinned down his shoulder with my boot. I was ready to pinion his pretty head against the wooden beam bracing the tumbledown stone wall behind him.

There was a horrible gurgle a few feet from where we struggled.

Hermund forgot me. With his free hand he clutched for his cousin's shoulders and I lifted my boot. He bent over to cover Urius' corpse and choked back a sob.

Urius released a sickening gush of body fluids. A rivulet of vomit trickled across his lips as his eyes rolled back into his head. Hermund screamed for help, knowing there was none to come. He started babbling in guttural Alemannic. For all he knew, he'd lost his sister and now his cousin—all the companions he had left in this festering camp of brutish raiders who'd laid siege to a Caesar and failed.

I lifted Hermund by his filthy fur collar. Yanking him up off the corpse, I dragged him through the low door and past the horrified inmates of the clogged alley. I pulled him, still weeping and cursing, past nervous prisoners too cowed to try and save him, all the way to the rear guard station.

Borrowing a pair of rusty shackles too large for his boyish wrists, I produced my insignia and cleared us both through the back gates.

Hermund was too shocked by Urius' death to struggle any longer. By the time I got the boy all the way around the fetid ditches of the camp, avoiding pools of stagnant water flecked with mosquitoes dancing in the dusk, I realized he'd abandoned his youthful bravado.

He wasn't much of an Alemannic prince, more a limp and hopeless child. I pulled him up onto the back of my horse without resistance.

I saw no point in explaining anything to him in Latin since his command of the language sounded far less fluent than his sister's. The relief on his face when he saw Gunda alive at the Castra would be worth the cost to me of the baths we both needed—immediately.

Chapter 6, Victory Takes Wing

—THE CASTRA PEREGRINA, MAY 26, 357—

Until Helena's miscarriage, Constantius had enjoyed a flawless state visit. Now the Emperor wished to memorialize his gratitude to Roma. But what do you give the city that has everything?

After many consultations with Roman engineers and sculptors he abandoned his grandiose plan to duplicate Trajan's colossal equestrian statue. Time and talent, it seems, runs shorter in our hectic times. You could see the relief on the urban planners' faces as they left the imperial suite after the third and last meeting.

That still left the Emperor's courtiers losing sleep. The Emperor must leave his mark, but original construction entailed supervision and responsibility. None of his advisers wanted to stay behind. The court's pressing business—not to mention all those rich opportunities and promotions—would leave Roma with the Emperor.

Still, Constantius II needed to make *some* impressive gesture to awe us denizens of the old capital as his imperial circus headed out the gates.

He needed something colossal—but off-the-shelf. The solution was a ready-made obelisk.

The first obelisks came down to us from a remote Egyptian age, before the average man could read anything but illustrations of imperial greatness or mystic wonder.

I'd spent my childhood in the shadows of two extraordinary columns dragged to Roma centuries ago by Octavian Augustus, the greatest of all emperors. Constantius' flatterers dinned into his ears that what Octavian could do, surely he could repeat. Happily for our ruler, there was a spare obelisk handy. His father Constantine had thought it would look better towering above his new imperial capital, Constantinopolis. The mammoth granite monument, one hundred and fifteen feet high, had been uprooted from its pedestal and floated as far as Alexandria, but then the old Constantine had died.

And there it still rested.

The order now went down to Egypt. Before too long, if everything went well and the gods gave Roman delivery ships fair winds, this fabulous needle of ego would be docking three miles down the Tiberis from our city walls, dragged through the Ostian Gate and the Piscina Publica, and deposited in the Circus Maximus.

With this flurry of planning, the Vicennalia struck its closing note.

But no, the Emperor did one more thing before departure. As far as I am concerned, one hundred Egyptian obelisks will never heal the wound he inflicted on our great city's heart that last week in May.

Long after the entire Castra had retired, a sentry woke me in my modest cell.

'Your old *dispensator* is pounding on the gates. He says it can't wait.'

Verus' bent silhouette appeared in the shadowed doorframe, pushing aside the weary watchman. The old man trembled with anger.

'Marcus, you got to stop these fanatics! You got to stop them somehow. I been listening to their planning and plotting for days. I can't stand it.'

'They're leaving in two days. They paid up their rent, didn't they?'

Given the status of our tenants, the modest fee had been more a point of principle than profit.

'This ain't nothing about rents, Marcus!'

I'd been deep in sleep but here he was, sitting on the edge of my narrow bed, practically on top of my bare chest. I smelled wine on his breath and the warm odor of his stained leather tunic.

'Verus, what are you doing here? What time is it?'

'It's time to get off your backside and stop this band of religious loonies from destroying the last of Roma, that's what time it is!'

I pushed him aside and splashed water on my face. He was agitated enough to pour the whole basin over me if I didn't show some sign of life.

'Light the lamp, will you?' I pulled on my tunic and tried to wake myself up. He'd broken into a deep, dreamless repose, the kind of rest I'd needed for weeks.

'There ain't no time for combing your hair, son! You've got to stop these vandals before it's too late.'

'Hush, Verus! You'll wake up the entire Castra. What can't wait until morning?'

He was already hustling me out of my room, forcing me down the narrow corridors toward the open court surrounding the main buildings.

A few torches lit the grand and eerie space, emptied at this hour of busy *agentes*, trainers, clerks, and slaves. I turned him around by his scrawny old shoulders to peer by moonlight into his distraught face.

'What is it? Where are we going?'

'To that *magister* of yours, that Apo-what's-his-face. If anybody can stop 'em, it's that one. Ain't he a *clarissimus*? Ain't he got the Emperor's ear?'

'I can't do that. Stop *what*?'

Verus shook his head with impatience and started off for the gates. 'Oh, I'll show you. We're too late already. Hurry up, or it'll be gone.'

I trotted after his wiry legs down the slope northwestwards, along the Via Tusculana toward the lower districts, housing the crowded apartments below. Even there, everything was quiet.

'We're too late, Marcus! But it's us that'll pay, I warn you! It's Roma that's going to pay the price! The city will fall and they'll lay the blame on guys like you and me. You'll see what those bastards are up to!'

I could have caught up with the old man, pinned him to the paving stones, and halted all this nonsense, but I'd never seen him like this. He was moving on those bandy legs like a bolt from Jupiter. He'd infected me with his panic. Kahina and Leo were safe in Ostia, so what would turn Verus into this frenzied Mercury?

A journey that might have taken twice as long during the busy hours of the day was nothing at this hour. Only the heavy cargo, forbidden from blocking the streets during daytime, trundled past unimpeded, delivering fresh fish, vegetables, and meat to the markets before sunrise.

We stuck to narrower pathways, overshadowed by ramshackle apartment houses tottering on unsteady beams. We dodged pools of sewage and rubbish until we passed the great amphitheater. Breathless, we emerged into the district of the imperial *fora*, one walled square after another, the echoing leavings of the greatest of our emperors.

I was hungry and sleepy, but most of all, riled.

'Verus,' I panted, but the old man was fired by some superhuman determination. He had crouched low to lead me through the street between the Temple of the Vesta and the Temple of Castor and Pollux. Their hallowed porticoes anchored the southeast corner of the oldest forum, the original forum, and the *greatest* forum of the Empire.

Standing in the moody darkness were all the other celebrated buildings stretching out on either side of this venerable space—the Temples of Concord and Vespasian and the Porticus of the Dei Consentes to the west, the Temples of Vesta and the Regia just on our right, and facing us, the Basilica Aemilia stretching its long facade down the northern side of the Forum.

Verus clenched my arm, pointing with his other trembling hand across the shadows to the Curia Julia—the Senate building tucked behind the far end of the Aemilia.

How many dawn mornings had I made this same journey as a child, running pell-mell behind the Senator in his full toga and cloak? My little arms strained not to drop my burden of office—his reference *codices* and written scrolls for another day of debate.

How many times had I nibbled at his midday-snack behind his back, as he raised his arms in full rhetorical flight? Crouching now in the dark, I could imagine the Senator again, gesturing with pride to the altar that stood at the end of the long Senate chamber, overlooked by the benign and confident gold statue of the Goddess Victory.

—THE DEADLY CAESAR—

Worn out by reading to him all his spare hours, I was indifferent to the diatribes the Senator intoned day in and day out, but I knew that small building was the heart of Roma's democracy and power and that the Altar of Victory guaranteed nothing would change.

Octavian Augustus set up the altar in 29 BC to commemorate the defeat of Antony and Cleopatra at the Battle of Actium. The statue itself was even older, captured in 272 BC during the Pyrrhic War. She stood perched on a globe, held a palm branch in her left hand, and extended a laurel wreath with her right.

Perhaps I would have taken more interest in our trips to the Senate building if the Senator had said just once, 'This is important. My words here matter. You are my only grandson, you fig-tree-climbing little bastard. On your shoulders I rest all my hopes.'

But he never said it. He was always holding out for the legitimate heir to come. And thanks to Kahina, he did. My own Leo arrived, the Senator's great-grandson. The Manlius heir who could inherit the family's great treasure and reputation had appeared, by an accident of love, legitimacy, and supreme discretion.

As for our senators now, they only drew ridicule from the modern imperial capitals. Our Senate was an impotent club of nostalgic blowhards, the empty mouthpieces of a discarded city.

It had been years since I'd spent more than a few minutes cutting through this hallowed space. What active *agens* had business in the crumbling old Forum? Yet tonight here I was sitting on the cold stone next to a near-hysterical family retainer.

'Listen!' Verus rose on his toes and snuck around the corner of the Temple of Castor. I followed him up the steep steps. From behind its columns, we saw thirty infantrymen march into the Forum and surround the Senate. Within five minutes, an unbreakable palisade of spears pierced the pre-dawn gloom. Who were these soldiers? Why were they carrying no standards or pennants?

'We're too late.' Verus fell to his knees and put his head in his hands.

'No, come on.' I pulled him back to his feet and we retreated and ran westwards, behind the courts, the Basilica Julia to the Temple of Saturn housing the state treasury.

The troops were moving in from the west, between the Porticus Deorum Consentium and the Temple of Concordia.

We inched forward and crouched behind a wide column fronting the Temple of Saturn. Now we could see straight across the Rostrum in time to watch a large ox wagon drawn by four massive beasts pull up in front of the Curia.

I saw no reason to hide any longer if this was a standard maintenance operation. Verus yanked me back out of sight.

'It's treason,' he warned. 'I heard them planning it, night after night.'

'What is it they're—?' I started to inch closer.

'Stay out of sight,' Verus said. 'You can't trust none of 'em.'

The first pinkish-gray light in the eastern sky sifted through the blackness covering the roofs and columns. The soldiers' torches waving in the night cut through wisps of mist rolling in off the river. The statues of the great and the dead were resuming their bright colors for the new day.

The secret work sped up. We heard pounding inside the Curia with hammers wrapped in thick cloth. Officers gave muffled orders for more ropes. Stone ground against stone.

The wall of soldiers stepped aside for the ox wagon and closed ranks again. Soldiers lifted a pallet off the wagon bed and carried it into the Curia. The soldiers became less stealthy as dawn's fingers revealed their task.

To the sound of a command, half the soldiers were ordered inside the Curia. Verus and I heard more orders from inside— coordinated, rhythmic and to our ears, criminal. I was now certain enough of their foul crime to bolt forward in protest.

Verus grabbed my boot and held me fast with all his strength.

'You want to get yourself run through?' he hissed.

Horrified, I watched the soldiers emerge from the Curia in two lines. The city's guardian muse, the Statue of Victory, lay on the long pallet, her head buried in a pile of blankets and her pointed wingtips catching the first glints of sunlight.

—THE DEADLY CAESAR—

'They're getting away with it.' Verus' bony chest heaved up and down from distress and disbelief.

I left Verus to climb back up the Esquiline to the townhouse. I headed straight up the Caelian to the Castra. Silent tears coursed down my cheeks. I would report that our own sovereign had ripped our city's soul from our bosom.

I wanted to tell the Emperor to his face what I thought of his Eastern Christian cult with its greedy bishops and simpering priests preaching meekness and resignation instead of strength and order.

I could not have guessed during that miserable walk that my chance to rebuke the Emperor would come within hours of sunrise.

☧☧☧

Apodemius and I were summoned to the Imperial Palace. Accompanied by Ahenobarbus and two *centenarii*, we arrived at the exterior gates and presented our insignia in a somber mood.

'I was summoned by name?' I asked the *Magister*.

'More than named. Called urgently. The imperial party will not stay in the palace for more than another day.'

Apodemius hated going out in public. He especially avoided the crush of crowds and the bright sights of Roma. He hated tourists, pilgrims, markets, and traffic. He was blinking like a mole blinded by the morning blaze reflected off marble and stone.

'Did they say why, *Magister*?'

'No but I'm worried. You need us as witnesses, Numidianus. If you were spotted in the Forum spying on a state secret, our *schola* must observe your interrogation and record any procedural anomalies. We can't keep you out of prison, but we can register injustice, if it comes to that.'

'I broke no law, *Magister*. No one saw us. And by now the entire city knows that Victory's missing. How can robbing the most important statue in the known world stay secret?'

Ahenobarbus rolled his eyes, 'Not robbing, Numidianus, removing.'

When our stalwart party entered a small marble chamber, I noticed centuries' worth of dirt encrusting the veins of the ageing stone and deep cracks in the mosaics of Justice and Mercy embedded in the floor. A few modern chairs and tables converted the ancient space into a modern meeting room.

Constantius sat in a wide, gilt chair brought from his court in Mediolanum. We five prostrated ourselves. Apodemius gave the hem of the Emperor's cloak a perfunctory brush of his lips. The ornate protocol of the Pannonian imperial family sat ill with Apodemius' conservative Roman manner.

The Emperor's heavy eyelids narrowed. His tight lips curled with distaste at the size of our delegation.

'Excuse everyone but Biarchus Numidianus, *Magister*.'

Our three 'witnesses' hesitated. This was exactly what Apodemius feared. A sense of solidarity ran deep among us *agentes* shunned by polite society and feared by the lower orders. We were the despised *curiosi* and we held fast for each other. My fellow agents intended to stick to my side.

'We dismiss you three,' Constantius repeated.

The Emperor's bodyguard Teutomeres and two sentries moved forward. Apodemius nodded to Ahenobarbus and the two *centenarii* to wait—and no doubt eavesdrop—from outside the great double doors.

I waited for my grilling to begin.

Constantius looked not at me, but through me. '*Biarchus* Numidianus, you testified in favor of the Caesar Julian during the Gallus hearings two years ago.'

'Yes, *Imperator*.'

'Perhaps the Caesar will look kindly on you as our messenger. You will personally inform him of the *Augusta* Helena's loss. This is a state secret that necessitates absolute discretion.'

Relief washed over me. In my outrage at Constantius' sacrilege to the Altar of Victory, I'd forgotten Helena's miscarriage.

'*Imperator*, it will be my sad privilege to carry a letter from this Palace.'

The *agentes* were, after all, the official managers of the greatest postal system in the history of mankind.

'There will be no letter. Even imperial letters carry risks. We do not wish to see a family tragedy leaked to all corners of our Empire like so much society tittle-tattle. This is more than women's business. The question of an imperial heir is of supreme political and military concern. You will convey this news yourself with no one present but the Caesar.'

It was a sensitive but simple mission. In my relief that I was not in trouble over my dawn espionage in the Forum, I hardly took in the rest of his order.

'. . . to attach yourself to the staff of the Praetorian Prefect Florentius and assist in the management of civilian affairs in northern Gallia.'

I couldn't help glancing over at Apodemius. His wrinkled face betrayed no surprise, but I knew he had not been warned of this. He had been genuinely worried I was to be punished for seeing too much in the Forum.

'First, you will proceed to Raetia where General Barbatio, the *Magister Peditum* is en route with twenty-five thousand troops in a pincer movement to join the northern troops. We are going to flush the Alemanni invaders back across the Rhenus. This *forceps* strategy worked well enough in the last fighting season. One more campaign will shove these tribes off Roman territory once and for all.'

'Yes, *Imperator*.'

'While attached to the Prefect's staff, you will discover what you can about Alemannic policies.'

Now Apodemius had no choice but to speak. 'Surely, *Imperator Domine*, military espionage is a job for army *exploratores*, men familiar with that terrain and language.'

The Emperor hesitated. 'There is also some *political* work, *Magister*.' There was something that Constantius was weighing with each word, but not saying.

'Is there then another, less *official* task than tribal surveillance?' I asked.

Constantius cleared his throat. 'Apodemius told me that you are becoming a respected analyst of dispatches copied for your *schola*, some of them including most *sensitive* reports. I wish you to observe the staff around the Caesar. You will watch his officers to assess their cohesion. You may find yourself spying on a

Roman, assessing his loyalty to our imperial venture, and the support he shows our standard.'

The Emperor must be reluctant to name the unreliable officer for fear of coloring my independent judgment. He had enough intrigants among his *consistoriani*, men constantly incriminating each other with accusations of treason. Why only recently, the relentless plotter General Arbetio had been caught up himself in a net of charges, but wiggled free somehow.

I suspected General Barbatio right away. He was an ambitious Dacian thug of no education. He bought and bullied his way up the army career ladder and harbored no personal loyalty to the imperial family. I knew he sought favor and advancement under General Ursicinus, soon to be back fighting Persians on the Eastern front. Perhaps Constantius had heard more of that treasonous alliance.

Or perhaps the Emperor suspected this Praetorian Prefect Florentius? He was no relation to the acting Magister Officiorum on Constantius' staff, Florentius, son of Nigrinianus. I didn't know this Florentius but I had read reports of disagreements between the Caesar and the Praetorian Prefect over tax policy.

And then there was the general replacing the resentful Marcellus, an aged veteran named Severus. Was he disloyal to the young Caesar?

Constantius moved his heavy head to gaze down at me. 'We are sure we need say no more.'

I wished he would say a great deal more. I dared to fish a bit longer in the Emperor's purple mental waters.

'Yes, *Imperator*, I receive worrying rumors from the headquarters of the northern army, gossip that the Caesar Julian does not have the fullest support of everyone reporting to him.'

There was a prolonged silence. I added, 'As you know better than I, there were questions as to his working relationship with General Ursicinus followed by the public breakdown in cooperation from General Marcellus.'

Constantius almost frowned. The Marcellus business must have troubled him more he let on. I fumbled along:

'But General Severus is an older man than Marcellus, full in years and reputation. He should be content to advise the young

Caesar and ride a polite distance behind him, showing due respect for the imperial family and your image, *Imperator*.'

Apodemius gave the Emperor a careful nod to acknowledge that our unexpected briefing was done. Yet I hesitated before kissing that draped cloak an unfound farewell.

Constantius didn't respond to my prompts. I flailed away, 'I will do my utmost to ferret out any sign of disloyalty to Caesar.'

'The Caesar's camp needs careful watching,' he said, as opaque as ever. Why did he persist with this enigmatic briefing?

'The Caesar's success may draw enemies,' Apodemius parried in a strange, hesitant tone.

Constantius sniffed. 'Our cousin has done well. Thanks to his victories in the field, he is almost esteemed a second Titus or a son of Vespasian, in the glorious progress of his wars as very like Trajan, while mild as Antoninus Pius, and in searching out the true and perfect reason of things in harmony with Marcus Aurelius, in emulation of whom he molds his conduct and character.'

'Very like all these great men,' I said, an uneasy chill rising up my spine.

'We are leaving for Sirmium soon. Is perhaps Julian too good to be true?' Constantius muttered. It was outside the chamber that I realized the awful implication of the Emperor's question.

※ ※ ※

My indignation grew on the long litter ride behind Apodemius back to the relative cool and calm of the Castra. He took little notice of me as he hastened away to his office to rest for the remaining daylight hours. Apodemius was a nocturnal animal. Like the bats, cats, and owls that stalk their prey by night, his vision pierced the dark minds of his men. But occasionally the man acted as obtuse as the dumbest cow on the Manlius estates.

'You can't expect me to muddle into a top imperial mission on the basis of such a clumsy interview!' I protested. We crossed the courtyard surrounding the main building. I had turned to face him and was bumping into by more than one fellow *agens* as I tried to slow him down.

He stopped and looked at me. 'What is it about this assignment that you didn't understand?'

'It's as layered as a banquet pie,' I said. 'First, it's a gold-plated messenger's job. Tell the poor man his wife lost her child. Is that it? No. Remain in Gallia attached to the Prefect's staff to pretend to assist in civil affairs, but actually to spy on the Alemanni.'

'It's very simple,' he said, with a shake of his bony skull. Strands of snow-white hair floated around his ears like a soft nimbus.

'But with everybody thinking I'm the *agens* working an administration cover to spy on the Alemanni, I'm *really* there to spy on a possible traitor within Julian's camp.'

'Perhaps you haven't got it right after all. Weren't you listening?'

I took his arm and assisted his old carcass into the building and up the worn stone steps that led, from one corridor to another, and through one creaking office into another. At last, with much sighing and self-disgust at his painful knees, we passed through his anteroom into his private sanctuary. He took a fresh linen towel, drenched it in a basin of cool water, stretched himself out on his massage bed, and laid the wet towel over his face.

'*Magister*, what did I miss?'

'You didn't miss a thing, Numidianus. You just don't like what you realize you heard,' he mumbled through the wet cloth.

I stared at his map. A thick cluster of army pins had moved up to Raetia. At least I could be thankful I was not attached to the military staff of my old acquaintance Barbatio.

'You know it yourself, Numidianus, from reading the reports and stolen correspondence. Everyone in authority up there answers to the Emperor. The Caesar took up his post with no one on his side but his book bag carriers. He knows we read his mail. His pen pals know it too. You've read his letters to his friends in Athens? He chafes under his elders. He knows who spies on him—or tried. Paulus Catena was the last man to tackle a subtle task like that—and failed. There's the eunuch chamberlain Eutherius who pretends to be his friend, but answers to the man who sent him—Constantius.'

'Constantius just *praised* Julian.'

—THE DEADLY CAESAR—

'What else can the poor sod do? Julian has recaptured Agrippina and secured much of the interior. He's a public success, handing his cousin laurels of victory and prisoners by the convoy load. But he's gathering the wrong men around him—Greek magicians, pagan philosophers, and strange doctors. He should be sticking to directions from the Emperor instead of freelancing up to Agrippina and off across the Rhenus and here and there.'

'I think I understand.'

I collapsed on the old stool in front of his desk used by *agentes* under daily review. 'The person I'm to watch isn't disloyal to the Caesar. It is *the Caesar himself*.'

From under his soothing towel, Apodemius gave a large sigh.

'You see, Numidianus, Julian started out well. Last year's actions were a great success. He's learned all the necessary military skills in a mere two campaign seasons. But has he learned too much? Could it be that we now have on our hands a deadly Caesar? Refresh this towel for me, would you?'

I rinsed off the towel in the cool water of his basin.

'I see. Because Julian is the cleverest man in the imperial family, I'm blanketed, *smothered* in cover stories to elude his suspicions? Why me? I'm still just a *biarchus*—first class,' I added with sour pride.

'Constantius has suffered the co-rule of his dissolute brother Constans, the upstart General Magnentius, the foolish old General Vetranio, his deluded cousin Gallus, and the vacillating General Silvanus. You happened to witness each disaster.'

'The Fates have made me their toy.'

'And you know General Barbatio from years ago in Numidia and Antiochia. But most of all, you must go because you earned Julian's trust in Mediolanum.'

'Send someone else. I can't get embroiled in yet another battle above my rank.'

'That's another reason you're ideal. You're ambitious ... and frustrated. You may attract treasonous offers, fellow malcontents, conspiratorial conversations.'

'And all this while I'm spying on that barbarian Chnodomarius? Or was that a joke?'

'Oh, that. No, no, no, not a joke at all.'

The *Magister* lifted that stupid rag off his face and tossed it back into the basin. He walked with creaking limbs around his desk and over to his map.

'Constantius must applaud Julian's victories over the Alemanni through here.' He swept his hand around central Gallia. 'But remember Constantius made a deal with them. He wants to drive them back across the river but at the same time, keep the peace that he forged with the *regi* Gundomadus and Vadomarius.'

'In short,' Apodemius lowered himself onto his cushion, 'we don't want Julian to become so heroic, he destroys imperial peace at the expense of the tribes, do we?'

'And how do I spy on the Alemanni?'

'You use that girl, of course.'

'Gunda? The one who tried to kill Constantius? Work with Gunda? She's a *barbarian* herself.'

Apodemius knew I didn't mean such contempt. I was short of temper and sleep. I'd spent most of the night traipsing around the old Forum and half the morning deciphering imperial riddles under personal threat.

I was furious at being sent again, still ranked *biarchus*, on another dangerous mission. There were other *agentes*—undereducated, corrupt, and insolent men—even ones who flaunted Apodemius' authority by going straight to the Emperor—like *Ducenarius* Gaudentius. They enjoyed higher prestige and pay.

'Barbarians are essential to this empire, Numidianus, like slaves, even though they aren't Roman. And might never be. But many of them will *become* Roman. Look at yourself, boy, in your smart tunic and perfect shave. We'll overlook those sloppy boots.'

'I hide your gift to me here.' I showed him the loops inside my boot cuffs holding a small, clever knife issued to *agentes* on difficult missions. A treasure of useful tools—a blade, a pick, a spoon, and a file could swivel out as needed and then snap back into the handle.

'Numidianus, I know your family tree. On your father's side are not only famous senators, but also the blood of your grandmother, his second wife. She was a Gallic woman whom the senators of Roma looked at askance. I was a young man when he brought her to the Esquiline Hill. She seemed a risky choice at the time. So you and I both know that your ancestors include Gauls who fought Julius Caesar stark naked.'

I knew what was coming next.

'We won't even go into your mother's side. How much Berber ran through her veins? You can be so stubborn, I'm not sure a mule doesn't figure somehow in your parentage.'

'So that's my assignment. Give Julian the message. Announce myself to Prefect Florentius as a spy on the Alemanni. But also spy on Julian and his staff. Is that all? Is that it?'

'Well no, not exactly. You saw Victory being dragged from her base?'

'My spirit rages even now.'

'Mine too, Numidianus.'

'It was not something that Caesar Julian would have done, had anyone asked him.'

'Indeed. There are few in power who understand the true heritage of our empire any more.' Apodemius' crooked back was turned to me. He fed his mice bits of stale bread, crumb by crumb.

He said in a low voice, 'As a fellow Roman, you have a personal mission from me—the most sensitive of them all.'

'Yet *another* task?'

'Yes,' he said, brushing crumbs off his bleached tunic. He leaned across his desk and reached out a gnarled hand, imploring me.

'If possible, save that brilliant, *foolish* young Caesar from himself.'

Chapter 7, Gunda's Song

—Roma, mid-July, 357—

As always, the imperial military campaign season began in July. From Sirmium, Constantius turned his face eastward to concentrate on the Persian threat. He left the West to his caesar, a youth under the surveillance of trusted men, both military and civilian . . . and myself.

I needed many weeks before departure to put the Manlius holdings in order for the rest of the summer. Verus and I summoned the managers of the Cisalpine lumberyard and cattle herd, the Sardinian cornfields, our five hundred acres of Falernian vines, the pig herd in Parma, the docks in Ostia, the oyster beds in Baiae, and the beehives in Hybla and Calabria.

We calculated the temporary labor needed for the corn harvest, paid off repair bills, agreed on the commissions for honey, ham, and beef sales, tallied the rents, and tested the grapes.

At long last, the family's fortunes were recovering from the ravages of civil war between Constantius and Magnentius. Unfortunately, the old Roman house on the Esquiline Hill was a mess, thanks to the careless tenancy of our courtier tenants. They had stained our cushions, cracked our recently restored black and white floor tiles with their heavy boots, and dried their sweaty palms on Kahina's wall hangings. With every careless gesture— from the broken ancestral memorial mask left half-hanging off the peristyle wall to rips in the *triclinium* couch covers— Constantius' Mediolanum party had left traces of contempt for us—'old Romans,' 'has-beens,' 'Senatorial left-overs.'

The one room they'd never vandalized in their offhand way was the late Senator's study at the back of the house overlooking the open garden and back alley. Verus had padlocked it three times over.

'Not that those there gents seemed the reading type,' our *dispensator* sneered as he tossed a wine-stained tunic embroidered with silver trim into the kitchen rubbish. Verus could have appropriated that costly trim for his own favorite tunic, but I didn't stop him. Perhaps the tunic's owner had offended Verus so much he would never want to see the official's finery again.

For all our financial distractions, the inflexible date to begin my mission loomed. I'm not sure which part of this assignment I dreaded most—telling the Caesar his unborn son was dead, reconnoitering the ruthless Alemanni, or spying on the Caesar himself. I almost hoped that the news of the dead baby would leak out, but in matters involving imperial females, state secrets were well kept.

I also dreaded working with the treacherous Gunda. For good reason I preferred to carry out my missions alone. In North Africa, my spy chief Leo's farmhand, Nico, had betrayed me out of jealousy. During the civil war, I'd been duped by the seductive Roxana, acting as a double agent in the court of General Magnentius for the Lord Chamberlain Eusebius.

And because I'd reported in Agrippina to the usurping General Silvanus, I'd alienated my superior, the *ducenarius* Gaudentius, when Silvanus put him under house arrest but let me carry on as a trusted adviser.

This Gunda promised trouble, starting with that lethal blade of hers. I could only hope the stifling Roman summer nights in a bare Castra cell had tamed her temper just a little.

Of course, I needed her help if my career were to survive this convoluted assignment. But I was damned in Hades if I was going to let any Alemanna barbarian realize that.

※※※

We traveled as far as Mediolanum without her saying more than thanks for the modest meals we ate in silence and a terse goodnight as we parted to rest in *mansio* rooms set aside for privileged *Cursus* travelers. I'd made the journey from Roma to the new court so often, I was a familiar face at every stop. I tipped well—perhaps betraying I had once been a slave eager for tips myself.

As before, Gunda sat well on her horse—although I'd hardly rate her a Goddess Epona. In addition to the traveling cloak, lyre bag, and small reticule of personal items, she'd got herself sturdy leather footwear. But whereas she had practically raced me back to Roma after her disastrous performance in Constantius' court, she now rode at no more than a respectable, steady pace. She wore a wary expression. Whenever we passed other riders, military or governmental, she slunk down underneath her hood.

We progressed without incident up through the refreshing mountain passes north of Mediolanum, through Comum and Curia, and downhill toward the fortress at Brigantium. I would have expected her to be impatient, if not eager, to reach the border of her father's territory in the Agri Decumantes just ahead.

Instead, her silence went from thoughtful to oppressive. I'm not fond of chatty women as a rule, but I grew worried. Was Gunda brooding on our enforced partnership? Was she plotting to escape my company for tribal protectors? I'd been riding ahead of her but after we passed through Curia, I insisted she ride in front of me. Hour after hour, her horse's flanks shifted underneath her generous hips. When she shed her cloak in the heat of midday, her long braided hair swung across her back in an echo of the horse's swishing tail.

It was not the worst sight to contemplate. The paved route through the passes was cool after hours on the sun-bleached plains. Sometimes we stopped at a stream rushing past the old road. Signs of other travelers—mostly soldiers—littered the mossy earth. My old sparring partner and now *Magister Peditum* General Barbatio and his twenty-five thousand troops had marched through here only a few weeks before us on his way to the fortress pitched over the ancient Colonia ara Augusta Rauracum. He and I had a checkered history, but I had little choice; at Augusta Raurica Gunda and I would take our first break in the journey to Julian's headquarters farther north.

The turf on either side of the road was rutted by convoy-wagon tracks, mule hoof prints, cracked eating bowls, discarded socks worn through—the humble detritus of infantrymen.

Combined into units, they formed the formidable fighting machine of the Roman Empire, but each morning a soldier washed, shaved, and shat like any blue-faced Celt or slinky Persian. As for Gunda, a barbarian woman could prove as fastidious as the finest socialite traveling between Roma and her Sicilian villa. Between evening stops, she did her woman's business, whatever it was, out of my sight off the road. But not so far, I ordered, that I couldn't reach her in seconds if we ran into brigands.

'Brigands?' She curled her lip as she remounted her horse. 'You mean my people?'

'I mean the brigands who have driven those poor Gallo-Romans we passed yesterday to do what farming they can manage, all crushed in together, behind town walls—for fear of what your people might do to them.'

'It's our land now,' she said. Those cool eyes narrowed. 'The Emperor gave it to us.'

When we descended from the foothills, I saw how little the Alemanni 'settlers' tended Roman irrigation ditches and walls. They distrusted towns. Even small *vici* seemed too civilized for them. Empty stables, weed-covered villas, and broken gutters trickling rivulets of snowmelt in all directions told me what had happened to properties once cultivated by diligent Roman citizens.

Gunda detected my disgust. Tightlipped she fought back some rude outburst all the way to Vindonissa. There three chilly Alpine rivers—the Araris, the Lindimacus and a river the Helvetii tribes called the Reuss—converged. An old fortress controlled access to the Rhenus less than ten miles to the north of us. At least here the depredations of the Alemanni were nowhere to be seen.

Our ancient legions might be gone but military cemeteries lining the roads spoke volumes of history to me. I read their memorial engravings. The *Legio XIII*, *Legio XXI Rapax* and two auxiliary cohorts, the *III Hispanorum* and *VI Raetorum*, later the *VII Raetorum Equitata* and the *XXVI Voluntariorum Civium Romanorum*, the *Legio XI Claudia Pia Fidelis* and the *Legio VIII* had all left Roman sons buried around Vindonissa.

Were these noble deaths for naught? When the border shifted northward, Vindonissa fell in strategic importance.

—THE DEADLY CAESAR—

Now Alemannic incursions made it important once again.

Tomorrow Gunda and I would continue along the *Cursus* on the left bank of the Rhenus to Augusta Raurica. Vindonissa was vital in the communications system between the armies on the Rhenus and the Danuvius. It guarded that part of the river frontier made vulnerable by the sharp bend of the river. Three imperial roads met there. There was another road to the valley of the Rhodanus via the river garrison at Tenedo and then Genava, as well as the southward route to the Via Aquae Helveticae and Turicum back to Italia.

A new *castrum* towered over the paved *fora* to shield its inhabitants from shifting tensions beyond their walls. As Gunda and I arrived, the open space bustled with civilians on sunset errands at shops lining all four sides of the forum. Trade looked brisk and the goods on offer abundant enough.

While daylight lingered, I would stop at the postal station on the far side of town for fresh news, if any, of Barbatio's progress farther ahead. I left Gunda to settle herself at a comfortable *mansio* where the ground floor housed a particularly good *taberna*.

'I will wait for you before eating, Roman' she said, her dusty face streaked with summer's sweat.

'We've made good time. Take advantage. There are good *thermae* here. Find the women's entrance and refresh yourself. And address me as *Agens* or *Biarchus*. We're adjacent to your father's territory. Passers-by should know I'm your imperial escort, so that your reputation doesn't suffer.'

'I am the daughter of Gundomad. My reputation cannot be questioned.'

She took my coins and looked across the crowded forum for the baths.

'You don't have to eat with me, if my company wearies you.'

'Does mine weary you?' she asked.

'I've known livelier travel companions.'

She swung her lyre bag over her shoulder and headed off to choose her room for the night, but turned and demanded, 'Give me back my knife.'

'You won't need it in the women's baths.'

She gave a petulant shrug and stalked off.

Apart from being my hostage, having no idea of our mission, and resenting her brother's captivity, I wondered what put her in such a sulk—but I didn't care. I intended to shave, bathe, and soak in Vindonissa's facilities without any apologies. But first, I must check things at the *agentes* station and then absorb the local gossip over one of the lively dice games under the shadow of a small portico along the Via Principalis.

It was hours later when I reached our *mansio*. I'd lost two or three day's pay but picked up much useful intelligence. Alemannic sabotage—mostly roadblocks of felled trees—kept Barbatio's army pinned down in Augusta Raurica. Skirmishing with barbarians along his own route had also delayed the Caesar Julian's arrival at the two army's reconnoiter point.

'Who is this General Barbatio?'

Gunda eyed me over her cup of watered wine. She had scrubbed and scraped herself until she shone. Bathhouse attendants had piled her hair into gleaming coils and braids and fixed a preposterous frill of crimped hair to her temple with that garnet-eyed fox. By the lantern lights of the *taberna*, the lightest strands of her hair gleamed silvery.

She seemed almost to be wearing a ceremonial parade helmet. All that was missing was the pounded tin mask with its dark eyeholes and unsmiling lips.

I told her, 'General Barbatio is a Dacian I knew in North Africa when he was nothing more than a middling lieutenant on border patrol.'

'He must be a man of great qualities to have reached *Magister Peditum*.'

'Qualities? None at all, unless you value ambition devoid of intelligence, greed devoid of moral values, physical strength devoid of courage, in favor of craven, obsequious pandering to officers of higher rank.'

'You like him a lot.'

'I don't want to talk about Barbatio.'

I dipped my cabbage roll into garlic sauce. Her penetrating gaze refused to release me.

'I dealt with him on a sensitive mission in the East involving Caesar Gallus' arrest. Let's say General Barbatio never fails to live down to my expectations.'

—THE DEADLY CAESAR—

'And yet?'

'What?'

'You are holding something back, Roman.'

I shrugged. 'He rescued someone from slavery for me—a Roman citizen.'

'Someone? Then it must be a woman.'

'Yes, a woman. Barbatio was taking his cut from the illegal trade in civil war prisoners. I threatened to report him for a crime against a Roman citizen.'

'This slave was your wife?'

'No. Do you want more to eat? I'm tired. We need our sleep. From here on, the journey will be more dangerous.'

Though Kahina was the mother of my child, the complications of Leo's accidental conception, Kahina's forced marriage to my former master and unacknowledged sire, and our inherited responsibility for Leo and his vast inheritance—none of these secrets were Gunda's business.

'Why not?'

'Why not what?' I pulled out my coin sack to pay for our meal.

'Why is she not your wife?' Gunda read my face too well.

'I don't need a wife. Anyway, she's a Christian. Very devout. I'm not a Christian. Not that I don't appreciate compassion, chastity, or charity. But most Christians are just like everyone else, only they worship the religion in power and they know how to use it.'

'Oh, I know all about Christianity from my bishop,' she said with a knowing chuckle, 'but I wouldn't say working for him taught me compassion, chastity, or charity,' she said.

'He mistreated you?'

'He tried, the horny pig.'

'A priest? I thought they—'

'He wasn't a priest, just one of those politicians who use bishoping as a political leg up. He had a wife, a hag he deserved.'

'Still, the bishop taught you Latin surprisingly well.'

She paused at that, then explained: 'I told you, my father wanted me to acquire *Romanitas* for marriage to a high-ranking official. The bishop wanted me to translate Christian prayers into my tongue so he could convert and subdue the settlers.'

She patted her lacquered hairdo, as if proving a point. 'Everybody has a use for Gunda. What is my use to you? Why am I here?'

I didn't take the bait. 'Did you translate anything?'

She leaned across the table and recited in a low voice:

Fater unser, thu bist in himile
uuihi namu dinan
qhueme rihhi din
uuerde uuillo diin,
so in himile, sosa in erdu
prooth unseer emezzihic kip uns hiutu
oblaz uns sculdi unsero
so uuir oblazem uns skuldikem
enti ni unsih firleit in khorunka
uzzer losi unsih fona ubile . . .

She finished her Lord's Prayer and gave me a self-satisfied smile by the lamplight.

'Your people never showed interest in Christianity before.'

She sucked on a pear core and spit the seeds on the floor. 'My people worship the one-eyed god of war Wodanaz, whom you Romans call Odin. Wodanaz gave us poetry for our songs.'

'As I said, I've never been drawn to the new Church and we Romans have enough war gods as it is.'

'Then you worship the Sun? Or the great Cybele?' she teased.

'The old gods are my guides. My prayers at the Castra Temple of Jupiter Redux are answered.' Yet my *schola*'s temple stood bolted shut against future offerings.

A Roman trader hailed us from the opposite corner of the tavern's dining room. 'Can your woman there give us a song?'

He reeked of arrogance, an urbanite lording it over provincials. But he gave Gunda a warm enough smile. He had noticed her lyre's stag-like horns poking out of its sack. The instrument sat like a third diner at our side.

'Yes,' Gunda said, but first she finished her dessert with ostentatious precision. After washing her fingers, she polished road dust off the lyre and, bending her ear low, tested its strings. The missing string had been replaced. The tuning was in order.

Gunda turned to face the other diners. She placed the lyre upright between her two knees. Steadying it with her left hand, she played with her right. After a few chords, she began to hum. No one ever played the lyre without singing, but for a few minutes, she sang only to herself. Just when a few of the audience shifted on their stools with impatience, she lifted up a voice as clear as a flute.

I'm not very musical. As a *delicatus* slave in the Manlius *triclinium* where the Commander entertained his military pals late into the night, I heard enough cymbals, flutes, and drums to last me 'til the Persians rule Roma. Raucous song competitions lasting into the wee hours were marathons of exhaustion for my childish ears. Then my life was filled with the harsh blare of *cornicenes* and *buccinatores* as I served Gregorius from one field posting to another

Since my life as an *agens* began, there hadn't been any music in my life whatsoever.

Gunda sang in her own tongue, sparing her audience the mediocre poetry of a typical Roman banquet. To me, it was just noise—but beautiful noise. Soothing tones bathing the dining room by the flickering light of the *taberna*'s oil lamps. It was like listening to someone weave sounds the way a spinner turns fine wool strands into fabric. Sometimes her pick strummed across all the strings to stress the beat. More often, it darted and danced from string to string in a pattern as intricate as an imperial floor mosaic. Travelers and servers alike fell silent, laid down their cups of wine and trays, and let their chatter fall away.

She finished on a low calling note. A man reached over to tip her, but she refused his coin, saying, 'I am the daughter of Gundomad. I sing for my art, not my bread.'

'What is your song about?' I asked, refilling her cup with chilled *posca*. 'It had so many verses.'

'A girl marries the prince of another tribe. At first she's happy and pleases him. Then she realizes that though she loves him, he does not love her. He loves himself and the glory of raiding, ambushes, and brawls.'

'Does he realize in time? Does it end on a happy or sad note?'

'In the end he sees that the passion of love is sweeter than the excitement of bloodshed.' She tossed me a scornful glance. 'Can you not distinguish the subtleties and harmonies of music? Some people are deaf to notes, just as deaf people are to words themselves.'

'I'm not musical, but you sang it very well.'

Some of the other diners clamored for more songs, but Gunda cradled the lyre in her arms like a sleepy child that had overstayed its bedtime and disappeared upstairs to her room.

'Are all her songs like that?' A serving girl cleared away our bowls.

'I suppose you understood better than I did.'

She looked more an *Alemanna laeta* than Roman to me. Wiping her nose on her stained tunic sleeve, she frowned at my insinuation that she wasn't a Gallo-Roman town girl and returned to the grill counter.

'Wish they was all that civilized,' said a gruff man passing my table to head back into the street. I detected an Illyrian accent. He was over forty, clean-shaven, with sagging muscles, and simple but clean civilian clothing. I'd lay money he was an army veteran who had settled along the river and put his pension to good use.

He wore a bandage around his head so as to cover one eye. It was a clean strap of bleached linen, neatly pleated and expertly tied. I'd seen enough of these arrangements since my days serving the disfigured Commander to know that whatever lay underneath the bandage must be an old wound. The bandage had become part of his wardrobe, cleaned and folded by his woman. But perhaps a man who'd lost an eye in these parts had no reason to praise Gunda's people for being civilized, no matter how haunting their songs.

⚜⚜⚜

We left Vindonissa rather late the next morning. We were on a race through disputed territory to catch up with Barbatio's troops and I was almost grateful for the girl's sullen concentration on the road. She'd shed the bathhouse styling of yesterday and looked more than ever like an Alemanna rustic, still bedecked with heavy jewelry but with hair in a simple braid again.

More important, she spoke the dialect of the tribes pressing in on these fields and towns. Given her father's standing as the regional *rex*, she was sure to carry herself proudly before any thugs we might encounter. Well before dawn, I had tipped the boys of the state stables to give us their freshest horses.

Gunda kept up and we made good time. By the end of the afternoon, I expected to reach a guarded *mansio* midway to Augusta Raurica where we could rest.

We had been following the *Cursus* due west, the wide gray waters of the Rhenus flowing past us a few miles out of sight. As the morning turned to afternoon, two riders kept pace with us using a rougher road—the usual substandard route that served travelers without state *diplomata* or *evectiones*—running parallel to the imperial highway. Their horses kicked up gusts of summer dust. Reddish hair flowed down their backs. Oversized round gold brooches glinted off their shoulders.

It seemed prudent to avoid crossing their paths at any upcoming junction. I told Gunda we would take advantage of the spreading plain along the riverbanks. At my signal, we doubled our pace.

Across the distance that separated the two roads, our Alemanni duo sped up.

For another two hours Gunda and I galloped like this, trailed by a cloud of road dust behind our left shoulders. We changed horses at a minor relay station. After ordering only snacks we could eat in our saddles, I ordered Gunda to remount.

She sensed my mood. To her credit, she said nothing, but cantered off ahead of me with a straight spine, her jaw jutting forward. She had no doubt spotted our 'shadows.' She might not mind bumping into her brethren, but at a ratio of two men to one, I did. She was essential to my mission—like it or not. I did not intend to lose her to friendly cousins.

We hurried on toward a thick forest. Alemanni peasants tilled some of the territory through which we'd ridden but even now, when a golden harvest should be rustling in the fading afternoon breeze, we crossed many weedy, fallow fields. Abandoned Roman villas surrounded by ruined gardens and overgrown pastureland dotted the horizon.

The *Cursus* cut straight ahead into those trees. We ducked as our horses slowed and entered a natural tunnel of lush, low branches. We reined in to catch our breath. Shade cooled my nervous brow. An inviting stream cut under an arched Roman bridge and rippled away toward the banks of the great river flowing out of sight.

In the heat of noon, Gunda had finished her goatskin bladder of *posca*. She slipped into the darker shadows behind the trees to relieve herself. I pulled both horses down a steep slope through a soft blanket of leaves to let them drink at the stream. My animal shook his muzzle with pleasure, jingling his bronze harness disks as he slurped.

I heard hooves pounding up the verge next to the paved road approaching the forest.

'Gunda?'

There was no answer.

I dragged our two horses farther down into the crevice of the stream's bed where it curved away from the road until I was satisfied that the men would pass by without stopping. I prayed to the gods that Gunda would stay hidden.

Instead, the riders reined in just where I'd led the horses off the paving and into the soft earth. One rider dismounted and spoke a few words of Alemannic—a harsh tongue. His companion answered no less hoarsely, as if clearing his throat mid-speech. In less than a minute, they would follow my tracks through the crushed leaves to discover me under a wide tangle of tree roots overhanging the stream.

They had followed us intentionally. We must have stopped in a spot targeted by brigands who knew how the inviting tunnel of cool leaves, the narrowed road, and the refreshing stream offered them a perfect trap for robbery.

Gunda began warbling to herself—damn the girl. Her song stopped. She said something in her own language. Male voices moved closer to the road. I tethered the two sets of reins to a sturdy root and snuck back up the muddy slope to observe unseen. The gurgling water drowned out the rustle of my boots slipping on the leaves.

I did not trust Gunda. Even though we held Hermund hostage in the Castra, his safety might only matter so far in her calculations. Perhaps she'd been hoping for just such a rescue by fighters from a *pagus* answering to her father. She might even encourage them to seize me as a hostage to trade for Hermund.

—THE DEADLY CAESAR—

If Gunda looked ready to betray me to enemy killers, I'd be back in my saddle and across that stream faster than a *ballista* shot.

She pulled out her purse and offered the few coins left from her bath in Vindonissa. Were they no more than petty bandits?

No, she put her money back. She tossed them a confident, offhand comment. She moved in my direction. I ducked down, ready to make a dash as soon as they came tracking me through the soft leaves.

She didn't get far. They raised their voices, questioning her harder. I peeked again. She wasn't answering but matching their hard gazes with dignity. Both accosters were taller than Gunda, though not as tall as the Franks of the north. Up close, their reddish gold hair tied in knots and plaits looked dyed.

These two weren't tribal settlers—that was for sure. They had never mucked through wet fields. They wore good riding trousers, not clumsy farmer's leggings. Their calfskin boots were brushed. Their hands were clean and their beards combed. They boasted thick torcs of gold around their throats and upper arms. They wore no cloaks in the summer heat so anyone could see they bristled with impressive weapons. These were not the mass-produced arms of a Roman *fabricae* equipping thousands of Roman troops and Germanic *federates*, but the handcrafted treasures of high-ranking Alemanni fighters, including an axe, a short dagger, and long swords in elaborate scabbards attached to baldrics girded with studded deerskins. Long bows and barbed angons dangled from their saddles on the gaudy harnessed horses hitched nearby.

None of this seemed lost on Gunda of the cool eyes and wry sneer. She stood erect and unintimidated, asking a tart question or two of her own. She did not like the shorter man's answer, so she questioned the taller man who leaned against a tree trunk and laughed in her face. She stepped back in surprised anger and slapped him full across his mouth.

My fear for myself dropped away. The daughter of our ally Gundomadus was courting danger herself.

She reached down into the folds of her skirts and then gave a little gasp. She had wanted her razor-like little knife, but it still hung from my own belt for 'safe-keeping.' She needed her weapon now. The two accosters saw her futile gesture and laughing harder, threw her back against the broad trunk. The taller pinned down both of her arms while the shorter began to manhandle her.

She was the daughter of one of their *reges*. Why weren't they showing her the respect *Germani* always showed their highborn women?

This wasn't what Gunda expected either. With panicked eyes and chest heaving beneath her cloak, she shouted in their guttural language. She was arguing fast but they were barking back at her just as hard. The short man turned her little purse inside out and the tall man stroked her thigh with his raised knee.

She kicked at them both and kept up her spitting, choking, scolding stream of curses.

I had not only her knife, but also our road license identifying her as my charge and travel companion. Gunda's name alone should command obedience from these men. Would it help if I claimed her as mine and not theirs?

I drew my *spatha* and scrambled up the bank, dodging from one tree to the next, working my way up toward the road under the cover of Gunda's indignant protests of their insults and retorts. She was twisting hard to free herself. The tall man she had slapped now whacked her across the jaw, stunning her into silence. I saw her eyes roll as she fought to hold her wits through the shock of a blow that could have knocked out a grown warrior.

The shorter man drew his dagger. He hesitated. The taller man said something. Within seconds, these two might murder her. I ran the last few yards. Before they heard me coming, I had stuck my *pugio* between the taller man's ribs. Still dizzy from his punch, Gunda staggered away behind the tree. The shorter man rounded on me with his dagger in his left hand pointed at my sword. It was a delaying move—his right hand reached for the axe in his belt. I held an advantage over that weapon for no more than seconds. I'd seen the head of a flying barbarian hatchet cleave a man's skull before.

I plunged my *spatha* deep into his gut and drew it hard leftwise and through the coarse gray wool until the stain of red guts pooled over his torso and his face drained white.

—THE DEADLY CAESAR—

There was a grunt and a scuffling in the leaves behind me. The second man was no longer down, though my dagger had gone in deep. He was about to grab my neck with his bare hands when a granite rock came down on his head from behind. He fell. I stood staring at Gunda, who dropped her weapon and brushed loose gravel off her hands.

She was shaking from head to toe. I dared not touch her but tried to explain my delay.

'Gunda, I'm sorry. I suspected you of divulging your name at the tavern in a bid to be rescued. I thought you planned to turn me over to them.'

I went to collect our horses and when I came back, I found her was kneeling next to the body of the taller man, grabbing at his neck with frantic hands.

'Get me to your army, Roman, fast,' she said with a wild sob.

'Gunda, why did those men abuse you? What did they say?'

She wrenched the thick gold neck ring off the dead man's neck and started working away at the second corpse, wresting his prized jewelry off him as well and stuffing her gruesome trophies into the sack hanging off her saddle.

'Please hurry, hurry! Someone at the tavern did betray me. Those two were sent to find me. They were sent to kill me. Get us away from here.'

'But you're like royalty to them, aren't you? Or did you lie to me?'

I jerked her back and forth by the shoulders.

'Are you the daughter of Gundomadus, one of the seven great *reges* or not? Or is your brother just some illiterate nobody? Are you nothing but an entertainer? A tribal whore in stolen jewelry?'

'I am Gunda, daughter of Gundomad,' she said, spitting in my face. 'And now those bastards told me Gundomad has been assaulted! Rivals attacked my father because he fights to keep his word to your emperor! Our family is fair game for any violent bastard. Rape? Murder? This is an ally's reward?'

Still choking on angry tears, she mounted her horse.

'Get me out of here, Roman. Get me safe!'

Chapter 8, Losses at Lugdunum

—THE LAST LEG TO AUGUSTA RAURICA—

So the Alemanni had spies of their own. Gunda had sung only one song—one song too many—back in that *taberna*. Her performance had betrayed not only her beautiful voice but also her pedigree and cloaked identity. She had announced her identity to the entire room. Had she been betrayed to an Alemanni network by the one-eyed man as revenge for his injury?

Unlikely. He was too tired and resigned.

Then I remembered the serving girl—envious and downtrodden—trying to pretend she wasn't an Alemannic immigrant.

We couldn't trust anyone when we stopped for food or fresh horses, even at the humblest *mansio*, and especially not bordering the *pagus* we had assumed was safe under the control of Gundomadus and his brother Vadomarius.

Vadomarius—where did he stand? Was he in danger as well? Or had Gunda's uncle threatened his own brother to prove that a worthless Roman treaty hadn't bought him out? Or did the menace come from one of the kings following Chnodomarius, their *supremus*?

Or even Chnodomarius himself?

'Alemanni' was supposed to mean 'all men,' but as usual, the *Germani* fought each other as deadly rivals for power between their vast tribes. Apodemius had assumed that Gunda would be useful to me in ferreting out intelligence about where these tribes stood in relation to the Empire. But Gunda would be of little use if she and her family were political pariahs.

She was too dazed to ride at full speed and refused to stick to the *Cursus* out of fear. We shifted over to a farmer's trail and lost many hours. We ended up napping rough by the side of an abandoned villa. Reduced to breakfasting on stream water and wild fruit, we crossed paths with a trio of army scouts searching the unpaved land for signs of Alemannic raiders. They delivered us that evening to a market hamlet less than a morning's ride from Augusta Raurica.

I watched Gunda closely that evening. The two brutes' attack had shaken her and she stuck close to my side. She showed no interest in perusing the market stalls selling ladies' knickknacks and perfumed oils or risking a bath without my protection. From time to time, she glanced at her little knife, secure on my belt, but I just shook my head, even when we retired to eat the main meal of the day.

The humble room at a 'villa' we'd requisitioned from a local tradesman had little to recommend it, but our host served endless pots of mountain honey, curds, and dried beef.

'And we always hear how well you Romans eat,' Gunda said, downing the rustic food with an unladylike appetite.

'You ate better at the horny bishop's, I suppose.'

'Very well indeed, Roman. Hare or fowl with different sauces every night, hard-boiled eggs with anchovy stuffing, boiled vegetables, dried fish, and fresh berries, peaches, apricots, elderberry custard—'

'That's what I like about Christians. Their devotion to poverty and self-denial.'

'Well, he was a bishop, not some Egyptian monk living off desert weeds. Of course he ate well.'

'Better than your mother's cooking, I suppose?'

My jibe didn't go down well. She gulped on her food and gave me an odd look.

'You forget my mother was the bedmate of the *Heerkönig* Gundomad. Such a man doesn't live in some hovel, but in a hilltop fortress built by you Romans and attended by hundreds of his *comitatus*. My mother never touched a cooking pot in her life. Before she died, she commanded over a dozen Roman slaves in her kitchen feeding my father and his noblemen?'

'How did your brother get caught raiding?'

'Hermund has looks and name, but he's slow-witted and impressionable. Unfortunately, he's just smart enough to know how dim he is.'

She shrugged as if she could disown her brother's foolish adventure.

'He joined those raiders to prove himself to our father. He was hoping for booty and praise like some lowborn Alemannus nobody. That's all those boys know! They have no schools, no disciplined infantry training, and no apprenticeships for skills or trade. Their only hope to make something of themselves raiding in war bands like their ancestors.'

She sighed and turned away, adding, 'I still hope to save Hermund from himself before it's too late.'

With her phrases like 'their ancestors' and 'their only hope' it was as if Gunda wanted to impress on me that she was not just another ignorant Alemanna, but almost Roman. She must have acquired her arrogance at the knee of a mother determined to out-Roman the Romans.

She wiped a streak of honey off her face with the back of her sleeve and asked, 'Where are we going? What do you expect of me? Will you drag me all the way to the northern sea?'

'I don't know yet. I'll need you—possibly to talk to the tribes we trust, possibly to listen to the tribes we don't.'

'I should risk myself just to win Hermund's release?'

'That was our bargain. Considering what you tried in court, you're lucky to be alive.'

'You think I should be satisfied now with Hermund's freedom?'

She swept her tangled hair from her brow and picked at her teeth with a silver pick from the little purse hanging from her belt. 'No, Roman, I want more, much more.'

'More?'

'I want you to arrange a commission for Hermund in your army, a good post, the kind they give to senators' sons and generals' boys. He's the only son of a king. He should be trained by a powerful commander.'

'I can't fix that. I'm not even in the army, remember?'

She stood up and straightened her tunic and *stola*. 'Then I won't help you.'

She left our table without any more explanation. By Hades, this girl played for high stakes! One minute she was trying to stab the Emperor, the next minute twisting my arm to make her brother into a jumped-up *adiutor*.

I should not have been so surprised. She'd upped the ante because her father was in danger. She was right to do so. Hermund was no longer safe at home if certain Alemannic tribes were turning against our allies. Our campaign must be provoking them into choosing sides fast. We Romans had had peace along these borders but now we risked war.

I was still pondering this as I settled down for the night on a makeshift bed of cushions borrowed from the merchant's dining room. The gentle plucking of Gunda's strings in her room upstairs sent me into a tired slumber. I woke up sometime after midnight to the sounds of dozens of hooves pounding past our door. I waited half an hour, listening to the hoot of an owl. Just as I was falling asleep again, a couple of horses returned.

The quarter moon crossed the sky outside the unshuttered window. A group of men exchanged words with our merchant host in his garden and he came back inside with two men.

While I closed my eyes and feigned sleep, places were found for the newcomers to catch some rest before dawn.

I overheard '... losses at Lugdunum ...'

Something was up. Lugdunum lay hundreds of miles to the southwest, far too deep in the heart of secure Roman Gallia for a barbarian strike.

It was hard to go back to sleep. I thought I had recognized the first officer as a tribune named Flavius Valentinianus.

I was sure I knew the other man—the Frankish tribune Bainobaudes, last seen in Agrippina in 355 consulting with his fellow Franco-Roman, the doomed General Silvanus.

These officers didn't report to General Barbatio. If they reported to anybody, it would be to General Severus up north, and in so far as he was no more than a figurehead, to the rising Caesar himself.

What were these tribunes doing near Augusta Raurica?

If a contest for command over the Western Roman Army was underway, young Julian had just shifted two key game pieces deep into Barbatio's half of the board.

—THE DEADLY CAESAR—

☧☧☧

The sky over the Rhenus dawned the color of cold, wet iron blades. The morning drizzle ran down our waterproofed cloaks. Gunda and I would have to race to reach Augusta Raurica ahead of the storm moving in fast from the Gallic west.

Across the small square outside the merchant's house, army squadrons were mustering for a day of sorties while the two tribunes barked out orders.

One didn't forget a man like Valentinian. Only a few years older than myself, he was a very well built Pannonian, muscular but not lacking in grace. His shining chestnut hair framed a high complexion. His jovial features were offset by a stern sidelong glance of deep-set gray eyes.

I could understand the wariness in his expression. He was the son of the disgraced Gratianus Funarius, a prominent commander during the reigns of emperors Constantine I and his brother Constans I. Gratianus was serving as *Comes* of Roman Africa the year I was born not far away in Numidia Militaris. Later he left our dry deserts for the fogs of Britannia. But after his retirement to Cibalae in Pannonia, he had once offered the hospitality of his villa to the usurping Emperor Magnentius. As punishment, Constantius II stripped Gratianus of all his wealth. He lived on in Cibalae still, scratching respectability from a soldier's pension.

Given how Magnentius' rebellion had dragged so many into catastrophe, Valentinian must have worked hard to distance himself from his father's political downfall. He was strict in his own comportment, rigorous with others and, to make up for his father's poor taste in emperors, loyal to Constantius II to a fault.

How did I know all this about the powerful soldier now rousting his riders into their saddles? I'd seen him once with his father visiting Magnentius' court. That hard set to his mouth and stiff spine hadn't changed.

Years later, while the blood of civil war dried and the skulls of casualties bleached white, I was sitting in the Castra analyzing reports from the Armenian front. I overheard another *agens* say that Magnentius' virgin 'Empress' Justina had landed under the protection of Valentinian's household. She was serving as a companion to his wife, Marina Severa.

I did not like to think of the brave Justina—barely out of childhood but wise beyond her slim years—subjected to the whims of any tyrant or brute. Worried for her, I had called up the Cibalean family's dossier from our Castra archives. From what I read, this Valentinian was not a brute—at least not to women.

The sun wasn't up yet, but all the stable hands were busy. Valentinian saw me struggling with my horse's flank strap.

He strode over and stared at me. 'You're an *agens*?'

If he wasn't a brute, he was certainly brusque.

'*Biarchus*,' I said, straining to cinch the swollen leather through its buckle while the unhappy horse sidestepped away. 'On civilian assignment to join the staff of Praetorian Prefect Florentius.'

'I see.'

I detected an instant's hesitation. He gestured through the gray drizzle to Gunda busy at the side of her horse. I had warned the Alemanna to prepare for an early start. She was wrapping her lyre in thick rounds of linen for the wet ride.

'You traveled with her from Roma?' he asked me.

Apart from concern for her beloved instrument, Gunda seemed indifferent to the lousy weather. A North African Roman like me shivered through the 'summer' of the Germanic river plateau. On a drenched morning like this, Kahina would have wrapped her oiled coiffure in silk or wool.

Gunda had grown up around damp fields, dank forests, and snowy peaks. Her thick pale hair, escaping its braid, collected drops of mist like tiny jewels. She adjusted her weatherproofed woolen cloak to cover the lyre sack strapped across her back.

We watched Gunda throw herself up into the saddle and look down her nose at the men bustling all around her.

'Oh, she keeps up,' I assured Valentinian.

Valentinian looked her up and down before turning back to me. 'Not bad looking, if you like wild rides. Is she "civilian business" too?'

'Gunda is the temporary charge of our *schola*, Tribune. She's the daughter of Gundomadus *Rex*, our Alemannic ally in the Agri Decumantes.'

'Why is she traveling north with you?'

'That's the assignment—at least part of it. *Imperial business.*' I raised a warning eyebrow.

'Oh, I'm just looking,' he said. 'I'm a happily married man and my men know the difference between a camp follower and a king's wench. We're riding to catch *laeti*, not tunic skirts. But what good is she to you, then, *Agens*?'

'When I know, I'll tell you first, Tribune.'

He was a careful commander. His jovial inquiry had been more than casual pleasantry, but he had more urgent matters to see to. He took my gentle rebuff in good spirit. With relief, I watched the muscle-bound officer stride away.

So Valentinian did not remember me after all these years. And why would a visitor to the rebel court have noticed a discreet postal officer spying on General Magnentius for Roma? An *agens*' job was to avoid drawing attention to himself as much as possible. I certainly had no intention of mentioning our previous encounter. The Manlius *gens* was just now escaping from the rebel taint of the civil war.

The Franco-Roman Bainobaudes had spotted me chatting to his fellow officer and took Valentinian's spot on the glistening pavement.

'Let me help you with that horse.'

'I've got it, thanks.'

He searched my face and glanced down at my insignia. He pulled on his long moustache.

'I thought I knew you. You were the *agens* in Agrippina two years ago? The one who came with the *magister* and that rough customer—?'

'*Ducenarius* Gaudentius. I'm Marcus Gregorianus Numidianus, *biarchus*, upper class.'

'That's right. The other *agentes* were detained, but not you. General Silvanus trusted you. Gave you the run of the governor's palace. Perhaps he made a mistake. Perhaps we all were wrong to trust a Numidian *curiosus*.'

The Frank's long, powerful fingers massaged the twisted silver and gold pommel of his *spatha*.

I would let him insult me with that *curiosus*—this once. Everyone hated our *schola*. We opened and copied their mail, monitored their rivalries, and reported their secrets. We held ourselves aloof and unscathed from the vicious fray of Constantius' court.

And Tribune Bainobaudes had lost a lot the day General Silvanus fell, slaughtered in the governor's private chapel in Agrippina. Franco-Roman officers in their long green-silver cloaks, with their flowing hair and combed moustaches—all these high-ranking second-generation barbarian officers woven into the fabric of the Empire—would not have forgotten in two short years their hero's futile, fatal bid for the purple.

Silvanus had been a loyal commander, justifiably resentful of calumny. Once Silvanus was cornered by vile accusations down in court, he'd twisted and turned. The bonds and careers of his personal *comitatus* had twisted and turned with him. I had counseled Silvanus to challenge his *consistoriani* enemies in person—just as I had witnessed the burly General Ursicinus do.

But I had begged in vain. Vicious tongues had goaded Silvanus into believing it was too late to change Emperor's Constantius' suspicious mind.

'I did not betray Silvanus,' I told Bainobaudes now. 'Your general betrayed himself.'

'Silvanus was a careful man.'

'Too careful. He vacillated too many times, Tribune. That was always his way. Commander Atticus Manlius Gregorius trusted Silvanus, but Silvanus changed his mind at the last minute and tipped the Battle of Mursa to Constantius. So Gregorius and tens of thousands of other noble Romans died because they trusted Silvanus. Perhaps they made a similar mistake?'

I would not confide that I was also Commander Gregorius' bastard freedman. All the same, he heard my bitterness.

Bainobaudes drew himself up. 'We will all die serving Roma, one way or another.'

It cannot have been easy for him to bury the Empire's leading Frankish commander and report to duty to the executioner General Ursicinus—Silvanus' replacement—the very next day.

'Indeed, we will and not all of us in uniform. I hope your daughter Clothild is well?'

—THE DEADLY CAESAR—

Bainobaudes' vixenish offspring had been shoved into Silvanus' path as a future empress, to the great distress of his mistress Roxana, not to mention his long-suffering wife held hostage in the imperial court.

'Clothild will serve Roma when her turn comes,' Bainobaudes said. He turned away to supervise the *decurio* leading away the first squadron file.

Bainobaudes was a noble man who prized loyalty above all else. I knew he respected me, at least for the day I had fought, blade for blade, by his side. He had bargained hard with savage Frankish tribesman in the dark forest across the Lower Rhenus from Agrippina. His secret purpose had been to request sanctuary for his 'Emperor' Silvanus from Emperor Constantius' revenge.

The barbarian Franks said no. Along with Silvanus' other negotiators, we two had barely survived their blunt refusal, issued with sharp axes and barbed angons.

It did not take long this morning to learn the details of the two tribunes' mission around Augusta Raurica.

While General Barbatio had been mustering his vast army in preparation for the march farther north, a rogue band of disaffected *laeti* some few hundred strong had swept across the border and plunged deep into peaceful Gallia. They'd sped all the way to Lugdunum and would have burned that prized city to the ground if the gates hadn't been slammed and bolted just seconds short of disaster.

The brigands had taken out their frustration on the surrounding countryside, pillaging estates and farmland, leaving havoc and rapine in their wake. Loaded down with booty, these thugs were now returning eastward to the haven of their scattered hamlets across the river.

Caesar Julian had consulted no one but, after studying the brigands' likely escape routes, he had dispatched three elite cavalry *turmae*, each thirty riders in three files, along the few roads passing between the mountain ranges between Vesontio and Augusta Raurica.

Already hundreds of *laeti* raiders lay slaughtered on Gallia's country trails and their loot restored to the unhappy victims of Lugdunum.

But one war band had escaped. Valentinian and Bainobaudes' squadrons were crisscrossing the plateau, determined to catch the marauders before they evaded justice.

Thinking back to my boyhood recitations of Julius Caesar for the Senator in his study on the Esquiline Hill, I could only shake my head at how ancient history haunted us in these modern times. Again, Roma struggled to manage our barbarian allies along these tumbling waterways, steep mountainsides, and crisp flower-strewn fields. Again, there were other, more hostile, *Germani* ranging up and down the river border ready to slaughter or rob us.

I knew our young Flavius Claudius Julianus had grown up pouring over the same books as me. These tribes were different in name but in three centuries, little else had changed. Julius Caesar had defeated his heroic enemy Vercingetorix. But if Gunda was right, Chnodomarius was no noble Vercingetorix. He was just a cruder bully than most.

Then I slowed in my tracks.

'What is it?' Gunda asked as her horse drew up to mine.

'Nothing, nothing.'

I had been struck by an awful suspicion. Was our eager young Caesar imagining the terrifying 'Gigas' Chnodomarius was his own personal Vercingetorix—just for posterity?

We needed to keep our barbarian friends, perhaps to awe or educate them, but not to enrage them.

Gunda and I raced our state horses onward to Augusta Raurica ahead of the Caesar's squadrons.

※※※

Our horses fought buffeting winds in the contest to reach the elbow bend of the Rhenus. Hurricane clouds racing all the way from the distant western coast gusted across Gallia and swept up the plateau. On the steep slopes lining our route, lashes of rain bent the pines. I hoped the sky would hold, but an hour before we spotted the aqueduct of Augusta Raurica, sheets of water poured down. We slowed for fear our horses would lose their footing on the slippery approach past Barbatio's encamped troops and up to the city gates.

Rainwater gushed along the rutted roadways between the thousands of tents pitched in full view of the ramparts. The army camp's Via Principia, some two hundred feet in width, was flooding. All pennants and standards had been rescued from the downpour. The last preparations for continuing up the Rhenus were at a standstill. Tens of thousands of soldiers huddled under leather roofs, each with his *contubernium*, eight men to a tent.

We trotted along the staked palisade toward the old curial palace used as the general's temporary headquarters. A few curious heads popped out in time to see us disappear through the city gates.

Midsummer's late dusk was at least an hour away, yet thick rain obscured the old town. Loose pottery, roof tiles, and city litter whipped in all directions. *Aediles* lit rain-proofed torches, lamps, and lanterns to guide unlucky stragglers to shelter. Not everyone found a haven. A blind beggar was trying to crawl into an overturned barrel as I rode past.

We arrived on General Barbatio's doorstep with hoods dripping into our eyes.

For all her pluck in the saddle, Gunda looked worn to the bone. It wasn't just the weight of those stolen neck torcs she insisted on carrying. It was the strain of confusion. She had regained some of her composure on the road, though I knew from her docility toward me that her spirit was sagging with worry for her father's uncertain predicament.

No doubt, she'd been quickly reassessing her political position. It seemed she had decided that Roman protection was the best she could do for now.

And our journey would only get more difficult for her as we traveled up the *Cursus* to our rendezvous point with General Severus and Caesar Julian.

Despite myself, I admired her when I saw her collect her forces to enter the palace with her bedraggled head held high.

When we reached the headquarters, I told Gunda to take advantage of the palace's amenities while I presented myself to my least favorite general in the Roman army. Once this town had been nothing more than Castrum Rauracense, a lonely garrison guarding a ford in a bend of the river. But for centuries since it had served as the strategic crossing between Gallia to the Danuvius and as such, the original headquarters of the *Legio I Martia*.

We were unlikely to be this comfortable for many days to come.

'No, I'll come with you,' she insisted.

'No, this is between Romans. Our talk involves sensitive information between an *agens* and a commander in the field.'

As she turned away, I thought better of it. There was little I was prepared to tell Barbatio that Gunda couldn't hear. Her presence might even provide an excellent excuse to tell him less.

'All right,' I relented, 'Join me here after you've bathed and changed.' I entrusted her to an adjutant to find a suitable room.

Almost immediately, I turned the corner and bumped into a Palatine tribune, Cella of the 'shield-bearing' Scutarii, and two others on their way to report to Barbatio. They were gracious enough to allow me the first audience and excused themselves to take care of other business.

Barbatio didn't rise to greet me, but stayed half-reclining on a couch, his armor digging into the brocade cushions and his heavy boots tapping on the priceless mosaic underfoot.

He stared up at me with piercing black eyes. The rest of us reeked of humid wool but he exuded his own dry, angry heat. The gaudy jewels on his wide belt sparkled by the lamp sconces lining the wall.

'You have risen high in the world, General.'

'Welcome, *Biarchus* Numidianus.' His stress on my rank, so long unchanged, was his personal vinegar in the wound.

'You catch me reading a letter from my wife,' he said. He had no letter in his hand and had certainly never been a 'man of letters' in the decade I'd known him. A meek scribe standing to one side nodded to me before continuing out loud, '... he promises to be as clever as his renowned father. We so long to see him well placed in a promising career safe from the dangers of the battlefield. Do what you can. Please also remember, my darling bed-beast—'

'That's enough! I'll read the rest of it in private.' Barbatio jumped up and shoved the poor scribe out a small side door. He tucked the letter under his armor and gestured me to sit on a humble wooden stool meant for a lady's maid.

'My wife Assyria writes to me of our cherished son, Gessius,' he explained. 'The boy is now old enough to choose his career.'

'Surely custom, law, and the example of his illustrious father conspire to make him the greatest of commanders.'

I imagined this Gessius as a skinny brute of a boy with less hair on his legs and chest than Barbatio but if he was lucky, more brains between his ears.

'Stop the flattery, Numidianus. We're alone. I know what you think of me. But I've swallowed my setbacks since Antiochia. Oiled a lot of palms and licked a lot of boots to get out of Moguntiacum. I've reached *Magister Peditum*. Imagine! Silvanus' entire personal household bows to my wife now—including his mother's slaves! Silvanus' infantry salute me, *me*, the Dacian lieutenant your precious Commander ignored back in Numidia Militaris.'

'Yes, General, you've acquitted yourself admirably.'

'Yes, I have.'

He circled the room, rubbing his stubbly chin with thick fingers. 'Listen, my Gessius shows promise, Numidianus. I did you a big favor once—'

'It was not a favor. Your reputation and career were on the line.'

'—when I heard you were en route to the Caesar's camp, I decided to ask you a favor in return.'

I stood up from the ridiculous stool and braced my shoulders. 'My mission is already somewhat complicated.'

The last thing I needed was a fourth commission to spy on someone.

'This has nothing to do with state business. I want you to recommend my son for admission to the *agentes*' training school in Roma.'

'What?'

The irony that General Barbatio wanted his own bright spark to join our *schola* while Gunda wanted Hermund reporting to a thickhead like Barbatio didn't escape me.

'I'll make it worth your while, Numidianus. You don't seem to be getting very far. Here's my offer; you see my boy through training to a confirmed appointment and I'll make sure you retire in style.'

'First, General, who said I wanted to retire? Second, I'm comfortable enough, thanks to the terms of the Manlius estate.'

'Oh, come on! You've always had your eye on the next rung but I hear things. I hear your superior, one Ahenobarbus, is looking to retire soon. *Ducenarius* Gaudentius is the coming man and he doesn't like you. The other senior *agentes* are dispersed and anxious, afraid of putting a foot wrong with whoever's in line to take Apodemius' place.'

'Whomever.' I couldn't resist.

'You don't make the right friends, Numidianus. You don't want to be a freedman estate manager all your life, do you?'

I shrugged a shoulder. 'Obviously, you're not familiar with the size of the Manlius fortune.'

Barbatio knew very well the extent of Leo's inheritance and he swallowed a retort. In a low voice drenched in phony sympathy, he continued, 'Is your lovely lady friend recovered? You can't count on employment for life when the mistress of the house is the object of fortune hunters from one end of the Eternal City to the other, can you? I imagine your public rooms are filled with *captatores* sniffing her skirts.'

Barbatio had taunted me in North Africa when I was a *volo*, a mere slave attending the Commander. Since then, he'd complicated my life whenever he got the chance. Now he insulted me by trying to buy his son a place in my service. Apodemius already had enough worries about seeping corruption and nepotism in his *schola*. We didn't need more Barbatios.

'I've got enough money to make it worth your while,' he said, misreading my silence. 'I'm keeping the rolls higher than the actual troop numbers and pocketing the difference. All the officers do it—including General Ursicinus.'

Gunda and I had ridden past his crowded army settlement outside the walls of the city before passing the temple, church, and amphitheater to get to his headquarters.

'The Emperor thinks you have twenty-five thousand men out there.'

'Well, let him. It doesn't take much fiddling to pad out a purse,' Barbatio said. With a smug heave, he adjusted the wide polished belt, supported with straining jeweled struts, corseting his impressive paunch.

'So, you won't look out for my Gessius?'

I said nothing.

Barbatio shrugged. 'No matter. I've already written to that philosopher Libanius on the boy's behalf in exchange for his transfer back to Antiochia. You were only a backup plan.'

He twisted a heavy ring on his left hand, barely hiding his displeasure.

'So, Numidianus, you're not here as my friend. Whose friend are you? And why are you here?'

Chapter 9, One Commander Too Many

—THE FORTRESS OF AUGUSTA RAURICA—

'I will show you, General.'

I found Gunda seated in the corridor outside, her face composed and her hair brushed now brushed into a neat pair of coils. She wore the heavy neck torc in addition to a pair of *fibulae* in garnets and silver, each pierced by a ferocious silver pin and linked by a filigreed silver chain. The jingly gold bracelets were back on her wrists. A Roman woman in a tasteful pin or two would have shaken her head at disbelief at the portable treasure weighing Gunda down.

'This is the daughter of the Alemannic king we call Gundomadus,' I told Barbatio. 'She is accompanying me to the court of the Caesar, where I will be attached to the Praetorian Prefect Florentius.'

Barbatio looked Gunda up and down, ogled her full figure, and then frowned at me.

'Attached to Florentius. Is that all?'

He knew Apodemius was unlikely to spare me for so vague and anodyne a task. I had no intention of confiding the news of Helena's miscarriage or anything else to Barbatio. The Caesar must hear it from my lips and none other's.

The general's brain caught up. 'He's our most trusted ally in mopping your people off the left bank! What are you doing here, then, girl? Why aren't you with your father?'

Gunda stepped forward. 'I might not be safe. There has been an attempt on his life, General. Some Alemanni now call

Gundomad a traitor.' I admired her aplomb in reporting a personal threat to her own family.

'He's supposed to be controlling his people on the other side of the river out there! Who is in charge of your tribes now, then? Your uncle? Or is he discredited as a traitor too?'

Gunda was nearly as tall as Barbatio and showed no hint of being cowed by his bluster. 'Surely you have your own military lines of intelligence, General?'

'All I hear from our scouts is "Gigas, Gigas. Gigas is moving south. Gigas is roving upriver." What happened to our treaties with your family? Are we exposed, even down here, to this savage Gigas?'

'His name is Chnodomarius, not Gigas.'

'Don't tell me what to say, girl.'

Gunda made one of her scoffing sounds. 'You Romans only call him Gigas to make the enemy bigger and inflate petty victories into triumphs you can stamp on coins.'

Barbatio wasn't taking this. 'I saw the man for myself across the Rhenus from the fortress at Moguntiacum. He was a head taller than any other man in his company, wearing a gold helmet with a brilliant mask, and looking just as vicious as his reputation.'

'You saw one Alemannus chief among many, wearing a helmet that caught the sun's rays—not some mythic monster.'

'Whatever his size, Gigas is our enemy and we are ordered to subdue his followers, to clear them off our land and—'

'Last year's campaign against us was not enough? Our signature on your treaty was not enough? Why? Your young caesar needs a war, that's why. We Alemanni have made no real trouble, just taken the land you offered us. Then a few no-goods surround that boy in Senonae and all of a sudden it's "a siege" from which he needs rescuing. The Caesar—or someone in his camp—is trying to make us all into your enemies so that he can blood himself on our young men and send captives like my brother and cousin as trophies to his imperial cousin.'

Barbatio glanced at me. I nodded in confirmation. Hermund was our prisoner. It might take a minute or more for Barbatio to deduce that Gunda might be my hostage. I didn't give him time to think that through.

'General, how long will it take your troops to get to the rendezvous with the Caesar?'

He waved his hand thick with rings. He had always liked gaudy rings.

'Send her out of here first and then we can talk.'

I escorted Gunda into the care of an *immunis* on guard duty outside, with orders she was to stay in her quarters under supervision where a meal should be sent to her.

'And no, you can't have your knife back,' I said before she could protest.

She shook her head in disgust. 'Gigas! Gigas! That Barbatio is an impressionable idiot. My father is no traitor, Roman, but perhaps he is a fool to place his trust in such commanders.'

I shoved her off without giving her the satisfaction of a reply, but for the first time, I almost began to like Gunda.

※※※

For all his bluff, I smelled Barbatio's nervous sweat. The news that one of our two allies across the water had been discredited shook his complacency. He escorted me into a smaller side chamber used by his staff during the day as a clearinghouse for logistics and treasury affairs. A small map lay pinned down at the corners on a marble table by oil lamps flickering through the falling gloom. Neat rows of polished pebbles represented the legions camped outside the town walls.

He summoned Cella who had been waiting outside. The tribune had Alemannic features, like so many Scutarii recruits, but with a shiny, shaven skull and no beard or moustache. He made no attempt to ape the modern fashions of military commanders of mixed background. No jeweled belt or finely wrought blade of twisted pattern, no embroidered *orbiculi* on his bleached tunic, not so much as a gold animal *fibula* set him apart from a Roman soldier of decades ago.

Seeing my lack of senior military rank, Cella outlined their plan to me with visible reluctance. He ran his hand along the line depicting the broad current of the Rhenus slowly, almost possessively.

'We will march along the left bank, passing Argentoratum and moving downstream to a point not normally served by a bridge.'

'The river level will be at its lowest by then?'

'Exactly. We will coordinate with General Severus' forces coming in from the west. They've already moved from Senonae to Durocortorum, here, cleansing the area of Alemanni insurgents as they progress eastward to Divodurum Mediomatricum and then along the Mediomatrici-Argentoraum highway, up to here, to the Tres Tabernae Cesaris at the mouth of the main entry route through the Vosges Mountains.'

Cella had dragged a long finger across Gallia toward the famous point where Julius Caesar had built three rest stops for changes of horse and oxen before the steep incline to the plateau.

'What is this large square, Tribune?'

'It marks the half-demolished fortress sitting on high ground overlooking the Rhenus valley.'

'The *forceps* strategy, just like last year?' I nodded.

'Constantius wants no war with these ragged war bands, just a show of Roman strength,' Barbatio said.

'And your pincer closes . . . ?'

'Here.'

Cella's index finger tapped a spot a few miles north of Argentoratum where the spreading river was studded with a few small islands.

'With the help of our Alemanni allies, a bridge will enable our troops to evacuate the barbarian settlers swiftly over to the right bank before their chieftains can organize any resistance.'

I was glad Gunda wasn't here. Cella's plan reeked of Constantius' policy toward the Alemanni—pulling them in as long as they were useful, then pushing them back out, and always keeping them divided and fractious among themselves. So far this strategy matched my briefing from Apodemius and my impression from the Emperor himself.

I'd just noticed something else in the briefing. Cella had referred to the other army as marching behind General Severus, correct as far as military protocol went, but a notable oversight of the rising caesar. One wondered how Julian viewed this ambiguous policy balanced between war and peace.

'Who's going to build this bridge, Tribune?'

'We are. We've brought the engineers, the boats, and sufficient rations for our men.'

'You'll need a supply of long timber.'

'We'll get the local Alemanni settlers to cut and dress the trunks. We'll pay them. And we won't be stealing food from the settlers. We're taking on enough feedstock, grain, and wine here in Augusta Raurica to keep us going.'

'It looks like a good plan—as long as your bridge engineers are real and not part of your phantom roll call.'

There was dead silence. Then Cella broke into a harsh laugh and slapped me on the back.

Barbatio wasn't smiling.

At that moment the arrival of Julian's squadrons led by Valentinian and Bainobaudes was announced. The two tribunes were waiting to present their credentials to Barbatio in the palace's main reception hall.

The Dacian's black eyes narrowed. He played for time as he absorbed the shock of Julian's two unexpected officers on his doorstep. With too-obvious deliberation, he kept Cella talking to me about the preparations for the proposed march north. He dragged our conference on for as long as he could until Cella was reduced to detailing the pay scale for barbarian woodcutters versus raft builders.

'They're gone, General.' An adjutant interrupted us.

Barbatio's face reddened. 'Where? Where've they gone?'

'They said they couldn't wait, that the *laeti* would escape over the river any minute if they didn't position themselves immediately along the roads to the bridge.'

'What *laeti*? What's he talking about?' Barbatio shouted in our faces.

He pounded down the corridor at double speed to an echoing hall, compelling us to follow. He threw open the wide carved doors. The two visiting tribunes had vanished in the other direction, leaving a pool of rainwater on an artist's mosaic of a basin filled with four dancing fish. It was proof of the impatient minutes they'd waited to make their report before leaving a trail of muddy scuffmarks toward the old palace exit.

I explained: 'Severus and Julian slammed Lugdunum shut against a *laeti* raiding army but not before the attackers devastated the unprotected estates outside walls. The raiders split up into separate war bands laden down with what loot they could carry. Most of them were caught. But the last bunch is making its way for the other side. This plateau is their last possible escape route.'

'I command thousands of men out there who can this block this pass. Why in Hades should I need his *turmae* when I have whole legions? How dare he?'

It was a fair question. No one dared ask whom Barbatio meant by 'he'—General Severus or Caesar Julian. We heard dozens of horses galloping away through the thick rain outside.

'There's no time to call up our troops,' Cella told Barbatio. Anyway, our horn signals would send the *laeti* into hiding, in which case, we might recover the loot, but they'd disperse, impossible to arrest.'

Cella turned to me, 'Where are those squadrons headed?'

'Wherever they can ambush the raiders before they cross the border.'

Barbatio's headquarters sat close to the amphitheater, with a view of both the army to the west and the town proper to the east. We followed on his heels up to the roof to gaze southward at the main road on our right.

The storm had returned, doubly cold and fierce. Both townsfolk and soldiers huddled undercover. Lightning flashed over the hills beyond, turning the pines blanketing the southern slopes an eerie blue-gray before falling back into a formless dark wall.

To our left, the river churned against the ancient Roman embankment. Boats tethered to the docks banged one into another or drifted away from the piers to be battered by tree branches tumbling downstream.

Augusta Raurica sat on a triangle of land facing north, framed by two tributaries that joined at the point to flow into the great river. Its Temple of Jupiter faced an imposing theatre and, along with the market forum slightly to the south, lay buried in the heart of this town of some twenty thousand souls. The southern edge of the town farthest from the river stretched about a kilometer wide bordered by a state road arriving from the west and abutting the low-slung Jurassien foothills.

With Barbatio's vast army planted across the tributary that formed the western edge of the triangle, the tribunes would cover the routes along the southern foothills below the 'rear' of Augusta Raurica. The *laeti* would most likely try to slip past using the main road to pass the great amphitheater and the triumphal arch on their left, but then dodge through the town's minor back streets to reach a wide road leading out the other side of town.

That route led to a secondary river crossing for townsfolk farming the wide fields along the river. The bridge there stood unguarded.

'I see the squadrons, General!' Cella pointed at a flickering line of torches fighting the rain to keep alight and threading up from the base of the foothills to a vantage point overhanging the southern road.

Julian's *turmae* had chosen a good spot for surveillance with a fast descent to the bridgehead. With the barbarians' backs to the river, Valentinian and Bainobaudes would chop them down in their tracks.

The furious, wet day was ending, but the only clue to the setting sun was a deepening haze closing in on all sides. I kept my eyes trained on that distant line flickering between thick pine trunks on the slope. If we could see the waiting squadrons, so could any *laeti* aiming to pass.

The wind turned colder still. The rain sprayed like needles into our faces. Water streaked crosswise across cloaks and helmets and we all peered from under our hoods to the southeast. I saw nothing there as the light dimmed and then failed altogether, but we still heard rattling empty wagons, bending trees, and thrashing fields.

Our god Jupiter had grown bored with the summer and decided to turn this plateau into a maelstrom of chaos and wreckage.

A crackling noise broke in the sky overhead. Ice pebbles pelted us like frozen missiles. Hailstones skipped across the roof, rattling down on the courtyard below the parapet, and bounced in all directions everywhere like crazy dice tossed in a gambling game of the gods.

This lasted ten minutes. As the downpour of stones slowed, we stepped closer to the roof edge, our boots crunching on ice pebbles.

Another flash of lightning bolted across the sky and zigzagged over the hills beyond the town. I turned just in time to see, lit up as if by an Olympian lamp held by a giant goddess, a thin line of stealthy figures climbing the southeastern ridge. Pulling horses laden high with teetering sacks and rolls, they were trying to steady their burdens in the high winds.

This was the elusive band of *laeti* brigands—perhaps a hundred—the last of their plundering army.

Julian's *turmae* had spotted them too. Their torches went out. The slope became a greenish-black curtain of forest.

The brigands were still at least half a mile off. They disappeared from view behind a bend in the long road leading toward the outskirts of the town. It was only a matter of time before they reappeared. As soon as they had cleared the last junction, the *turmae* would race back down the mountain path down and cut the *laeti* brigands off from any other routes. They would be trapped with their backs before they reached the narrow bridge.

We were about to witness a bloodbath.

Barbatio's huge figure stood rigid, barely covered by a cloak grasped tight in both meaty hands. He could not have missed the sight of the skulking *laeti* but his gaze fixed on the elbow of river bending north.

Then he turned and looked down on the rain-lashed triumphal arch. He wore a peculiar expression of pleasure in defiance. It reminded me of the day in Numidia he'd been commissioned to burn the body of an assassin, a fanatical Circumcellion. He took pleasure in stoking the pyre in full view of a threatening mob of religious fanatics held back by our camp palisade.

That perverse expression had also distorted his features in the prison cell in Pola, Istria after he'd beheaded the doomed young Caesar Gallus on orders from Constantius. In absence of all reason and restraint, Barbatio had mutilated the Gallus' face in a savage outburst that availed no one.

Seeing that look now, I almost laid my hand on his arm but stopped short. I was still ranked *biarchus*. Through bribery, bravery, or sheer bullheaded persistence, Barbatio had risen to *Magister Peditum*. If he had secret orders from the Emperor, I was in the dark.

He chuckled to himself. 'The Caesar thought to steal credit for yet another meaningless encounter with a nameless gang of ruffians, Numidianus,' he muttered. 'But he forgot—there is only one commander here.'

He pushed away Cella's outstretched arm tracing the distant line of brigands. 'Recall those squadrons, now! Have Valentinian and Bainobaudes report to me.'

Cella stared at Barbatio through the pounding rain. Two junior officers who had followed us onto the roof exchanged glances of alarm. We were all drenched. Clinging to our hoods and helmets in the high winds like that, was there any chance we'd misheard Barbatio's order?

But Barbatio was leaving the roof and the stormy drama beyond. Cella had already dashed past him into the palace. It was hardly five minutes before we heard a single horn summon Julian's *turmae* off the slopes and to the headquarters where Barbatio waited.

I stayed on the roof with two remaining officers. It was too dark now to distinguish the squadrons' horses picking their way down through the distant trees until their lines reformed at the base of the slope. Once out from cover, they crossed the very road down which the *laeti* might yet slip around the town.

The other men excused themselves to join the assembled staff inside.

I huddled against the parapet with my eyes trained on the barely visible road. The hailstorm had started to wear itself out. Heavy rain slanted down, overflowing the roof gutter, and drowning my boots up to my socks.

Hundreds of lamps glowed through the slats of shuttered windows below. I envied the citizens of Augusta Raurica eating their lentils and eggs in the warmth of snug apartments and villas. Behind me, the army shifted and turned on their bedrolls, chewing limp flatbreads and dried fruits or gathered around some cooking pot filled with meat rations in wine and garum sauce.

I waited and waited. The *laeti* had not reappeared, perhaps alerted by the signal horn or the shock of seeing the vast army camp spreading across the northwestern fields.

The winds picked up again, brushing my cheeks. The rising moon winked at me from behind racing clouds. I did not know what Gunda was doing but this was not the night or weather in which she'd attempt an escape. I did not care to be in the main hall below where Barbatio would receive the visiting tribunes for a full briefing as to the width and breadth of his command over the plateau.

I hoped I would catch sight of the *laeti* again. I was a patient man, an ex-slave used to attending, waiting, and watching.

And then I detected suspicious movement on the southwest edge of the town. I had not wasted more than two hungry hours in that wretched position in such an exposed spot.

I slipped out of the palace and hurried to a sheltered alcove to watch the junction up close. The brigands must have sent scouts to sniff out the dormant army camp and the unguarded southern road. They'd reassembled their straggling train and were making their way in dead silence around the city's modest suburb.

As they came within view at last, I was no longer certain how easy Valentinian's bloodbath would have been. These men were armed to the teeth. They rode strong, obedient horses that kept a disciplined pace, despite their burdens. All the horses and men were dressed for the foul weather. They were making good progress.

It was not only too late to send up an alarm, it would be foolhardy to countermand Barbatio's orders with any alert. The *laeti* seemed to know this territory well. They avoided the road bordering the eastern quarter where not even a dog stirred from his snug bed and slipped forward toward the narrow bridge. At last they returned to the main road and were only a few hundreds yards from the imperial border.

But they weren't foolish. They didn't make an open dash for safety. They took cover for another twenty minutes. I strained my eyes, bewildered as to where such a large group had disappeared, but then three scouts slipped out from behind a cluster of barns and warehouses. I could imagine them holding their breath, waiting for a shout from the palace ramparts.

But no shout came. I was the only witness. Nothing broke the sound of whistling wind.

One by one, their scouts slipped across the bridge. When all three had reached the far bank, they lit up a signal torch and extinguished its flame just as quickly.

The rest of the brigand force followed in orderly fashion scarcely twenty feet away from where I hid. Broken into groups of a dozen, they disappeared by handfuls leading booty-laden mounts into the thick forest beyond the Rhenus. It would be a short ride for them to reach the first *vicus* under the protection of Gundomadus or Vadomarius and beyond the discipline of either Julian or Barbatio.

I closed my eyes and prayed to the gods to grant them a safe retreat. For what I had seen had filled me with a deep and unexpected melancholy. Among these thieves, I'd recognized at least two faces—senior rebel Roman officers turned outcast. Six years ago, they had stood proud, shouting commands to the Western Army under the standard of the Emperor Magnentius. I had seen them in a meeting tent reporting to Silvanus, Gregorius, and the usurper's *magister officiorum* Marcellinus.

This is what their loyalty to the army reformers had reduced them to. They'd run away from certain death in the front lines on the Persian front for a squalid existence among the settler renegades.

Through no fault of their own, they were two good men lost forever to the Empire. There were probably more such men in this barbarian company sneaking out of the Empire as I watched.

Out of respect for what had been a noble cause, I was grateful Barbatio's stupidity had spared their lives.

※ ※ ※

I had already seen enough of *Tribunus* Cella—his battle-scarred arms, straining calves, and thinset lips—to guess he was a soldier who did not make mistakes.

However, he might be a soldier who would recognize a misstep when he saw one.

It was not hard to locate him, but it was hard to get him alone. He received me only after the general staff had been dismissed and Barbatio had retired with his wife's love letter still pressed to his bosom. Even the storm had fallen away in exhaustion.

The moon shone in through the window. Cella received me alone in the logistics room. The map was laid out as before but the markers representing the legions' encampment were gone. The army was under orders to move.

'You wanted a word with me, *Agens* Numidianus?'

'Tribune, you let the *laeti* make it over the border. I watched them from the junction just before the bridge.'

Cella took a deep breath. '*Agens*, we all follow orders. Without a clear line of command, the Roman Army would not prevail.'

'It did not prevail tonight.'

'Valentinian and Bainobaudes will answer for the *laeti*'s escape. The General has already drafted his report to the Emperor. Both tribunes are to be cashiered.'

'Cashiered? Valentinian and Bainobaudes did their duty until Barbatio recalled them!'

'The Caesar's tribunes will take the blame.'

Cella did not move from his chair. His fingers cupped a white glass goblet, drained of wine.

'You know they're not responsible. You conveyed the recall order yourself.'

'I know, *Agens*.' He glanced at me and then returned to his study of the empty wine vessel. 'If you know another version, I encourage you to file your own report.'

'May I ask the General's reasoning?'

'General Barbatio hears rumors that Caesar Julian intends to discredit him, just as he painted the noble General Marcellus as derelict in his duty. As far as this attack on Lugdunum is concerned, Barbatio foresaw that Julian's squadrons would apprehend the brigands only to place the final leaf in Julian's laurels.'

'But General Barbatio hasn't discredited the Caesar. If anything, he has discredited himself.'

Cella took a deep breath. 'Numidianus, have you ever seen our general play *latrunculi*?'

'I have been acquainted with Barbatio for a decade. I've never once seen him touch a game board.'

'It shows, doesn't it?'

Cella rose from his chair, stiff and tired. 'When some men play *latrunculi*, they anticipate their opponent's moves many turns ahead. They might even sacrifice a pawn or two to encircle their opponent's king later. Others play the game move-by-move, piece-by-piece. Our *Magister Peditum* is one of the latter.'

'How does General Barbatio intend to explain tonight's move to Julian?'

'He doesn't. As of tonight, we follow a different strategy. We use the bridge here to cross the river and then march down the right bank instead of the left. We pass through the *pagi* controlled by our Alemanni allies to the point opposite our designated rendezvous point. We'll make good time, using the current to carry our boats loaded with the heaviest supplies.'

'Then what?'

'We build the bridge and clear out the Alemanni on our own while Julian dawdles taking on one skirmish after another on his way to the rendezvous.'

'So instead of waiting for Julian to form the coordinated pincer formation, Barbatio takes all the credit.'

'Our General is under orders of his own, you know.'

This was too cryptic for me until I realized that the *laeti* had arrived home in the *pagus* of Gunda's father, to whom Constantius had promised peace, not war.

'You mean Barbatio's eradication of the Alemanni settlements will be carried out by negotiation, not violence? Barbatio didn't want a slaughter here tonight.'

Cella allowed himself a wry smile. 'We live in confusing times, do we not, Numidianus?'

'It's not that simple, Tribune. I know Tribune Bainobaudes very well from two years ago in Agrippina. He has survived too many political battles to be cashiered over this trifle. He will not accept dismissal.'

'You're right but there's nothing I can do about Bainobaudes. Tribune Valentinian is less emotional, but no less proud of his service record. He's heading home to Cibalae at dawn to consolidate his position. When the time is ripe, he'll lobby Constantius for a new commission. Meanwhile, your Frankish acquaintance is leaving tonight to rejoin Julian in complete defiance of Barbatio's decision.'

I'd taken enough of Cella's time. 'I'll file my own report, as you suggest. My thanks, Tribune.'

I could write my report in the morning. All I wanted at this moment was a hot bath and a steaming bowl of *puls*.

'I would not dawdle too long over paperwork, if I were you. I would not even eat that supper you missed keeping watch on the roof. I'd pack up your Alemanna noblewoman and ride out with Bainobaudes tonight. She may be incidental to your posting up north, but if she is essential to your mission, move very quickly.'

Startled, I turned at the door, waiting for an explanation of his warning.

Cella walked over to me, close enough for me to see the pinkish-white stripes of old blade cuts crisscrossing his right forearm gleaming by the torchlight.

'That Alemanna whom I saw in the corridor—am I right in thinking she is traveling under your escort?'

'Yes. We hold her brother in the Castra and she is cooperating with us to win his freedom and restore her father's authority.'

'You have spoken freely to me, *Agens*. Let me speak freely to you. Tomorrow Barbatio will lead our column over the border. Why miss the chance to march through Alemanni-held territory with a highborn Alemanna at his side? I overheard him give orders that your proud Gunda was to be put under his personal custody as of dawn.'

Chapter 10, Gunda Makes a Choice

—THE ROAD TOWARD ARGENTOVARIA—

I wasn't waiting to discover how Barbatio intended to use Gunda— certainly not as an interpreter. He had hundreds of soldiers, crack Raetovarii troops, sleeping out in those tents. They could speak Alemannic dialect—if negotiations were part of Barbatio's plan, that is.

I knew the man too well. He would relish flaunting Gunda as his hostage as his army moved northward through the allies' *pagi*. He would force her to demonstrate her submission—even humiliation—to a barbarian public.

I didn't warn Gunda of Barbatio's intentions to lay claim to her. Disagreements between Roman officers were hardly her business. I merely roused her without apology three hours earlier than promised, plunked her on a horse between Bainobaudes in the lead and myself trailing, and told her that a late breakfast would be waiting for her at the old Celtic fortress of Mons Brisiacus across the river facing Argentovaria.

She said nothing. Thank the gods, those valuable golden torcs were safely packed away with her lyre. Her thick rolls of gleaming hair sat pinned into modest coils under her hood. It was easier to travel with a nondescript female than with an Alemanna noblewoman decked out in a year's salary of gold and a towering coiffure topped with a fox hairpin with garnet eyes.

Still, this docile departure seemed a bit too easy. It was not the first time on our journey that the spitfire who'd pulled a knife to stab an emperor surprised me with her cooperation. I scored it up to concern for her brother's welfare or insecurity about her father's place in the current political climate. But was there more going on behind those frost-blue eyes?

I kept her knife sheathed with my *pugio*.

Both Bainobaudes and I knew this paved stretch of the *Cursus Publicus* running straight north up the Rhenus valley. Now that the steep ascents and vertiginous descents of the mountains lay behind us, the long stretch of fertile valley would take us past hamlets, a few towns, and innumerable borderland estates. I had last ridden this north-south route—back and forth, back and forth—only two years ago during the crisis over General Silvanus, the so-called 'Emperor of Twenty-nine Days.'

Those urgent races between the Mediolanum court and the usurping general's base in Agrippina had exposed any traveler to the cost of Constantius' invitation to the Alemanni to harass Magnentius' rear flanks back in 351.

What had the Emperor imagined would happen once the usurper's head twirled on the tip of a Roman spear? Had Constantius assumed these illiterate immigrants would sign up as fresh fodder for his diminished infantry? Had he considered the wailing distress of Gallo-Roman landlords facing hungry, savage faces who claimed their fields, gardens, and vineyards for themselves? Had he priced the losses to the tax rolls? Or the menace of robbery, brigandage, rapine, and waste?

Riding on missions to the Lower Rhenus, I'd been on the alert for Alemanni raiders seizing good land from Gallo-Romans or robbing merchants on brave sorties to get their hard-won harvests to safer markets inland.

Roma's recovery efforts continued. General Severus and Caesar Julian had cleared Agrippina of raiding Franks. Julian had retaken the towns of Augustodunum and Augustobona Tricassium. He had just saved Lugdunum.

Was not this progress?

Yet I rode behind Bainobaudes and Gunda with apprehension. Last year's campaign against the Alemanni in central Gallia had brought Constantius only a temporary peace. This summer was riled by uncertainty, rumor, and aggression—on both sides.

—THE DEADLY CAESAR—

Uneasiness roiled my more private thoughts as well: ruminations on Kahina and Leo in Ostia, my worries about the Manlius estates, my friend Roxana healing her wounds in secret sanctuary, and my resentments at my stalled career. It was hard to concentrate on the mission at hand, so ill defined and unpromising.

The wide road ran straight ahead. The summer skies sat low overhead, dark and heavy with swollen rain clouds. I couldn't shake off the chill from my evening's vigil in Augusta Raurica. I was ready to travel, but to fight? The lanky tribune was far more experienced in combat than myself. Like me, Bainobaudes carried a sword and dagger, but before any Alemannus killer came within reach of us, the tribune would no doubt neatly sling his tribal brothers' favorite weapon—the heavy-headed axe-like *francisca*—deep into the attacker's forehead from twenty feet.

In this, the Franco-Roman officer and I, the Numidian freedman, were Roman brothers through and through. He was certainly no friend of wild Germanic cousins with red-dyed hair. I'd seen a merciless Bainobaudes maul tribal Franks outside Agrippina. Though they were men who shared his blood and dialect, they were barbarian enemies from across the border.

We rode fast—not quite the *agentes*' professional relay pace, as I'd been trained ten years before, but a good swift army clip. Even at a gallop, I noticed the weed-covered fields, clogged irrigation ditches, collapsing roofs, and crumbling road verges. If Roma spoke of itself in the vocabulary of walls, aqueducts, arches and paving, these sad sights confessed disorder and decay.

High and proud, Mons Brisiacus waited for us on an overhanging plateau well chosen by wily ancient Celts. From the left bank town of Argentovaria, we crossed the low-lying river on a large raft to a dock on the right bank and climbed the slope to the fortress' main gate. I negotiated fresh horses on presentation of my papers while Bainobaudes sought out the officer in charge of border defense. Along with Vesontio, Noviodunum, Aventicum, and Augusta Raurica, Mons Brisiacus was one of the five cities of the diocese Maxima Sequanorum in the Gallia Prefecture.

'And our friend in charge works hard to keep it that way,' Bainobaudes told me on his return from a drink with the officer.

'He warned we'll have to be careful from here on until we reach Brotomagus.'

'We only need to reach the northern army—wherever they are.'

'The gods help us if I'm not reinstated,' he said. 'I won't accept such treatment from that brute Barbatio.'

This was the only indignation Bainobaudes voiced, though he was still seething. I'd seen him command thousands of Franco-Roman infantrymen up north, men wearing the signature helmets and furs of the ferociously proud Cornuti *auxilium*.

On the best imperial roads, the state-franchised *mansiones* stood about nine to twelve miles apart—one reason why *agentes* on postal relay could deliver messages as fast as birds, some exaggerated. This was not the case now, and had not been on this route for some time, fractured by fighting for at least half a decade.

The next such rest stop stood empty, its courtyard fountain clogged with rotting leaves, its iron stable hitches broken off the wall, and the front door to the small *triclinium* hanging crooked off a stubborn hinge. It would take more than one pacification of the Alemanni, perhaps many summer campaigns to come, to bring an innkeeper and his family back here.

We were making good time over these days, yet tiring and only halfway to Tres Tabernae. Our latest horses had proved themselves laggards. I checked my *schola* guide and suggested we would arrive soon at a *mutatio* I recalled from the Silvanus days.

Toward the early evening, these being 'summer hours' when the daylight seemed endless, we crossed paths with a fellow *agens*, a junior *circitor* carrying the civil postal bag from *curiae* north of here down to Mons Brisiacus. I flagged him down.

'Any news of the northern army?'

'Almost to Durocortorum,' he said. 'Delayed by action around Lugdunum.'

'So I heard. Are they still aiming for Tres Tabernae?'

He told us Julian had dispatched an advance party to assess Alemannic damage to that old fortress and start repairs. It was another hour to the next *mutatio*. The *circitor* shot off at full gallop.

—THE DEADLY CAESAR—

When we reached the relay station, I saw why the boy had fled further questions with a guilty glance. We found only an old man and a 'hand' of no older than eight.

'We just had a rider through, Tribune. He took the best horse we had,' said the guileless child.

And we had just seen it gallop past less than an hour before.

The stable boy offered us a mean selection: two retired army nags—complete with scars, limps, and only three eyes between them, and a couple of draft horses abandoned by Roman farmers fleeing the barbarians.

'I'd rather walk than ride into the Caesar's camp on one of those,' I said.

'I'd rather crawl.' Bainobaudes turned to me in disgust. 'I thought your service maintained these stations in war as in peace.'

'Any service is only as good as its empire,' I retorted, 'and the Empire depends on your defenses. I'll take one of the farm horses. At least he can see the road.'

Gunda made no complaint. She fed her chosen mount bits of dried fruit from her small sack. Her composure was beginning to unnerve me. The farther north we rode, the more concentrated the expression on her inscrutable face. We were putting many miles between her and both brother and father. Yet she seemed more assured than ever.

We plodded on now, unable to make our target and reluctant to overnight in the rough. We rounded a slight curve in the *Cursus* and came upon a freshly-built *vicus* of Alemanni settlers around a former Roman estate. Three or four houses sat sunk waist-deep into pits, their smoky fires belching into the threatening sky through crude circles cut in their thatched roofs. The main house was a third century villa adapted to *Germani* taste, with a timber roof and some improvised pillars adding a lopsided, cockeyed look to the lost elegance of the original dwelling.

'We're stopping here,' Gunda announced, dropping to the ground on determined boots. She walked through the villa's ramshackle garden overrun with feathery vegetable fronds and spiky green onions. The barbarian residents had annexed a sunken entrance and Gunda loped down the earthen steps, her cloak hem dragging behind her until we saw only her head and shoulders. She pounded on the door and shouted something in her dialect.

Bainobaudes turned in his saddle to ask me, 'Who holds the *potestas* over that woman?'

'Her father, I suppose.'

'There's no husband?'

'She told me her father sent her to a bishop's household to learn Latin and our ways. He hopes to marry her to a Roman officer—or better,' I couldn't resist adding.

Bainobaudes frowned. 'Yet this woman does not carry herself like a maiden. *Germani* women are known for their upright behavior, even those roguish tribes.'

'She has done nothing inappropriate.'

He stroked the ends of his moustache. 'Yet, for all her correct comportment, I say our female companion is no blushing innocent.'

I didn't challenge him. After all, Bainobaudes was the father of Clothild, one of most coquettish *bona fide* virgins I'd ever tangled with. I was no expert with 'maidens.' My dealings with women took me elsewhere. Like any healthy, unmarried Roman male, I frequented and appreciated the generous charms of tavern girls. I sheltered the *matrona* Kahina, the mother of my only child, with respectful affection. And I'd admired and had enjoyed knowing both the courageous body and brains of my fellow *agens* Roxana.

But virgins—not really. Bainobaudes knew their ways better than I. There was an ambiguity about Gunda that troubled me in ways I didn't want to acknowledge, even to myself.

A startled woman opened the door to Gunda who addressed her in clipped sentences. The settler raised an eyebrow, holding firm to the edge of her door. She scrutinized me, a tall stranger with more than a hint of North Africa in my complexion and hair. I wore my working tunic, bordered in red and blue embroidery at hem and sleeves, with nondescript leg bindings and trousers.

Gunda next pointed to Bainobaudes, standing even taller in full military glory. His segmented helmet was polished bright and studded with garnets. His belt stiffeners were solid silver. Large

—THE DEADLY CAESAR—

bear-headed *fibulae* linked with a filigreed chain across his bold breast pinned his green and silver cloak at both shoulders.

Taking in this warrior bristling with weapons, the woman made to slam the door shut but Gunda placed a neat leather boot in the doorframe and added a few more guttural words.

I was certain she talked of money.

The woman hesitated, then opened the door wider. A rough-complexioned girl on the cusp of maturity and an indifferent little child covered in so much grime and hair, its gender might remain a mystery for years to come, cowered behind their mother.

'We can stay here for the night,' Gunda said. 'We pay her in advance. Keep the horses tethered close.'

She disappeared into the dank interior of the rotting villa.

'I don't like it,' said Bainobaudes.

'The newest Romans in the Forum,' I answered with a shrug. 'We have to trust someone sooner or later.'

I glanced up at the threatening sky. 'If she tries to rob us, we can uproot her last carrots in revenge.'

Gunda called out to us from a small vestibule window that had lost its covering long ago. 'She welcomes you.'

'I have known warmer welcomes,' the Frank muttered.

'Just 'til the storm passes,' I told him out of Gunda's earshot. 'We have our weapons.'

I glanced around for smelting equipment or other heavy implements. 'I don't see any trace of a man in this place. The other huts seem empty. There's no smoke.'

We settled as best we could on the broken tiles of the old *triclinium*. The courtyard that had once flourished with potted plants and flowers stood overrun with weeds and tangled vines. The fountain had stopped running but the woman filled it with rainwater from a wooden cistern outside. We washed off before eating. I stared through filmy water at blue and green *tesserae* that had once portrayed dancing fish. The eyes of the fish had been plucked out—no doubt for their gold.

We ate a watery turnip soup, unflavored by *garum* or salt and washed down with a thin beer—tasteless but filling. It left a bitter aftertaste. The females did not drink.

The young girl ladled out each share and then disappeared to slurp her bowlful up somewhere around a corner. The child stared at me until the woman grabbed the dirty imp by its ragged tunic and ordered it to stay at her side with a gruff, '*Dohärcho, Hunno.*'

Gunda offered to entertain the toddler who made strange little sounds like an animal. I admired the way she fashioned a little toy soldier from loose twigs and crumpled leaves, complete with a tiny sword from a splinter of wood. I still felt feverish from my night's vigil in the rain back in Augusta Raurica and longed for solid rest. I hated to think what this poor supper was going to cost us in coins.

I thought longingly of the freshly skinned game hanging outside, ready for salting. There must be hunters nearby. I told Gunda to ask our grubby hostess where they were.

'Their men have gone north to build your general's bridge. He has promised good pay for long timbers. They're already logging now. When the army engineers give the signal that the pontoon of boats is ready, the logs will be floated downstream.'

'So these men are waiting for Barbatio to join them on the left bank? Don't they know he's marching up the other side?'

Gunda asked the woman a question. Our hostess answered with a phrase halfway between spitting and disdain.

'What different would it make to her men?' Gunda translated. 'Logs are logs, once they're in the middle of the current. Her man hopes to appease the anger in your Caesar's heart by doing good work. These settlers want to keep this land, as Constantius promised, and to avoid returning to the far side. They'll log planks for your bridge, Romans, but only if they don't have to cross it themselves.'

The woman had seen Gunda's *lyra* poking from its sack. She demanded a song as partial payment. Gunda's expression changed from practical to wistful. She took out her instrument and, with that now-familiar gesture, tested and tuned the strings. With her pick, she plucked out an introduction to a variation of the tune I'd heard before, the song about the princess who married the warmongering prince from next door. Gunda's fingers danced again, in and out, along the strings and her bell-like warble echoed down the empty corridors of the old villa.

Then the song changed. Gunda strummed fat chords with an angry and discordant stroke. Our rough hostess nodded with approval at Gunda's strident phrases.

—THE DEADLY CAESAR—

The toddler, worn out by slaps and pushes, had nodded off under a stool by the cooking pot and slept right through the song.

Gunda finished her last chorus and packed up her instrument.

'The same song as before? Why did it sound so painful this time?' I asked.

'A different ending this time—not so sweet,' she said. 'I'm going to sleep in the back. The woman will bring you cushions. You can sleep on those low beds in the other room.'

There was not much comfort to be found in the old villa, but we would manage on two ancient Roman couches, thankful for what roof we had when another violent storm passed overhead. We pulled the horses under cover of the roof, just before one of the gutters lining the courtyard gave way, releasing a hail of tiles shattering on the peristyle walkway.

ℛℛℛ

I woke up just as the sunrise was chasing the shadows on the flaking plaster ceiling. I was eager to rise and get going, but jerked helplessly on top of the couch. My ankles were tightly bound to the wooden legs and my wrists firmly fastened apart to the sides of the couch frame.

A dull, heavy ache pressed down on my forehead. I had been drugged.

'Bainobaudes!'

The Franco-Roman's mouth was gagged. He was sitting up, but powerless, bound by stout ropes to the base of a wooden pillar behind his couch. He sat only a few feet from steps leading down to the overgrown, dank peristyle garden. He tried to say something through the stained rag cutting around his jaw.

His glittering helmet, finely worked sword, *pugio* and *francisca* were gone, along with the sword belt he'd loosened before dropping off. His solid boots and even his socks were gone. I'd fallen asleep too exhausted to pull off my own footwear, thank the gods.

The only sound in the villa was rainwater dripping down from the broken gutter. Through a crack between the clumsy beams over the broken roof above us, a pink morning glowed.

Gunda and the woman had either fled or were fetching men now to do worse. Logging might keep them busy, but robbing sleeping Romans was far more profitable.

My couch was light, just four legs supporting four light crossbars, a few straps for support, and a worn cushion. I jerked. It moved. There was hope, but escape was going to take time. I jerked again, inching toward Bainobaudes. After five minutes of this, I'd worked my boots to within inches of his elbow.

He'd been working away at that gag. By rubbing his bristly cheek against the ridges of the pillar, he'd loosened it enough to talk.

'I woke up when they were tying you down. Gunda and the woman together. They'd already done me. Got this gag around me first so I wouldn't warn you.'

'I slept through. There was something in the beer. I tasted it.'

'Their beer is made of all kinds of plants and herbs—known to induce sleep. I should have thought . . . the bitch! Our weapons are gone.'

'So is she. They must have been in a hurry or they would have gagged me too.'

The last of the rainstorm dripped into the villa, punctuating the silence. Not a creature disturbed the hamlet outside.

'They were in a hurry to trade our things, maybe catch up with their men, or get to some other settlement nearby.'

'At least they didn't murder us.'

Bainobaudes gave a rueful chuckle. 'There's still time.'

'She wouldn't dare while we hold Gunda's brother as hostage in Roma.'

'No, but they can take us as slaves in return. And Romans don't come back from those black forests once they're seized.' Bainobaudes looked down at the ropes binding his waist to the pillar. 'I wonder if that brother means so much to her after all.'

I jerked the end of my bed forward again, again and again.

'We have no weapons,' Bainobaudes repeated to himself, taking it in.

—THE DEADLY CAESAR—

'We have one. I'm going to work off my boot and you get hold of the knife hidden inside the cuff,' I said. I rubbed the back of my boot up and down, trying to work it off my foot, using the couch's lower rail as a lever against which to push the leather cuff up and over my heel. At last the boot loosened, dangled, and fell on the ground.

My hidden reserve blade lay folded up inside, within Bainobaudes' view.

The Frank had to get his hands lower and to the front. Using his bare feet on the grimy floor stones, he inched himself around the pillar. It looked like a painful process. He'd been tied very tight and the crumbly stone ridges dug into his back as he rotated away. Slowly, his bound wrists and straining fingers came into view. He tried to position himself but it was impossible to get his bound wrists any lower than they were. My boot lay a full hand's span too far from his straining fingers.

I jerked again, trying to kick the boot into his clutches but to our dismay, one of the couch's outer legs sent the knife spinning free of its leather loops, spinning around and around, to drop down a flagstone step and out of view.

The tribune laid his head back against the pillar. I cursed. Fastened like a prisoner on a rack, how I could rattle down the steps?

There was the sound of a single step. The dirty toddler stood watching us from across the open courtyard.

'Come over here,' I said in a gentle tone. The child only watched me with eyes like dark almonds. It rubbed its grubby nose. I tried again, but my Latin was no good. I scoured my memory for the words I'd heard the woman use the night before, but I'd been too weary to pay much attention to her impatient barking.

The child was our only hope. It could give us the knife. There might be only minutes before the men of the village returned.

What had happened to my memory? Me, who could memorize whole volumes read to the blind Senator as a child, couldn't muster a few words of Alemannic I'd heard only the evening before?

I remembered something now, but when I tried, 'Donnato, Hunnus,' the child laughed. I tried again. My Germanic dialect classes at the Castra had been based on a useless Gothic translation of the Bible.

This and that, one word and another, nothing worked. I kept at it.

It was no good. No matter what I said, the child gave me that placid smile. Bainobaudes tried all the snatches he'd heard his Alemanni recruits use, '*Donarch, Hunu, Honnu, Donharr,*' but it was no use.

He looked at me. 'That's the way with dialect. These people may have come down from the steep peaks.'

We listened to the last raindrops plunking into a barrel set to catch water from a broken gutter overhead. The child settled down on the cold stones and watched us.

It hardly needed more rest. It had slept soundly last night, worn out by Gunda's amusements and the excitement of our arrival... sleeping under the stool while Bainobaudes, the mother, the sister and myself listened...

We'd been wasting valuable minutes. The child was deaf.

No words would have brought it over to us. The mother had spoken out of habit, but had dragged the child by its rags.

I made a comical face, crossing my eyes and twisting my mouth like the kind of lunatic beggars crowding the steps of Roman basilicas.

The child gave a high-pitched giggle and covered its dirty mouth.

I stuck out my tongue.

The child laughed again.

'What in Hades are you doing, Numidianus?'

'That brat is stone deaf. I'm trying to make friends. Make a face at the knife. Pretend its a toy.'

Bainobaudes just stared at me.

I leered in the funniest way possible at the folded knife sitting on the step out of our reach.

The child followed my gaze and crawled over to the knife. I wiggled my eyebrows and bulged my eyes. A pudgy fist closed around the thick handle, the sharp blade still folded safely into its body.

—THE DEADLY CAESAR—

'Keep trying. The mother can't be far if she left her child untended,' Bainobaudes said. 'She'll be back soon and she won't be alone.'

Frowning with mock curiosity, I pursed my mouth and nodded and then I stretched out my fingers.

The child was either naughty or just smarter than I. I had no means of opening and using anything with all my hand bound down like that. With a mischievous laugh, it thrust the knife handle straight into Bainobaudes' grasp, ran a few feet away, and giggled with triumphant at having thwarted me.

'Swivel the blade open and free yourself first,' I said.

Bainobaudes was soon working hard at his bonds, awkwardly twisting his hands back and forth to swing the blade on its hinge and get purchase on his cords. At one point, he lost hold of the knife and struggled with his hips to nudge it back into his fingers.

'They must have taken our horses as well.' I watched him sweat at it, able to see what he could only feel from the other side of the pillar. 'Keep at it. The twine is fraying. You're halfway now.'

'My wrists are raw.'

'They're bleeding. Keep going.'

Hooves pounded up the road.

We froze, caught halfway to escape. It was too late for Bainobaudes to rotate back to his original position at the pillar or for me to shuffle my couch back many feet. We were trapped.

There was a light step or two, then silence.

We waited.

Gunda entered the courtyard. She stood panting, exultant in her victory over us. She looked a barbarian princess in full, with that mane of pale hair flying free and wild. Her cheeks flushed the color of wine from her ride through the chilly morning.

She looked at me and chuckled with pleasure. Shaking rainwater off her cloak, she reached into her belt sack and brandished her polished *Germani* dagger—stolen from my sheath along with my own *pugio* and all our other valuables.

She tested the blade with her forefinger.

'Free us and we'll reward you with gold and loyalty,' Bainobaudes said.

'Gunda,' I said, my voice a desperate croak, 'I don't know what you're planning, but you still have a choice. Don't do anything you'll regret. Remember, we hold Hermund as a guarantee.'

'Gold? Hostages? You both show your usual contempt for the stupid barbarian girl.'

'We hold you in high esteem, Gunda—for your intelligence and art.' I said. 'You're no fool. You're not like these ignorant settlers, trading a life for a battered helmet or two.'

'You're in no position to bargain now, Romans. I have my knife back.'

She mounted the steps and sank to her knees not far from where I lay helpless. She wore the expression of a girl who enjoyed taking revenge on men. All her cooperation, docility, and tempered comportment had been a sham after all. She was the same Alemanna who had tried to kill Constantius, maybe even an Alemanna who wanted to kill all Romans for breaking promises to her endangered father.

'You Romans love your Games. So, we can bargain, for the game of it. What is this choice you offer me?' she asked in a taunting whisper. I smelled scented oils lingering in her hair, fresh sweat from her hasty return, her fear and excitement—all rising off the thick, wet wool of her cloak.

'You can sell or kill us, but your brother will pay a steep price. That's what hostages are for, Gunda. He won't have a quick or easy death. Or, you can leave us here to rejoin these people you've help to rob us. Or flee to your father's side. No one would blame you for going home.'

'Those aren't choices *you* offer. Those are choices I've already seized for myself, Roman.'

She held the knife in front of her, not far from my left eye. I tried not to flinch.

'Or you can continue with us, serve your father's Roman allies, see your brother made an officer with honor, and see yourself restored in our eyes as the leading *matrona* of your people.'

I was promising her dreams. The gods knew if our *schola* could deliver.

—THE DEADLY CAESAR—

She leaned back on her haunches and gave a glance at Bainobaudes on the other side of the pillar. She saw his bleeding wrists and the knife in his grasp.

'I've already made my choice, Romans.'

She twisted her knife in the air and now I flinched, ready for her to plunge it into my side.

But first, she sharpened its edge using the worn corner of a marble pedestal as her grindstone—first one side and then the other. She licked the edge clean and smiled.

Then she started sawing away at my bindings. In a few minutes of concentrated work, she'd freed my hands and cut my feet free. She helped liberate Bainobaudes who had resumed as fast as he could with my swivel knife. I secreted her knife down my tunic as soon as I was free.

'They've gone to barter your things for the highest price,' she said, glancing at Bainobaudes' bare head where his glorious helmet with its red studded jewels should have sat. 'In the hands of the right warrior your weapons will draw much Roman blood. They know they're going to lose everything if your Caesar and his general have their way. A bag of coins will help them start their lives over on the other side of the river.'

'We don't want a war, Gunda.' Bainobaudes drew himself up, hissing at the pain of unfolding his stiffened spine.

'Well, someone does,' she said.

'We need horses,' I said.

We two Roman officers followed Gunda out of the wretched villa as obediently as children. We left the scrawny Hunno playing with dead leaves blown into an unswept corner of the courtyard.

'What did you tell the others? Did you say you'd come back to watch the child?' I asked her. 'Was that your excuse while they look for a buyer for our weapons?'

She glanced over at the brat. It smiled and gave her one of its strange giggles back, perhaps remembering their games of the evening before. Gunda did not smile in return. She gave it the indifferent glance of a veteran warrior, not a young woman. The ice in her eyes chilled me. I would not want to find myself facing any such opponent in the field. She was her father's daughter.

We couldn't find more horses, but there was an old mule tied up behind one of the other huts. As I had been raised the son of a Numidian mule breeder, I volunteered to leave the horse to Bainobaudes and Gunda and ride the smelly, bad-tempered brute to the next *mutatio*.

If this mission had been confused and contradictory from the very beginning, it had now reduced me to this—trailing behind a bankrupt, cashiered Franco-Roman *tribunus* and a treacherous Alemanna, my face brushed by the tail of their horse and my miserable bottom bouncing on the back of a mule.

Chapter 11, The Death of a Dynasty

—The Fortress of Tres Tabernae—

Many relays later, we three emerged from a thickly forested stretch of the *Cursus Publicus* to find ourselves on the outskirts of Tres Tabernae. The fortress, charred from recent Alemanni fires, sheltered in the embrace of low-slung foothills below the Vosago Mons.

The fields stretching to the east and west of the road should have been waving gold with ripening grain in July. Instead I gazed across a trampled blanket of barren brown stalks, yet another landscape of futile desolation and haphazard recovery. Why were these barbarians so determined to hold land they could barely cultivate and to dismantle governance they could not replace?

It took more than seized land and a ready sword to make someone Roman. What did such people know of all the wisdom and wit locked up in the old Senator's Roman library of treasured scrolls and *codices*? Gunda's passionate songs could never replace the poetry or rhetoric of Roma, the wealth of centuries. It was that library, not my blood, that made me a true Roman.

How ironic that Gunda's father sought alliance and more from us Romans. Did he imagine himself attending a *curiales* meeting in braided hair and animal hides?

Julian's army camp sprawled between where we halted and the fortress. My practiced eye said the camp hadn't been in place for very long. I had served for years as a *volo* attending the wounded Commander Gregorius and I knew army routine as well as any soldier. Several thousand men had just staked their tents in precise lines in front of the fortress. The sewage trench was still nearly empty, the tent cords taut, and the cooking fires neat.

But setting up camp took only hours and already the army had moved on to repair work. Army engineers and construction experts scurried along the fortress walls above the camp. Soldiers stood on ladders, manned bucket brigades, and slapped the reins of ox wagons groaning with stone and lumber.

From the height of her saddle, Gunda lifted her chin and surveyed the thousands of soldiers obeying each swift command. I felt nothing but pride in seeing that, even with supplies short and marauders threatening at every turn, the army's discipline produced such order and efficiency.

We never know when we are happy until too late. Sometimes those years of sleeping on an army blanket just inside the leather flap of my father's tent had been, if not the happiest, certainly the simplest and most innocent days of my life.

I was just taking in this familiar scene with admiration of our military tradition when Gunda sneered. 'It's as I told you when we left the prisoner camp, isn't it, Roman? You all live in camps of some kind, you Romans, behind walls and trenches, in neat rows and streets—like obedient little ants.'

I swallowed a retort and we set off down the final stretch leading to the main gates of the camp. Perhaps it was too much to expect an Alemanna to understand. I trotted behind the stiff-backed Tribune Bainobaudes, thinking of what the Frankish barbarians had done to win *their* place in the Empire.

Unlike Valentinian, Bainobaudes had no private estate, even a reduced one in Cibalae, to fall back on. His family roots were sunk deep in the devastated lands around Agrippina, barely recovered by Julian and Severus from Frankish raids.

If there was no future for him, much less for his ambitious daughter, in Agrippina, there was certainly no alternative for his family across the river among the savage Franks. He was no doubt worrying how to provide for his Clothild. With her Roman hairstyles and Latin education mixed with Frankish fertility amulets and heavy, northern robes, she was the embodiment of his Romanized family's future.

He needed his commission back.

—THE DEADLY CAESAR—

The cashiered tribune still wore his insignia. He intended to report immediately to General Severus before the old man returned to his own camp back in Brotomagus, some ten miles due east on the riverbank. What lengths would he go to in order to get himself reinstated as officer with his original unit of Cornuti? Bainobaudes would plead his case hard, even if that meant blaming a fellow tribune like Cella—or even General Barbatio. The Dacian's foul temper had done Bainobaudes an injustice.

Our pace quickened—but only as fast as that damned stubborn mule now following on a lead behind my horse would go. He wasn't used to the *Cursus*' paving stones and for hours had kept veering onto any soft track that tempted him. My mother had always said I was as stubborn as a mule, but this beast had proved my match. I intended to teach him a lesson as soon as I located the army stables by handing him over to pull a wagon of mammoth boulders.

Bainobaudes left Gunda with me and trotted away for the camp's central Via Principia to find Severus. I wished him luck.

Officially, my attachment was to Praetorian Prefect Florentius, but I was eager to get a look at the 'new' Julian right away. I immediately spotted the Caesar on the ramparts. He was shouting down orders to engineers to shift fallen rubble away from the winding climb up to the fortress gates.

Where had the round-shouldered, pimply scholar with the straggly, downy beard disappeared? I recalled that odd night in my rough cell off the finance annex in the Mediolanum Palace when Julian had appeared in the shadows. He'd carried a sack of books on his back and was fleeing the dangers of court to study his beloved philosophy in Athens.

If he still had the reputation of a scholar, he wasn't bent over war manuals by Julius Caesar today. Though he wore no bright cloak or shining helmet, he looked even at that distance like a man transformed and in charge—erect, clean-shaven, and confident, his shoulders and chest braced for authority.

He gestured at two surveyors at the base of the fortress wall. He swung his arm around, waved, and pointed. They answered—and then turned and worked their teams all the faster.

It had been many weeks since my briefing at court. It seemed almost incredible that the confident young man overseeing ramparts repairs was still not aware that his imperial wife had miscarried. But the battlefield was its own world, a sphere far removed from ladies' inner chambers, imperial medical attendants, and dynastic family matters.

I entrusted Gunda to the care of an *adiutor* and promised I would check up on her later. The first of my assignments must not be delayed. I had thought until now it would be the easiest of tasks, far easier than spying on Alemanni or lying to Julian about my ulterior purpose of spying *on him*. But as I approached this Caesar, younger than I, but in joint command of thirteen thousand soldiers, I fell back in my saddle.

I suddenly felt older than my thirty-some years. I had read as many books as Julian. I had learned as many lessons as the philosophers could teach. Yet nothing I had recited out loud in that dusty Roman study—my knees to my chin as I hunched on the bench at the feet of the blind Senator—nothing prepared me for this.

It should not be easy to tell any man his unborn son had died. To break it to a Caesar, for whom that infant promised an entire imperial future, suddenly seemed very daunting indeed.

※※※

Imperial government hierarchy dictated that the *schola* of the *agentes in rebus* reported to the *Magister Officiorum* who sat on the *Consistorium*.

I would be nominally attached to Florentius as the senior *agens* posted among the civil service officers around the Caesar's 'court.' But here, deep in disputed Gallic territory, all protocol seemed a world away from the prostrations and hem kissing in Mediolanum or Sirmium.

Soldier or civilian, Florentius and I were both men serving on the troubled borderlands. The Caesar considered himself as on campaign even during his winter 'respite' in Senonae. His 'court' was little more than a book-filled tent at the nexus of the army surrounded by other prominent tents housing advisers and officers.

I noticed immediately from the pennants and sentries' insignias that the largest tent was for meetings, while the most activity enlivened the fifth tent along the Via Principia. This must be Julian's.

Smack in between were three other tents, one of them belonging to the Prefect, the others to tribunes. I was announced. I waited, watching the snap of *dracones* in the rising winds overhead. There were no *consistoriani* in court dress here and far fewer delays and identifications than wherever Constantius resided—Arelate, Mediolanum, or Sirmium.

Everywhere these days, the fashion among civil officers had long been a strong nod to military costume and practice. My visit to Florentius for presentation of my credentials had all the trappings of an army secondment.

On cue, I pushed aside the leather flap to find the prefect's back turned to me. He was reviewing messages, tossing one after another aside in impatience. He turned to greet me with that same statuesque, studied style of Emperor Constantius. His boots, tunic, embroidered trim on hem and sleeves, the large purple and gold *orbiculi,* the sturdy, but fine-woven trousers and even the mathematically even legging wraps mimicked Constantius' meticulous style.

All around us officers were letting their hair grow longer. Many encouraged moustaches to affect a rakish, barbarian flair. Florentius' hair was ashy blond—lighter than Constantius'—but cut in the same perfect bowl and curled in a pipe-like fringe an inch above his eyebrows, just like the Emperor's.

For a moment, I thought I was staring at the Emperor himself, for the Prefect had modeled every detail of his attire and manner on our sovereign— apart from the full purple cloak forbidden to all but the semi-divine Constantius himself.

Florentius mirrored his supreme commander in other little ways, too. I saw he fixed his cloak in the exact spot on one shoulder where Constantius always pinned his *fibula*. He steadied his nervous right hand by resting it on his hefty, polished belt just as Constantius did. And there was that trademark rigidity with which he moved his head as one with his shoulders, his nape fixed by an invisible pike through to his midriff.

I had been trained to observe details that might reveal a man's personality, origins, education or purse. All I could conclude so far was that the Prefect had obscured his self behind a caricature of our sovereign.

Florentius glanced through my *agens* identification document on thick vellum, my road license, and a letter from the Emperor himself endorsed by *Magister* Apodemius on behalf of the *schola*. He reread the letter, lingered on the coda, and then looked me up and down. My letter of appointment mentioned that I carried a private message for Julian. Florentius didn't betray any curiosity, only a touch of imitation-imperial disdain.

'They send me an African?'

'Born in Numidia Militaris, Prefect, but raised in Roma, in the *domus* of the Manlius family.'

'Gregorianus. You're a *libertinus*? Answering to . . . ?'

'As an *agens*, I report to *Magister* Apodemius of my *schola*—'

'Yes, yes, but your original master, your *patronus* was . . . ?'

'The late Commander Atticus Manlius Gregorius.'

I stood all the straighter, adding only in my mind, 'my father.'

'He was the one who was badly wounded taking Constantine II? The one who went over to Magnentius, with Silvanus, and that treasure-hunting Marcellinus?'

'The Commander suffered his injuries some years before, in a skirmish with barbarians, but yes, he fought in the conflict between the late Constantines. He served the Empire as honorably as his venerated ancestors would have wished.'

'Really? After Constantine II died, your Commander chose the rebels over Constans. Hardly the kind of loyalty my ancestors would wish. I suppose you're at least good at the basics?'

'I'm excellent at managing the post.' I didn't need to add *and reading and copying it in secret.* An *agens*' reputation preceded him wherever he went.

'Useful at accounting? Any experience auditing tax rolls? Or are you one of those *agentes* who pokes his nose into everything and just takes his cut?'

'I have passed all our accounting classes. I am, perhaps, better employed away from a desk.'

'In other words, you're no use to me at all. I'm in over my ears in revenue and harvest shortages as well as tax collection problems. Neither the poll-tax nor the land-tax meet our targets. On top of that, there's political confusion on every side.'

'The *schola* has been asked that I assist you as best I can, but with a special eye for the analysis of Alemanni—this political confusion, as you just called it.'

For a moment, Florentius looked confused. Then he recovered with a crack of a smile. 'Political—you thought I meant the Alemanni? They're just a rabble with more fights between themselves than with us. Once this fortress is manned again, their last route inland will be closed off. They'll be forced across the river. Gallia's prosperity will take longer to restore.'

He imitated Constantius. He answered to Constantius. He'd let slip the real problem in his own mind. When he mentioned political confusion, he'd meant confusion over *internal command*—not barbarians.

This confusion had reduced even the great General Ursicinus to a resentful and useless funk in Durocortorum until his transfer. It had rendered the resentful General Marcellus speechless with rage in Mediolanum over the siege at Senonae. The 'confusion' prompted a question hovering in everyone's mind but on no one's lips—*who was in charge of this army?*

And now I could see for myself—*who was in charge of administering Gallia?* Constantius' professional veterans of battlefronts from Britannia to Assyria? Or his young cousin, a raw-shaven bookworm lifting his battle strategies from a well-thumbed copy of Julius Caesar?

'Rabble, perhaps,' I said. 'Yet this Alemannic rabble has a hierarchy as clear to them as it is opaque to us. *Reges, reguli, optimates, comitati* of their own, though these are not their terms.'

'I say rabble, some with dirtier or redder hair than others, Numidianus. I'd prefer you spend time on my tax rolls than waste it on reporting Alemannic squabbles.'

'Our Caesar is waging a major campaign aimed at reclamation of Alemanni-settled territory. The Emperor seeks peace and stability. Let's hope their two objectives are not mutually exclusive. I have brought with me an Alemannic noblewoman, the daughter of Gundomadus *Rex*. So far, Gundomadus holds his alliance with the Empire close to his heart. His daughter's knowledge of Alemannic intentions and ties may help you govern.'

Prefect Florentius wasn't interested in barbarians. He waved at a table laden with documents and mail packets.

'You'll work with my chief scribe and sort out all that backlog.'

A tall official with a cadaverous face and a sly expression entered the tent. I stepped back with a feeling of repellence. This man was Pentadius, a powerful *notarius* of the *consistorium*, last seen up close in that fetid prison cell recording the interrogation and brutal execution of Julian's half-brother, Caesar Gallus for the imperial files. The other two men arriving to oversee how our *schola* handled the affair had been the Lord Chamberlain Eusebius and the Frankish king-turned-Roman courtier, Mallobaudes.

'This is *Agens* Marcus Gregorianus Numidianus,' Florentius said.

'Yes, I know you, *Agens*.' Pentadius moved closer, the way a feline takes one slow and careful step after another toward his prey.

I rallied, '*Notarius* Pentadius, I am freshly attached to this court.'

'Then you report to me, for the Emperor has sent me here as acting *Magister Officiorum*, to be confirmed no later than when new consuls are named,' he said.

Whether he was the Lord Chamberlain's man, another Constantius spy, or had managed this key promotion from some new political constituency, Pentadius was a stroke of ill luck for me. He was a watchful type. If my every move was reported back to the chief eunuch Eusebius, my task of assisting Julian and watching his court while pretending to monitor Alemanni allies had just turned trickier.

My unease eluded Prefect Florentius. 'Deliver your message to our caesar now, *Agens*. You have to meet the rest of his personal staff anyway. Here, take your papers.'

Pentadius raised a questioning eyebrow at the mention of an imperial message. Such a rising official would have his own means of uncovering secrets. It was for this reason that Constantius was using me—hoping that Julian would be so busy resenting Pentadius' obvious prying, he'd take an *agens*' Alemannic mission at face value.

Still, I braced myself for an inquisition from Julian, who was so long acquainted with watchers, traitors, and toadies.

'Go on,' Florentius said, pointing Julian's tent. 'Get on with it, then report back to me here with that barbarian woman you think so useful.'

'Yes, I thought, let's get it over with. And Mercury help me if Julian condemns the messenger for the message.

※※※

The Caesar was not in his tent, but someone else was. Remembering the bustling figure rushing along the parapets of the fortress, I was not surprised that Julian had to be summoned. I waited—correct, discreet, and silent as a slave—but my comportment seemed a polite provocation to a stranger in Greek civilian dress reading a heavy illustrated *codex* at Julian's camp table. Other volumes—by Marcus Aurelius, Julius Caesar and the Greeks—stood stacked around his knees.

'You have a purpose here, *agens*?' He addressed me with the accent of the Far Eastern shore of our great sea, perhaps Pergamum or thereabouts, but tinged with the affectation of the Alexandrian elite.

'*Biarchus* Marcus Gregorianus Numidianus, carrying a personal message for the Caesar.'

'If it's a military matter, tell General Severus without delay. No one should keep you waiting, not even a Constantine,' he said with an oily smile.

'I will wait.'

'If it's a civil matter, you can report it to the Prefect's staff.'

'Thank you for your concern.'

If I let him whittle away at the nature of my message like this, he'd be announcing Helena's miscarriage himself within twenty minutes.

'So it's not military or civil?'

I saw no insignia, telltale jewelry, trim, or belt feature to identify this swarthy foreigner so at home using Julian's stool, table, and tent.

'Is the Caesar's library of interest to you? He came to his posting carrying a valued library from the Empress,' I parried.

Resting my gaze on his reading with seeming indifference, I asked, 'Homer?'

I knew it was not Homer. I'd long ago acquired the knack of reading upside down, one of the tricks for which Apodemius first recruited me. The tome was an illustrated work on theurgical 'divine-working.' I admired Plato and all the Greek philosophers cramming the shelves of the late Senator Manlius' library, but in my opinion, the school of magic and theurgy was a suspect realm.

'No. It is not Homer.' He stood up and washed his hands in an ornate basin on a tripod. 'I leave heroic tales to the impressionable.'

There was a sound of running footsteps, the swish of the tent flap, and the cry, 'Numidianus! My old friend! The book-loving *agens* from Mediolanum!'

The Caesar gripped me in an enthusiastic welcome. His thick neck ran with sweat, rubble dust, and swipes of wet mortar. Over his shoulder, the older man smiled with indulgent but unfeigned affection for the exuberant Constantine.

'You've met Dr Oribasius?'

'We've just met, Flavius Claudius Julianus.' I fell to one knee, observing a modicum of protocol.

'Get up, Numidianus. I don't go in for Constantius' prostrations and slipper licking. Today you dine with my closest advisers and myself. We'll talk of books and ideas, not marching orders or weapons stocks! But I warn you, only coarse, healthy rations. I eat what the soldiers eat.'

'Roman soldiers always dine quite well.'

'Too well. Remember Cato of Tusculum said, "Great care about food implies great neglect of virtue"? So no pheasants or sow's udders for us, all right?'

—THE DEADLY CAESAR—

He no longer looked like a bearded student from Athens in a homespun tunic and sandals. He wore the same woolen tunic as middle-ranked officers, with baldric, a wide, strutted belt, and a workaday cloak.

That stammering student's quaver, the tic that had earned him the nickname 'the chattering mole,' had diminished. He now tried, with a modicum of success, for a commander's confident delivery.

He was styling himself a soldier's soldier, not a pampered image-bearer. Indeed, looking at Julian up close, I would have thought him no higher than another tribune, albeit one who liked mucking in with his men for collegiality's sake.

His coarse diet had made him heftier in full military gear than that first night we talked of Plato in my grubby *agens* room behind the Finance Building. Two years' campaigning had broadened his shoulders, making his thick neck less obvious. The northern winter had ruddied his cheeks, shorn of their adolescent fuzz, but could do nothing for the weak chin that had once benefited from the cover of a student's beard.

If he still retained in my own eyes some trace of a bobbing, hairy goat, snorting through that long nose of his, at least he'd assumed the hirsute mantle of a proud goat acquiring imperial authority.

He was filthy, covered from head to toe with the dirt of the broken fortress. But at least he gave off the honest smell of exertion, not the sour smell of an unwashed boy.

Without a hint of modesty or protocol, he had already pulled off his boots and sweat-stiffened socks and was dropping his trousers for a clean pair. Before my startled gaze he sluiced himself down with the entire contents of his basin and tossed the empty container out the tent door for that chamberlain Eutherius to refill.

Wrapping his hairy torso with a worn *susurna*—the soldier's answer to blanket, rug, and rain gear—he sat down on an army bedroll devoid of covering or cushion. His bushy eyebrows gave a knowing wriggle and he wagged a finger at me.

'Numidianus, you are here because they think I trust you, unlike that vile Paulus Catena they sent before or the acting

Magister Officiorum Pentadius out there now, not to mention all those other spies lining up to watch me.'

'I have a letter of introduction and attachment to the Praetorian Prefect Florentius.'

'Oh, the gods help you there! That man wants to raise taxes on these poor Gauls to twenty *solidi* from each landlord, which means a little bit on the side for you as well, doesn't it, *Agens*? Don't count on it, my friend. They can hardly manage seven or eight per estate.'

'I bring you news of private importance.'

His jovial expression faded. 'Am I being recalled to loiter in some tedious suburb for another six months while Constantius deliberates my loyalty all over again?'

I looked over at Dr Oribasius but said nothing.

'I don't have secrets from Oribasius,' Julian said, pulling his *susurna* tighter over his hunched shoulders. 'He's my personal physician, my friend, and my teacher.'

'But others deem certain state secrets for your ears only, Caesar.'

Julian scowled. 'Very well. Leave us, Oribasius.'

The doctor slipped out of the tent. Oribasius struck me as too easily and too confidently excused. He'd know of Helena's misfortune by dusk.

'So why are you here, Numidianus? To deliver more books from the Empress? To bring me private letters from the true friends I miss? Or more instructions from my august cousin on when to pray and when to shit?'

I fell to both knees as the weight of my message demanded and lowered my head. 'It is my deepest regret that I must inform you that your consort, the *Augusta* Helena, lost her unborn child during the Vicennalia tour of Roma.'

There was a deathly silence. I dared not raise my eyes to see his reaction. I heard a curious snort. The Caesar blew his dust-clogged nose on a linen towel.

'Was it a boy?'

'There were signs, yes.'

'The last one was a boy, too.'

'An *agens* dare not express personal condolence over such a private, imperial matter, but—'

'Oh, yes, of course, thank you. I hope the lady does not suffer?'

I hesitated, recalling Helena's wan, pious figure fighting back a faint at the vertiginous 'Hundred Steps Stairs.'

'In the opinion of the doctors, the tour tired her. The visit to *Rupes Tarpeia* might have caused her emotional distress. They question whether she is capable of carrying another pregnancy to term.'

'I see . . . Was she well attended?'

His cool reaction to my warning she might not bear a child ever again shocked me. As long as Constantius' Eusebia produced no rival infant, Julian's possible heirs would inherit the known world. Had he not just lost hope of his future dynasty?

'Empress Eusebia never left her side and was both solicitous and generous with medications known best to females.' It was the farthest I could go to hint at Eusebia's dangerous meddling. Coming out of my mouth, it sounded like an audacious indiscretion.

'Good Eusebia! My only friend at court!'

'I can return later to report on other important, but less distressing affairs, Caesar.' I made for the exit to leave him with his grief—well hidden as it was.

'Why would you go in the middle of our conversation?'

'Surely, Caesar, you wish to be alone?'

'Numidianus! I was sent up here with very few friends, less trust, and no command whatsoever. I need to know every last detail of your assignment.'

'Perhaps you need time to write to the *Augusta* . . . or the Empress Eusebia?'

'What could I say to make Helena feel better? She'll find comfort in her Christ.'

I thought of Kahina. Julian showed far less resentment at losing a beloved companion to adoration of the 'Savior' than I felt at times.

'As for the Empress,' he said, 'I hope the *Imperatrix* won't blame herself after all the expert female advice she has bestowed on poor Helena. Someday I'll write an encomium praising Eusebia above all women.'

He brightened. 'Now, settle yourself while I finish today's business. Then we will debate great ideas over our meal.' There was no irony and no trace of the suspicions Apodemius had confided to his Castra officers.

But I heard something in his voice.

Those lonely years of cold imprisonment in the Macellum fortress, with only eunuchs and a semi-stable half-brother for companions, would have sharpened Julian's animal sense of danger. Though the Caesar might be mocked behind his back, disdained by experienced veterans, and fruitless at fatherhood, this young man was no longer everyone's pawn.

How would I make sure I did not become his?

Chapter 12, The Goat of Glory

—TRES TABERNAE—

After settling in, shaving, and brushing off the dust of the road, I went to meet Julian's 'court.' Seated at the lowliest end of a dinner party being set on small tables in a spacious dining tent, I listened to his trusted aides.

I had not forgotten the Emperor's order to assess the loyalty of the men around Julian. I'd already witnessed how little Barbatio was inclined to cooperate with his Caesar. Tribune Cella had followed Barbatio's orders without question and the tribune's disdainful asides had chimed with his superior's. Florentius readily criticized Julian for dragging his feet on raising taxes. Pentadius could only be on the spot to spy for Constantius, Eusebius or—knowing his history—both men.

This evening I sat among men Julian actually trusted.

The rabbit stew on my plate was certainly no distraction. You'll hear Roman soldiers complain about road conditions, weather, local women or lack of same, but usually you won't hear complaints about food. If an army marches on its rations and the bounty of its local hosts, Julian seemed unaware of this military tradition. Rarely have I eaten so badly in an army camp, even during the most adverse campaign and even as a *volo* slave scraping the leftovers of Commander Gregorius' supper.

Julian seemed determined to imitate the Stoics when it came to his stomach. Looking at my small portion of tasteless muck, I regretted begging off Prefect Florentius' invitation to supper a few tents away. There I might have found the roasted fowl, rich sauces, expensive wine, and fresh fruits that had been exiled from the Caesar's diet.

But rich conversation made up for a mean menu. Oribasius led a debate on the nature of the relationship of religious ritual to good fortune—was a favorable outcome a reflection of the purity of the sacrificer's intention and actions? Was it proof that the gods were pleased? And if bad fortune came instead, who was to blame?

I found some bread and kept listening. Which was better—Christian prayers or pagan rites? The intervention of Christian martyrs in heaven? Or the protection of pagan gods in their shrines?

The Caesar encouraged disputatious argument as if it were the spice our stew lacked. No one stood on ceremony in foisting his opinion on the imperial youth. Julian never pulled rank, but answered each opinion with a quote pulled from one of his precious books.

I had already met the calm and confident medic Oribasius, trained in Alexandria just as I had suspected.

At the far end of the tent sat the aged *Magister Equitum*, General Severus, facing a middle-aged *quaestor*, one Saturninius Secundus Salutius. Though self-effacing in manner, the Gallo-Roman Salutius proved well versed in Greek philosophy and informative on his native region. He had served under Emperor Constans before Constantius. He had both the governorship of southwest Gallia and of an African province under his career belt.

Salutius said he was drawing up notes in his spare time to write a manual of pagan theology. As I scraped up the last of my stew, the *quaestor* fell into a polite debate with a younger Roman from Hispania. This was a deputy prefect with a similar name, Flavius Sallustius. Sallustius was, I took mental note, yet another pagan.

Squeezed a few feet away from the *quaestor* Salutius, prefect Sallustius, and General Severus was Julian's Alemannic adviser-cum-translator. This enormous barbarian was a *Germani* nobleman-turned-Roman and a non-commissioned *tribunus vacans*, Hariobaudes.

Hariobaudes sat taller in his camp chair than some of the young slaves standing at his elbow.

I could not imagine a group of imperial advisers less like the intrigants of Constantius' *consistorium*: the property-hungry eunuch Lord Chamberlain Eusebius, the ambitious Consul Arbetio, or the serpentine forger Lampadius.

While Hariobaudes and Severus said little, the chat between the other four bounced in and out of Greek, especially when talking of the gods without bodies, or *asômatoi*, and their problems of communicating with us mere mortals trapped in the realm of the physical *sômati*. How and when a divine spirit crossed from the realm of the gods into ours was a question that excited Julian enormously. Could the gods occupy earthly *agalmatôn* such as statues?

This was the liveliest question of the *mensa secunda*—plain apples.

There were no cakes.

With nothing more to satiate my persistent hunger, I sipped my watered wine. Nobody much cared about me, which was refreshing. As a *curiosus* despised by social classes both high and low, I wasn't used to being treated as a straightforward dining fellow—least of all by a Constantine.

I watched Severus the most closely, as he was only here for a few hours before returning to his separate camp. His every gesture conveyed submission toward our young Caesar. In return, Julian deferred to the old man, although nary one single point of strategy or military preparedness arose during the entire meal. The gnarled veteran's comportment could not be more opposite to that of his predecessors Generals Marcellus or Ursicinus. Severus was not a man to be caught by allegations of rivalry or disloyalty to the Constantines.

I could never imagine General Ursicinus sitting through this talking shop of Platonic metaphysics.

And would General Marcellus in his cups not have wanted to strangle the Caesar at being forced to listen to: 'But Salutius, remember Aristophanes' *Birds*? A physical barrier between the heavens and the earth prevents the gods from receiving the smoke of sacrifices. So Aristophanes assumed that our gods could be far away from their altars and statues when sacrifices and the accompanying prayers are performed.'

If warfare, not politics or theology, was Severus' strong suit, tact and discretion followed close behind. He did not point out, between his refrain 'Please pass the garum sauce', that our Caesar pretended to be a practicing Christian.

I sat there, silent and astonished. How would such an openly pagan debate, even academic, be excused in the suspicious court of Constantius? Protecting Arian Christian orthodoxy was the only thing that distracted the Emperor from the Persian threat.

Julian called my name—not for the first time, it seemed.

'You ignore your sovereign, *Agens*? The food is not that good, we know!'

Everyone laughed.

Julian leaned over his table. 'I asked you, Numidianus, what is your opinion? Do you believe that a statue could come to life? Can ritual evoke the presence of a god? Can we unite with the divine to achieve *henosis* and perfect ourselves?'

'Yes, Numidianus, tell us,' Tribune Hariobaudes muttered. 'Could any prayer or sacrifice summon divine energy into cold marble, as our Hellenophile friends would have us believe?'

The massive Alemannus turned to Severus, 'If statues can breathe, they can listen. If they listen, what tales do they report back to the *agentes in rebus*, hey? All our secret prayers and plans?'

'Easier than reading our mail?' Severus raised his empty cup to Hariobaudes in agreement.

Julian's heavy lower lip twitched at their banter over *agentes*.

'All *agentes* are scoundrels excepting this good fellow here,' he said. 'Numidianus must be spared our contempt for he has been schooled in the ancient greats and is truthful in testimony. I owe him much.'

They kept on debating the animation of statues. The only break in the collegial banter was the delivery of a message for Tribune Hariobaudes. He betrayed no reaction but after the *adiutor* left the officers' dining tent, the Alemannus' searching gaze rested on me far too long.

Nevertheless, I felt welcomed by Julian. No doubt it was a combination of his warmth and the day's weariness that led me to blurt out, 'I know of one statue, the greatest statue of the Empire, that moved.'

—THE DEADLY CAESAR—

All eyes fixed on me. Drinking cups froze mid-air. Old Severus, jowls waggling, slurped up his soup to dead silence on all sides.

'A statue really moved? Tell us, Numidianus.' Julian leaned forward.

'It was only a few nights before the Emperor left Roma—on May 26, to be exact. The *dispensator* of the Manlius *domus* and I were in the old Forum. We witnessed the Statue of Victory leaving the Senate House, in secret and without warning.'

'Where did the statue go?' Salutius asked.

'Only the Emperor knows for certain.'

'You say it moved, but surely not of its own accord?' Oribasius asked.

'No, Doctor, not of its own accord. I'm sorry to disappoint you all. It was carried out of the Senate on Emperor Constantius' bidding. Yet if the great spirit that protects Roma ever inhabited its stone, I am sure it wept that night to be evicted from its sacred altar.'

My news sobered up their sophomoric ramblings. Even Severus stopped belching. All the ruddy color drained away from the Caesar's thick features. I could not be mistaken at reading his heart. This was a loss that stabbed him in his soul. The removal of the Empire's spiritual guardian shocked Julian far more than the death of his own heir.

I waited. Would he defend his cousin's sacrilege?

An adjutant appeared at Julian's side bearing a message for the Caesar's ears only. Julian rose from his table, turned his back on us, listened, and then exploded, 'That idiot!'

He returned to his seat looking older than his twenty-six years.

'Tell me, friends, has General Barbatio ever won a real battle? How did this brute rise to such power with no single victory to his cursed name?'

No one answered. Barbatio enjoyed no reputation as an outstanding battle commander, but had bribed and wangled himself so high into Constantius' favor, he was a dangerous man to slander before witnesses.

'What is wrong, Caesar?' Sallustius asked.

Julian laid both hands on his table to steady himself. 'It appears that General Barbatio is starting the bridge without us, but the damn fool has pitched his camp on the wrong side of the river! Does he think that by avoiding our agreed rendezvous, he can claim all victory for himself?'

Severus lifted his lined face to growl, 'Use Barbatio's vanity to your purpose, Caesar. If we merge our armies, it will be General Barbatio—not you or I—who's in charge. So let him build his bridge from over there. We will be the ones escorting the settlers across it. We will be victorious.'

It seemed obvious now that the thick-skulled Barbatio—with his superior troops and supplies—had been designated supreme commander of the conjoined campaign. Knowing Barbatio as I did, the line of command seemed absurd. But what soldier had known Barbatio as long or as well as I?

Julian gave a high-pitched giggle of disbelief at Severus' counsel. 'We'll take stock of our situation,' he said, collecting his cloak and weapon. 'Barbatio bungled the *laeti* brigands' arrest. Let's pray he doesn't bungle the bridge.'

'Perhaps bad luck attends your campaign because the Statue of Victory was moved,' Oribasius joked. 'If only it weren't against the law to make a sacrificial offering in penitence . . .'

This was not a jest even Julian could allow.

'If my good Christian cousin has seen fit to remove the Statue of Victory,' he said, 'then we do not question his wisdom.' He adjusted his sword belt. 'Come with me, Severus. We mustn't slacken our preparations. Good-night.'

⚓⚓⚓

Before I retired to my tent positioned within reach of the supervision of Florentius and his deputies, I checked on Gunda. I heard her lyre music yards before I reached her small tent at the farthest edge of the encampment, among the camp followers' families.

But her song was mournful. It was a variation on the same melody as before, but both early gaiety and later stridency had drained away. It had turned dirge-like. Gunda's spirits had reached some low point in our adventure.

'Is that the song you sang to us in the tavern? How different it can sound.'

She brushed back a curtain of silvery gold hair and used her *plectrum* to clean a fingernail.

'I vary the lyrics to suit my mood,' she said. She kept her eyes on her lap as she fidgeted.

'Still about a girl who marries the prince of another tribe?'

'Yes.'

'When you sang it near Mons Brisiacus, it ended harshly.'

'The clash of armies, the fury of battle, the horror of mutilation,' she said.

'And now it's mournful from beginning to end.'

She squinted into the lamp's glow. 'Why are we here, Roman? Have you tricked me? Am I a hostage to exchange for Roman prisoners across the river?'

She had been brooding too hard. Her dark speculations explained her mood of defeat.

'No, of course not, Gunda. We are going to find out what the Alemanni are planning. Do you agree to help me?'

'Will I see my brother made a high Roman officer?'

'You must deal with us honestly and get information we need. I am not asking you to risk falling into the hands of your enemies, but to plumb your friends for ways of preventing war.'

She rallied a little. 'It will be difficult to help if you get yourself tied up in stupid knots again.'

'That's the Gunda I know. You agree? Even if it holds some danger for you as Gundomadus' daughter?'

'What is the first step?'

'That we trust each other. You rescued Bainobaudes and me. You have earned my trust.'

I laid her knife in her lap. 'Don't try any of your tricks on Caesar Julian.'

Never once had she met my eyes. She seemed worn out by uncertainty and loneliness. Her feisty pride found itself reduced by camping among the lowest type of imperial wife who could still call herself honest—and all the sluts who couldn't. These were the females Roman soldiers nicknamed 'their infantry,' lacking any dancing or flute skills, education, or beauty. Squalling babies, the urine stench of laundry vats, and some brawling nag nearby reminded me of the squalor around Gunda.

I longed to hear her full-throated and confident voice soar like that night in the roadside *mansio*. But I must not admit I felt sorry for her as I left. I had just reached the tent flap when she caught my shoulders and trembled against me in a sudden embrace.

'Roman, believe me, what I do is for my father, not my brother. The honest and noble Gundomad is the greatest Alemannus of them all. He is wronged by anyone who calls him a traitor.'

Her strong, lush body pressed full-breasted and soft against my chest. I could have run my fingers through her marvelous mane of moonlit hair glinting by the lamplight.

I was a lonely man. I could have gone a great deal further. The Tribune Valentinian's practiced eye had called Gunda right. Though she was an upright *Germana*, I would not feel such unwanted lust if she had been untouched. She was no innocent.

'Good-night, Gunda.'

I pulled her off and did not look back.

'Good-night, Roman.'

As I walked back toward camp headquarters, her lyre's silence reproached me.

※※※

'*Agens* Numidianus?'

The smell of an Eastern unguent floated through the close air of our tent. Reaching for my *pugio*, I peered over my blanket at a dark silhouette of Oribasius.

'The Caesar's asking for you.'

'What happened to his army messengers?'

'Each hour is precious to him. You're lucky he makes time for you at all.'

I pulled on my riding trousers, socks, and boots and followed the doctor already padding ten feet ahead from the Prefect's section past silent tents and ebbing campfires toward Julian's alley.

Oribasius left me outside the Caesar's tent flap. The interior flickered with dancing shadows cast by lamps and torches.

'Numidianus.' Julian was dressed against the night chill only in his underclothing and that ragged *susurna*.

'You have a task for me, Caesar?'

'It's been a long time since I was in what we would call civilization. I've got many questions for you.'

The moon was easing down into the western sky. It must have been around three hours past midnight. Was I dreaming?

'How do you stay awake after such an active day, *Domine*?'

'Alexander the Great's trick. He set a bronze basin beside his couch and with outstretched arm held a silver ball over it.' Julian held a bronze set of *strigiles* over his basin, 'so that if he fell into a doze, the noise woke him up.' The curved scrapers clanged into the metal bowl.

'You admire the Macedonian, Caesar?'

'I have received a spark of his very spirit, Numidianus. Do you believe in the transmigration of souls, the teachings of Pythagoras and Plato?'

'One can acquire many admirable habits through emulation—'

'But unlike Alexander, I wake up whenever I wish. Once I'm done with business, I turn to poetry, philosophy, and prayer.'

I spotted no private altar in his mobile household and I did not imagine him on his knees night after night in this rude tent.

'I pray to Mercury for swift understanding. The gods are intermediaries between ourselves and The One, whom Plotinus teaches us is supreme and transcendent, containing no division, multiplicity or distinction; beyond all categories of being and non-being.'

I could no answer him. Unfortunately, Plotinus had not been one of the 'modern' philosophers favored by the blind Senator Manlius when I read to him in my childish voice.

From underneath his blanket, Julian smiled without a hint of guile.

'I was accused of treason in Mediolanum and only walked free because you told the truth. Unusual in an *agens*.'

'But you dislike our *schola*?'

'I hate it. The *agentes* slither around and spy on everyone like reptiles. They absolve themselves of all wrongdoing but take a percentage of everything.'

Apodemius was right to worry about corruption within, but dozens of honest *agentes* would have taken rightful umbrage at Julian's dismissal of our entire service.

'You see, I want to trust you, Numidianus. I believe you to be one of us. You have read the great books. Your Greek is fluent. You feel the loss of the Statue of Victory as keenly as I do. Don't deny it. I saw your expression.'

'That statue must be restored to its rightful place.'

'I agree, Numidianus. To do that, we need sound men who understand the past so as to forge the future. These Christians embrace a faith that has nothing divine in it. It only exploits that childish part of a man's soul that loves fable. I cling to the ancient search for purity and truth—'

'If you prefer to speak Greek, I am rusty but—'

Julian's illuminated gaze came back to earth. 'If I can still speak Greek, it's surprising. I've become such a barbarian up here in the wilds of Gallia, but no, no, Latin will do.' He gave that high-pitched, nervous snort that undid his military bearing.

'You've assembled an educated set of companions.'

His eyes shifted away. 'Oribasius warned me you were another Eutherius, here to report on me.'

'No, Caesar. For starters, I'm not a eunuch. But you are too harsh toward your chamberlain. Eutherius is honest. I heard him tell Constantius in Mediolanum that General Marcellus' accusations against you were lies. He staked his life on your loyalty. Surely, as *praepositus cubiculi*, Eutherius is your most trusted servant.'

'Eutherius risked nothing in telling the truth. He is Constantius' spy.' Julian spoke with the weariness of constant suspicion.

'I am no spy for your cousin.' I lied with ease. I might be a *biarchus* nobody, but I was a *biarchus* nobody with five years' experience on Julian.

'Officially I'm attached to the Prefect to assist the acting *Magister Officiorum*. There are others who can spy on you better than I.'

Alluding to Pentadius and imperial surveillance in the same breath was hardly subtle. Julian poured me some *posca* from his beaker. His cups were not bejeweled Frankish glass or respectable red ware—just soldiers' tin.

'And unofficially?'

'Unofficially, I'm here to spy on the Alemanni. Constantius wants to strengthen his ties with those who sign treaties, like Gundomadus and his brother, and break up the alliances of those who shun Roma's protection.'

'I have Tribune Hariobaudes for relations with those barbarians.'

'Hariobaudes can parlay, parry, bargain, and trade with the Alemanni for you. No doubt he translates their dialect better than any other Roman on your staff. But how can he *spy*? He is the most recognizable Alemannic officer serving the Empire today. I bring you an invisible agent, not a conspicuous Roman.'

'Who?'

'The chieftain Gundomadus' daughter.'

Julian sat in silence, displeased.

'They're all illiterate savages. If they smell weakness, they pounce on us, devastate our fields, and enslave our citizens.'

Would he dare contradict Constantius' policy of accommodation, negotiation, and evacuation? Not to me.

'How do they speak of me in court these days?'

'They see your captives arriving in shackles. They number your victories and acclaim Constantius' wisdom in appointing you here.'

'Yes, while he takes the credit.' Julian stood up and paced his tent. 'Do you remember how we met, the night I fled the court, feeling lucky to have escaped the torture cells that swallowed my brother?'

'It was an honor to assist your passage.'

'But can you guess how hard I've worked, only to find myself struggling against another kind of slavery?' He emptied the beaker as a student might drain a skin of cheap wine.

'Numidianus, you saw me dragged into court on suspicion of treason two years ago and your testimony cleared me. But you don't know the rest. From the first moment of my arrival from Greece, Eusebia kept showing me the utmost kindness through her eunuchs. When the Silvanus affair ended, I was given access to the court at last, but a little "Thessalian persuasion" was pressed on me. You know what I mean.'

I did indeed. It was his second reference in one evening to Alexander the Great. When the Macedonian conqueror met an unfriendly reception to his imperial claims to Thessaly, he reminded his opponents of his ancient relationship to them through Heracles. He spoke 'kindly words' and made 'rich promises,' until the Thessalian League gave Alexander leadership of Greece.

Julian meant that Constantius had used the claim of blood as leverage on the young man to forget the murders, exile, and continuing dangers.

'Then it got worse. Constantius' lackeys marched into my room, shaved off my beard, dressed me in a military cloak, and transformed me into a parody of a soldier.'

'I saw you then, Caesar, from a distance.'

'Then you saw I couldn't strut along like them, staring down my nose at the crowd.'

He'd cut a pitiful figure drowning in an imperial cloak many sizes too large but I did not tell him that tonight.

'Then Constantius sent me up here with instructions in his own hand in a little booklet, like you'd give a stepson leaving for school. He gave me only two hundred *scholares*, some battered *cataphractarii*, and a few mounted archers—perhaps three hundred and sixty men—undisciplined, *phaulotatous*—as my escort through a wilderness where Silvanus required thousands for safe passage only two years before. I'd barely reached Taurini when we heard that a Frankish horde had ransacked Agrippina.'

'Is that when you decided to retake the city?'

He gave a bitter laugh. 'Then? Hardly! I wore the title and robe of a caesar, but I was a *slave*. I wasn't allowed to pay or assemble troops. When the besieged towns begged me for protection, I sent them what few troops I had, praying no one would attack my unprotected staff. Constantius had sent express orders to Ursicinus, Marcellus and the others to watch me more vigilantly than the enemy.'

'They didn't watch the enemy very hard,' I said, 'or the towns and fields would not have been so ravaged.'

'You have it right. Ursicinus and Marcellus couldn't decide on a single strategy between them. While they bickered, the Alemanni were gaining ground on the left bank.'

He tossed his cup aside. 'But about me, they agreed. They locked my doors, left warders as guards, searched my servants for letters to my Eastern friends, and allowed me two boys and two old men as personal attendants. I feared for my life. I knew I shouldn't interfere with Ursicinus, except when I saw something serious was overlooked or something was being attempted that ought never to have been attempted at all.'

'General Ursicinus doesn't like being second-guessed.'

'I got nothing but contempt from Ursicinus, even when I bit my tongue over his decisions. For the sake of my self-respect, I contented myself with parading Constantius' imperial robe and image. I got worse from Marcellus. His neglect was nearly lethal.'

I was not convinced that the 'siege' of Senonae had been as lethal as all that, but certainly Gunda's testimony had confirmed neglect.

'Ursicinus is gone, Caesar. Marcellus is gone. Severus seems deferential and cooperative.'

Julian shook his head in disgust. 'That old fart Severus is too cautious, always saying, "Wait for the bridge, Caesar, wait for the bridge." The gods know better! Hariobaudes says there could be as many as twenty thousand Roman captives across the border. We should be making onslaughts on these tribes while they're still fractious and weak.'

'We all want peace.'

Julian's personal safety lay in cooperation with Constantius' policy. But my comment sat unanswered.

The lamps flickered lower. No fire heated the tent but Julian glowed with the warmth of anger.

'Numidianus, I trained hard. While I marched in pyrrhic measure to the harmony of those military pipes, I repeated that letter from Cicero to Atticus about the oxen and the saddle—'

'*A pack-saddle is put on an ox; this is surely no burden for me.*'

'Yes! Yes!' He sighed. 'How you understand! It takes weeks for my letters to reach friends in the East.' He giggled. 'Do you know why Oribasius is here?'

'No, Caesar.'

'Only because Constantius has no idea he's my friend.'

I did not envy Julian's plight, beholden to the murderer of his entire family for his life, current position, and limited freedom.

'But during the campaign last spring, Caesar, you seized the field.'

'I did better than that. Once the *forceps* was complete, I kept moving north and retook Agrippina from the Franks. I tackled these Alemanni. How can Constantius swallow the savagery of such "allies"—forty-five towns and dozens more forts demolished? The tax coffers are empty. The farmlands harbor only snakes and toads.'

'Has the *Imperator*'s confidence in you grown since?'

Julian snorted again. 'If Constantius heard I was killed in battle on some desolate Gallic plain tomorrow or that my body was floating down the Rhenus to the frozen north, I do not think he would shed one single tear.'

Their rivalry over succession reminded me of Helena's lost pregnancy. 'I'm sorry for your loss, Caesar.'

'Do not dwell on that.' He pulled at his chin where his beard used to be and I saw him steal a suspicious glance at me. 'This afternoon *Magister* Pentadius told Tribune Hariobaudes that you witnessed the death of my half-brother Gallus.'

I was on my guard. Comradeship with a Caesar only went so far, it seemed, even just before dawn.

'I did, Caesar.'

'You never told me you were party to his murder.'

'I was his appointed escort from Antiochia. But rest assured, Caesar, the indictment was based on investigations and interrogation. I saw his governance in Antiochia. Caesar Gallus was not a well man. He was unfit to govern in the opinion of men far wiser than myself.'

Julian spat out, 'All the more reason to spare him, exile him, anything but slaughter him on trumped-up charges in the same dungeon that saw the murder of my uncle's firstborn, Crispus!'

'The fortress in Pula was not my choice.'

'It was the foul joke of your *Magister* Apodemius. How I hate that man.'

'We serve the Empire.'

'All I see is that you serve yourselves, abuse the taxpayer with your run of the *Cursus* and ride state animals until they drop dead. If I were emperor, Numidianus, I would prosecute your *schola*, burn that awful Apodemius at the stake, and padlock the Castra Peregrina for good. In fact, I'd dismantle the entire road network, clogged up with spies and bishops.'

How ironic that it was Apodemius' order that I assist this youth and how ridiculous I could not enlighten Julian without compromising my superior.

'Prove to me that you're loyal, Numidianus. Prove to me you *agentes* serve the Empire. Serve our gods, not yourselves! Serve *me*, not that corrupt, foul city of eunuchs and notaries parading their so-called Christian fables! I've only ever known two genuine Christians—my beloved tutor, the eunuch Mardonius . . . and Helena.'

'You'll find me more loyal than you expect.'

'Then do something more useful than lining Florentius' purse with cuts from the *annona*. Penetrate those Alemanni in their foul nests and hidden caves. Bring me their secrets instead of selling mine. Bring me that daughter of Gundomadus, now, here!'

'Now?'

'Yes, go and fetch her!'

He had worked himself into a rage fed on self-abnegation, suspicion, sleepless nights, and lonely prayers to the gods in their Olympian pantheon. I left him waiting there alone, wrapped in that soiled blanket.

The vast camp of thousands lay quiet, the clanging music of armorers' anvils, signal horns, and final orders buried in sleep. I trotted away from Julian's tent down the pounded alley leading as straight as the surveyors could stake it.

I was not alone. A giant figure loomed up at me along the Via Praetoria. He grabbed my arm before I could unsheathe my *spatha*.

Hariobaudes brandished a flaming torch an inch too close to my nose.

'Is the Chattering Mole done with his metaphysical ramblings for the night? Most of us find some way of begging off.'

'He wants to see my traveling companion,' I said.

'Gundomadus' daughter?'

'Yes, how did you know her name? I'm going to collect her.'

He chuckled. 'Does she want to meet him?'

I shook him off. It was another half-mile run, all the way past the baggage train and on to the squalor of her tent lane.

'Gunda,' I whispered. There was no answer.

'Gunda?' I called in a normal voice. I felt my way to the far end of the dark space without stumbling into her sleeping form or even a bedroll. I dashed outside, grabbed an ebbing torch from its holder and thrust it through the open entrance.

Gunda was gone.

Chapter 13, The Search for Gunda

—SUNRISE OUTSIDE TRES TABERNAE—

The discovery of her empty tent sent me raging. As if in someone else's dream, I watched myself flipping over Gunda's discarded bedding, examining the ashes of her fire, and thrusting my hand into every corner of the small tent. I was desperate for a clue to her disappearance.

I checked the latrines, the water barrels, and the alleys leading away in all directions from that camp quarter.

A feeling of betrayal surged into my breast. The vivid memory of her fervent embrace overwhelmed my reason. I thought of how Gunda had bid me goodnight. I had not realized she meant goodbye.

What in Hades had happened?

And why flee now? If she wanted her freedom, she could have left Bainobaudes and myself to our deaths at the hands of that brutish Alemanna and her thuggish fellows days ago.

Perhaps she had not meant goodbye. The blunt Gunda seemed too frank for that. She must have decided to run away after I left her tent.

What had happened? Had she learned something that endangered her? Had she clung to me for the protection I carelessly denied her by relegating her so far from the headquarters? Had she recognized someone in the camp? Had someone recognized her?

The camp was full of strange soldiers. Most of them were *Germani* but even if a handful harked from the distant Agri

Decumantes, who would recognize Gunda under a hood slipping through the busy camp at dusk?

Or had that fervent clutching meant she'd grown to care for me during our long days of travel? Had she hoped I would hold her back, even make love to her there in the privacy of her borrowed tent?

No, she was too proud, even hardhearted, to submit herself to chance like that. Her embrace had been a contrary farewell, a last gesture in that strange arrogant contest she'd waged against 'the Roman' ever since we first met in the prison camp.

And she had had time to take all her things—including her lyre.

The pink-gray gleam of the new day blossomed into a broad orange glow over the fortress above us.

I sent a slave to tell the Caesar's staff that Gunda could not be found. I collared the rest of families settled near her tent as well as the sentries walking the palisade bordering this insalubrious part of the encampment. I begged everyone I saw for information. The ragged, rough women I interrogated were too busy heating up stewpots and swabbing down mewling infants to bother with a *curiosus* hunting for a missing beauty with a lyre slung across her back.

I offered bribes to barbers and slaves alike. Though tempted by my coins, none had seen Gunda leave. Perhaps they thought better of telling tales to a tall Numidian bearing an *agens* insignia—whatever his bribe.

I accosted Tribune Hariobaudes as dawn burned away the last dew clinging to the tent ropes. He dressed as strictly as any Roman officer but the sun caught the gold of his hair, the shine of his *fibulae*, and the glitter of his buckle. He cut a colorful figure even without barbarian torcs or armbands and he knew it.

'The Alemanna's gone.'

'So I hear.'

'You knew something was afoot last night. Why didn't you warn me you suspected something?'

The *tribunus vacans* flexed his shoulders. Perhaps he made up for his lack of commission by throwing his looming weight around.

—THE DEADLY CAESAR—

'What did you know of that female, *Agens*? What do you know of my people at all? Did you think you could employ such a woman to Roman purposes?'

'We hold her brother hostage at the Castra. For his sake, she vowed to assist us.'

'She might have higher loyalties.'

'Yes, to her father and to his alliance with us.'

Hariobaudes gave a thin smile and straightened his helmet strap. 'Then I meant, she might have *lower* loyalties. That kind cares nothing about alliances between kings and princes. Women worry about alliances closer to home—even the highborn ones.'

With this enigmatic dismissal of Gunda's 'kind,' he strode off for the exercise field spread out beyond the camp perimeter. He had hinted something, but would say no more. He resented my meddling in Alemannic affairs, assignment or no. He had enjoyed toying with me.

That barbarian chieftain had achieved much to be ranked *tribunus vacans*. While some Alemanni inside our borders were happy as praetorian officers or just recruiters profiteering along the *limes*, Hariobaudes looked ready to risk more to rise even higher in fame.

Both Hariobaudes and I knew the hurdles those born on the margins of Empire leapt over for acceptance and promotion. And even then, what? The career of a highflying *Germanus* in the sacred *consistorium* of Constantius would be precarious. Look at what had happened to General Silvanus because of treachery and envy in court.

Hariobaudes wasn't just flexing his muscles in my face. He was flaunting hard-won power at a North African colonial outsmarted by a wild-haired girl from across the river.

And it wasn't only an African freedman *curiosus* like me that Hariobaudes resented. It was Gunda herself. She was a highborn Alemanna, fluent in Latin, and dabbling in Roman politics. She might try to play the intermediary between Julian and the tribes on both sides of the river. She might contradict Hariobaudes' advice to harass and hound their people.

I understood the man better than he guessed.

Hariobaudes had wanted to discredit Gunda. His first tactic had been to use the unpopular Pentadius' tattling about Gallus' execution to distance Julian from my counsel—and Gunda's.

What had happened overnight? Had Gunda defected of her own free will? Or had Hariobaudes threatened her? Had she raced home to her father in the Agri Decumantes? Or been lured away under false pretenses for ransom?

Why else did Hariobaudes suggest that Gunda might not meet the Caesar—if he hadn't got rid of her himself in stealth? What did he know about Gunda that he was keeping to himself?

Had Hariobaudes gone even further? Was Gunda still alive?

I couldn't dwell on the worst. To get away from camp, she'd have needed a horse. Without the *evectio* I carried, she'd risk being shoved off the *Cursus* onto side roads and rough paths. That wouldn't stop Gunda from reaching her destination—wherever it was.

At the army stables, I learned she'd worked her sweetest wiles on a stable boy no older than eight. Well before dawn, they'd chosen her a strong horse complete with good saddle and inconspicuous harness.

I didn't want to see the child punished. I bought off the *tribunus stabulensis* and took the youngster for a walk halfway up the rubble-strewn hills under the crumbling fortress walls.

'... asked me where I was from, *Biarchus*... if I had any brothers or sisters. Said she was mistreated by a Roman she'd trusted too much. The lady was homesick. Like all of us. She wanted to go home to the *pagani*.'

'Which direction did she take?'

'Didn't say. They've got *vici* all over the place, but nowhere's I'd want to live.'

'Neither would she. Where's the nearest big settlement?'

'Not far. I heard one of the scouts who'd come back from some bunch of 'em cutting logs for the bridge. The rest just live in huts or rundown villas.'

'Where is this logging camp?'

'To the east, in the forests along the river between Brotomagus and Argentoratum. I guess she headed for them. You see, I listen to the scouts as they come and go—I like to know where they're headed and what they saw. But please, don't punish me if I'm wrong.'

I gave him a few *nummi*. 'Punish you? You're what our service looks for—boys with big eyes, bigger ears, and powerful legs for riding. What's your name? Where are your parents?'

'My name is Tonantius. The Alemanni captured my parents in a raid.'

'Tonantius, I need you to bring a good horse to me behind the Via Praetoria at the back end of the Prefect's section in ten minutes.'

He frowned. 'Are you the Roman who treated the woman bad?'

'No, your lady friend is important to the Caesar's plans. I'm attached to the Prefect's staff.'

Prefect Florentius didn't interest Tonantius. 'Have you met the Caesar?' he asked with a brightening expression. 'Is he going to lead us to great victories on this campaign?'

'Wouldn't peace be better than bloodshed?'

'No. The Caesar's right,' Tonantius said. 'We must drive every last one of them off Roman land. I want my parents back.'

※※※

Those two Alemanni fighters had attacked Gunda in a *pagus* where she should have been safe. Our Alemanna 'hostess' had nearly slit our throats in Roman territory for a few weapons. Beautiful and defenseless, Gunda rode alone now and, apart from that silly paring knife, weaponless. I hoped she would stick to the *Cursus* for as long as she could.

I equipped myself with a better-than-average sword from the armorers, along with a *pugio* sharper than the one I'd lost on the road. Both weapons came from good state *fabricae*, though they lacked the twisted sheen and expensive finish of a handcrafted Germanic product. My swivel knife stayed hidden under its tall boot cuff.

I had one other advantage over Gunda. Every *agens* carries a concise table of the roads, *vici*, towns, cities, *mansiones*, *caupones*, and relay stables of the region he crosses on duty. This includes the distances, watercourses, and road quality—from military highways down to private toll roads and rustic unpaved paths. It was all copied out from our Castra-issued *itinerarium* as needed. Unlike the tourist scribbles used by pilgrims and merchants, an *agens'* guide was under constant revision as the political and physical situation changed.

From this, I saw there was a *via vincinale*, probably a lightly graveled dirt road, cutting from on a diagonal from Tres Tabernae to Argentoratum. If Gunda sought shelter with the nearest Alemanni, she'd be working her way due eastwards, passing the military camp in Brotomagus, and only then riding southwards along the riverside toward the logging camp.

But the logging camp couldn't be far from Barbatio's army waiting for logs on the opposite side of the winding waters. I had to retrieve Gunda before Barbatio's scouts delivered her into his eager clutches as his own political pawn.

I packed enough dried food for two days' ride and left a message for Florentius that I would return without fail within the week. Anyway, the Prefect would not mourn an untrustworthy nuisance he had to keep out of mischief.

Horns signaled the start of exercises and construction just as I rode away. I knew from the lingering heat of her ashes that Gunda had less than two hours' advance on me but I harbored one small fear—that she'd taken a more desperate tack. She might have turned inland for the shelter of her dubious bishop or headed down safer detours through central Gallia to reach her brother at the Castra.

In which case, she was not only lost to me, but to the mission. Who knew what course the untrained mind of such highborn, high-strung woman might take?

I paused to analyze these possibilities from what I knew of her. It was not like Gunda to retreat and hide with a cleric she despised. She had no friends or supplies to see her all the way back to Roma.

No, it was more like her to advance and claim her place in the fray. The attack on her in the forest was a warning that her father was in peril. The tame Alemanni settlers laboring for Roma might put her in touch with friendly tribes across the river.

Contact with them offered fresh information on where things stood for her father and uncle.

I put my money on the logging camp. I turned my horse onto the graveled trail cutting southeast across the ravaged fields. If that old Greek Pythagoras was right, my route was shorter than the *Cursus* leading Gunda due east and then south. It was worth a try.

Once clear of the camp, my spirits lifted. I told myself I did not care for her, desire her, or fear for her. My task was to bring her back—that was all.

※※※

Whatever progress I was making, it had to be faster than Gunda's. Apart from a low range that separated Tres Tabernae from the Rhenus valley plateau, the path stretched flat ahead of me. It was easy miles of dry riding along a well-marked, empty trail that had once teemed with market wagons, postal riders, and local traffic. I galloped past small farmers, mending walls and clearing weeds— trying to get their estates back on their feet. I skirted a few walled towns that looked bolted up tight against Alemanni harassment. It wasn't much of a journey for a hardened rider, but all the same, I wasn't the eager flying *circitor* who'd once worn a *petanus* pinned with the white feather of express mail, trying to set a record as he circled the postal routes between Sirmium and Mediolanum.

You can always spot an army site before you see the tents. You almost feel the deep rumble from unseen wagons, heavy-footed oxen, and tramping horses underneath your horse's hooves. Smoke from distant campfires, ironmonger's blazes, and bonfires burning the detritus of thousands of men with their trailing women and children swirls into the clouds in the sky ahead.

I spied the logging base at midday. Their setup wouldn't have passed muster as an army camp, but there was a respectable gesture toward a palisade and a straggly grid of tents. Enough soldiers for two squadrons were eating their day's rations in the warm sun. They'd be there to guard the project from attack. I had only to glance at the river behind the carpenters and carriers to see why protection was needed.

The loggers had chosen a spot richly timbered and conveniently close to the bank. But I'd never seen the Rhenus current so shallow. Instead of a confident transportation artery, the river drifted and sprawled in a caricature of a mythical lagoon. Its summer nadir exposed half a dozen small islands and oxbow lakes. Runnels, streams, and eddies swirled and whirled, churning up the silt. The deeper crosscurrents would prove tricky for a boat, even trickier for a horse, and downright dangerous for any swimmer sucked into the muck or caught in an undertow.

I watched the nearest island, bustling almost as much as the loggers' camp. Hovels and lean-tos melded into the green. One after another, dirty brown barbarian silhouettes emerged or sank back into the foliage. A second island downriver shifted with activity in the shimmering sunlight and beyond, a third. I felt the chill one gets when the rough bark of a tree under your hand suddenly shifts form and becomes a camouflaged creature poised to sting.

Alemanni warriors, with their telltale red-dyed hair in knots and braids, their imposing height, and their trademark ferocity in stance and style were nowhere to be seen. Unlike the barbarian nobles who occupied abandoned, crumbling, Roman fortresses on hilltops farther eastward, these island campers were the poorest and most desperate of their people. Hungry and dirty, they were lurking and poking around our defenses, hoping for fertile land in Gallia or biding their time for a better life out from under the tyranny of tribal chieftains.

I would have been happier to have seen their fighting-age men loitering around these aimless, hapless folk. The absence of males older than ten across the shoals hung like a threatening question mark over the Roman squadrons guarding the loggers. Guard or engineer—every Roman on this left bank had to be primed to leap into action at the whisper of a raiders' attack.

Some of the teams were working scattered throughout the forest on either side of my approach. Drivers and cutters lifted and secured mammoth trees onto heavy *clabularii* wagons and whipped them back to camp, their towering pyramids of trunks strapped down tight. Oxen plodded back and forth between the forest edge and the river camp where the timber was measured and dressed under the supervision of engineers.

I skirted these teams and trotted closer to the center of the operation. An *immunis* working on dry ground above the river bank looked official enough to help me, yet not so high-ranked as to hinder me.

I showed him my insignia. 'Numidianus, *Biarchus*.'

'Ennius. *Architectus*.'

'I'm expecting a woman to ride in here, an Alemanna. Seen her?'

'All these guys left their women behind. We've got work to do.'

'Who's in charge of them? I could ask around.'

'I don't know their names. I leave that to the sub-engineers. Right now they better get a move on shifting the timber.'

Ennius was leaning over a mess of plans sketched on the cheapest *taeneotic*. Pinned down by rocks at the corners, they flapped and spilled over his camp desk and his stool. I jumped off my horse and rescued a sketch of a bridge with keystone arches snatched up by the river's breeze. I returned to Ennius' side and laid his plan on top of minor sketches showing measurements for watertight wooden sheaths to be sunk into the undependable riverbed.

'That looks to me like the Pons Aelius in Roma.'

He grimaced at my comment. Perhaps a comparison with Hadrian's ancient bridge on the Tiberis did not flatter such a modern technician. I was wrong.

'Yes, a beauty.' He flattened the plans. 'With cofferdams packed with clay and pillar sheaths as tight as a virgin's pussy. You scoop out the water and the mud of the river from this cylinder so that a concrete foundation for the pier can be constructed on firm ground.'

'Won't that take time?'

'This bridge here? Months, at least. Unfortunately, *Agens*, we're not building *this*. We're going with the *Dacian* model.'

Ennius rotated a sketch of a crude wooden crossing supported by a line of boats of very shallow draft so that I could see.

'Hardly the same thing.'

He shrugged. 'I keep the other sketch to inspire me. This project won't be anything to be proud of.'

'Speed is the priority, not posterity.'

'Well, where's the challenge in speed? You know the place called Confluentes?' He pointed a gnarled finger downriver.

'The junction of the Rhenus and the Mosella. I've ridden through it a few times. Saw a burnt-out bridge there in '55.'

'Right you are, *Biarchus*. Did you know that Julius Caesar threw up a timber model at Confluentes in only ten days with forty thousand men? *Four hundred years ago*! As soon as the great man crossed back into Roman territory, he tore the bloody thing down, just to show those *Germani* what Roman engineers could do.'

I tapped his rough sketch for Barbatio's pontoon bridge. 'You don't think that's going to impress the barbarians as much?'

He rolled up the clumsy design. 'Mine'll be better. But the river's a mess. It's impossible to control the passage of the planks with all these crosscurrents, sandbars—you name it. They should have driven protective beams in by now, on a slant, into the riverbed. No time for proper—'

He'd spotted a problem with one of the teams. 'Sorry, but we're running behind schedule.'

'What about my Alemanna?'

He grabbed a measuring rod and ran toward a fresh wagonload of logs, calling over his shoulder, 'Try some of the *vici* downstream.'

Rope slings powered by men working a treadmill lowered huge logs into the water. On the opposite bank somewhere downriver, Barbatio's team must be linking up the pontoon boats to receive Ennius' timber.

There was no point in waiting. Gunda hadn't got this far. Better to take Ennius' advice and head her off along the north-south highway alongside the river. I cadged some fresh snacks off the kitchen team and set off again.

Behind me, a fresh load of planks hit the river at an angle with a terrible splash. They stuck fast into the riverbed, their raw ends poking up out of the mud.

'Damn your greasy mitts!' Ennius shouted at the team as I rode away. Tempers were fraying. If Gunda did reach this camp, she'd find no one with time to waste on an Alemanna unless she was handy with a pulley.

I wasn't keen to dismount alone and find myself surrounded by a band of settler toughs. But there was no other way to find out if anyone had seen Gunda riding past without stopping, again and again, at settlements along the *Cursus*.

The Alemanni had indeed seized crops and villas all along the river route. Struggling farms and ragged crops dotted the low slopes of the river valley. No doubt these poor immigrants assumed that by putting themselves on the Roman bank, they would enjoy our laws and protection. Hadn't the Franks got to keep their empty Toxandria up north, Gunda had protested? Weren't the Samartians welcomed in the east for their infantry recruits? Why couldn't the Alemanni stay too?

The afternoon sun warmed my left shoulder and my horse grew weary, plodding past dull-eyed barefoot children and mothers with blistered hands. They weren't as foolish as the Frankish savages, seizing Agrippina only to flee and leave Julian a so-called 'victory' over an emptied shell of a capital. These settlers were staying away from the towns where Roman officers and bureaucracy still held sway. They were keeping their heads bowed.

Yet Julian intended to build his reputation on conquering such gullible, downtrodden clusters of humanity.

From time to time, I got fresh water at a well and put my question across. But even a bronze coin or two only got the same answer in gestures and broken Latin—no Gunda.

Halfway to Brotomagus, Roman work teams blocked the *Cursus*. With ropes and hooks flailing away, they directed the floating timber that Ennius was sending downriver to the bridge site. My stomach rumbled but I wouldn't stop until I caught up with Gunda. I could distract myself all I wanted, but I knew that my own guts were telling me something I had fought off. It was an admission to myself that I'd denied until now.

I wanted more from Gunda than information. Her silvery-gold hair, her dancing fingers, her lilting voice, her sharp-eyed jibes, her rapier knife, her graceful hips and proud, independent carriage—yes, I thought of these and I wanted more.

Kahina's slow, incomplete mental recovery and then her humorless, chaste submission to Christian obsession had built a wall between us that all my patience and intelligence couldn't breach. Her youthful sweetness had matured into sanctimonious piety. Her devotion to Leo risked sacrificing him to an institution that only grew fat and dishonest under the indulgence of the throne.

The more I saw the danger her religious 'gratitude' posed to Leo's legacy—with one Roman family after another signing away their treasure to Constantius' greedy churchmen—the more I was set against everything Kahina worshipped. This was one point on which our new Caesar, lip service to Constantius aside, would agree with me.

But Gunda thought for herself. At times, she even thought for both of us. She challenged, fascinated, and aroused me. She wanted to be Roman in all the ways I cherished. She comported herself like the noblewoman she was at home. Was it so unthinkable that I should win her? How had my respected Roman grandfather felt when he brought home his second wife, a Gallic noblewoman? Hadn't the Senator breached an old social divide in the heart of ancient Roman society between the old *gentes* and the provincial arrivistes?

Yet by all accounts, my beautiful grandmother had adapted, thrived, and conquered not only Senator Manlius' heart, but all the wagging tongues of the Esquiline Hill as well.

After all, Gunda had been designated by her father to marry a Roman officer—only not a common *biarchus* like myself. She aimed higher.

Well, so did I. I was determined to advance, for all our sakes—Leo and Kahina's—as well as my own. This mission was going to see me promoted to *centenarius* or I would quit the *schola* to keep the Manlius estates well clear of avaricious priests and their gold-encrusted bishops.

The thought of declaring myself to Gunda quickened my pace. There was little distance left to the next *mansio*. The innkeeper might provide sensible directions, hot food, and a basin of steaming water. He was less likely to know much about Gunda's whereabouts.

On that score, I was dead wrong.

—THE DEADLY CAESAR—

'Oh, I wouldn't forget her,' the *manceps* said, squinting into the late afternoon's summer haze. 'She wanted a boat to get across from that pier out there.'

I had caught her—or at least a reliable scent on her trail.

'Did she cross?'

'Well, you don't see no boat, do you, son?'

He pointed at a dilapidated wooden extension jutting high over the river in the distance, its boat rings hanging slack.

This part of the river lay as low as the rest, but I saw none of the islands infested with refugee families for a quarter of a mile in each direction—just a wide stretch of flowing water made treacherous by the shifting bed, a clutch of muddy meads on the far side, and the jutting roots of old tree trunks cluttering the near bank.

'I'm surprised a boat could get through that.'

'Oh, she paid well enough, she did.'

Where or how had Gunda got any money? My heart recoiled at the possibilities, but she might be desperate to escape Roman territory. I cursed her for not confiding in me. She must have known very well where she was going.

'How long since she crossed?'

'Not many hours ago.'

The *manceps* took the exhausted horse off my hands and, jingling my coins in his palm, promised to reserve a fresh horse for my return.

'Make it two horses. You've got another boat?'

'Yes, but I don't want to lose a good customer. Can you swim?'

'If I have to.'

Swimming is not something a Numidian desert boy transferred by slavery to the walled confines of a Roman townhouse practices often. Stolen dips into the Tiberis hanging on to ropes and barrels with other frolicking slaves had earned me too many punishments to call swimming a favorite recreation. *Agentes* were trained to swim, but I stuck to gymnasium pools for aquatic exercise.

'Right then, there's an old one-man boat hidden in that gorse hedge,' he said. 'Thieves don't bother to look there. Here, I'll take you down.'

I strained my eyes down the slope, but for the first ten minutes of walking through tall grass and then reeds, all I saw ahead was a dense wall of bright yellow high and dry above the soggy bank. The hedge's pea-like flowers disguised vicious dark green spines that my innkeeper trusted to keep bandits at bay.

He helped me lower the leaky tub into the silty water. I clambered aboard next to a splintered oar and a fraying rope on the bottom. He watched me and counted up my coins.

'What's across the river?' I asked.

'Well, you want to go there so bad, I figured you knew, being an *agens* and all.'

'I'm bringing the Alemanna back. I just want to know who might be waiting to stop me.'

'Oh, if you're lucky, you won't meet anyone. But if you're looking for company, that's the *pagus* of Mederichus.'

'Mederichus?' I asked, fumbling with a rusty oarlock. An eddy six feet away from the shore caught and twisted the little craft around.

'The brother of Gigas,' the innkeeper shouted, waving me off with his free hand and clutching my money with the other. 'Use the current, son, don't fight it. That way, you just might make to the other side in dry trousers.'

He laughed as I fought for control of the boat, turning in dizzy circles. I got it straight and by the time he was out of sight beyond the yellow hedge, I was halfway across the river.

The boat slammed to a halt on a hidden sandbank. I tried working it this way and that with my oar but it was jammed hard. The bow had got itself wedged in a cleft between two submerged rocks. I climbed out of the boat and slogged knee-deep up to the front to check the damage and tried to push the boat free. But there was a splintering sound as the rocks sank their pointed edges like teeth deeper into the fragile wood. Water started to seep into the bow through the ripped planks.

I considered walking the last hundred feet to the far shore. But only six feet away, the rippling water turned an ominous black where the riverbed gave way to a steep drop. The river's flow was cutting a deep gully where a deadlier current rushed along at twice the speed.

—THE DEADLY CAESAR—

A dark form appeared on the water, outlined by the sun setting over the barbarian bank. I feared it was a loose tree or barrel but was relieved to see it was one of the loggers' rafts bearing three standing men struggling with a convoy of deadly planks ropes to their platform. About a dozen loosely linked giant logs bounced wildly alongside—sweeping ahead of the raft until the men pushed them back and then tossing in their wake.

The loggers spotted me, stuck in the center of their path like some straw target set in a field for trainee *Sagittarii*.

'Look out!' they called.

As if I had a choice. I jumped back into the boat for protection and waved my oar to warn them away from where I floated, marooned and sinking by the inch, thanks to the damaged planking. I might have to dive and swim out of their lethal course.

'Move, man! Move!' they shouted. The loggers steered as best they could. If I was lucky, their raft was going to slide past me at a deadly clip by no more than a lucky few yards.

They were less than fifty feet away and seeing the edge of their elevated raft racing level with my neck, I saw I had no choice. I scrambled back out of the boat and ran to the very edge of the sandbank beyond which I feared for my life in a torrent of colder water rushing over my knees. I fought for balance and prepared to dive in. I only looked back when I heard a logger hailing me.

They'd grounded themselves on purpose, punting themselves to anchor for as long as it took me to recover my breath and slog back to their raft. The troublesome logs floated past us, tugging on their ropes and hooks while the men came to my rescue.

A few minutes later, they'd set me back on my feet in the shallows of the right bank and floated on. I collapsed on the wild grasses covering the slope, panting hard. I wrung out my socks and laid back, closing my eyes against the bright afternoon sun.

I had had little sleep the night before and this was turning out to be a very long day. The next minute promised worse.

Five Alemanni were blocking the sunlight.

'A runaway?' they asked in Latin.

'No.'

As wet as I was, my good quality clothing and decent footwear argued in my favor. I'd been so determined to catch up with Gunda, I'd failed to prepare a cover story. If these were Roma's allies, and not brutish raiders, I'd be all right. I fished out my insignia, wondering whether they recognized the emblem of my *schola*.

They took my *spatha* and *pugio*, tied me up, and blindfolded my eyes. This was not the behavior of allies. I smelled the rider in front of me, the sweat of his horse, the last summer flush of wildflowers, and the receding gurgle of the river. After about an hour, I was yanked to the ground and jerked forward.

I cursed my lousy luck, wasting valuable hours as Gunda's trail went cold.

I was shoved forward as one Alemannus pushed my head low to avoid a doorframe. My boots struck flagstones and then pounded earth. I smelled a cooking fire and male bodies. There was an exchange in dialect—possibly some explanation for my presence.

Then the blindfold was pulled off. I blinked into thick smoke.

A statuesque Alemannic youth faced me over a fire in the center of a large room of unfinished wood walls built over the remnants of a Roman stone foundation. His *paenula* hung from large *fibulae* in the shape of gold eagles. Underneath he wore a rich suit of Roman armor decorated with green stones set in filigreed gold around the hem and wrists. His reddish-blond beard was short and soft—almost downy.

He was not only the youngest but also the tallest. His long cloak barely reached the top of his boots. He was not handsome in our Roman or Greek sense—no soft eyes, generous lips, or high and noble hairline. His appearance was arresting for its light blue eyes, wide forehead, high cheekbones, long nose, and jutting chin.

He reminded me of a hawk.

There were other details that spoke of contact with the Empire—luxury tokens that our side handed over during negotiations to signal Roman regard. Garnets in cloisonné work decorated his *pugio* hilt, gold buckles of chipped work fixed the joins of his sword belt, and gold embroidery trimmed the hem of his dark indigo tunic.

—THE DEADLY CAESAR—

I tried to gauge the strength of this Germanic band from the look of its lofty officers, all clothed in different versions of the same raiding gear: a *sagum* or short rectangular cape over well-made tunics of woven animal hair mixed with wool, and riding trousers of animal hide bound to the calf with leather strips.

Barbarian chieftains were known among themselves as 'ring-givers' and their bartered gifts included Roman goods that trickled down from man to man. This party stood practically radiant with secondhand booty reflecting the firelight.

One man sported a necklace of gold imperial coins. Another wore a double stranded *torc* in the Germanic style around his neck and two gold bracelets with knobbed ends. This is what they did with good *solidi* in lands where there were few regular markets and little to buy but Roman glass, mirrors, dinnerware— and prisoners.

My capture had interrupted an intense debate. They resumed huddled in conference around the flames that kept the old stone enclosure dry. Only one stood apart with arms folded in a defensive posture and face shadowed by a long, thin cloak hooded with rich otter fur.

The boy leader saw me scrutinize his men. This was my job and I should not forget it. I was memorizing faces, ready to report to Apodemius the mood and intelligence of Roma's allies or enemies—but which were they?

Seeing the scrutiny I gave to each of his men, their leader came up close to me and announced, 'I am Agenarich, *heerkönig* of nine hundred men who answer to my family along this shoreline. This is my *comitatus*—men you Romans call *optimates, armati, fortiores*—'

'Agenarich? We Romans know you as the *Regalis* Serapio, re-named by your father in memory of his introduction to Greek culture while a Roman hostage.'

'The same.' Serapio said, 'And this is my consort.'

Gunda turned around and pushed the otter trim away from her pale brow. She gave a slow nod, but no more. Reeling with confusion, I forced my eyes back to Serapio.

He was not one of Roma's allies—at least not so far.

How could I explain myself now? I had planned to declare myself a state escort for the honored daughter of Gundomadus, engage their aid, and sound out their deliberations.

But she was already here, the consort of Serapio.

Would I endanger Gunda if I said I'd tracked her this far? Was her astonishing composure a feint to protect me? Or disown me? Was there no end to this female's duplicities?

All I knew, as I struggled to invent a completely fresh explanation of my intrusion, was that her cold eyes warned me off.

I'd saved her brother's life in Roma and saved her from execution as an assassin. She'd saved Bainobaudes and myself from slaughter on the road.

As far as Gunda was concerned, we were even. It was now every Roman for himself.

Unfortunately, I was the only Roman in the room.

Chapter 14, Gunda's Lament

—Nightfall, the Pagus of Mederichus—

'Explain yourself, *Agens*,' Serapio said, the last trace of cordiality dropping away from his features. 'My men picked you up miles off the old Roman road. If you are trying to deliver imperial mail, you are the wrong side of the water.'

He repeated his joke in dialect. One of his warriors clipped my shoulder with a meaty fist and chortled in broken Latin, 'Where's your post bag?'

'I was sent by Tribune Hariobaudes,' I lied. 'The Western Army of Roma is moving down the Rhenus on both banks. They are constructing a bridge nearby. Hariobaudes wishes to warn all the *reguli* of a plan to force the Alemanni settlers off Roman land and back to the right bank.'

Serapio almost smiled. Next to me, a stout fighter with breath reeking of herbed barley beer muttered in Alemannic. There was a brief exchange between Serapio and his followers. I watched their expressions as he answered each man in a low, patient tone. Tensions eased a little. One unclenched his right hand from the gold hilt of the *spatha* hanging off his sword belt. But he still looked ready to slice my head off, if only to amuse Serapio.

'So you plan to drive our people off land that is theirs by right? If you tell the truth, *Agens*, then why not come to us honestly by open road with an escort or even a squadron? Why skulk, wet and alone, in the broken reeds? Perhaps you came to spy on us, to count our numbers, or to locate the hostages we keep—all those *curiales* and merchants we took from your towns.'

'My boat was unreliable. I was dropped on the bank by loggers.'

'So that is your story?'

'Yes.'

Gunda's eyes never flinched. Serapio followed my glance and scowled. She stood as tall, rigid, and silent as that obelisk Constantius was planting in the center of Roma. She was even more hardhearted, it seemed, than Egyptian granite. Only she among our audience understood my terse, rapid Latin exchange with Serapio.

Only she could save or condemn me.

'You bring a meager message for such effort, *Agens*. We have already heard of the Caesar's march eastward to Tres Tabernae. We know of his headstrong campaign to reclaim the towns and fields Constantius gave to us. Do you bring anything else, say, a token of Tribune Hariobaudes' goodwill?'

Like any *agens*, I dressed in a spare, anonymous style to keep a low profile. I was not a man who carried trinkets in case of last minute barbarian-wooing. Years ago, I'd carried three rings from the hand of a slaughtered rebel *magister officiorum* off the muddy battlefield of Mursa, intending to return the treasure to his widow. In the end, those three rings had saved my Kahina, my son, and myself.

But random treasure didn't drop into my lap every day.

'No, I carry no tribute or token.'

'Not even a sword ring? . . . Too bad.'

Serapio uttered a few low words to the stout, eager man at my side, then turned back to me. 'You'll stay with our other Roman "guests." You won't be lonely. Hundreds of them are collecting the harvest a day's ride east of here.'

One of the men who had hauled me in from the riverbank now yanked me forward, lifted my under-tunic to expose my naked belly, squeezed my upper arms, laughed, and punched me hard above my belt.

I folded over, gasping for breath.

Serapio's cool voice added, 'A healthy Roman soldier brings eight *solidi*. You're neither young nor fighting fit, but if you're of any value to your *schola*, we might get something. Tribune Hariobaudes, whom we know by reputation, will no doubt become worried by your absence, will he not? He will send word to claim you back. Otherwise, you till the land with our other captives and fend for yourself, as they do. For the moment, they pull up just enough roots to survive. Work hard. Who knows? You might be with us for good.'

Not once did Gunda lift her gaze from the crackling fire to face me. Not once did she look me in the eyes as Serapio ordained my fate.

His men tied me up again and dumped me in an empty hut next to their meeting house. Their rumbling voices reached my dark corner reeking of human filth where I fumbled for my bearings for at least another hour. I heard other voices, too, but apart from Serapio's hardened coterie, the hamlet sheltered only old women and children.

Huts were left unattended and livestock pens empty. These barbarians worked almost as hard as their slaves to bring in the crops and game. Ordinary people were hungry on both sides of the river and they had to forage and fight for what crops there were. The working villagers would only return from their fields and pastures after dusk.

Meanwhile Barbatio's army convoy was groaning with enough food for thousands of hungry soldiers. Julian's troops were eager for their portion.

As the last summer light penetrating the planked walls of my prison faded away, more and more *pagani* passed my bolted door. Serapio's debate with his men was over. Freshly stoked cooking fires burned nearby. It became clear no one intended to feed me. I had dozed off my exhaustion in less than an hour. My stomach rumbled.

I had to escape before hunger weakened my wits and limbs. The hut offered nothing in the way of a cutting edge, but it wouldn't be hard to work the knife hidden in my boot cuff into my grasp. Only, Gunda knew full well of my hidden weapon. She'd seen me using it on the ropes that trussed Bainobaudes' ankles only days before.

Happily for me, her mind seemed focused on Serapio for now. Floating through the *vicus*' smoke, the barking of dogs, and the mewling of small children, Gunda's voice rose into the night air. She was singing the familiar tune, but had changed it yet again. Once mournful, then shrill, her theme tonight turned seductive and insinuating.

If I'd still worn that stupid blindfold, I would have pulled it tight round my ears to muffle her siren notes. She had turned into a singing Circe, addressing her love song to that callow, gaudy Serapio.

Though my hands and ankles were tightly tied, I managed to get the knife into my clutches. Even through my furious effort to cut myself free, my dream of drawing Gunda close to me would not go away. Her drifting serenade mocked and taunted me, curdling my fantasy.

And didn't her song last longer, now that she had the audience she'd wanted all along? It was tormenting to hear her lilting words through the hush of the village, broken only by the cackling of hens fighting over their evening grain and the spit and snap of roasting meat outside. I had to tear my thoughts from Serapio's cozy fireside. There was only this one night to escape before I was transferred farther east and shackled to other Roman slaves.

There was one consolation. As long as she sang, she wasn't coming for my knife. But she might have warned one of the *optimates* to take it off me. When a pair of boots tramped close by my door, I held my breath.

But no one entered. As far as Serapio's minions knew, there was no reason to take any more notice of me until my transfer to the captives' fields at dawn. Nevertheless, I kept my ears cocked. If someone knocked, I'd hide the knife and scurry back into the darkest corner where I'd been dumped.

Gunda's song rose higher. She was the triumphant sorceress luring Ulysses to her island of amorous consummation. I hated him for having her. I hated her for making me listen to their reunion.

The fraying hemp bit into my bleeding wrists but I was only halfway through the ropes. I had not kept the knife sharp enough.

Her song stopped. I froze and listened to Serapio and Gunda exchange brief words. She resumed her song, but, impatient, he cut her off. It was bound to turn more intimate. I braced myself to endure the sounds of their incipient lovemaking.

I set to working again at the last ends of split hemp that bit into my flesh like a spray of needles. I heard them still talking, their voices rising.

—THE DEADLY CAESAR—

Finally the blade broke through. With a last yank at the threads of reluctant twine, my wrists flew free. I worked faster at the ropes around my ankles and after many minutes unfolded my stiff knees and bruised stomach. But I was nowhere near freedom. My captors had closed a crude and rusty padlock through a hinge on the hut's only door.

From Serapio's hut, Gunda gave a sharp cry followed by the sound of a slap. Another cry and another slap followed. If this was barbarian lovemaking, I felt no more jealousy. Wooden furniture scraped the floor and something thudded against a wall. Another slap followed.

Gunda retaliated in a hoarse outburst. A long silence. Another blow. More weeping. Those two noble Alemanni ruffians had outraged me by abusing Gunda in that leafy forest byway, but Serapio's cruelty this evening aroused even deeper rancor in my heart. If the lyrics of her refrain were true, Serapio was the man she loved.

Her variable lyrics had a haunting reality ... *marries the prince of another tribe ... he does not love her as much as he loves himself and the thrill of raiding, ambushes, and skirmishes ... passion of love is sweeter ...*

But something had gone wrong. Serapio's love, meted out far from the family's hilltop fortress—that rude and lawless *herrschaftszentrum*—was violent, not sweet.

Gunda's wails cut through the indifferent grinding of a mortar and pestle close by and the evening hum of crickets in the grasses beyond. No one went to Serapio's hut. In an Alemanni settlement, what went on behind a warrior's bolted door was nobody else's business.

There was no window in my hut. I heard all this through an opening in the roof to let smoke rise free. Orion's starry sword dangling from his celestial belt twinkled down at me through the dark circle cut in the thatch.

Virgil's words came back to me ... *with swift-rising flood the stormful season of Orion's star drove us onto viewless shoals, and angry gales dispersed us ...*

In my haste to get loose, I'd just demolished my sole means of escape. Why hadn't I realized before I'd cut the rope into pieces that, if more carefully unwound, it could have served as a hoist onto the roof above? Like most *Germani* houses, the sunken hut stood about four feet below the surrounding ground. It would have been an easy leap to freedom.

I was tying the rope back together when I heard women's voices, soft footsteps, and the rattle of the padlock. Within seconds, I'd scuttled with the rope bits back into the blackest corner.

The door swung open. A girl with only buds for breasts peered in by the light of a lamp extended by a second female only half visible on the upper steps behind her. The child inched forward in the dim light. She found me kneeling there in the shadowy crud with my hands clasped behind my back.

With trembling fingers, she fed me by spoon from a hand-hewn clay bowl. I downed another tasteless mush of meat scraps, broth, and lentils with no hint of wine, *garum*, or spice to help it down. I swallowed the mess, pretending helplessness but feeling genuine gratitude. As soon as I'd drained the bowl, she hurried back toward the doorway for the protection of her taller, shadowy companion.

The other woman descended the last few steps and regarded me from the obscurity of her dark hood.

'Why did you follow me, Roman?'

'To prevent you falling into Barbatio's clutches. He would have mistreated and exploited you. Why did you lure me here? To make me your hostage? To trade me for Hermund?' I couldn't help adding, 'Or to listen to your love song?'

'I warned you from the beginning, *when you find I'm the wife of an important man, I'll put in a word for you.*' Her voice hardened. 'You laughed at me that evening in the *taberna*. I meant to help you.'

'Help? You didn't say anything today. I know how they treat Roman captives inland.'

'I know even better than you. You lied to Serapio. Tribune Hariobaudes didn't send you.'

'How would you know?'

'Hariobaudes has no messages for Mederichus or his son.'

'You seem so sure. The tribune recognized you in Julian's camp, didn't he? That's why you fled.'

'Yes. He threatened to hand me back to Serapio for punishment as a runaway. I had no choice but to race here first to offer my own excuses.'

I glanced at the youngster quaking in the doorway.

'Don't worry about her, Roman. She doesn't speak Latin. Serapio sent her to protect my honor.'

'Isn't it late for him to worry about us spending time together?'

Her voice sank lower and colder. 'He has no idea you traveled with me.'

'Then why did he beat you?'

She pulled the hood forward over her brow. She was too proud to confirm what I'd heard. Her acceptance of that vain young man on any terms disgusted me.

'Isn't it time you explained your other lies, Gunda?'

'What do you mean?'

'Did you really live with a bishop?' I asked, trying to detain her one more minute. Though every second risked discovery of our acquaintance, I wanted—I needed—to goad her, pin her down, and shame her with her deceit.

'Did you really overhear General Marcellus say anything about the siege at Senonae? Or was that also a lie? Why did those men rough you up in the forest? Because of your father's loyalty to Roma—or did you say that to keep me on your side? At the Castra, we're taught that war is mere sport to your tribes. Romans don't have to conquer the Alemanni, just set them at each other's throats. Maybe those two men were your husband's rivals, abusing you to score one on him?'

Gunda took one step toward me, then checked her rising temper.

I badgered her: 'Is Hermund your brother? Or is that another lie? Is Gundomadus even your father? Or should I ask your mother? Maybe you never had a father to claim you!'

Gunda clutched her hood while the nervous girl waited in the doorway and turned that lumpy bowl around and around. She might have heard tales about the dangers of Roman men, just as Roman children heard fantastic warnings about the gigantic 'Gigas' and his bloodthirsty barbarians. Had she known the hands behind my back were unbound, she might have fainted in terror.

For a minute I considered pushing past them and that padlock dangling off the clumsy hinge to bolt for my life. But the girl would scream. Serapio's men carried heavy arms, including my own confiscated *spatha* and *pugio*, as well as the barbed *angons* and *franciscae* acquired from the Franks. Their skills might not be as honed as those of their northern cousins, but they weren't carrying deadly axes and barbed spears just to set off their jewelry.

'I'll never see you again,' I said, suppressing my outburst to a whisper, 'but if I offended you by not treating you as nobly as you desired, I certainly treated you better than that brute in the next hut. And the Castra has treated Hermund better than what lies in store for me to the east.'

From that moment in Apodemius' study, when the *Magister* had guessed she was Gundomadus' daughter, she'd responded with candor and a grateful air of recovered dignity. Was it all a pose? Was any of her story true? Or was she nothing more than a lowly assassin sent to kill Constantius?

'You ask too many questions,' she said. 'We're going to leave you now. But first, hand over that knife you have hidden in your boot cuff. You loved fingering my blade, so now I'll play with yours.'

That was why she'd come. She could hardly have explained to her husband why she knew me well enough to have seen my hidden blade. The girl and her bowl were mere excuses to collect my last weapon so she could sleep soundly tonight by Serapio's side.

'Get it for yourself,' I said, keeping my hands clasped behind my waist.

She knelt on the dirt. Beneath her fine otter cloak, she was wearing that old indigo skirt from the day we met. She started to unlace my boot to loosen the cuff.

'Why did he strike you?'

'To show his men I was back under his control.'

'For the gods' sake, you could do better than him!'

'My father chose him, not I. Our union strengthens the alliance along the river.'

'Did your sacrifice pay off?'

—THE DEADLY CAESAR—

'The only territory between our *pagi* and Serapio's is that of Chnodomarius. With my husband to the north and my father and uncle to the south, we have the giant encircled. He is bound to behave himself with Roma.'

She'd pulled off the boot and fished around inside but found nothing. She froze for a moment and then replaced the boot and laced it back up. She checked the other boot cuff. She kept herself hunched over my knees, blocking the view of all this from the girl, still waiting and watching.

Gunda realized my knife was missing. She said nothing and avoided my narrowed gaze.

'You could do better, Gunda. You were toying with me, letting me think you were unmarried. But you could still declare yourself divorced from this barbarian pact and legally marry an honorable Roman—one with a future and a fortune.'

She leaned back on her haunches and gave me a sour expression. She suspected I had the knife somewhere. She might even have guessed my hands were free.

'And I suppose you know a Roman who would take me?'

'Yes, a man with a promising career, a respectable social position, and a reasonable fortune.'

'A Roman citizen?'

'Not a citizen. A freedman who would take you—tonight.'

Gunda stared at me from under the shadowy hood. The lamp flame flickered. The girl by the door whimpered and shivered. The night wasn't chilly, but the wind carried the wet breeze of the river flowing northward.

I ignored the danger of Serapio's suspicious men, so close at hand, and plowed on. I fought to keep desperation from queering my pitch. At least she was still listening.

'Come with me, Gunda. It wouldn't be the first time you ran away from him. I figured out that much sitting here on dried turds and bones. You did take sanctuary in a clergyman's household, didn't you?'

'I told you.'

'But not because your parents sent you to prepare for marriage. You were already married. And not to learn Latin. You already spoke good Latin. I realized that the minute I heard Serapio's Latin today. Your parents and his—all you noble families—keep Roman captives as tutors. Your noble families learn Latin to emulate the Franks, supply the army with officers like Hariobaudes, and win better treaties with us. A Roman must have raised you. Who else would have taught you to play the lyre?'

'I didn't lie about the bishop.'

'You might have lied about many things to me, even to Apodemius, but someone worked out the Christians' prayer in your language. Someone taught it to you.'

'Why not this captive tutor you imagine?' she said, practically taunting me.

'Because that's not something your father would have permitted. You Alemanni don't have any interest in the Arian cult. Only a Roman cleric would waste his time on it.'

'So you believe me.'

'I believe you fled to a bishop but not to acquire *Romanitas*. A Christian refuge was the one place Serapio wouldn't think to hunt for his wayward wife. You don't love that man, do you?'

'What business is it of yours?'

'I don't know why I made an offer to you just now. You're a complete liar—not worthy enough to wash the underlinen of that honest girl standing there. Is that why your beloved welcomes you home with a beating?'

'Shut up!' she burst out and gave me a wallop that twisted my head sideways. My dim vision of her disappeared for a dizzy instant. When my wits cleared, she'd pushed the girl into the night and slammed the door shut behind them. The padlock rattled as their footsteps receded.

I laid my head back against the rough wall and released a deep sigh of relief. My assault on her Germanic sense of honor had paid off.

First, she'd left the knife in my possession.

Second, was it possible she hadn't snapped the padlock shut on purpose?

※※※

—THE DEADLY CAESAR—

I was twenty minutes down a dilapidated Roman road that cut through Serapio's meeting point and navigating my weary steps for the Rhenus to the west by the setting moon. The open road left me more vulnerable to recapture than any obscure route, but in this blackness it was the fastest hope of escape. And on the disintegrating paving, I was bound to hear anyone coming after me in the short summer night.

Somewhere and sometime along that bank, preferably before the exposure of dawn, I would stumble into Barbatio's vast encampment. I kept my eyes trained for smoke whirling into the charcoal night. My ears strained for the music of a sleeping army—the braying of a mule, the odd flute, or the shout of a sentry changing shifts.

Only wisps of innocent cloud brushed the moon. I kept stumbling over ancient ruts in the paving stones underfoot. The overgrown Roman markers showed this was an abandoned stretch of the *Cursus Clabularis* built for oxcart traffic between the river and our old inland garrisons. No Roman engineers had done repairs here for at least a century. I risked spraining an ankle on these lethal potholes. There was no other track or path through the dense brush hedging me in on both sides.

My thoughts were in a jumble. A hooting owl mocked my utter failure to make any sense of this mission's contradictory tasks.

It had been easy to see that Julian discomfited envious military rivals who wished the young upstart ill. So much for Constantius' 'unofficial' commission. As to my 'cover' story, I'd told Julian I had come equipped to spy on the Alemanni, only to discover my trusty Alemanna mediator was nothing of the kind. I'd learnt nothing about these barbarians except the depths of their deceit.

According to Apodemius, I should help Julian, no matter what his cousin emperor or his military 'superiors' had in store for the young caesar. But now I'd seen Julian's policy up close. How I could endorse his eagerness to crush ragged brigands as if they were disciplined armies or to launch professional war on shoeless peasants and petty warlords?

Something rustled in the thicket on my left. Sudden panic eclipsed my melancholy. After many miles, my wrists were still bleeding and my legs were weakening. I made tempting prey for any starving predator with a good nose. I braced myself for the attack of a wolf or mountain cat but only a wild piglet dashed across the road on its sticklike legs in front of me.

I kept on half-trotting, half-trudging, wondering how I could have imagined this mission would ever succeed, much less earn me promotion to *centenarius*.

I'd been on the road for some two hours by the moon when I detected the clatter of horse hooves on old rubble. Ahead or behind me? Army scouts out for predawn surveillance? Or Serapio's *comitatus* coming to seize me just a few miles short of Roman protection?

I tried to run, but my boots felt weighted with lead. More than one horse was coming up from behind. I knelt in the old roadside trench and flailed at the dense brush until my hands managed enough space to thrust in my torso like that frightened baby pig.

I was too slow to squeeze myself entirely out of sight. I waited for the whoosh of a barbed *angon* to pierce my shoulder blades.

The horses' hooves stopped a few feet away from where I pushed at the thicket.

'Get up,' Gunda said.

I reached for my boot cuff and pulled out the knife.

'I don't want to harm you, Gunda, but you'll have to find some other way to please your man.'

'You Romans think you're so cultivated. Yet you can't tell the difference between a love song and a lament?'

She fell silent in the saddle. I waited for her to match me knife for knife, and though I knew I'd win, it was not combat I relished. I did not want to be another man who hurt her.

She pulled herself up with a deep breath and threw back her hood so that I could see by the blue-white moonlight what Serapio had done to her face with his fist. Never had I seen a woman so proud and so humbled in the same instant.

'You made an offer to me back there. Then you took it back.'

'I made an offer.'

She exhaled with an audible convulsion of relief and, for an instant, hung her head in relief over the pommels of her saddle. Then she sat up straight and nodded.

'Take this horse.' She tossed me the reins of the second animal tethered to her saddle.

We galloped forward, saddle-to-saddle, flank-to-flank, with the rising August sun warming our backs. As the sky lightened from pinkish-gray to orange, I saw the vivid bruises on her face and dried blood on her swollen lip. Serapio's wife had good reason to lament.

My spirits rose. Her arrogant, resentful tone hadn't improved one whit, I had to admit, but at least Gunda now trusted me with a sliver of the truth.

Chapter 15, Disaster on the Bridge

—Barbatio's Encampment Opposite Saliso—

We rounded a crest and gazed over the languorous waters of the twisting Rhenus. The general's tent city spread out before us.

Less than a mile away, some twenty-five thousand soldiers trained and toiled within staked palisades in a neat rectangle stretching for many miles along the right bank. If my dog-eared *agentes*' guide was correct, the dilapidated ruin on the heights across the river was the ancient Celtic lookout point of Saliso.

I had exhausted myself for days trying to keep Gunda from becoming Barbatio's pawn and now I had no choice but to surrender us both to his protection. Gunda closed her swollen eyes with relief, so I told her nothing of my private hesitation.

The morning breeze carried the sounds of horses, men, anvils, carts, and even outbursts of good-natured song. Cooking ovens, smelting fires, rubbish dumps—all poured smoke and smells into the brightening sky.

Like any Roman, I inhaled the stench of the Roman army with the joy of arriving home. For the regularity and rhythm of any such camp—from the Antonine Wall in Britannia to the wastes of African Mauretania spelled home to a man who'd served in the ranks—even a *volo* armed with no more than a sack, tin bowl, and blanket.

A modest tower was rising, level-by-level, stone-by-stone, to anchor the pontoons to the near bank. The bridge teams still worked by the light of night torches that lined the tracks leading from both ends of the sprawling camp to the bridge site.

A mule train loaded with buckets of mortar staged a stubborn, braying protest down the sloping banks to the water's edge. Fifty feet back from the soggy bank, army masons chipped more stones to anchor the bridge. Squinting by the dawn light, carpenters measured and trimmed broad planks as they were lifted out of the water and placed on tethered barges that collected deliveries from upriver.

Everywhere there were pulleys and cranes, timber barges and rafts, and two-man saws. The air hummed with the grating of metal teeth and grindstones.

A string of pontoon boats floated from our side of the river across the rippling water to the Roman side, little more in this light than a misty line silhouetted against a background of mud and trees. They bobbed and swayed as the current caught them. The boats in the center tugged both sides slightly downriver, as the river's deepest current urged the sluggish shallower waters to speed up.

A chain boom to protect the pontoon boats stretched into the water and then sank below sight mid-river. Two barges, their crewmen ready with hooks and nets to receive the timber arriving from Ennius' team, punted away from the shore.

In a few days, this scene would resemble the engineer's sketch up at the logging site. Then Mederichus and Serapio would be summoned to this bridgehead to receive their refugees. Or would they slink into the forest depths to stage a less peaceful response?

Thanks to my days with the Commander, I knew my way forwards, backwards, and sideways through any encampment, no matter how vast, that had been staked out by a Roman army surveyor. I handed over our barbarian nags to a stable boy and led Gunda straight for the Porta Praetoria at the eastern end. We washed in warm water steaming from army basins and ate a decent soldier's breakfast, thanks to the cooks. The stables, latrines, and quarters for the sulky camp followers were situated downwind but this time I determined Gunda would be sheltered upwind with me.

—THE DEADLY CAESAR—

She read my mind. 'You will not hide me away again, Roman.'

'I agree, but it's still a risk to present you a second time to Barbatio. He has no talent for political nuance inside our empire, much less beyond. He will not grasp the delicacy of your family position.'

Gunda's split lip broke into a painful smile. 'I am prepared to earn his respect. There are things I can tell him now—useful things. Your general must listen.'

'I have a better idea—or rather, a better listener.'

The imminent transfer of the refugees across his bridge promised a notable victory for Barbatio, especially if Constantius' entire *forceps* strategy came to a peaceful close without Julian over on the left bank stealing the general's limelight.

I doubted the general would want to spare time on a mere *agens* this morning. But just in case I was wrong, I would lay the ground with Tribune Cella right away to forestall Barbatio from trying to exert his baleful authority over Gunda and myself.

I'd been trained by the best experts in the Empire to read men at a glance and I'd noticed Cella's reaction to his general's rash commands down at the Castrum Rauracum. I was certain that if Cella ever found himself under oath in a proper Roman court, he would declare the order to withdraw the tribunes Bainobaudes and Valentinian from the *laeti's* getaway route a strategic error by Barbatio. I'd held that impression of the Scutari tribune's levelheadedness in reserve for just such a day as today.

Cella worked in a makeshift wooden barrack not far from Barbatio's own headquarters. Gunda and I interrupted him in the middle of a conference with two fellow Palatine officers bent over a table. There was no drawing of the bridge in front of them, but a hand-drawn sketch of the entire Middle Rhenus marked by symbols and initials for the various Alemanni kings positioned along the bank. I smiled to myself, thinking of a far finer specimen of planning, the expert map of Apodemius' down in Roma, with its Empire-wide forest of pins, flags, and tacks marking whole peoples, armies, espionage stations, courier stops, communications posts, and roadways of every classification and use.

Still Cella's crude guide seemed to be serving some purpose, for the tribune's irritation at our interruption was obvious.

'What are you doing here, *Biarchus*? You're supposed to be attached to the staff of the—'

'Acting *Magister Officiorum* Pentadius, reporting to the Praetorian Prefect Florentius. Yes, I know, Tribune. I'm here to appeal for your protection as we pass on our way back to the other side. We must report our findings on the Alemanni forces to the Caesar. He is expecting us.'

It seemed that when it came to the *Schola* of Bluff, I'd learned a lot from Gunda in a very short time. After all, I had left the Caesar clutching his blanket and waiting for me to return with Gunda to his tent over a day ago. The gods only knew what Julian had answered to my hurried message apologizing for Gunda's disappearance.

Cella kept one hand on his work and the other pointed at my bruised companion in her soiled cloak and dark blue skirt. She looked nothing like the bejeweled noblewoman who had passed through Augusta Raurica.

'This is the daughter of the *rex* Gundomadus, our ally?'

I had expected to speak for both of us. But Gunda stepped forward with a bold bracing of her shoulders.

'I am.'

She was inches taller than Cella. Despite the vicious bruises blooming purple and green across her face, she intended to impose her person on these Roman officers with as much dignity as she could muster.

'You can see this woman has suffered injuries and needs attention,' I said. 'I would not expect her to suffer questioning in her condition.'

Cella raised an eyebrow to his fellows leaning across the table.

'What do you know, officers? Would you have predicted that a *curiosus* would show gallantry to anyone, much less an Alemanna tribeswoman? If you've learned nothing to help us, then admit it, Numidianus. Don't excuse the failure of your mission on this woman's bleeding lip. Anyway, Julian has Hariobaudes to explain his people to us. We're building the bridge to send them all home. We need not bother this lady.'

—THE DEADLY CAESAR—

I took his insults without flinching. The truth could not be denied. I was a failure. I had learned nothing useful, only facts about Gunda I could hardly accept myself. If I had to skulk back to the safety of Florentius' mobile camp office with its humiliating paperwork, so be it.

'On the contrary, *Tribuni*,' Gunda said, 'Bother me all you like. This worthy *agens* delivers me straight from Serapio's council. I have been privy to his latest deliberations. As the daughter of your ally, I should keep nothing back from you on any excuse.'

She extracted a bothersome twig from the long braid barely containing her thick mane. 'Apart from some scrapes and bumps, I am in excellent health. What is it you need to know?'

This was a breakfast surprise Cella hadn't counted on. Neither had I. More important, it promised nuggets of information for which Barbatio couldn't claim credit at the next general staff meeting.

'Then look at this chart, *Matrona*, and if you can, explain the locations and relations among your chieftains.' He tossed a smirk at his subordinates and waited.

Gunda studied the crude lines and markings on Cella's sketch.

'This is Mederichus and Serapio's domain, not far from here, but all the way up to here,' she said. 'To the south sits Chnodomar, then my uncle Vadomar and finally, opposite your Castrum Rauracum, my own father's stronghold, here.'

She laid her finger on an unmarked space well behind the curve of the river's knee.

'I see you have marked already the locations of the *reges* Hortar and Suomar farther north. But they are not so closely allied with each other, much less with the Empire. I do not know the boundaries between Macrian, Ursicinus, and Hariobaud to the very far north, but from what I overheard, Macrian is the wiliest and most respected of all the northernmost chieftains. You would do well to bind your interests to his. He is no keener to accede ultimate leadership to Chnodomarius than my father is.'

The officers took in a collective breath.

'What are their warrior numbers? Can you tell us?' Cella asked.

'There are discussions, of course. And I am a careful listener. Each of the *pagi* in this vicinity, eleven to be exact, could send one thousand warriors to aid another under threat.'

Unsurprised, Cella nodded but Gunda checked him with a raised palm.

'But if you reckon on only eleven thousand men opposite you, Tribune, you forget we Alemanni have relations with war bands roaming toward us from the distant east. Through tribute and obligation, there are some one to two thousand other fighters who could be drawn in at our summons.'

'So that makes the maximum army of the Alemanni from twelve to thirteen thousand?' asked one of the subordinates with a shrug. 'Hardly matching what Julian and Severus command between them. With our own twenty-five thousand, that leaves us of an advantage of at least three Romans to every Alemannus.'

'Yes,' Gunda smiled, 'Our tribes would be foolish to confront the combined Western armies of Roma—unless—'

'Unless what?' Cella asked.

'Even if the great *reges* in the far north do not personally ride into battle against your men, they would be bound to contribute warriors eager to join in such a fight. That would add perhaps another two to three thousand? There are messengers moving northward down the Rhenus right now, all the way . . .' her finger traced the winding river up, up, up ' . . . to the cold waves of the great *Mare Germanicum*.'

Cella's braced stance did not falter, but his eyes flicked up at me. These numbers were larger than he'd estimated, but perhaps still not a lethal threat. We all knew the weaknesses of barbarian fighters. They preferred one-to-one combat on foot, even placing infantry amid their cavalry ranks, forcing everyone to dismount. For centuries they'd eschewed trained mobilization in units. Their leaders could exhort and encourage, but hardly expect to command in any fray mixing so many different tribes.

When we broke their first assault, they lost courage and took flight, while Roman soldiers regrouped and tightened their lines. The *Germani* from across the Rhenus just didn't have the well-honed, disciplined fighting tradition of their Roman-trained cousins—including those of Alemannic parentage.

— THE DEADLY CAESAR —

Again Gunda read our thoughts. 'And something else,' she told Cella. 'You Romans think our people cannot unite under one man, that it goes against our character—'

'You *Germani* are all so proud of your independent natures, *Matrona*.'

'That may change, *Tribune*.' Her voice turned as hard as Noric steel.

'You're saying that your proud leaders might agree to fight us as one?'

'I am sorry for my father's sake to report that I heard some seven names mentioned—all respected ring-givers, nobleman of great authority—willing to ride behind Chnodomarius.'

'Talk, just talk!' one of the deputies scoffed.

'The plan is centered *here*.' Gunda used that deft right index finger I'd admired dancing on the lyre strings to point to Argentoratum on the left riverbank. 'And they are gathering . . . now.'

'They're already banding, knowing we command superior forces?' Cella was taking Gunda more seriously than his colleagues did.

'They're more than talking of it. Supposing they joined battle with you on the fields outside Argentoratum? Your kind of military formation is no secret. If it came to a fight, they're prepared to position the braver part of their men, including their cavalry—'

'Such as it is!' scoffed a Scutarius.

'*Such as it is*, against your better troops, near the riverside, here. Also, they would strengthen their wing upland, opposite your left flank here with a reserve of warriors concealed . . . there.'

She laid her finger on a spot of rotund clumps indicating a thick swathe of trees away from the river.

'But what's to conceal them?' the Cella asked.

Gunda smiled. 'Your scouts should learn this terrain, Tribune. Your chart does not include a marshy, elevated watercourse here, due north above your road and overgrown with reeds. The enemy would be well hidden near this aqueduct. They'll be crouching there, lying in wait.'

Cella had heard more than enough. 'That's valuable information indeed. But let's hope this plan will never be put into action.'

'You can rely on my father to keep his pact with your emperor, providing you refrain from indulging in useless bloodshed. Let our settlers inside the border keep their land. Their fighters kept their word and fought Magnentius and Decentius for your empire. We resigned ourselves last year to Constantius' renewed campaign in Raetia. We signed a treaty with him then. We have a right to expect peace.'

Outside the barrack came the great hum and rumble of the Western Army—thousands of men busy at exercises, weapon repairs, construction, and all the other business of our imperial military machine.

'This is your last chance. Tell the Caesar to keep the Emperor's pact with us and we will keep faith with him,' Gunda said.

The officers looked at each other. A sliver of relief crossing their faces hinted at a debate among them that could not be admitted in front of a barbarian informer.

Was perhaps General Barbatio not so keen on cleansing the left bank of Alemanni as his fellow commander, the all-conquering Julian? Was the bridge to be the Dacian's proud monument to a peaceful border, rather than bloody conquest?

I had guessed it. These officers wanted peace as much as Gunda and her father. Hardheaded Romans preferred to recruit raw Alemanni boys into their ranks, not run them through with spears. And I knew Barbatio well. He was no imperial visionary, just an undereducated, slow-witted career man. He entertained no ambition to push Roman borders deeper into barbarian territory like Julius Caesar or Marcus Aurelius.

Barbatio's biggest ambition—as I knew—was to get his only son into the Castra training school at the prodding of that wife, Assyria, so uneducated she needed a scribe to write her hysterical love letters to her husband. Barbatio would never have ever thought to compare himself to Alexander the Great—although the infatuated Assyria might.

The conference drew to a close. Cella excused Gunda, but detained me.

'You've done the *schola* proud, Numidianus,' he said with admirable grace. 'She was very well-informed. Perhaps too well-informed?'

He left that question with me, almost as a command.

I caught up with Gunda. 'Come to my tent,' I said, pulling her out of the path of a wagon groaning under a load of iron struts and nails. With one hand around her upper arm, I led her down the length of the Via Praetoria to my quarters. My *contubernales* were absent, as I expected, with jobs to do. Thanks to Gunda, my day's toil seemed already done—but not quite.

Cella's doubt was clear. Was her briefing to be trusted?

'Was all of that true? Was any of it true?'

Her eyes narrowed. She shook off my hand.

'You will never trust me again, Roman?'

'Answer me this: did you overhear General Marcellus at any bishop's house, yes or no?'

'He was there, more than once.'

'Did he "shake with amusement" telling the bishop, "I'll leave for Senonae only when it's obviously too late"?'

'I made that up. I overheard you in the camp. I listened to them outside that court chamber. I guessed how to answer.'

'Then you libeled a senior Roman commander? You ended that man's career on a whim and risked the integrity of our *schola*?'

'Marcellus had pawed me more than once. He was arrogant and presumptuous. He was the type to leave your Caesar in the lurch. He deserved to be discredited.'

'Why risk ruining yourself just to ruin him?'

'To enter the court, of course.'

'To assassinate Constantius?'

'To *execute* him for betraying my father.'

'And get killed in the bargain?'

'It would consolidate my father's place in the hierarchy of our people.'

'Is Gundomadus under threat now? Or was that also a lie, back in the forest?'

I held both her shoulders and pulled her closer to me. She wrenched away from me, but I was tired of her twistings and turnings and held her fast.

'My father is in great danger. You Romans must pull back from this campaign or my father will be sacrificed by men as deadly as your Caesar Julian.'

'You would have gone to the torture chambers as a regicide for Gundomadus? Do you know what the Constantius' notary, Paulus Catena, does during his interrogations—even to women? It is Hades on earth.'

'I would go to anyone's underworld to prove I am worthy of my father—your Hades or our *Hel*—you choose.'

'Though he married you to an arrogant brute?'

I was holding her by the back of her head and whispering into her ear. I could smell her hair oil. A scent of the forest, pine resin, and field flowers, carried by her womanly warmth dizzied my senses, but I kept on. I had to get it all out of her—wash out all the lying with one angry question after another.

'My father's honor belongs to every one of us. He led our tribe into submission and you repay him with brutality. He takes the blame. The other *reges* and *reguli* are turning against him.'

'And your uncle? Vadomarius? Is he also a turncoat against the alliance?'

'My uncle is trapped between my father and Chnodomar. He sees Serapio is already arming for resistance. How long can he hold out without a gesture of peace from you Romans?'

'And that's why Serapio beat you? Because he loves war? He wants war now? And you challenged him in front of his *comitatus*?'

I was pressing myself against her now. My worn trousers, thin and dusty, could not disguise my desire.

'Yes. Serapio wants war, no less than your caesar.' Her hand descended to my thighs and found me, eager and insistent.

My hopes leaped. 'You tried to persuade Serapio with your lyre?'

'I tried. I failed.'

'He refused your song?' I muttered, pressing my mouth against her temple, kissing her hairline, and sinking my nostrils into the tender skin of her neck.

When she nodded, I felt her thick braid tug underneath my grasp.

'He refused your love?'

—THE DEADLY CAESAR—

I didn't wait for that answer. I pressed my mouth against hers, bruised and bleeding as it was. I was hungry for this, for a woman who knew how to couple. Valentinian had watched these hips and known—she was no innocent maiden. I'd known Kahina in her virgin wide-eyed resignation and then the *agens* Roxana hardened by professional seductiveness. I'd relieved my long loneliness with countless clumsy bargirls and smelly camp whores, who accepted any Roman man with indifference and impatience. Humor was an occasional bonus.

There could be no more answering or explaining with Gunda today, only peacemaking. I could not wait to be inside her. I carried her to one of the soldier's camp beds. She lifted her indigo skirt above her pale knees. There was nothing more but an Alemanna's plain underlinen, soaked through with her moisture, between us.

As the army churned all around the taut walls of that tent, Gunda met me, brow to brow, breast to breast, thigh to thigh, and sigh for sigh—personal, passionate, and uncompromisingly. There were no more questions or answers now, no more lies, and no more excuses—only small exclamations escaping her open mouth.

She was panting. I heard myself groaning and slowed myself to a musical rhythm all her own. She made love the way she sang, with infinite variation, surprise, and devotion to my lust. There would be many ways of hearing her sing with her entire body.

⚜⚜⚜

Gunda bolted upright and shook me out of my satiated nap.

'What is that sound, Roman? What does that mean? An attack?'

The light seeping underneath our tent wall slanted across the packed ground. It was not yet evening, but dozens of horns sounded an alarm, calling the troops to defensive positions.

'Wait here.'

I grabbed what equipment I could and followed a stream of curious men strapping on belts and helmets, pulling on leggings and boots, ripping off work aprons and pulling on tunics. The horns kept blowing. Everyone was shouting for the next set of orders, but no signal for battle came.

With hundreds of other men, I pushed behind other off-duty officers down the camp alley and toward the riverside where the attack had sounded.

I joined a throng of thousands lining the soggy waterfront. I strained to see around or over the cranes, vats, and sawhorses of the bridge construction. The tower, half-built, stood overhead.

There rose a cacophony, 'The boats! The boats!' Through the maelstrom of shouts and horns, there was the sound of heavy crunching, as if gods were sparring with giant trees.

I shoved my way right to the edge of the water and stared. Barbatio's pontoon bridge was nothing more now than a mass of jutting timbers, roiling logs, crashing timber, and dozens of ropes slithering through the water like white snakes released by unseen hands.

The pontoon boats, moored to both banks, straggled downriver with the current in two separated files. In their place, a logjam of timber pushed past us, with hundreds more planks and trunks unhindered by any boom chain or rope tumbling through the current past the unfinished tower.

A unit of men linked by belts, ropes, and hands slid into the water to salvage whatever boats within reach had survived whole. They stood with backs exposed just as an unexpected flotilla of more loose timber came rounding the bend and heading straight for their spines.

The man farthest out from the shore screamed for help—he'd lost hold of the next man and, trapped in the sea of lumber, was clinging to a single log in the dozens rushing past the camp. He was beyond rescue and still yelling until the river of wood crushed him and then flushed him out of sight.

'Get out! Get out!' The other soldiers scrambled to pull their fellows back up the bank before they were crippled or carried off by this fresh onslaught of lethal logs.

'Get moving!'

'Lend a hand!'

'Get hooks!'

'We need poles! Where're the rafts? More rafts!'

—THE DEADLY CAESAR—

Thousands of men rallied to save what they could of the boats that hadn't been shattered or pierced by the inexorable press of raw trunks.

'What happened?' I shouted to one engineer.

'Accident upriver. They were almost finished! Got too impatient! They lost control of the stock piled up on the bank.'

Was it an accident?

Julian would have said it was barbarian sabotage, but I was ready to believe it was sheer bad luck. I'd seen the short staff slaving upriver in a rush to supply the site. I'd seen half a dozen pyramids of freshly dressed planks tottering to precarious heights on the oxcarts and barges. I'd seen docile *pagani* working for the engineer Ennius for pay—not politics.

Accident or not, it put paid to the bridge and anyone who expected a peaceful exodus of Alemanni settlers. It looked as disastrous as any accident I'd ever seen in a Roman camp, as if one of angry Germanic gods had unleashed an entire forest downriver in indignation at our Roman engineering. For at least half a mile, wood was rolling, bouncing, and sliding the entire width and span of the Rhenus.

And if it was not an act of the gods but a declaration of war by the Alemanni, then my 'too well-informed' Gunda sitting in the middle of a camp filled with angry, frustrated Romans was in grave danger.

Chapter 16, Burning Boats

—BARBATIO'S ENCAMPMENT—

Barbatio insisted his troops stay on the alert for a possible attack. The army's harsh instruments joined each other in chorus, legion-by-legion, sending gusts of noise rolling down the riverbank. The tumult ran through each man's body, merging him into a single body ready to obey without question, thought, or hesitation. Jumping to these horns made us Romans, whether we spoke Latin, Frankish, or Alemannic. It made us stronger than any barbarians we faced.

Thousand of men tossed off their work aprons and grabbed their weapons as they followed the shouts flying from officer to officer and infantryman to fellow fighter. Thousands of tents emptied out. Each alley streamed with warriors racing to positions around the palisade.

It rushed back to me from the past—the stampede of boots, hundreds of fires stomped into ashes, cooking pots overturned, the flash of metal and slap of leather, the thudding of hooves. But I had no weapons, no station to report to, no line to join, no armor to don, and no shield to hoist. *Immunes*—technical officers with no fighting role—remained behind. *Agentes* were excluded from battle.

But I was still a member of the *praefectus'* staff. I raced to the headquarters to learn every move Barbatio intended. I had to know if Gunda was in danger. I trotted full pelt past that bloated sea of floating wood.

Not all pontoon crafts were sunk outright. The majority had slid over to our bank. The insistent pressure of the heavy logs had tugged a few free of their ropes and these were gliding downstream toward the northern horizon. Some were beached on the distant islands where Alemanni settlers sheltered from the confusion.

The most damaged boats dragged their tackle and ropes through the reeds clogging the banks.

I caught up with Cella's officers entering a barrack already filled with dozens of other officers.

'Where're they coming from?' Barbatio bristled with full armor as if anxious for a fight.

'No engagement so far,' Cella said.

'They destroyed the bridge. They're coming for us next,' said a nervous *domesticus*.

Doubt clouded Cella's eyes. 'The river level is too sluggish to count on such destruction. If this was sabotage, they were lucky the logs gained any speed at all. It was the weight and number of trees that overwhelmed the booms and crushed the boat line—not the speed.'

'They've stacked felled trees across the roads to slow us down before this,' another tribune muttered. 'Why wouldn't they sabotage the bridge next?'

Barbatio dispatched scouts to locate the barbarian attackers' whereabouts—north, south or east of the camp? Until they were sighted, there seemed nothing else to do but wait for the enemy to make his move.

We stood there for many minutes in silence waiting for a fresh alert or signal. The rush of fear and readiness that had surged through every man's breast gave way to a dispirited frustration. Barbatio slumped down in his camp chair and polished off a jug of watered wine.

The whole camp fell into a pregnant hush—alert and sweating. Where would the Alemanni appear? When? Under which chieftain's banner?

After an hour of this, Barbatio barked at his staff. 'How long to finish a bridge without the boats?'

'Weeks at most,' I said from the back of the assembled officers.

'What in Hades are you doing here, Numidianus? I want to hear that from an engineer.'

—THE DEADLY CAESAR—

'I talked to the engineer Ennius preparing your timber supply upriver. Julius Caesar had forty thousand men when he put up a timber bridge across the Rhenus in ten days. Ennius could do it again.'

Barbatio didn't trust me. A sour curve to his thick lip hinted that my encouragement was unwelcome. We all shifted our boots in silence until a quaking team of *immunes* appeared, dripping wet up to their muddy belts from commanding the salvage operation.

Distant cries of men still shifting the logs on the river broke the fearful silence. They were trying to rescue what they could, despite the constant fear of a fresh assault.

The sun sent slanting rays through a crude window past our boots. Soon the late summer's afternoon glare would be roasting those men standing outside in full battle gear. A pregnant breath held the assembled army as one man. Exasperated with inaction, Barbatio marched outside with his immediate subordinates. It was almost autumn, the end of any campaign season. A triumphant summer for Barbatio didn't require bloodshed, especially when good Alemanni recruits, handled right, could replace the 'ghost' soldiers in his fraudulent payrolls.

On the Via Praetoria, I waited with a few adjutants listening to the hush of half the Western Army, *ballistae* loaded and *spathae* poised, waiting for a fight.

No one attacked.

Apollo's flaming orange sank below the western hills sending soft golden light across the splintered wood still rolling through the water. The returning scouts reported to Barbatio's tight group. Even from fifty feet away, I read their gestures. There were no barbarians lying in wait.

A glowering Barbatio gave no command to relax. The troops would stay in position throughout the short night.

'And tomorrow, General?' Cella asked.

Cella wasn't like Barbatio. He played *latrunculi* many moves ahead. He was always mediating, anticipating, and using an intelligence that could see beyond the next hour.

Barbatio drew up his beefy shoulders. 'We signal retreat, Tribune. We return to Mediolanum. This campaign is at an end.

Burn what's left of the boats and any supplies we can't transport by road. The Alemanni can't use what we destroy.'

As the officers, bewildered and grim-faced filed away, we heard shouts from the riverbank. One small craft carrying five officers struggled through the floating wood from the far bank. All eyes watched them with discomfort. They were sitting targets for any hidden barbarian marksman with a good axe-throwing arm.

Barbatio's infantrymen raced out and pulled them to shore.

Their leader was none other than Tribune Bainobaudes. His companions brandished the standard of the Cornuti under Julian's command.

Bainobaudes strode up the bank just as army slaves were lighting the torches to mark out the paths in the dusk. With an exultant confidence, he greeted the general who'd cashiered him. Barbatio made no effort to disguise the displeasure crossing his unshaven face made scruffy by the uncertainty and heat of the long day.

'I come from Caesar Julian's camp, General. He asks what you intend to do about the bridge.'

General Severus' scouts near Brotomagus had reported the disaster.

Barbatio started to vent a rude reply, but checked himself in time. He'd risen this far by playing things safe, greasing the right palms, and staying within the bounds of any commission from Constantius. Instead of making a fresh blunder, he rubbed a thick palm over his black stubble.

'I cannot recognize a man I dismissed from service.'

Bainobaudes said, 'I answer to a Constantine now. I ask my questions in the Constantinian name.'

'How dare you?'

'Presuming that the bridge project is a lost cause,' Bainobaudes sighed with feigned and insulting regret, 'the Caesar requests any boats you have salvaged for his use as well as the supplies you were meant to deliver some weeks ago.'

'Boats? With what intention?'

'I know no more than that but I see your men preparing to break camp. If you retreat, you leave the Caesar and his troops open to attack. Our army needs food. The harvest on the other side of the river is poor and belongs to the farmers we seek to appease and transfer across the river. Surely you don't begrudge your fellow commander a few boats and wagons of grain?'

Barbatio grunted. 'Can't you see what's happened to the boats?'

'Any man can count. You had dozens. Give us seven of those left.'

Barbatio turned his massive body to face us all and roared at the Franco-Roman. 'You give the *Magister Peditum* orders?'

Cella placed a hand on Barbatio's shoulder, but the raging Dacian shook him off.

'That brat, that stinking, pontificating, wisp-bearded, round-shouldered runt thinks that because he can debate and philosophize in Athens' lazy sun, that he's got the makings of the great Constantine?'

Barbatio turned to his listening staff officers. 'Do you hear the audacity? Do you recognize the madness that infects this family's more withered branches? Our emperor was right to weed out the weak and diseased stalks.'

Cella turned away, eyes dropped with embarrassment.

Barbatio took no notice. 'Don't forget, Bainobaudes, I was Master of the Guards in Antiochia. I've seen this before—the posturing, the overruling, the scheming, and the insubordination to men of experience and seniority. This *boy* Julian is no better than his whining, sniveling, crazy half-brother.'

'Seven boats, I ask with the gratitude of Flavius Claudius Julianus,' Bainobaudes said.

I admired his calm invocation of his commander's pedigree, but Bainobaudes was hardly the best envoy Julian could have chosen. Knowing Barbatio had cashiered the tribune so recently, insult was implied.

And insult had been taken.

Barbatio growled to Cella. 'Burn the boats. And keep only enough supplies for two weeks' march south.' He grimaced with cruel satisfaction at Bainobaudes. 'You can tell the Caesar that his toy campaign is over.'

'Then we will move quickly to save the boat on which we crossed,' Bainobaudes answered. 'You already tried to pin the blame for the failure to seize the *laeti* brigands on Tribune

Valentinian and me. There will be a reckoning, sooner or later, General Barbatio, and I will be the first to offer myself as a witness. You refuse us a mere seven boats.'

'You think I can't explain myself to our sovereign? I will do so within the month by letter and then in court, if necessary. Let no man speak against my judgment that our work here is done. The Alemanni are cowed. They're already shifting their family and goods to the islands. Felling trees to slow our march, yelling insults at our troops across the river—these are the actions of a weak and divided people.'

Cella glanced at me. He remembered Gunda's briefing about the gathering of the *reges* and *reguli* numbers, their strategies and their traps.

But Barbatio had recovered his composure. He had set his face toward Mediolanum and resolution had calmed him.

'You refuse our Caesar seven boats, General?' Bainobaudes had to be sure.

'I do.'

'And the food supplies?'

Barbatio said nothing more and disappeared for his private quarters. The general's staff fell away, silent and troubled. I flew down the Via Praetoria after the Cornuti leader heading for the Porta Decumana. I grabbed Bainobaudes' arm.

'What's going on across the river?'

'I saw you back there, Numidianus. The Western Army is splitting in two. Decide which side you serve.'

'Barbatio is a stupid thug. He regrets half his decisions after an hour's reflection. I've seen it time and again.'

'Then reflect, yourself, Numidianus. Barbatio doesn't have the guts to expose the Caesar to danger from the Alemanni unless he had instructions from above.'

'Will the Caesar go into winter retreat?'

'I don't know. Are you coming with me?'

'I need to fetch the Alemanna.'

'We need her more than ever,' the Cornuti tribune said. The glint in his eyes chilled my blood. 'I give you a few minutes, no more,' he said. 'It'll be too hard to get through that mess on the river after dark.'

—THE DEADLY CAESAR—

The thousands of empty tents we passed spoke of *contubernales* standing at attention along all four palisades—disciplined and tired but still at their posts. The crack and roar of fire burst up from the river. Barbatio's conflagration had started. Within minutes, flames lit up the fading sky and danced across streaks of engineers' oil pooling on the water's surface.

I was only a few feet from reaching the flap of my own tent when my ears picked up an incongruous sound. Through the summer heat and confusion, Gunda sat alone, waiting for me. She was singing. To comfort herself? To celebrate our love? To ward off the churlish or uncouth interruptions she feared from strange soldiers?

'Did you hear my song?' She rose to her feet, her face flushed with relief at my return.

'Gunda, pack your things. We're leaving.'

'I composed a new song, different from the old one. But look,' she held the lyre up. 'I snapped a string. Yet the song came to me. It will sound much better with a new—'

'Gunda, did you hear me?'

'Yes, we must leave. I'm happy to leave.' She reached to embrace me. 'Because of you.'

'Hurry, please.' I grabbed her cloak and sack of belongings. 'Bainobaudes is waiting for us with the last boat headed over to the left bank.'

'The left bank? Why *there*?' She frowned. 'Surely we're going south. We go now to my father.' She insisted, 'It was in my song. Our life together.'

'We're returning to the Caesar's camp.'

She took a step back. 'Why? Our mission is finished, Roman. I gave them all I could. My father will welcome you as his imperial adviser. You'll be honored and revered as his right hand counselor.'

'Gunda, I can't abandon the *agentes* in the middle of a mission to serve Gundomadus. I don't know him.'

'But he will listen to me—'

'Pack your things.'

I began to stuff everything into her traveling bag. I was bent over on one knee, praying Bainobaudes was still waiting, when Gunda's foot shot out, kicking me hard on the shoulder.

'Leave my things alone! You will come south. We will see my father and then go to Roma to recover Hermund from your headquarters. I have kept my side of our bargain. I told that tribune everything I know about the strategy at Argentoratum. Are you no better than your caesar across the river? Reneging on every honorable deal we make?'

'Stop it, Gunda. Stop!' I drew the strings of her bag closed tight, picked up her lyre, and dragged her out of the tent, retracing my steps along the route to the riverbank. 'I have no future like that. I must complete this mission. I'll be able to do more with a promotion in Roma than as some half-baked adviser to a barbarian chieftain.'

'What is in Roma?' she wailed, digging her heels into the dirt.

'Do you think I could leave Leo or walk away from my responsibilities to the Manlius estates or Kahina?'

'*Who is Kahina? Who is Leo?*' she screamed. She jerked herself free of my grasp. Behind her pale hair, the flames of Barbatio's burning boats shot into the sky. Her eyes gleamed—not with the mischievous twinkle of love—but with the burning fire of pain and confusion.

'My family, my *schola*, my whole life belongs to Roma. Keep calling me "Roman" because that is all I am.'

'Those are people in your past,' she cried. 'You will be a prince among the Alemanni.'

'I'm a Manlius. You can't understand now but you will. Let me finish this mission, get the promotion—'

'You have enough money.'

'I don't serve for money. I serve for honor. Returning to complete my posting is honorable. If you're going to live among us, you must learn how a Manlius values the privilege of serving the Empire. If my Gallic grandmother could learn, so will you. Protecting the Empire is not a sport with us, not some game of skirmishing or frivolous test of manhood.'

'I won't come with you.' She planted her boots apart in the pounded dust.

—THE DEADLY CAESAR—

This was impossible. There was no time to explain. I could not lose her like this.

'Then where will you go 'til I come for you? You can't stay here. You can't go back to Serapio.'

'I'll wait for you on those islands in the river—between your empire and my people. Now do your duty and then hurry back for me.'

I kissed her hard and held her, as the roar of the burning boats drowned her murmurs of love. Something wooden at the top of the half-finished bridgehead tower caught a spark and the tower exploded, shooting iron filings in all directions. Gunda dashed out of my arms.

I raced down to the river and leapt into Bainobaudes' wavering craft. Horses would be waiting for us on the opposite bank to speed us through contested territory riddled with roadblocks and angry *Germani*.

₽₽₽

As we approached Julian's camp we passed teams of infantrymen stripped to the waist, loading grain and reaping tools into army wagons. The army was hungry and they were foraging for whatever was left. The fields on both sides of the road lay stripped clean. Brown and broken stalks jutted like thousands of broken teeth into the late summer sky.

The Alemanni settlers had fled the area, but how far had they gone? Mounting their horses with relief were two thirsty squadrons of light cavalry who'd stood guard all day to protect their fellows assigned to harvesting. Teams of men had spread out in all directions from Tres Tabernae to stock Julian's garrison for the coming winter. Hunger, not enmity, had driven the Roman troops to break their peace with the immigrants. The power of the *spatha*, not negotiation, would satisfy their starvation.

We six sped on to Julian's camp. Barbatio's mobile city of twenty-five thousand robust, well-equipped men made the fifteen thousand left to Severus and Julian look underfed and vulnerable. The old general and the young caesar had conjoined their troops below the fortress hill into two distinct camps—staked within palisades along classic grids—but for all the effort to maintain standards, they looked far less impressive than Barbatio's massive presence.

The cooking pots we rode past contained no more than broth, and the small bones of trapped birds or forest animals. Decent bread looked scant. These forces faced an impossible winter's retreat up here without the grain that had been entrusted to Barbatio's baggage train. I shuddered to think what would happen when they heard the grain would never come.

When we turned up at the kitchen tent for sustenance, Bainobaudes accepted no larger portion than any given to his Cornuti infantrymen and I took the same.

Happily, I could not find the Praefectus Florentius before Bainobaudes and I received confirmation that Julian would receive us at first light. The only 'civilian' I saw in the camp was the solitary Dr Oribasius. Garbed in his Alexandrian robes, the Greek seemed to float past on some other plane, untouched by the troops' misery. I'd forgotten he was even part of the Caesar's 'court.' Given Constantius' dislike of Julian having any personal friends, this might be a good reason for discretion.

Oribasius took no part, then, in military deliberations. Nor did he seem attached in any way to Florentius and his struggle to keep the civil administration of Gallia in order. The Greek buried himself in the shadows of Julian's life, burrowing away at his collection of Galen's teachings, Bainobaudes told me. He occupied that place where Julian hid his secret leanings and deepest thoughts about family, religion, and destiny.

With such power, Oribasius might be one of the more dangerous men in the Empire.

Julian's routine was nap, study, and prayer through the night. He would be deliberating his next move on practically no sleep. I needed sleep but dozed fitfully, haunted by Gunda's song—a song I'd cut short.

The dawn broke cooler than in previous mornings. The northern summer was slipping away. I surveyed the long stretch of swaying standards—Julian's three guard units, the targeteers Scutarii, the Armaturae, and the Gentiles—Goths, Scythians, and Franks—each a heavy infantry unit some six hundred strong.

—THE DEADLY CAESAR—

Beyond those units were his light horse cavalry, five hundred Dalmatae javelin experts and heavy-armored *cataphractarii* mingling with the heaviest of all, the formidable 'oven men.' The *clibinarii* were riders encased in suffocating armor from head to foot mounted on horses draped with blankets and masks of mail—a fighting style Constantius copied from the Sassanids riding against his Eastern army.

The camp held other legions—the Petulantes five hundred strong teamed up with the Celtae of the same number, the Primani, Ioviani and the Herculiani—each of those about one thousand men. The Caesar's *auxilia palatina*—the Regii, Bracchiati, Batavii, Heruli, and Bainobaudes' Cornuti, gave him another five hundred each.

An archer from the Sagitarii—massed archers trained to cover the infantry from behind—gave me a brisk salutation as I went to wash myself down. My heart rose several notches at the sight of these pennants and flags of all these disciplined, hardened men. These thousands were going hungry and unpaid, yet they rose as one each morning with stout spirits and unfaltering routine.

The first hint of autumn—a cool draft carrying a warning of winter—hit my naked chest as I lifted off my tunic. We were some eight weeks away from the first snows, if my memory of Treverorum was any guide. My North African half longed for my early childhood's desert vista—the dry, balmy air of Numidia, the abundance of the colonial grain fields, and the reassuring trickling and turning of irrigation wheels.

I splashed myself out of my reverie, washed, and shaved with a borrowed razor outside the tent. Perhaps there had been a moment, after the civil war, when I could have gone back to Numidia with Kahina and Leo. We could have turned our backs on Roma and started over again, flush with Manlius income, but free of Manlius melancholy.

I'd let that moment slip away. In less than an hour, I'd report to the Caesar again. My only hope was to serve Roma as best I could.

※※※

'An *attack*?'

Julian's staff had assembled to decide the punishment of a Scutarius who had murdered a fellow targeteer during the night. Julian had only just received Bainobaudes and myself when proceedings halted for a fresh report. *Exploratores* crisscrossing the many miles between the fortress camp of Tres Tabernae and the river had investigated fresh smoke trailing Barbatio's exit route.

'Yes, Caesar, an *attack*. A costly one, too.'

The thickset Petulantes' scout was still panting. He swabbed nervous sweat off his balding pate with his woolen Pannonian cap. His trousers were wet with river water.

'How costly?'

'General Barbatio has lost most of his baggage wagons.'

'Didn't he fight them off? Recover our supplies?'

'No, Caesar. The few survivors said Barbatio lost all his baggage, pack animals, even his camp followers and their children.'

'Camp followers to Hades! What about my boats and food?'

Julian turned to Bainobaudes. 'Tribune, have you got the boats I requisitioned?'

'No boats, Caesar.'

An astonished Julian stared at Severus who had claimed the privilege of age to remain seated. As usual, Severus proved himself neither insubordinate nor overbearing. The elderly man gave only a sagacious nod, as if to say, 'What else did you expect?'

I admired Bainobaudes' cool blood. The Franco-Roman knew better than to embroider what could not even be patched. There was a long pause.

'Explain yourself, Tribune. I asked for seven craft, no more!'

'After the collapse of the bridge, Barbatio burned all his remaining boats a few hours ago, Caesar,' Bainobaudes said. 'And any supplies that couldn't be transported by road.'

Julian was the youngest man in the group, an untested Constantine facing down veteran professionals. He planted both boots apart, his hands on his hips, in a feeble imitation of a taller man's stance. It sat ill next to his other pretensions—the humble army tunic and careless shave.

—THE DEADLY CAESAR—

'So, transport them! There's a road straight here from Brotomagus. Those supplies were meant for my men! We've been waiting for weeks!'

Behind Julian stood selected tribunes and all the favored adjutants and aides who could squeeze into this privileged space—more than twenty-five men in the makeshift barrack thrown up by Julian's engineers.

Bainobaudes was taller than Julian and the tribune drew up his full height to withstand the bleating dismay of his imperial commander.

'Has Barbatio sent me no explanation? What exactly did he say?' The Caesar's eyes landed hard on me, standing just behind the tribune's right shoulder. None of his previous collegial friendship welcomed me this morning.

Bainobaudes and I both demurred. Which one of us dared repeat the insults the outraged Barbatio had heaped on Julian's head? ... *brat, stinking, pontificating, wisp-bearded, round-shouldered runt* ... Barbatio was no friend of mine, but I would not dare repeat his slurs.

Detecting our guilty glances, Julian came right up to us and thrust his heavy lower lip at me.

'What did Barbatio say, *Agens*?'

'No doubt his horns reached your ears, Caesar—'

'Of course our scouts heard his horns! Did he need an Olympian fanfare just to mobilize against some band of barbarian skirmishers The man commands twenty-five thousand troops. He couldn't slay every last one of the raiders?'

Bainobaudes said. 'Barbatio had ordered his legions to break camp. He was speeding the army southwards at fast pace. The Alemanni seized on his retreat as a show of weakness. Within the hour of his troops forming into columns, the enemy separated his ox wagons and camp followers from the main convoy.'

'Break camp?' Julian stared.

'The supplies he lost this morning were all he had retained to sustain his force until they reach Mediolanum. He put the rest of the supplies to the torch.'

'Mediolanum?' Julian started.

I was an *agens*, reporting to the *Magister Officiorum*. If worse news must be delivered to the excitable Julian, better it come from someone even he couldn't immediately cashier on the spot. I took over from Bainobaudes.

'Forgive us, Caesar. The boats, the supplies—they are not the point. General Barbatio has declared the end of this year's campaign,' I said.

'End-d-d-d of the campaign?' What is the coward's excuse?'

'The loss of the bridge, Caesar.'

Julian looked to the impassive Severus, to no avail. The old veteran was doing his best to obscure his standing and demote his authority in favor of Julian.

As for Julian, he was still only inches away from Bainobaudes and me, close enough to detect a spark light up his eyes. His chin twitching, fist clenching, boot stomping—all signs of distress suddenly dropped away.

He jerked his head with a sudden realization; Barbatio was a general in flight, a *Magister Peditum per Gallias* abandoning the Gallic field. The hated killer of his half-brother Gallus was tossing his field laurels to the Caesar.

Julian shook his head. 'Fellows, this is what comes of dishonoring the Altar of Victory in Roma.'

He turned and asked me, '*Agens*, where's your informant, that Alemanna?'

I wanted Gunda safe from Julian, no less than from Barbatio. Eyes blinking with sudden eagerness, Julian looked capable of anything. He mustn't realize that a royal hostage, a bargaining chip right off the dicing table of war, was within his grasp. Only I must know her hiding place.

'Returned to her father Gundomadus, our ally,' I lied.

'Why? Why?'

'Gunda served our purposes with honor, Caesar.' I answered. 'She proved a faithful interlocutor. She gave Barbatio's tribunes useful strategic information. She advised them to keep the evacuation of warrior Alemanni as peaceful as possible. Let the civilian settlers stay on our lands won by fair combat and diplomatic promise.'

'Why would I do that? Why would I harm my reputation by compromising?'

'Because it serves the Empire's purpose, Caesar. The tribes are a fractious, uncoordinated, distended jumble of minor kings and renegade chieftains. Each man seeks to make a name for himself among his own people. They bicker and weaken themselves. But antagonize them further and you risk unifying them into a fighting force.'

'What kind of army could those illiterates muster?' Julian waved the idea away.

'Do not play into Chnodomarius' plans to use us as foils for his ascendance to domination over fellow *reges*, Caesar.'

'Gigas himself thinks to fight? The giant barbarian will take us on?'

Before the grim gaze of all, Julian gave an incongruous skip on his bandy legs. He had digested the news of Barbatio's retreat and the loss of the boats and grain. The field was now his and his alone.

'This is something to avoid, Caesar,' I said. 'They do have a war plan, a strategy to ask their allies and rivals for troops to resist us. Gunda's counsel influenced Barbatio's decision to end the campaign before it was too late.'

I risked the fair assumption Cella had briefed Barbatio at the right moment.

Julian gave a high-pitched giggle, trying to sound superior. 'He lost courage when he heard he might have to fight, not just because the bridge collapsed.'

'Perhaps his decision complies with his instructions.'

Julian's eyes darted at me as if betrayed. 'Instructions, *Agens*? What do you know of *instructions*? Has your petty spying inflated into phantasmagoria of imperial *dicta*?'

I stayed silent, humiliated before every man there. I spotted Hariobaudes behind Salutius and Pentadius. The *tribunus vacans* smiled with satisfaction. Gunda's warning would go unattended here. No Alemannus or Alemanna would eclipse Hariobaudes.

Julian's tangible disdain enveloped me. No one took my side. We *curiosi* stood apart in society. Our privileges carried costs and suspicions. And indeed, my surmises were only based on my long acquaintance with Barbatio. Ambitious to the core, he would never dare halt an imperial campaign of his own accord. His departure signaled absolute confidence that Constantius II didn't want a war this season with the Alemanni.

It was obvious, but Julian refused to see it.

It was also not an *agens'* place to point out the obvious.

Julian could have asked me to detail the barbarian strategy explained already to Barbatio's staff but his thoughts were fixed on something else. We watched him pulling at his chin where his wispy beard once sprouted.

He looked up at his *explorator*, still standing by.

'Fetch me one of the local scouts. For the sake of morale, it is my men who will retrieve Roman honor from Barbatio's muddy trail.'

The local scout looked like a promising young man from a *vicus* of *laeti* settlers. His rough trousers and simple tunic spoke of poverty, but he belted his shirt with a wide Roman *cingulum* with polished struts and clutched a respectable Roman felt hat.

'Is there food on those islands where your rabble shelter?'

The scout looked confused. 'They fish and hunt, Caesar.'

'How many boats would we need to reach those islands?' Julian continued.

He hesitated, wide-eyed at the bobbing figure of his commander-in-chief.

'Boats? None, Caesar.'

'None?'

'No, Caesar. At the southernmost island, drought and silting have reduced the river to its lowest ebb in years. Men could ford across, floating on shields, if necessary.'

Julian gave a jerk into the air with both arms, clenching his fists with satisfaction, as if receiving a salute from the Arena. General Severus still said nothing.

'You're sure? All the way to the islands?'

'The current can be managed, Caesar.'

'Redeem yourself from your failure over the boats, Tribune Bainobaudes. Lead your bravest through the shallows to the islands. Burn their villages down and seize their boats. Bring back all the food you can plunder for good measure.'

'You misunderstand me, Caesar. There are no soldiers on those islands,' the scout protested. 'Just women and children sent there for safety.'

'Slaughter them to the last,' Julian ordered Bainobaudes. 'Slaughter them like . . . sheep.'

—THE DEADLY CAESAR—

He raised a palm in the air to cut off further debate and made straight for the exit, forcing junior officers to step sharply to one side as he passed.

Then he stopped and turned, pulling on his chin for a beard that was no longer there.

'History must not be thwarted,' he said.

Chapter 17, The Broken Lyre

—THE ISLANDS OF THE MIDDLE RHENUS—

The staff meeting broke up for routine duties across the breadth of the camp. With his career hanging in the balance, Bainobaudes set off with a grim expression to choose light-armed auxiliaries for his raid on the islands.

I had minutes, not hours, to save Gunda.

I found the stable boy Tonantius squatting in the shade of the stables. He was washing down a breakfast of hard tack *bucellatum* with gulps of *posca*. He gobbled fast, as if he'd stolen the food, but his furtive air dropped away when he saw me. There was a raw and ugly gap in his smile.

'What happened to your tooth?'

'*Stabulensis* knocked it out.' He grinned.

'Where did you say your family was, son?'

'On the other side of the river, *Agens*, shackled to their neighbors and slaving for the Alemanni kings.'

'Are you sure they're not on the islands in the middle of the river, working for the settlers who fled these lands?'

'If they was on the islands so close, I'd have swum to 'em myself,' he said, wiping his nose with an oily sleeve. 'Or they would have swum back, looking for me.'

'Of course they would have.'

'No, I got word they're far away.' He paused and looked at his bare feet, 'but not forever.'

'Of course not. Listen, Tonantius, I need a horse—'

'Is it true that after we clean them off our lands, we're crossing over to rescue our families?'

'I'm not sure. It would mean building a good, strong bridge to get the army across. That would take time.'

'Julian's different from those old men in charge.'

'Who tells you that?'

'I've got friends... in the Petulantes. You'll see. Julian will lead us across the river.'

I pondered that prediction as he saddled me a strong, fast horse. With proper Castra training, this sharp-eared youngster would be worth three of Barbatio's offspring. I tipped him safely out of the sight of his *stabulensis* who was overseeing the distribution of horse feed and slowly wending his way toward us.

Tonantius worked fast with the bridle and bit. I had just hoisted myself onto the horse when someone gripped my left ankle.

I looked down into the placid smile of Dr Oribasius. '*Agens Numidianus*, shouldn't you be catching up on the papers the Prefect Florentius set aside for you so many days ago?'

'I have urgent business related to the wishes of the Emperor,' I kicked his hand away. 'Florentius knows I'm not my own master.'

'Reconsider your actions, *Agens*—' He held the horse fast by one of the bronze-covered saddle horns with surprising strength.

'Let go!' I laid my hand on the hilt of my *pugio* in warning.

'Hear me out. Whatever you are doing—reconsider. Despite his hatred of your *schola*, the Caesar favored you as a man who understood his reading, his meditations, and his learning. But your absences have been noticed—even recorded.'

The sinuous figure of Pentadius sprang to mind and indeed, seemed to be on Oribasius' as well: 'If your official duties are to assist the Acting *Magister Officiorum* or Prefect Florentius, then I'd do whatever those officers ask—and no more.'

'My commission is none of your business.'

He released the saddle horn with a wave of false apology. 'Florentius expected assistance in clearing his revenue accounts and speeding up communications with the *curiales* of this region.'

'I'll get to it.'

He cast a cool eye at my weapons. 'Yet you're dangling a *spatha* off that ring in your sword belt and you've borrowed a shield from the Petulantes,' he chuckled, 'though I had not noticed anything *petulans* about you—not until now.'

He was wasting his irony on me.

—THE DEADLY CAESAR—

'Not all our *schola*'s work revolves around postal routes and customs accounts, Doctor.'

'So they say, so they say. I hear you duplicate wax seals and break into the mails for information to add to your secret reports, that you not only arrest and escort the accused, you are trained in poisons, codes, hidden weapons, and *illegal executions*. Keep in mind how much our Caesar hates your *magister*. He blames Apodemius for the death of his miserable half-brother.'

'I'm in a hurry—'

The Greek lowered his voice a notch. 'Please, take my well-meant advice. The Caesar needs men of learning and philosophy around him, no matter their *schola*. You can prove your worth and that of your *schola* by doing your job well, serving under Pentadius and Florentius. If I were you, I would leave the heroics to Homer. For men like ourselves—men of education, I mean—bloodshed is for ritual sacrifice, not mindless suicide.'

'I have no interest in sacrifice of any kind, Doctor. I dislike the ritual version and I abhor the human.'

I spurred my horse into a trot and was soon well clear of Oribasius' lingering gaze.

But was I out of his thoughts? He'd just tried to enlist me as his ally—but against whom and what? If someone was recording my absences for later use against me, was it a personal enemy or an enemy of Apodemius and our *schola*? Could this enemy keeping track of my loyalties and actions be none other than Dr Oribasius himself?

I'd been exhausted when Bainobaudes and I had arrived at the river shore. I was hardly feeling better today. By the time I located the exact spot where we'd landed, I saw that our 'last' boat, that precious survivor of Barbatio's conflagration, was no longer there. No doubt some quick-witted settlers had dragged it off the bank minutes after we disembarked. We might never have been there, save for the telltale matted grass and broken reeds trailing away from the hoof prints of our horses.

I shaded my eyes against the morning glare and stared across the water. There were three islands in view, one close to where I halted, the other two farther away and closer to the barbarian shore, but all teeming with Alemanni refugees. There were no trees on these 'islands,' which were really just outcrops of land usually submerged by Alpine runoff in the early spring. But now, in late summer, thick sun-bleached vegetation covered each refuge.

I crouched and watched. I caught only glimpses of movement, but I could number their fires by the smoke that circled up from the brush obscuring their humble shelters. Rags hung out to dry from low-slung foliage. The faint singing games of innocent children and the calls of their anxious mothers punctuated the morning peace.

They had no hope of farming these barren hillocks. They'd had no time to ferry livestock. Miserable and invisible, they could only subsist in such desperate enclaves until Julian and his troops had followed Barbatio into winter quarters.

Perhaps their predicament had sunk in by now. For the moment, their ragtag youths and angry old men had stopped shouting insults across the sluggish waters at the Roman forces. They'd gone to ground like terrified rabbits—hardly the noble foe of Julian's bookworm fantasies.

Which island was Gunda's sanctuary? The nearest island seemed the largest but distances could deceive. From where I stood on the bank, I made out at least three small boats tethered to the shoreline and possibly the brow of a fourth peeking out of the overgrowth. One had been used for fishing, judging by a sagging net draped to dry in the sun. Not one of these craft could support more than four men, but the army of Julian was in no position to quibble. Once he saw those boats, Bainobaudes was sure to head to that island first and then use them to coast downstream to raze the other two islands.

The scout had told Julian the river was low enough now to ford. I gauged the current and walked two hundred feet upstream until I'd reached a departure point that would land me on the diagonal at that first island. I had no wish to follow Barbatio's logs all the way to the great German Sea in the north.

I stuffed my socks into my boots, tied the leather laces around my neck, hid my insignia in my hat, and waded into the shallows. I tested the borrowed shield in the brown, silty flow. Though the boss in the center was heavy, its leather covering was taut and the wood dry. I eased myself down on my stomach along its diameter. It wobbled for a moment as I kicked off, but by grasping the pounded leather rim for balance and kicking off the shallow riverbed from time to time, I could control my progress.

Without warning the riverbed dropped away from my foot's reach. I was paddling as best I could, my underlinen soaked with muddy water, my *spatha* sheath dragging in the current. The island seemed to recede from me and the river's sluggish appearance was deceptive. The calm surface hid a powerful undertow that frustrated my crossing. The river gripped me in a hidden vice and seemed determined to keep me centered midway, rushing past my destination.

I fought to free myself from this deadly inner stream. Any minute now one of those young toughs left behind by the proven Alemanni fighters might emerge from the island brush. He'd look across the water and discover a floating Roman with upturned back inviting axe practice.

Suddenly, my frantic kicking propelled me free of the river's clutches and I surged forward. I reached the shallower waters of the first island's southern shore and now half-crawled, half kicked my way forward until I could stand and lift the shield out of the water.

Back in my boots and crouching low, I followed a trail of broken reeds and dented earth, a rudimentary footpath into the interior. Smoke from a cooking fire drifted up into the sky not more than fifty feet ahead. I circled what I presumed to be a hamlet of some kind until I found cover from where I could watch the settlers going about their business. The fire belonged to a clutch of rude huts watched over by two youths and an old woman.

Gunda wasn't there.

Another second track behind their huts led to another thin column of smoke. This time, I'd stumbled on a true *vicus* consisting of at least twenty shelters of branches, blankets, and skins. Perhaps as many as a hundred of Alemanni had set themselves up here—old men guarding gaggles of grandchildren while their hags pounded grain. There were dozens of young wives of absent fighters working away, dangling wool from spindles, or stirring their messes in a battery of coarse pottery and dented Roman vessels.

This was worth a wait. Surely it was the main camp. Sooner or later Gunda would pass my line of vision. But how long would it take for Bainobaudes' men to find this same place? I was sure in my heart that Constantius would not have authorized the coldblooded slaughter of these *Germani* but it was too late to stop those killers.

I was losing valuable minutes. Where was Gunda? I watched the bedraggled, trailing skirts of one woman after another, but unless Gunda was ill or hiding, I'd wasted half an hour scrutinizing every female there.

A dog tethered to a stake lifted his muzzle to the air. He sniffed and bared his fangs with a low growl. Had he caught my scent? He got a swat across his stiffening ears for his pains, for the scrawny crone at his side assumed his unfriendly snarl was aimed at her skeletal neighbor. She told a grubby, naked cherub with reddish curls to calm the dog with a scrap of discarded fat.

The dog was not appeased. He ran to the full length of his hemp tether and, bracing his legs in warning, barked out sharp, insistent warnings straight in my direction.

A horse whinnied from the distant bank behind me. My blood turned cold at that thin but lethal warning. The dog had detected real danger. Bainobaudes and his men had reached the left bank shore. The Alemanni took no notice. They were used to hearing the passing traffic of mounted Romans.

I grabbed my shield and scrambled through the brush and around the hamlet to the farther side. It didn't take long to reach the edge of the island directly facing the barbarian bank. Now I perceived what had not been visible from the Roman side.

The first two islands were connected by a long deposit of silt, forming a natural causeway hidden from view by less than half a foot of water. It ran less than twenty feet parallel to the Alemanni bank. The settlers had reinforced it with rocks and pebbles lining both sides. Gunda must be on one of the other two islands. I faced the bright colors of my shield to the ground so that no glimpse of Petulantes gold or blue would catch the Romans' sharp eyes. I dashed as fast as I could from the first island to the second.

This island's foliage was sparser. I was drenched up to my knees again and more visible than before. I searched in vain for signs of any settlement.

—THE DEADLY CAESAR—

Then a familiar sound—slight but clear as a flute—wafted on the breeze to my ear. It was Gunda's innocent song of hope. I climbed up the slope of the island and thrashed my way through shoulder-high weeds with no inkling of what I might stumble into.

Her song stopped. I dared not call out her name. Someone else might have heard me coming. If she were in the care of protectors, then I could expect to land myself smack into a well-meaning ambush.

I moved more stealthily now, poised for a clumsy barbarian weapon to fell me at any instant. The brush got thicker. Thorns snagged my trousers. There was no longer that bell-like voice to draw me in the right direction. I slashed with my sword and used my shield to push away the brambles blocking my progress. A snake slithered out of my path.

I stopped short. I was wasting valuable minutes, thrashing this way and that. I stopped and waited for dead silence to settle over the island once again.

It was an excruciating wait, but after a minute or two, Gunda began to sing once more. I plunged ahead now, keeping my bearings fixed on that brief snatch of song. She must be hidden in a stand of high bushes some fifty feet away, closer to the island's northern rim.

I plunged through the thickets and reeds like a frantic animal to discover Gunda alone, cross-legged under a lean-to of branches draped with her traveling cloak for shade. Her graceful fingers were plucking out a series of notes along her lyre strings just as I burst into a small clearing.

The settlers had shared their meager food with her. A small clay pot and dented tin cup dried on a rock in the sun near a campfire snuffed out for the day. Small items of clothing dried on a low bush.

She looked thin, unkempt, and tired. The bruises on her face from Serapio's blows had turned a rainbow of colors. All traces of the proud daughter of Gundomadus had gone. Even weeks of ferrying food to her brother in a fetid Roman prison camp had not reduced her to this.

'Gunda!' I whispered, hoarse with fear of discovery.

'Roman!' She looked up, startled. 'You've come for me so soon?'

'We must run! This island is a death trap.'

I dragged her cloak off the lean-to and wrapped it around her shoulders. Her familiar reticule was already in my hand and I was pushing her toward the shore facing the last island. The lyre dropped from her arms, but there was no time for packing up that clumsy instrument. Her travel bag full of golden trophies and jewels was forgotten. I raced ahead, my hand like a blacksmith's vice pulling on her slender arm.

She was protesting and dragging her heels, but I gave her no chance to slow down. Bainobaudes men must be fording the river by now, on shields if they had to, just as I had.

The slaughter was about to begin.

I used my sword to cut us a path through thick reeds to reach the northern beach of the island. Our feet plunged down into sucking mud for many seconds of frantic scrambling. This time nature had provided no easy escape.

'Can you swim?'

She turned white and pulled back from the water lapping the graveled beach. 'No! I came here by boat!'

Then the last island was out of the question. The Rhenus spread out between us, flowing its darkest and deepest.

I pointed to the right bank. 'Then I'll swim and you must float on my shield.'

Gunda turned away, pulling me back up the shore. 'We'll borrow a boat from those kind people. Even though I come from a rival tribe, they sheltered and fed me here. They'll—'

'Gunda—!' I dragged her back toward the water.

'They showed me respect and generosity. Let me go back!'

'Forget them,' I shouted in her face. I leaned into her bewildered face. 'Bainobaudes is coming here to kill them all. They're doomed. Fated. Do you understand me? They are as good as dead.'

She read disaster in my eyes and twisted back hard, escaping my grasp. Her overtunic ripped off one of the *fibulae* at her shoulder.

'Gunda, we mustn't delay.'

'Why didn't you warn the settlers?'

'And be taken by them as hostage to sabotage an imperial operation? They're your people.'

My cold political loyalty shocked her—I could see it in her eyes.

'Gunda, an hour ago there was time for you to save them all. Now there's only time to save yourself.'

We heard the first screams, terrible and piercing. Gunda jerked her head up, listening wide-eyed with horror. The cries, the shouted protests, the futile appeals—only Gunda could understand the words, but my heart could translate.

We froze as one. The river water lapping around our boots was turning red as the blood of Bainobaudes' victims on the first island upstream mingled with the green-brown current.

Gunda looked over my shoulder and her mouth opened with soundless shock. The body of a child floated face down past us. The vicious spiked tip of a Roman's lead-weight *plumbata tribolata* stuck out through its tiny shoulders. The cherub's red curls swayed with the current.

'The children. They're killing the children?' Gunda screamed, 'What are they doing? Why are they killing children? Is this your great Empire? Is this what you mean by "civilizing" barbarians?'

'You can't save them now,' I said. 'Hold on to my shield as if it were a raft and I'll swim by your side.'

'My lyre!' she cried.

Before I could stop her, she was dashing back toward the mud.

I stumbled after her across the gravel and onto the muddy slope but my shield and sword got in my way. I almost caught up with her and grabbed at her skirt, but missed, and she plunged into the thicket to retrieve her instrument.

I stood, panting and stunned by her stupidity over a plaything of wood and string.

Screams came closer, like wails from the belly of Hades. The settlers who had escaped Bainobaudes' first assault were making a dash for their lives through the shallows of the causeway leading straight to Gunda's lair. We heard the slash of swords and Roman shouts as other settlers tried to swim straight for the right bank.

Around the edge of the island where I stood, some of the Cornuti attackers slid into view on the very fishing boats I'd seen moored to the first island. Lethal darts whistled through the air and brought down the aged, the infirm, and the young. The boats, already low in the water with the weight of infantrymen and snatched booty, were coasting toward the causeway now. The men at the helm were aiming to cut off the train of refugees struggling through the current.

'Gunda! Hurry!'

She re-emerged through the dry brush seconds later. Dozens of her fellow Alemanni sprinted around her in all directions. The tranquil hideaway where I'd found her alone only minutes before had turned into a trampled scene of panic and carnage.

She dashed through the mud and toward the water's edge, holding fast to that damned *lyra*, as if she had rescued nothing less than her own soul. Seeing me waiting in the shallows with the upturned shield floating ready at my knees, she signaled she was coming to me. Jostled by panicked settlers on either side, she raced toward me, her lyre held high in her right arm.

She lifted her skirts with her left hand and waded into the water, ready to trust me with her life. She was less than six feet from where I waited when a circling Cornutus' axe swung through the air and plunged into her upstretched right arm just inches from her shoulder.

I caught her as she fell, pale with shock. Her eyes rolled in her head. Her grip on the lyre went limp as her fingers loosened, powerless and unresponding. The axe had made a savage gash right through her white flesh and deep into the pink muscle. The current around us turned livid with her blood. I lifted her onto my shield and pushed, kicked, and paddled as fast as I could for the safety of the barbarian bank.

More than one injured settler tried to grab hold of my shield or my arm before they sank under the current forever. I shoved one viciously mutilated body after another out of our path. I endured an eternity of deafening, flailing minutes of this, my right arm slung over Gunda's waist and clasping the edge of the shield and my left pulling against the current in frantic circles so as not to get pulled out to sea.

Finally my boots struck ground.

The lyre had long since drifted out of sight.

Chapter 18, Unexpected Brothers

—THE WRONG SIDE OF THE RHENUS—

Roman soldiers trained for years on end to summon up discipline and teamwork in the face of imminent death. Normal human beings just fought like animals to survive.

Panicked Alemanni settlers jostled and pushed each other out of the way to claw on all fours up the steep slope of the eastern riverbank and reach the grassy bluff overlooking the river. Ahead of Gunda and me, some fifty settlers staggered to get past the last few feet of swampy muck and stony beach.

Settlers who had reached solid ground were screaming for family or yowling out wordless grief. Some were coughing out water or choking on smoke. Others cursed and shouted. Many stared, silent, glassy-eyed, and bewildered, waiting to be wakened from a daylight nightmare.

The three islands behind us erupted into a chain of bonfires. Bainobaudes' men had finished their looting, loaded their boats, and laid their torches to every last hut and lean-to. A breeze rising behind us carried the crackle and roar of flames. Acrid smoke filled the sky overhead.

Closer to the water's edge, some women had collapsed into the silty mud. Old men were trying to start a fire but the kindling was too wet. There was a piercing shriek from a young woman as her little girl succumbed to her wounds.

But their suffering seemed nothing to the butchery that drifted through the current flowing past our horrified eyes.

Would Bainobaudes and his men pursue us here with their pronged darts and dripping *spathae*?

By sheltering my eyes against the glare of the western sun, I made out the hunched-over backs of Julian's Roman slaughterers as they paddled back to the left bank. The stolen Alemanni fishing boats were close to capsizing under the weight of stolen supplies and armed men. At the bow of the first rocking craft sat Bainobaudes—once my trusted traveling companion—now the desperate tribune who would do anything to re-instate himself after Barbatio's scapegoating.

Dozens still flailed with Gunda and me through the water—some wounded, others shocked but unharmed. Some poor souls were unable to keep their heads above the water and sank to their deaths, even in that sluggish current. Some, reaching the beach, just fell to their knees to find themselves alone and bereft of any comfort, much less rescue.

Gunda was alert enough to stagger through the shallows toward dry land. She and I were a stone's toss from safety when I lost my footing. Someone had tumbled into my back and pulled us both backwards into the current. I struggled to regain my balance and shook off a grasping girl of no more than sixteen.

Ashes streaked her forehead. A livid purple and white patch of burnt cheek was swelling into a fat blister. She must have fought her way right through the smoke and flames.

She jerked at my soggy sleeve.

'Krokus, Krokus,' she sobbed.

She bent over the muddy water and fished with desperate hands up to her armpits. She was hoping to catch something or someone under the surface but she brought up empty hands and stared at me, then at Gunda. She spoke to us in her dialect and holding her palms apart, measured out the size of an infant. She grabbed at my sleeve to slow our progress. She insisted we help find her babe until she saw Gunda's wound gape open again and stream fresh blood into the eddy around our knees.

In their common distress, none of the settlers had yet remarked that a Roman enemy was leading a wounded woman onto barbarian turf. Perhaps it was because I wore no battle armor and my clothes were soaked through. But my North African complexion, bright weapons, and dark bronze hair trimmed short would betray me as soon as the general turmoil died down.

—THE DEADLY CAESAR—

Somehow I had to stanch the blood pouring out of Gunda's arm. A couple of older boys helped me lift her up over the overhanging bluff and across a level field of wildflowers until we were some hundred feet away from the other survivors along the riverside. With each jog or swing, her arm's dark pink muscle opened to show the white bones of her joint swimming in blood.

We fashioned Gunda a bed from new fallen foliage under a copse of young oaks. Her silver-gold hair and gushing blood mingled with the green-orange of the late summer leaves. I used my short cloak to make a windbreak against the curiosity of other refugees, but it was unnecessary. Moaning and shouts had turned to a chorus of keening wails as the survivors tallied their missing and dead.

We had no *acetum* at hand, not even a bladder of wine, to cleanse Gunda's terrible wound. Youthful years around the medical tents of Commander Gregorius' troops had taught me how lethal an unwashed gash could become. The Rhenus did not run clear—even before the contamination of all those fresh corpses, there was the refugees' sewage and debris trapped in low-lying pools.

I used my linen undershirt to bind up her shoulder. Numb in mind and body, Gunda had managed to clamber with me out of the water, but she was struggling to stay alert. I'd never known how determined she could be until I saw her so weak, yet fighting off the oblivion of fainting.

A settler near the bluff shouted out a warning, pointing to two Alemanni warriors on horseback galloping out of the yellow-tipped forest behind us.

The men rode past the four of us huddled under the oak branches. They reined in their horses at the edge of the bluff. Looking down on the slope up which settlers still crawled and panted, they barked out hurried questions. The more senior man wore full Roman armor and helmet over his red braided hair. His saddle rings bristled with weapons.

He pointed at the fires filling the sky with black clouds over the middle of the Rhenus and demanded an explanation.

Bainobaudes and the other culprits were well out of sight. No doubt they were already galloping back to Tres Tabernae with their scavenged booty to announce their 'victory' to Julian.

Gunda had seen the riders passing. She said in a hoarse whisper, 'They're *optimates* of Chnodomarius, Roman. They mustn't find you here. They mustn't know who I am.'

'You have no other chance.'

I stood up and bellowed for help—and the gods only knew with what despair I foresaw that my bid to save Gunda condemned me to the whims of Serapio's formidable uncle.

'Why? Why? Oh, Roman, you fool. Now one is coming here. Run!' Gunda said.

I stood firm. My eyes were soon level with the gilded harness disks of a snorting war charger. I was only a foot away from a pair of fretworked leather shoes topped by tight-wrapped leg bindings around dark indigo trousers that ballooned free above the knees.

The second rider had lingered behind at the river to hear names of the dead and accounts of the islanders' catastrophe.

Squinting up into the late afternoon sun, I examined the features of a hardened *Alemannus* veteran. A whitened scar twisted across his high cheekbone like a pale snake. His hair was brilliant but dyed—its glinting copper unnatural for a man of his sallow coloring, dark brown eyes, and heavy brown eyebrows.

He gestured the two settler youths who had helped me to rejoin the others at the riverbank. When they hesitated, he laid a threatening hand on his *spatha* hilt. They dashed off.

'What are you doing here?' He spoke clean, simple Latin.

'Please help this lady without delay. A *francisca* has nearly taken off her arm.'

The old warrior gazed at Gunda's soaked and muddied calico skirt hem. Her linen under-tunic lay exposed—brown with river water, but of a fine-gauge weave and trimmed with worn gold and silver embroidery. Her hair had tumbled undone at the back, but two combs of carved tortoiseshell held hanks of it above her crown. Her favorite fox with the garnet eyes sat pinned to a shabby ribbon.

He frowned. 'This woman is a *laeta* settler from the Roman side?'

'Yes.'

He leaned over in the saddle. With the tip of his long barbed spear, he lifted her delicate under-tunic to register the good quality of her traveling boots. He knew I lied—Gunda was no immigrant farm girl.

'What are you doing with her? Are you one of the attackers?'

Gunda tried to lift herself on her good elbow in protest but fell back. 'No, no,' she shook her head. She started whispering in her own tongue, forcing the proud man to dismount. He knelt down in the grass and lowered his ear to her lips.

'She says you are a friend. You brought her a message from the Roman camp?'

'That is true.'

'What was your message?'

'To warn her of the attack.'

'To warn *her*? What about the others?' He was as shrewd as he looked.

'You waste her time. She's losing blood fast. She will die if we don't get her care. The wound must be washed and bound tight.'

The rider hailed his junior fellow back. The two men conferred some ten feet away from our shady copse.

The second man removed his helmet and knelt next to Gunda's shoulder on the leaves. Already my linen bandage was soaked through. Her face was ghost-white. Her strength was draining away.

The rider glanced up, startled. I expected him to urge haste. Instead he spoke with a sharp hiss of recognition to the older man. The deadly name 'Serapio' passed his lips.

He had recognized Gunda. We were both lost.

The older man gave a wry smile that crinkled up the wormy thread of his scar.

He switched back into his rough Latin to include me: 'We bear good news, wife of Serapio and daughter of Gundomad. We come from Chnodomar's camp. The *reguli* Vestralpus, Urius, and Ursicinus, together with your husband and his father, as well as the chieftains Suomar and Hortar—they have dispatched the flower of their forces to follow our leader. All our peoples hail Chnodomar as "Gigas" far and wide, and for good reason. His superiority in strategy and his determination to defend our assembled peoples is greater than that of any *Alemannus* alive.'

'That is a lie,' Gunda whispered. 'My father will never break his word to Roma. The others cannot have fallen under your chieftain's domination so easily.'

'Oh, perhaps they are not all there yet in person, but they've promised men and those men are on the way.'

'My father is an . . . ally . . . '

'Yes,' the younger rider broke in. 'Only your uncle and father reject our cause. They persist—stubborn and loyal to the Emperor and his butcher cousin.'

He gestured at the fires still crackling through stands of sun-bleached reeds and brush. 'See back there? See what your allies have done!' He looked at me. 'See how your Roman soldiers do us a favor? They make us all hate you.'

My anger burst out of me. 'They have done no one a favor today, this woman least of all.'

'Listen to him! Are those fires not fuel to our cause? Is there anyone now who would stand up and claim that Romans keep their word? Could anyone claim that Romans are grateful for our support against Magnentius, the Usurper? We follow the man who defeated the Usurper's brother, Decentius, in the field. Let there be no more doubt that your Constantines are faithless to their word.'

'She needs help. Stop making speeches!'

He leaned over Gunda again and I feared he was going to spit on her. Instead he said, 'Send a message to your father to join us or pay the price.'

My fear turned to anger. 'Don't threaten her! She can hardly keep her wits for the pain!'

I picked him up and tossed him by his shoulders into the tall grass.

'If you delay any longer,' I shouted at them, 'she'll be in no position to send any message to her father—except a plea that he honor her memory.'

Neither man intended to summon help for Gunda. Their appearance out from the forest had been too quick to be a reaction to the smoke spiraling into the skies and too fortuitous to be in answer to our plight.

These two men were on a separate mission.

—THE DEADLY CAESAR—

'Why are you here, if not to save these wretched people?'

I tore off fresh strips of my own linen. Something had to slow Gunda's blood loss.

'Get help yourself, *Agens*. We are like you—envoys, not fighters. We have no interest in interfering with a brother messenger. That would be against the customs and usage of war,' said the man with the scar.

'*Envoys?*'

'We ride to meet your Caesar. This is Gibuld. I am Makrian,' said the younger one, recovering himself from my assault. His pride in being an envoy reminded me of myself in my first years of riding the *Cursus Publicus* circuit, carrying imperial mail at high speed, brandishing the honor of a feather in my *petanus* to signal top priority.

'You tend her like a loyal friend,' Gibuld said. 'Show us the same honesty and we will treat you justly.'

He moved closer. 'One of Julian's soldier has fled to our protection to avoid execution.'

'I have heard of the murder. The culprit is a Scutarius.'

Gibuld nodded. 'That is the man. The scoundrel tries to buy us with Roman secrets. He claims that, with our defeat of your General Barbatio, the Caesar has only thirteen thousand soldiers left in his army. Is this criminal making up a tale to win time or does he speak the truth?'

'I am an honest man. And anyway, truth is easier than a lie. I see no reason to deny what can be of no comfort to you. When it comes to the Roman army, numbers in the field mean less than quality. Flavius Claudius Julianus commands the unquestioned loyalty, discipline, and fervor of every man numbered. His thirteen thousand troops are worth twenty thousand of yours.'

'Go with these envoys to the Roman side, Marcus,' Gunda said softly. 'If you stay within reach of Serapio, you will die.' Despite her agony, I smiled to hear her say my true name.

'Give me your drink,' I ordered the two Alemanni. 'Wine or *posca*, whatever you're carrying that's fresh and plentiful.'

With their jeweled flasks in hand, I knelt down next to Gunda and said nothing until I'd given her something to drink, then washed and redressed her foul injury. Even the two riders flinched when they saw the savage slash, its gaping edges like white lips that opened and closed, speaking of death.

The bitter sting of the cool liquid coursing over her wound gave Gunda fresh strength.

'Marcus' she gasped, 'guide these men to the Caesar. Bring me back a doctor to close my wound with needle and thread. Our only hope for my father, my brother, myself, is a firm peace and a stronger treaty. Convince these men to beg some gesture from the Caesar to prevent complete war.'

Gibuld understood her. 'You're free to come with us, *Agens*. Show us the fastest route to the Caesar's camp.'

Despite his bluster, he seemed relieved to acquire an official Roman escort through imperial territory. The two men returned to the other settlers to complete their assessment for an eventual report to Chnodomarius.

I bade a gentle farewell to Gunda. We both realized her only hope of surviving was expert Roman care.

She whispered, 'Make sure they sue for peace. There is something else, something the island settlers told me, but that these envoys may conceal from you.'

'What?' I nestled her close, her blood seeping across my tunic.

'Chnodomar has fortified a secret base for himself inside your territory—between Concordia and Tribunci. If my father's treaty with Roma carries any weight, tell the Caesar that this secret comes from the daughter of his faithful ally, the *rex* Gundomadus, ruler of the Agri Decumantes. Now go and let these people move me to shelter somewhere safe until you return.'

Some Alemanni villagers from the nearest *vicus* had arrived with mules, carts, and litters for the wounded. I waited until Gunda was lifted onto a wagon bed and then set off north with Chnodomarius' envoys for a raft crossing to the Roman side of the river. As hard as it was to separate, I could do no more for her than plead for her father, the fraying alliance, and a peace between the Empire and her tribes.

Once we reached Roman territory, we got an extra horse for me. I took the lead and galloped hard. I was racing away to distance myself from Serapio's shackles and dagger. I was racing to get a *medicus* for Gunda.

—THE DEADLY CAESAR—

But Gibuld and Makrian had confirmed my worst fears; the fractious Alemanni had united for war. Recalling Apodemius' last words to me, I was also racing to save Julian from himself.

₽₽₽

To show his disdain for Chnodomarius' messengers, Julian declined to receive them until sundown. They did not strike me as bad fellows, but to leave them the liberty—even for an hour—to survey the Romans' camp struck me as imprudent.

By the time I led Gibuld and Makrian to the command headquarters, they'd had ample opportunity to assess their enemy's situation. We passed enough soldiers scraping at half-empty pots or hauling in rotting vegetables to show the steep cost of the Alemanni's destruction of the *Magister Peditum*'s supply convoy.

We found Julian's tent as Spartan in comfort as ever—yet overstuffed with documents, *codices*, and his copies of Julius Caesar, and Plato. However, the Caesar was dressed, not for study or meditation but for battle—even at the end of a peaceful day. Like all the Constantines, he had an almost theatrical understanding of costume, whether it was the Athenian student-philosopher's short tunic and long beard or now the shining gold-trimmed armor and imperial purple cloak he had so recently disdained.

He was happy to impress any Alemannic ambassadors as the reincarnation of Alexander the Great, even by accident. They would report to Chnodomarius that the barbarians faced a foe superior in learning, strategy, and physical condition.

Julian and two adjutants led the three of us to the larger meeting barrack where the senior army and civil staff stood waiting. Severus was seated to one side, as usual. He comported himself like an elderly household god, ignored and gathering dust on a *lararium* pillar.

When the two barbarians stood freely before Julian and his court, he gestured immediately to a guard that they be forced by an unsheathed blade to perform a full *proskynesis*. How quickly he had learned from Constantius the purposes of intimidation! Only when their stomachs and noses were pressed flat against the floor, did Julian nod for them to proceed.

'My name is Gibuld, Caesar. Makrian and I come from Chnodomar, conqueror of Decentius, the False Caesar, and brother of Roma's late enemy, Magnentius the Usurper.'

'Rise and deliver your message.'

'Our great leader is known far and wide as "Gigas the Giant" for his superhuman stature, his prowess in battle, and his swelling command. In the name of all the Alemanni peoples, he protests your plunder of our lands, the rape of our harvest, and the stripping of our trees. These are lands won by the valor of our swords with the express approval of your Emperor.'

Julian flipped the corners of some army accounts stacked on a nearby table. He tossed Severus a satisfied smile and then glanced at Gibuld. 'Your chieftain's brigands robbed our convoys of supplies intended for our soldiers.'

Gibuld said: 'That was an impetuous attack by renegade malcontents. Do not use a minor skirmish to deflect us from our justified grievances. The departure of more than half your army shows Roma has reconsidered her unjust campaign against our settlements. Our scouts retrieved the shields abandoned by your army in its cowardly flight. We laughed to see that emblems which had once made us tremble were so easily conquered.'

Julian took this badly. Barbatio had killed his half-brother and now disgraced our army. He pressed his lips together and waited.

'Chnodomar expects no more than his due—to till the fertile fields of the left bank as guaranteed by *Imperator* Constantius.'

Julian gave a loud snort. He strutted past their bowed heads.

'Don't you dare quote my own cousin to me. Were you there at my elevation? I think not. May I remind you of how Constantius addressed me when describing your kind? I quote him thus: "These savages, as if sacrificing to their wicked Manes with Roman blood, have forced our peaceful frontier and are now overrunning Gallia. They are encouraged by the belief that dire straits beset us throughout our far-flung empire. If this evil, therefore, which is already creeping beyond set bounds, is met by the accord of our and your wills while time permits, the necks of these proud tribes will not swell so high. The frontiers of our empire will remain inviolate".'

Julian straightened his shoulders, mindful not to succumb to his student slouch.

'*Inviolate frontiers*. The Emperor and I are agreed. Tell your petty kings that we push them back across the river where they can squabble all they please. Feel free to award each other pounded arm coils and clunky necklaces for vanquishing your own cousins. But do not challenge Roma any longer.'

Gibuld stepped right up to the Caesar without invitation. He stared down his nose at the goatish younger man. From within the confines of his battered mail, the Alemannus produced a package of thick vellum bound with golden cord. He extended it to the Caesar.

'I present this as proof of the Empire's guarantee of lands and freedom on this side of the river.'

A murmur of surprise ran through the gathered officers. Prefect Florentius' expression darkened. *Magister* Pentadius lifted his chin with a jerk of recognition.

Julian gave the barbarian a cruel smile. 'Read it to us.'

Without untying the cord binding the document, Gibuld recited: 'This proves that you are contravening the determinations of your senior colleague and must confess as much; that you must either abide by his written guarantees or expect to fight us.'

Julian chuckled. 'That is not what the document *says*. I invited you, barbarian, to read it out loud.'

Gibuld hesitated. The overconfident Chnodomarius had misstepped when playing political chess with the young Caesar. He'd sent articulate men who rode fast and loomed over Julian in height and strength. The elder envoy spoke direct and grammatical Latin.

But poor Gibuld could not read.

I had promised Gunda to make every argument for peace. There could be no debate here today if Julian's assembled officers did not hear Constantius' guarantee for themselves. The sooner we got Julian to accept Chnodomarius' message, the sooner Gibuld and Makrian could speed a *medicus* and myself back across the river to save Gunda.

'Procedure demands that my *schola* assess the veracity of this document,' I said, stepping up to Gibuld's side. 'Forgery, which we saw only recently corrupt the unhappy case of the former *Magister Peditum* General Silvanus, has no place in sensitive negotiations. It was my own service that identified that deceit, but sadly too late. We must not make the same mistake.'

I unfolded the vellum carefully. If I had entertained any doubt it bore the signature of Constantius II, the Emperor's favorite salutation was under his name—an affectation so full of boundless self-love, it once made Apodemius' eyes roll heavenward in disgust.

'Yes,' I said, looking hard at old Severus. 'This is the Emperor's agreement allowing the Alemanni under Chnodomarius' rule free use of the lands contiguous with the Rhenus in exchange for support in arms against General Magnentius and his brother Decentius—signed five years ago.'

I held the long vellum strip open and, circling the tent, pointed to the bottom of the treaty for the gaze of all the assembled officers. 'This is the Emperor's particular signature, "Our Eternity, The Lord of the Entire Universe", the very phrase I have seen him add underneath his signature in Mediolanum.'

Julian hesitated. Would he have the audacity to pry the offensive document from my fingers? I handed it back to Gibuld. The Alemannus would die before he relinquished so valuable a treaty. Surely this was the moment Julian must back down from glory-seeking adventures. Nothing less than Constantius' word was at stake.

But Julian was more audacious than I reckoned. I had underestimated the fires of his ambition. We all had.

'These men are spies. Put them in chains,' he told his personal guard.

General Severus rose heavily to his feet and, with ponderous reluctance, placed himself in the center of the assembled officers.

'Forgive my raising a point born of long experience in the field, Caesar. We do not know where this "Gigas" lurks. Our army messengers will seek him out in vain. Any rebuff you make cannot reach this villain's ears unless you release his envoys. It is the hallowed custom of enemies to ensure the channel of communication remains open. This tradition has saved lives—especially Roman lives— throughout history.'

Julian half-turned to Severus and told him over his shoulder with the contempt one might fling at a down-faced military aide, 'Surely, Severus, you see my plan. As long as Chnodomarius assumes we are in negotiation, he relaxes his grip on his sword. His motley coalition malingers—frustrated, restless, and querulous. Their fragile unity frays.'

Severus looked unconvinced, but Julian would have the last word.

'The barbarian giant rests his blades on this worthless vellum, while we sharpen ours.'

※※※

Before any of the civilian superiors could detain me, I fled the barrack. I had to hunt down a medical officer who would accompany me back across the river before the last summer daylight had gone. Who would dare the raft crossing to bring his skills to save Gunda? I toured the medical tents and offered one year's pay in *solidi*. I was ready to leave my treasured *agens*' swivel knife as a guarantee of payment until we reached home. Yet each medical officer refused to leave his station.

Even after a dozen refusals, I clung to hope. Each legion had its separate medical team. I refused to believe no one would save her, even after hours of pleading within their fastidious tents, man after man, from the chief *medicus* to the lowliest *capsarius* rinsing out bedpans. Some were Greek slaves. Others were freedmen trained in the East. None was ready to slip through the dusk with me to save a wounded Alemanna beyond the border.

The troops were not yet on a war footing, but word was coursing through camp that Julian had imprisoned the two barbarian envoys seen trotting by so confidently only hours before. From unit to unit, I heard the grinding of whetstones and saw men polishing their armor by torchlight as they joked and chatted.

My heart started to sink only when I saw I had arrived at the perimeter of the camp near the edge of a cremation ditch. Two *capsarii* supervised the pyre on which the corpse of the murdered Scutarius lay burning. The atmosphere was thick with smoke and anger. The victim's *contubernales* watched from twenty feet upwind.

I went straight up to a small man, barely twenty, supervising the slaves tending the flames.

'Can you close an axe wound so deep that, without your needle, a shoulder might never move again?'

He turned a startled face to me. Torchlights flickered across his dark thoughtful eyes.

'That depends how deep the blade went.'

'This deep,' I gestured with the edge of my left hand. 'All the way to the joint.'

He looked reluctant. 'I can try to save the limb. But I can't guarantee he'll pull a bow or throw a dart again.'

'It's a woman, across the river.'

He sniffed at the risk. 'Sorry, *Biarchus*, I can't help you.'

'A year's pay in gold.'

'Actually, I'm too inexperienced. I'm only a *discens capsariorum*.'

'A trainee? That's okay. Willing to try?'

He hesitated. 'Payment now?'

'When we get home. I'm good for it.'

'Where is she?'

'There's a raft crossing downriver. Are you a good rider?'

He hesitated. 'I'd have to get instruments from the surgeon's chest. I've never done—'

'But you know the procedures?'

He nodded. I returned to the camp with this Ludovicus in tow as quickly as was decent to the murder victim and his mourning tent mates. The junior *capsarius* was just packing up the hollow spear-shaped *plumbus fistuala* that would drain Gunda's wound while he operated when I heard my name called out.

'*Agens* Numidianus? I have been hunting for you in all corners of the camp.'

I pretended not to recognize the *adiutor*. 'Not now. Later.'

'Now, *Biarchus* Numidianus, now. The Caesar wishes to speak with you—alone.'

Chapter 19, Blood on the Altar

—The Caesar's Tent, the Via Principia—

I was ordered to wait for the Caesar outside his private tent. I obeyed for many agonized minutes until I could no longer bear the thought of Gunda lying, tormented or delirious, on the floor of some filthy *vicus* hut with Serapio's men enjoying her suffering. I pushed past the imperial guards and burst in on him.

Dr Oribasius and the quaestor Salutius stood on either side of Julian. The three of them looked up at me with shocked faces full of guilt. Their hands were plunged together into a wide copper basin standing on an iron tripod.

The basin contained the guts of an animal so freshly butchered, it seemed still to heave with life. But no—the lifelike shiver was merely the swish of fresh blood and slippery entrails.

They abandoned their ritual examination in haste. I stared at Salutius, whose maturity and intelligent dinner conversation had not led me to suspect such practice.

The quaestor returned my questioning expression with a retort: 'Prayers divorced from sacrifices are only words; prayers with sacrifices are animated words.'

Julian rinsed off his hands in a second basin and wiped them dry.

I could hardly pretend I had not seen and understood that Oribasius and Salutius had just supervised the Emperor's cousin in a pagan sacrifice.

'Leave us,' Julian ordered his confidants. Salutius and Oribasius nodded. The doctor slipped past me with an insinuating smile. His Eastern robes and manner were as incongruous in that

Gallic leather tent as a Persian dancing girl attending a German boar hunt.

Salutius looked more uncomfortable. Unlike Oribasius, he was an active senior civil servant, bound to obey the Emperor's interdiction of ritual sacrifice of all kinds. To be caught red-handed—literally—by a Roman *agens* risked adding some very damaging information to his dossier at our *schola*.

I had just made a powerful enemy—the last thing I needed.

Julian gave a nervous giggle. 'You are surprised to find me carrying out my prayers? Do not look too shocked, Numidianus. I know you share my fealty to the true gods.'

'You are a *cultor deorum*, Caesar? You show yourself to the world as a practicing Christian.'

'Our troops are Christian, are they not? Our Emperor leads the Arian Church. And I admit Christ to the pantheon of gods who lead us to The One,' he explained.

'Yes, of course, Caesar, but—'

'My private meditations remain private.'

I did not like the conspiratorial smile he gave me. Though it would not hurt my standing in his court, he enlisted my sympathetic discretion with too much confidence.

'Does the Emperor know of your rituals? No doubt he would have you worship the Galilean in private as well as in public.'

'He will never know unless you report it. Constantius must think I am with the Galileans, but you and I both know that they worship a mere man—and a dead one at that.'

I stared down into the gory basin of guts without responding, remembering Apodemius' order to protect the Caesar from himself.

Julian took a cleansing breath and laid his damp towel over the basin.

'But I have not called you here to discuss sacrifice or theurgy. You are commissioned by your *schola* to supervise my court's procedures of official escort, exchange of messages, and so on. Naturally, you must protest my treatment of the foreign envoys and their so-called treaty. I consider it done.'

'General Severus knows the practices of warfare. He has already advised you well. History judges such things—not *agentes*.' If he hated our *schola*, he was still sensitive to history's verdict.

'I am deliberating my next action. We will not let the removal of the Statue of Victory cast its shadow over the Empire's destiny, will we?'

'No, Caesar.' He aimed straight for the patrician sentiment in my loyal Manlius heart.

'I spilt blood on this altar to know what the gods—Mercury, Mars, and Bellona—would have me do next.'

'This basin an altar?'

Was this what Senator Manlius' life defending Roman pagan traditions came down to—this sloppy, steaming abattoir in a caesar's tent?

For all my revulsion at the pieties and greed of certain Christian priests who preyed on Kahina's infantile credulity, the stench of Julian's pagan offal triggered a surge of disgust.

A nauseated anger seized me. I lifted the soggy linen off the basin and emptied its contents on the pounded earth. The entrails were still warm. I dangled the disgusting organs in the air in front of his long nose and quivering chin.

'You regret the loss of a statue in Roma? The loss of ritual blood in the temples of our fathers? Some would say that as of today the Caesar has much innocent *human* blood on his imperial hands.'

He stared up at me, stunned by my insane impertinence. I had insulted his 'triumph' over the Alemanni. I had added yet another layer of hatred for our *schola* to our account.

But Julian had learned through recent years of political sabotage to mask his temper.

'We shall have to rectify such talk, *Agens*.' His curt tone hid his embarrassment at my discovery of his illegal sacrifice. 'We must turn this shabby campaign of minor skirmishes and island raids into one substantial victory. You told me earlier that an Alemanna in your employ gave you information about the enemy.'

'I must leave you now to save that very lady.'

'First, I will have her information.'

'Information will do Roma no good if used to wage more war.'

'What do you know of warfare?' he chided.

'Over the restraints of my profession, I fought at Mursa.'

Julian shifted from one boot to the other He did not dare ask whether I had fought for Constantius or the rebel Magnentius. It was the entire Western Army that had paid the price. Constantius had saved the Empire but lost half his army and Magnentius two-thirds—a total of more than fifty thousand men in one day and one field.

I had survived mayhem lasting into the blackness of a night from the Underworld, slithering through the blood, mud, and carnage all around me. Our youthful Caesar still revered the roar and clash of man against man. He would never find himself pulling his own dying father through the slime of a futile hour. And I would never again read the *Iliad* or Caesar's *Gallic Wars* like this impressionable youth dazzled with the idolatry of battle fame.

'The memory of that single day has dulled your appetite for glory, *Agens*?'

'Reconsider, Caesar, I implore you. For every slaughtered Alemannus four more emerge from the forest, welded together by your campaign. There has been enough bloodshed already. I witnessed Bainobaudes' massacre—the corpses of babies torn from their mothers' breasts and dead children floating downriver.'

'Babies, mothers—! Did babies and mothers stop Julius Caesar from conquering Gallia? Pompey from Egypt? The great Alexander from marching to the uncharted edges of the East? You know imperial history as well as I.'

'Then think of your own dead boys and your Augusta's grief—'

'Gods! To mourn an unborn child or even a beloved infant aged one or two years is sheer bad taste! It happens every day! You think I mourn the loss of Helena's unborn children? Why? A dynasty lies nascent inside me, waiting to be fulfilled, just as the gods predict.'

'Then, Caesar, at least uphold the spirit of the Emperor's policy. Shift these peasants if you must, but do so without supplying barbarian rabble with more oil for their flames.'

'What noble rhetoric for such a lowborn creature. A freedman *biarchus*? You should have been a senator in the old Republic!'

He stroked his chin where his scrawny philosopher's beard had once curled. 'Numidianus, I thought at least you, of all your underhanded service, understood me.'

'Move the settlers over the border peacefully.'

He turned scornful again. 'So this is the advice of your costly network so valued by my cousin? To relinquish my greatest victory yet at hand over nameless barbarian infants?'

'Yes, that is my counsel. You may hate us *agentes*—'

'Oh, do I. You abuse the privileges of your postal network. You overrun the *Cursus Publicus* with corruption and waste. You ride state animals to their deaths. Apodemius has turned his department into a power unto itself just as despicable as the thousand eunuchs who slobber over Constantius. Yes, I hate your *schola*, just as I hate the Lord Chamberlain Eusebius who watched as your *Magister* Apodemius conducted the interrogation and execution of my brother Gallus. Even today, the eunuch poisons my relations with the Emperor.'

'Do not catalogue our *schola* with the Lord Chamberlain's beehive of eunuchs. Apodemius is as far from a friend to Eusebius as is possible. My *Magister*'s last and most sincere admonition to me on departure from Roma was to advise you wisely.'

'Then advise me!' he spat out and sent an adjutant for Bainobaudes and Hariobaudes while I waited, every minute in private anguish for Gunda.

How long would that *medicus* Ludovicus wait for me?

The tribunes arrived. I found it hard to look Bainobaudes in the eye. Hariobaudes grimaced with displeasure at discovering me in privileged consultation with his Caesar.

'Now, *Agens*, tell us everything you know.'

'What map do you have, Caesar?'

Julian and his two most trusted 'barbarian' tribunes watched as I bent over his *itinerarium pictum* of the river region stretching from Brotomagus southwards to Mons Brisiacus. It was an elongated drawing of the fortresses, roads, and layovers running north to south along the *Cursus Publicus* skirting the Rhenus and branching off westward as far as Tres Tabernae. The army *agrimensor* had indicated the domains of the *reguli* under Chnodomarius' thrall with dotted lines leading from the river into the narrow margin of the scroll representing the eastern barbarian bank.

Gunda was lying somewhere unknown in that featureless margin. No mark stood for the sheltering copse of young oaks or the nearest hamlet where she waited for my rescue.

Even Julian's map was not as richly detailed as my *schola* guide. But my life had depended on its protection during many risky solo rides. Fearful of exposing and thus losing my document, I let the Caesar's serve for my purposes.

'Chnodomarius is surreptitiously repairing the ruined Roman fortress near Tribunci, here, as his forward base inside our territory. He has seven of the Alemannic kings sending reinforcements, although not all have agreed to ride in person behind his standard. Only Vadomarius and Gundomadus are holding fast to their treaty with us, but the pressure on them and their families is mounting by the hour.'

Julian took a deep breath and straightened up. 'Is there a way of estimating their combined forces?'

'It must not come to that, Caesar. They know the terrain here too well. They enjoy growing support from the *laeti* who've dug in their heels. You must keep these people divided among themselves by strengthening your alliance with Gundomadus and Vadomarius. Seek friendship with the northern *rex* Macrianus, who is of independent character.'

'Is that all your Alemanna can tell us of their strategy?' Hariobaudes was no more interested in pleas for peaceful tactics than Julian. His expression conveyed contempt for anything Gunda said.

After another moment's examination of the drawing, I added, 'If pushed to it, Chnodomarius will wait in force for your troops, here, about eleven miles north of Argentoratum.'

I had impressed the Caesar at least. He looked more like an eager student than a blustering commander. 'Why there?'

'According to Gundomadus' daughter, it offers Chnodomarius the landscape for a trap. He will hide part of his army in thick reeds surrounding an old watercourse built north of the road, somewhere around an aqueduct, here. He will also anchor boats close by, perhaps behind this bend in the river, in case of a retreat with his *comitatus* to the old fortress in Tribunci.'

'It is an opportunity not to be missed, Caesar,' Bainobaudes said. Though the Cornutus tribune had re-secured his commission, he stood there covered in blood and river water, still hungry for glory.

'It's a trap that could backfire on our troops,' I warned. 'Our men are hungry and reduced in numbers. Gunda overheard Serapio briefing his *optimates*. Chnodomarius has a core of nine thousand at least, a minimum levy of another four thousand, and allies of perhaps two thousand from parts far beyond our exploration. There is a slim chance our troop numbers would match theirs, but the danger is that thousands more Alemanni have answered his call. They could overwhelm us.'

Julian was deaf to common sense. He gave Hariobaudes a broad smile. 'We may never again have them all gathered in one place. How much easier to vanquish the Alemanni horde in one encounter than to endure years on end of this harassment and sabotage.'

Happily, Hariobaudes could not stomach his role as chief adviser of Alemanni thinking being so easily usurped by a wild and absent girl.

'I see a trap already, without leaving this tent, Caesar. Why should we believe anything this female told him? *Agens*, confess. Haven't you known her to lie and dissemble before?'

And now Hariobaudes had me. The *tribunus vacans* had been at my side when I discovered Gunda had fled the camp without warning.

'You know I have. But her only motivation at all times has been to support her father. And Gundomadus has not failed the Empire yet.'

'So you believe this woman?' Julian's eyes flashed with the pleasure of a strategic debate.

'Yes, Caesar. I repeat, this "Gigas" seeks to engage you in battle here.' I pointed again to the unmarked spot on his map, 'drawing up his forces some eleven miles north of Argentoratum.'

I braved out Hariobaudes' sniff of disbelief.

'And I believe he will plant troops, hidden by the marshy thickets overgrown with reeds, here, behind an elevated watercourse.'

Hariobaudes stood back, hand on the hilt of his sword and chuckled. He gave Bainobaudes a conspiratorial glance.

'It is so easy for the *agentes* to listen in corridors, read our correspondence, and lurk behind pillars. But do they ever suffer the consequences when their counsel proves wrong? Do they not then hang apart, aloof, above judgment and safe from harm—legal or military?'

Bainobaudes was torn between us. He said nothing.

'Tribune Hariobaudes, Roman law protects our *schola* in order that we may see Roman law carried out and thereby protects the Empire from its flaws and fools.'

'How convenient,' Hariobaudes said with a sneer. 'But, Caesar, will you ask this informant to stake his life on his Alemanna's information? Because you're asking your troops to stake theirs.'

Could I trust Gunda? I closed my eyes and drew courage from the memory of our weeks of companionship culminating in so much passion.

Then I opened my eyes and saw all the resolve and tradition of Roman power ranked in front of me. I remembered Gunda's assassination attempt on Constantius to fortify her father's tottering reputation. I remembered her strange evasion in the forest and her sullen resentments of her brother's detention. And most of all, I resented her deception about her brutal husband, the proud Serapio.

Had she lied to me yet again? Had she conjured up Chnodomarius' watery trap only to set one for me even more devious? In her agony, had Gunda revenged herself on all Romans by planting false information on me?

Despite his distrust of my *schola*, Julian had seen me act in the cause of unprejudiced truth. He had so few around him who did not resent him, laugh at him, or plot against him. We shared a love of ancient Roma, its books and its gods, but I had lost his friendship when I emptied that basin at his feet.

Julian wanted to trust me but Hariobaudes had cast fatal doubts.

—THE DEADLY CAESAR—

'We shall test you, *Agens* Numidianus,' he said after a considered pause. 'If your information is correct, then it demonstrates some worth to your murderous service. If your information proves false, then my condemnation of your *schola* is justified.'

I fought back a dart of panic. Had Gunda loved me enough to tell me the entire truth—or in the end, did she love her people more? I already knew I was staking my own career on the word of a brave and beautiful, passionate and independent woman.

Now things had turned far worse. Julian had placed the standing of all my colleagues, my *Magister* Apodemius, and the future of our service in the balance.

I made to leave. Gunda needed that surgeon.

'Where are you going?' Julian signaled a guard to block my exit from the tent.

'Excuse me, Caesar. I must attend to the Alemanna. She may die from her wounds. It is an emergency.'

'The only emergency you heed is my call to march. Your information will be put to the test and you will not escape the result. You will not leave my staff from this minute on. You will stay to watch events unfold as you promise,' said Julian.

'I must beg your leave, Caesar, with my vow to return.'

'Not yet. Tribunes, inform General Severus we march as one army tomorrow. Alert the rest of the staff. Numidianus, you will repeat your intelligence to them. We face Chnodomarius and his so-called army at the spot you have designated.'

The two tribunes left me facing Julian. 'Surely there are scouts and others you wish to consult, Caesar?'

'I consult only the gods. You will remain in camp—under guard—Numidianus. If your information proves unreliable, you must be on hand to pay the penalty—for treason.'

He turned to his *adiutor*. 'Conduct this *agens* to my officers. Who knows what other military secrets he may recall now that he stops ricocheting from camp to camp?'

I reeled. I was no longer so much Julian's trusted informer as his prisoner. Before I could protest, an army messenger burst in on us.

'What is it at this late hour?' Julian barked. 'It's time for my sleep and private study.'

'Caesar, Gundomadus, *Rex* of the Brisigavi, holder of the Agri Decumantes, has been murdered.'

It was everything Gunda had feared. Constantius' ally had failed to impose peace on his people. Now he had died for his loyalty to Roma and his faith in the Empire's word.

'What shocks you, Numidianus?' Julian smiled at me. 'This is excellent news.'

I mourned already with Gunda and wondered if the terrible loss had reached her ears. If it had, could she comprehend through her agony? She was in greater danger now, if possible, than even she realized, lying and fighting for her life in some hostile peasant's hut.

Julian cared nothing for my distress. He stripped off his detested outer garments to wrap himself in that worn *susurna* for his vigil of study and meditation.

'You do not seem surprised, Caesar.'

'I am not. Our books tell us how Hercules escaped from the Styx through Minerva's interposition. The tokens of Heaven's good will toward me have been there from the first; when Constantius sent me out of Italy in the dead of winter, the sunshine was so cheerful my paltry escort called the November weather "spring-like" . . .'

While Gunda bled, Julian kept me a captive listening to his self-absorbed reminiscences '. . . And passing through a Gallic town, a crown of branches such as the folk hang from pillars, dropped loose and landed upon my head, fitting me just like a crown.'

His opportunistic hubris was an offense against Roma's pagan deities. His policy toward Gunda's people was an obscene caricature of ancient conquests and laurel-strewn Triumphs from history texts. This was a mockery of the Altar of Victory he claimed to worship.

I choked out the words, hiding none of my resentment. 'And you view the murder of your ally Gundomadus as a sign from the gods?'

'Of course.'

'It dashes any chance for peace. It shreds any hope of using a cooperative Alemannic king as an example to civilize the others.'

'Precisely.'

—THE DEADLY CAESAR—

How was I to protect this headstrong Constantine from his own legend-filled imagination?

'I will go brief the others now, as you order, Caesar.'

'Good, Numidianus. And spend your last hours before dawn in prayer. Reflect on this—when one finds an alliance turning inconvenient, how convenient when that alliance shatters. You see, the gods do listen to our prayers. At least, they listen to mine.'

₽₽₽

The Caesar Julian's sea of tents stretched to the east, where a livid orange streak sharp as a lance pierced the gray sky. Black and featureless silhouettes of eagles and *dracones* tilted and flapped overhead against the pinkening sky.

Frustrated and tired, I doused off in a cool basin of water and forced stale bread down a sour stomach devoid of appetite. The air was still fresh but the reddening dawn promised a scorching September day. Beyond the outer palisade and trench marking out the encampment, the fields stood shorn of their last crisp husks. Distant forests were turning from yellowish green into crackling gold.

Our *cornicenes* blew hard over the camp. Julian's army was awake. Like a single soul with only one thought of obedience, it mustered into marching formation.

On the jutting hill behind the dismantling camp, the ancient bulwark of Tres Tabernae loomed overhead, ramparts restored, rubble cleared, and solid new stonework welcoming the morning glare. Julian had closed the barbarians' last entry gate into Gallia and re-settled other garrisons along the frontier line to the north and south. He had also done all in his power to supply them with provisions, despite Barbatio's losses.

Now he signaled his men to turn their backs on their summer's labors. At the trumpeters' next blare, we marched off at a measured pace into the sun.

All weapons—lances, darts, swords, and axes—traveled sheathed or fastened in their holdings along with shields, daggers, bows and arrows. But every fighter was on alert. I understood the wary mood but, despite the disastrous raid on Barbatio's retreating convoy, I did not expect harassment on this journey. Gunda had said the enemy was gathering at the Rhenus twenty-one miles away.

I had to believe her.

I'd slept scarcely fifteen minutes while waiting under guard before the march. Every hour's passing was excruciating. What was happening to Gunda across the river? I'd sent messengers through the legions to locate the medical orderly who had offered to help—to no avail. If the *capsarius* Ludovicus had heard such a summons, he must have changed his mind. I'd made every excuse to escape detention to search for his medical unit myself but failed.

I had no choice but to travel under the 'protection' of Julian's praetorians. To the men who rode on either side, I was the Caesar's trusted 'adviser' who had survived the famous debacle at Mursa and had delivered the Alemanni battle plan in advance.

But the tribunes Hariobaudes and Bainobaudes knew better. I was Julian's prisoner, no less than the envoys Gibuld and Makrian shackled to a wall back at Tres Tabernae. My fate hung hostage to the truth of my report. If Gunda's information were false—if the Alemanni were not where she predicted and if the hidden units expected next to the watercourse were lying in wait elsewhere, Julian's guards would not hesitate to carry out his preordained punishment. Retribution on the rest of the *agentes in rebus* would follow in due course if ever Julian grew powerful enough to exact it.

My failure to serve Julian, rather than Constantius, was all the excuse the Caesar needed to begin his revenge for Apodemius' action against his half-brother.

For a time I rode squeezed between tight-lipped, hardened fighters, a far cry from the ragged, hapless 'escort' Constantius had provided his scholar cousin marching into a ravage Gallia two years before. Julian had recruited tirelessly for his legions and reconstituted the *limitanei* regiments that had dissolved during the province's years of anarchy. From where I trotted along, I took a closer look at the men he'd chosen for his escort cavalry—two hundred Scholares, half the number of *palatini* that Constantius would enjoy, but with a fierce combat record nonetheless.

—THE DEADLY CAESAR—

For a while, Julian asked me to ride at his side, and regaled me with his recurring dreams and various omens of his greatness. This morning, the 'chattering mole' was in his element, the very portrait of the armored Alexander he so idolized—the flea-bitten *susurna* discarded and the philosopher's fuzz freshly shaved. His *draconarius* rode behind him, supporting the long lance fixed at the top with a purple silk dragon. The windsock streamed in the wind with a sinister hissing noise like a snake shedding its skin.

Praetorian Prefect Florentius rode at the Caesar's side for more than an hour. The two men conversed in a confidential manner I found troubling. Given their simmering differences over governance, taxation, and other policy matters, it seemed curious that Julian would favor Florentius, of all men, in the business of warfare.

I glanced back at the endless column. Behind the officers marched Julian's enthusiastic thousands, many Gallo-Romans but a large proportion of them Germanic by blood—especially Alemannic. I could see the first many miles of it. It stretched at least yet another five out of sight.

No matter their bloodlines, the tedium and hunger of this hot, disrupted, disorganized summer had welded the men's impatience and frustration into one single weapon aiming straight at their barbarian cousins this morning.

Just behind us, the *auxilia* proudly marched. Bainobaudes rode at the head of his tramping Cornuti with the formidable Bracchiati right on their heels. I'd seen these *auxilia palatina* exercise under the command of the doomed General Silvanus. I'd heard their terrifying *barritus*, practiced that day in celebration of payday as the *donativa* was handed from the treasury box to thousands of eager palms. This morning they led the other *auxilia*—the Reges, the Celtae and the Batavi.

The legions—the Moesiaci, the Pannoniciani, the Primani, the Ioviani, and the Herculiani—kept in file underneath their *dracones*. They were, to a man, straining ahead this morning like racing horses with the bit in their mouths, held back only by the trainers' cage. They were eager to abandon their frustrating weeks of harvesting and construction for honest fighting.

The men on foot made good time on the east-west road. Given Barbatio had abandoned dead soldiers, ravaged supplies, and captured camp followers to Alemanni ferocity, the march was primed to repel any ambush; the infantry marched in the middle of the train, flanked on both sides by the protective columns of the mounted Scutarii archers on one side, and the heavy cavalry—the helmeted, masked and armored *cataphractarii* and *clibinarii*—on the other.

These last, the so-called 'oven men,' would be broiling under their airless articulated armor in this morning's intense heat.

Yet no man faltered.

Julian had at least thirteen thousand fighters attached to him by my count, but judging by the river of smartly moving warriors reaching to the western horizon, there might be even more. There were two thousand alone marching at the rear of Julian's infantrymen under the ponderous command of General Severus.

My mount was not the finest horseflesh available but *agentes* don't engage in combat. My survival would not depend on the fearless wheeling and charging of my steed. Knowing that even the cheerful Tonantius couldn't favor me on a morning like this, I'd settled for second-rate transportation.

'Are we going to fight, *Agens*, fight at last? Perhaps the Caesar's victory will bring my family back across the river?' The stable boy lisped through his gap-toothed grin when he saw me among the crush of men ready to saddle up.

'You're not going to fight at all, child,' I said. 'You're going to follow the orders of your *stabulensis* and stay well clear of danger.'

I had patted his bony shoulder with a pang of longing for Leo. Thank the gods it was not my precious boy, the heir to all Manlius fortunes, who was skipping between flying hooves and swinging harnesses to the curt barks of his officer.

I was riding many miles ahead of Tonantius, rumbling behind in a humble wagon as part of the army's vast baggage train. If the army's coming engagement succeeded, Julian might bargain for the boy's parents and the other Roman prisoners on the far side of the river. But my thoughts stayed with Gunda as I had last seen her. Her right arm lying limp on a bed of wildflowers in the oak shade was my private nightmare.

Florentius' glances of displeasure grew irksome to me. I trotted ahead to join the vanguard and engineers. This group was

—THE DEADLY CAESAR—

behind the scouts and skirmishers, but well ahead of the Caesar and escort riders, that parade of stiff-necked *legati* and *tribuni*, followed by his resolute legions and *auxilia*.

We were one hour short of midday and had traveled twenty-one miles, with only a brief stop at Brotomagus before turning south to continue upriver. We crested a rise and halted. The Rhenus' cool surface taunted our thirsty, tired men. They gazed down at it, sinuous as a sluggish snake, its murky waters at their lowest ebb yet.

An alert sounded. Our eyes followed the gestures of scouts a hundred feet ahead. A dark mass filled the eastern horizon, shifting north and south across the Rhenus. A sinister, seething, fluid body—chthonic and primeval—eclipsed the hills beyond our border. Thousands upon thousands of men and horses faced us with the sun slightly behind them, leaving all details and individual features in shadow.

The new Alemannic army stood facing us.

Chapter 20, Deadly Odds

—September, 357 AD, near Argentoratum—

Horns signaled the troops to fall into assembly formation so that Julian could better address them. They fanned out from the road, hundreds by hundreds, thousands by thousands, trudging across the crisp brown fields.

It was hotter than Hades. I dismounted, found nothing left to quench my thirst, and searched the thousands of helmeted heads and waving standards for a sign of Bainobaudes—or any other familiar face—among the officers surrounding the Caesar.

Even the taciturn docility of General Severus would have been of some comfort to me then, but the elderly man was still guiding his own troops forward from the very rear.

We stood on the verge of a great battle, but as far as Hariobaudes was concerned, we were poised on the edge of a judgment as to whom Julian should trust in his war against the *Germani*—the malodorous *agens* parroting the daughter of a fallen ally? Or the Empire's Alemanno-Roman adviser *primus*?

The horns summoned back the vanguard of scouts and skirmishers. This gave time Julian to ready himself, but as I drew closer, I detected no nerves whatsoever. He smiled with an unnatural poise.

The new formation was complete at last. The horns signaled for silence. At the point past which Julian's words could no longer reach the ears of his men, officers positioned across the broad slopes holding his sweating troops would relay his message. With a studied casualness, Julian faced his troops from the height of the impromptu podium of a baggage wagon.

The Caesar found his voice. 'A worry for maintaining our common safety drives me to beg you, my fellow soldiers, to trust in our courage. But we should choose caution over haste if we want to stand fast and repel what's coming.'

How he differed in stance and phrasing—in every respect—from the stiff-necked posture and florid Eastern rhetoric of his cousin! He glanced ever so slightly at Prefect Florentius standing twenty feet away. Then he continued:

'It's normal that young men should be eager and bold. But in the face of danger, they should be able to hold back. Be circumspect.'

The front ranks shifted in their boots, squinting up into the pounding glare of the sun passing its zenith. That scrawny, downy, pimply, round-shouldered, stammering youth laden down with his bag of borrowed books back in Mediolanum stood transformed above our heads.

'Let me therefore tell you what I think and you men tell me whether you agree and whether your justified anger can hold.'

Ah, I began to perceive what was happening. The words 'justified anger' gave Julian away. Full to the brim with his studies, he was employing the advice of ancient commanders to rouse troops on the eve of battle by engorging their hatred, indignation, and anger at the enemy beyond.

'You can see, men, the day is just past noon. We're exhausted by the march. There are steeper, blinder paths ahead; in a few hours, night will be relieved by no stars . . .'

This theatre of Julian's imagination lacked only the scenery, the toe marks on stage, and the *deus ex machina*.

'. . . when the enemy's swarms rush upon us, refreshed as they will be with rest and food and drink? What resistance can we offer with limbs weak from hunger, thirst, and marching? Therefore, since even the most difficult situations have often been surmounted by wise timing and careful planning, heaven-sent remedies will restore a situation which threatens ruin.'

And the drama took its course with less prompting now, because just as Julian had expected, his proposal to build a rampart, palisades, and trench around a camp were drowned in the racket of spears and lances rattling and slamming against impatient shields and knees.

—THE DEADLY CAESAR—

'... let us advance our triumphant eagles and victorious standards at dawn tomorrow.'

And if the shouts from the Petulantes ranked in the foreground—that they placed their trust in God in Heaven and in their own skill and in Julian's valor—if their clamor wasn't enough to complete this dramatic performance, none other than Prefect Florentius stepped forward as the Caesar's supporting player.

'It is risky, Caesar, but why not fight while the savages stand before us massed together?' the Prefect shouted. He pointed at the sluggish, formless mass of barbarians crowding the horizon. More of them were arriving every minute in a dark straggling line like an animal's tail laid across the eddying waters of the Rhenus.

'If we allow the enemy to scatter, Caesar, how can we survive the resentment of your soldiers whose hot tempers would be rightly inflamed to see victory wrested right out of their hands?'

The Prefect was word perfect. What brave Roman soldier could resist such flattery—to hear he had a hot temper that would be justifiably aroused if some inevitable prize were snatched away?

A standard bearer climbed up on the shoulders of a comrade and shouted, 'Forward, lucky Caesar, wherever your star leads us! You will see what your soldiers can accomplish under the command of such a warlike general—'

Cheers drowned out the rest of his rousing outburst. It was all too neat and orchestrated for my taste. I'd read the same histories of great campaigners as Julian. This 'spontaneous' call to attack was a classic—right down to the last lucky star.

Julian did not allow himself a satisfied smile. He braced his shoulders to take up this heavy burden placed on him by the Fates. He extended his arm and passed it over the heads of his excited men, signaling the advance to face the Alemanni, no matter the blistering heat or the late hour.

There was the deafening clatter, then thunderous pounding as thousands of men remounted, rearmed, and resumed march formation.

No one hesitated.

No one hung back.

No one consulted General Severus.

The line of authority reaching back to Mediolanum, for all intents and purposes, had just snapped. Julian had cast aside at last all semblance of cooperation with the Emperor.

I vaulted back into my saddle only after scrutinizing Florentius' expression as he resumed the lead in Julian's immediate party. He had longstanding orders from Constantius and defiant new instructions from Julian. The Caesar had marked him out today for this test of submission.

I lost sight of Florentius as my horse faltered and fell back into the embrace of the bristling Scutarii, favoring their horses' hooves on the soft verge of earth while Primani boots marched on the paving stones of the *Cursus*.

Not much later, we saw the determined movements of the Alemanni stretching out their lines inside the left bank. And they could see us with our standards and armor glinting in the brunt of the afternoon sun. Julian's senior adjutant signaled that I ride forward to secure myself inside the Caesar's body of guards.

'The *Germani* have been amassing over three days,' Julian told me. 'Our scouts say more are still approaching the river. Is that the watercourse, over there?'

'Yes, Caesar.'

Half a mile from where we had halted an aqueduct missing two of its arches spilled water onto the rolling slope beneath. Just above and to the left of the head of our column stood the promised forest. Its edges disappeared into a sunken landscape blanketed with thick reeds. I peered hard at the overgrowth for some glint of metal, hint of movement, the slightest clink or muffled command betraying men lying in wait. I saw nothing. I heard nothing.

There was no trap.

Gunda had lied to me.

Hariobaudes advised Julian to concentrate his strength in the open pastureland where our right wing would be exposed to the most ferocious charge.

'Then we'll position General Severus and his men over there,' Julian ordered, pointing directly at the forested slope. They would put old Severus and his troops in front of the motionless reeds, farthest to the left. With that, I knew the Caesar no longer expected any trap of hidden archers or crouching savages. Not if Severus was the man sent to field Gunda's 'ambush.'

Our army began to assume its battle formation. Hundreds of yards from us, the *Germani* horde circled, twisted, and turned, all the time in loud debate. At their rear, they were still absorbing thousands more in manpower, noisy stragglers and under-armed mercenaries from afar. Battle had not begun, yet the cacophony from their side was daunting as their bloodlust rose.

Despite my humiliation over the ambush in the reeds, I had to stay with the Caesar's guard force as ordered. I wanted nothing more than to ride away—to save Gunda and file my last report to the Emperor. There was nothing I could do after this to save Apodemius, Ahenobarbus, Cassius, Rufus, and all the *agentes in rebus* from the *schola*'s coming disgrace. Those great weakeners of all men—love and desire—had thrust me into the arms of a barbarian woman. My grandfather Manlius had loved a 'Gallic barbarian noblewoman' and flourished. Gunda had betrayed me. With sick despair, I knew I would believe her all over again.

A behemoth of a man, crisscrossing the front ranks of the Alemanni, caught my attention. He dominated their scrambling and jostling like a formidable god.

This must be 'Gigas'.

All the denigrations Gunda had uttered against this giant seemed vain and envious today. He rode a pale gray stallion as heavily armed as its rider encased in a gold-plated helmet topped by a flame-colored plume. It was impossible to read the chieftain's mood or intention—his features were obscured by an astonishing mask such as our own *cataphractarii* wore—but his dazzled with gold plate, not iron, in the merciless sun.

He reined in his magnificent steed at the edge of a ravine and waited for fellow Alemanni leaders in Roman-style armor to join him. I spotted young Serapio. Who could miss a young man of his energy and good looks? I did not know the others. None of us did. Hortar, Suomar, Urius, Ursicinus, Westralp and all the members of their *comitati*—these were mere names to us, faceless men lurking high in the hills of Germania abandoned by Roma over a hundred years ago.

Hidden, that is, until today.

These bejeweled fighters occupied our old garrisons, created new boundaries, and bartered power between themselves. Now here they were, no longer faceless. They were united against us for the first time in imperial history.

Hundreds of wary Roman faces glanced across the long expanse of open land. More Alemanni swelled the rearmost ranks of their brothers. Who could have numbered the tips of long bows moving into position beyond our view? We could safely assume they included bold young *armati* sent from the Agri Decumantes by Gunda's uncle, the reluctant Vadomarius.

Chnodomarius' best warriors would come from the *reguli*, those ring-givers who organized war bands notorious for acting like madmen in combat, using double-handed swords and fighting with their shields tied to their backs. They were mixing right in with mounted fighters. The only comfort to be found in this rippling ocean of men sweeping so close to our position was that they had fewer horsemen than our side and foot soldiers with little to no armor.

Only the most important Alemannus could keep a warhorse. And even if he did, the thick forests covering his home territory offered scant space for large cavalry exercises.

But those without armor could move all the more quickly. And floating above their heads were the standards of at least ten noblemen per chieftain.

Thousands of their infantry looked uncertain of their place. Of ragged quality, these would be temporary untrained levies, ignorant of formation maneuvers. Some carried long, barbed *angons*. Others brandished throwing spears and shields with rows of serried darts like our own men. But some had only shorter throwing-spears or simple *franciscae*. I spotted some with nothing more than *seaxes*—long, pointed knives of unhardened iron.

Our men could have taken courage from the confusion and disunity driving the enemy this way and that. Only, these barbarians were so numerous, they were blotting out the sun sinking behind them.

General Severus shifted his men northwards to form the utmost left wing closest to the swampy reeds at the base of the aqueduct. Next to him, Julian sent the two *auxilia* Petulantes and Heruli of five hundred each to the leftmost edge of his own front line. In the center front were the legions each one thousand strong—the Moesiaci, the Pannoniciani, the Ioviani, and Herculiani.

On the right end of the center front flank, Bainobaudes galloped back and forth in front of his Cornuti infantrymen and next, their *auxilium* brothers of the Bracchiati, another thousand men all told.

To the farthest right, where the land lay open and even, Julian sent his crack troops designed to shock the waiting enemy—the Dalmatae bristling with javelins and the Sagittarii who specialized in harassing attacks, pursuits, and ambushes on horses prized for speed and maneuverability in front.

Just behind the Sagittarii were ranks of over one thousand of those terrifying heavy cavalry, many with their inhuman masks. The air over their fierce heads was a thicket of *conti*, long heavy lances to match their ready swords.

To the left of the cataphractarii were five hundred Gentiles, and to the right five hundred expert bowmen, some mounted, others on foot—the Scutarii archers—led by a tribune famed for his daring named Nestica, took up the far right end. They stood—bowstrings tightened, right hands clutching a fistful of arrows, ready to rain the skies with death.

Two hundred mounted escorts circled Julian who was centered behind the Ioviani and Pannoniciani. His eagle standards and imperial dracones flapped in the light breeze off the water.

At the Caesar's back stood a wall of hardened fighters—two units of the *Auxilium Celtae* of five hundred each, one thousand Primani legionaries, and on their right, the two *auxilia*, Batavi and Regii of five hundred each.

It was a formation straight out of the textbooks designed to withstand anything Chnodomarius might throw at us. Despite the fading hour, our men stood erect in trim *calcei* and gleaming helmets and carrying their brilliant, painted shields. But even as they obeyed their horns' instructions, straightened their lines, and readied their weapons, they saw the mass of barbarians writhe and expand. Their signal-bearer's impatient bid for immediate victory had faded from their minds. The Alemanni enemy was more numerous than anything they'd ever faced.

How long would the morning's bravado endure? In the past, Alemanni bands had shown themselves nothing more than cowards. Once the Romans got past their towering barricades of tree trunks blocking the *Cursus*, not one Alemannus stood fast to defend his own home against our army. They panicked and melted back into their wooden fastness. They sent timorous suppliants to sue for peace.

Today our men expected to put the ruffians of 'Gigas' to flight after the first savage engagement. But in their impetuous clamor for engagement against Chnodomarius, had our troops considered how much they faced that was new?

A year ago, Constantius' 'forceps' hedged the Alemanni in from the south. Constantius was far away in Sirmium today and Barbatio's men heading into winter quarters in the south.

In previous encounters, the Alemanni war bands had fractured and fled in all directions. Today the army of barbarian thousands only consolidated itself into a single, almost mythical beast.

Three of our mounted scouts dashed after a handful of Alemanni, some mounted and at least one on foot, who were spying on our formation from the highest point of the forested hill. Our men caught up with them. After a struggle, they seized one straggler from the riders and pulled him, screaming and struggling at the end of a rope, to report to the waiting staff surrounding Julian.

The enemy spies who'd evaded capture reached the cohort of ring givers encircling Chnodomarius. Leaning down from his gilded saddle, he listened to their report. Then he raised his towering lance and bellowed out fresh orders.

A division of his light cavalry trotted down from the heights on the northern slope at the back reach of the impassable woods. Their hooves sent up clouds of fresh dust above the heads of the thousands of infantry barbarians spreading across the horizon. They rode to the opposite end of their army and formed disciplined ranks facing our right flank.

Foreboding rose in my chest. The Caesar had underestimated this foe. The barbarian giant was responding strategy for strategy, without having read a single word of Julius

—THE DEADLY CAESAR—

Caesar. He had just repositioned some four thousand of his best warriors, on foot and horse, directly opposite our best fighters.

We all could have anticipated that the Alemanni would learn from their defeats at our hands, but a fresh shiver chilled my spine as I saw Chnodomarius re-sculpt his bands of stragglers and family clusters into *cunei*, the wedge-shaped battle units the *Germani* had favored since Marcomanni times.

My hands started shaking. I gripped the reins tighter and glanced to either side. No one noticed my tremors. But I knew what they meant and I fought down a cold convulsion to vomit. My mind had flown to the nightmare fields of Mursa. I heard myself imploring my father, the Commander Atticus Gregorius, to keep breathing, to hold on to life, as I pulled him through the gore toward the medical tents. I heard the scrape of his shield, roped tight to his mutilated hand, as we made our way by inches over the weapons and bodies of dead comrades who had followed 'Emperor' Magnentius to their deaths in the name of reform.

I closed my eyes and steadied myself.

Agentes were not soldiers. I would not be fighting today. I had been disciplined once for entering the fray. Today I would remain safe inside the escort squadron. Knowing this did me no good. Now I saw a thousand bleeding Gundas in my imagination, a thousand more bodies turning white, a thousand deaths that Julian could still avert.

Julian would say the Empire must rid Gallia of Alemannic destruction. Roma must become whole, intact again, after years of civil war and mayhem.

Yet today the Empire's unity of command, the loyalty between Emperor and Caesar that bound our governance from Hadrian's Wall to Constantinopolis, was being sundered by his overweening ambition for fame and revenge.

The enemy's formations tightened. Their seething and whirling slowed. Had Julian not yet realized Chnodomarius was no ordinary barbarian? Was he asking himself now, as the chieftain mirrored our Roman battle formation, whether this was the gods' expected response to his basin of bloody entrails?

I had not lied to the envoy Gibuld back in that copse of oaks. A Roman army would always prevail over an untrained enemy through discipline and training, superior weaponry and wise strategy.

But this enemy was no longer untrained and what he lacked in weaponry, he enjoyed in superior numbers. The great plumed warrior, survivor of so many pitched battles against Romans, must have learned hard lessons. He had enjoyed his many victories—notably that over the reigning 'Caesar' Decentius, brother of Magnentius. This brutal giant would never have gathered an army here today, were he not sure of his supremacy.

That sinuous serpent of fresh arrivals kept crossing the Rhenus to push their way into the ranks from behind. Julian's army, many of them new recruits wielding second-hand weapons rescued from the Gallic fields, realized by now that they were outnumbered. Was it possible we were about to be outmaneuvered as well?

I inhaled the stench of excited soldiers mixed with thick dust clogging the air and underfoot. I was not the only man who felt the threat of Chnodomarius' proud carriage and assured command. Oh, gods—it was hot. The horses grew jittery. Their neighing filled the air and their champrons slapped as they shook their restless heads.

The enemy numbers were still multiplying.

This was not how Constantius had envisaged a campaign waged by the combined forces of Barbatio and Julian—that pincer strategy that Apodemius had outlined on his study map—some forty thousand stout Romans battering the life out of ragtag rivalrous bands.

'What's that Swine Head doing now?' asked a praetorian riding next to me, using slang learned from our own *Germani* auxiliaries.

Chnodomarius was weaving his light-armed infantry right into the ranks of his re-positioned cavalry. They would run low and stab our horses' flanks, forcing our riders out of their saddles and into the blades of barbarians waiting beneath. To see this enormous man in his flaming plume so deftly mix Roman tactics with barbarian practice felt ominous.

Over the rumble of horses and horns, there was a cry from one of the Pentulantes on our left, an impatient call for the Caesar to give the order to attack. Julian dashed forward, trailing at least three dozen of us galloping protectively in his wake. To my horror, this caesar was so innocent of battle outside the pages of his beloved histories, he did not realize he was dragging us within reach of barbarian missiles.

'The day has come to wash away our dishonor and restore the majesty of Roma,' he shouted.

He circled with us to the rear of his formation and reminded his men of Barbatio's ignominious retreat. He urged the infantry to hold back until the right signal came and only then to attack the barbarian lines at preordained points—not so soon that we would capture only a fraction of Chnodomarius' forces, but not so late that we would face even more overwhelming force.

But were we ready? Julian shifted the right wing of cavalry to the very edge of a ditch behind which the *Germani* clusters churned.

Over on the left flank, Severus had reined in his two thousand at the edge of a ravine facing the thick reeds and the forested hill. He was waiting for Julian's orders as alertly as a man half his age but his cautious halt left our defensive end tailing off in a susceptible curve.

Julian was within seconds of giving the *cornicenes* and *tubicenes* the final order when a roar from the enemy ranks checked his hand.

Hariobaudes shouted from his saddle to Julian. 'His fighters are worried that when we Romans get the upper hand, their kings will abandon the foot soldiers to our swords. They've demanded that "Gigas" relinquish his horse.'

We strained our necks to make out what was happening across the plain. The smirks on the faces of our praetorians vanished when we saw the great flaming plume of Chnodomarius sink from view into the crush of men on foot and his ghostlike stallion led off the battlefield. Then his *reges* and their *reguli* obeyed and packs of horses were cleared off to the side—so confident were these numberless barbarians of victory over us today.

Then from both ends of our army, the long trumpets blared and the brass *cornua* tooted. Our first volleys of arrows flew from the rear of the right flank and missiles of every kind of barbarian invention plunged into our front lines. My horse staggered underneath me with the shock of the assault. I pulled him closer to Julian's escort as thousands of Alemanni came racing at our center, their hair streaming and eyes wide with murderous fire.

I tried to keep my horse in step with Julian's guard. We followed the Caesar first right, then left, and right again, tracking the mayhem clouded in dust and noise.

With a great clack of wood meeting leather, the legions braced into protective *testudi*, shields interlocked over their bent heads to absorb the coming onslaught. As one man, they fought back the Alemanni in mathematical rhythm with lethal javelin thrusts.

My trembling had vanished. The rage and roar of battle smothers a man's fear for as long as the clash of blades comes straight at him. With a scrap of linen wrapped around my mouth to keep the clogging dust from suffocating me, I leaned forward in my saddle with my sword and shield at the ready, just in case.

The cavalry to our right was already regrouping after an initial assault. We moved backward as our infantry kept close and tight, but they were losing ground, yard by hard-fought yard, to a wall of barbarians slamming their weapons into Roman shields and using their knees, thousands of them, to press against our solid defenses.

We Romans showed coordination and control—just as I had boasted to Gibuld—but to my horror, many of the barbarians were taller and hardier than our men, even Romans of barbarian stock. Discipline and resolve struggled against wild, robust turbulence as clearly as those ancient soldiers depicted on the friezes of Trajan's column back home.

Only the blood that flowed was wet and the stumps of missing hands, the axes cleaving through breastplates, and the stares of the sightless as they sank dying to their knees were horrible and real.

The nausea of Mursa returned. The months of nightmares so hard suppressed sprang back to life like demons sprouting from the reddening earth around me. I saw again the terror of a man rolling into the clotted earth to watch his own entrails spilling under the hooves of his own horse. I watched as a pike lifted up a man by his jawbone and left him swinging, helpless and dying, suspended in the air.

—THE DEADLY CAESAR—

Julian raised his left arm through the dusty swirls. His left wing, those redoubtable Petulantes, his most loyal of *auxilia* had regained dozens of yards with the Heruli close behind. Hundreds of Alemanni bodies now writhed underfoot as our men advanced in parallel with the line of the *Cursus* separating them from the forest slope.

Only Severus' wing stood fast, paralyzing our left end at the edge of the swampy reeds.

Any minute something must go wrong. Our inferior numbers could not hold out forever against wave upon wave of Chnodomarius' screaming, streaming warriors. My ears filled with bellows, screams, wails and commands, the clanging of weapons and the clunk of shields, and the whir of arrow volleys almost more sinister than the honest thud of axe on bone.

A single horn—insistent, repeating, alarming—pierced the tumult. Julian's most trusted *legati* led us in a race to investigate. A hundred yards ahead to the right, part of our line had collapsed. The Alemanni were racing through our defense, leaving our agonized wounded clawing at the pounded ground.

'What is it?' Hariobaudes yelled into the fray.

A commander of our heavy cavalry had taken a slight wound and slipped over the neck of his own horse, both man and animal sinking into the chaos. His confused unit had panicked and turned like a machine of metal slamming straight into a wall of our infantry who tried in vain to hold their panicked fellows in the field.

Chnodomarius had broken the Roman line.

The Western Army faced the loss of Gallia within the hour.

Racing my horse away with the others from the massacre embroiling our right wing, I galloped toward patient old General Severus. He was finally taking matters into his own hands. His caution had rested on my briefing that danger hid within the reach of the old aqueduct and he had employed the patience and prudence of his years. Now he led his units of *auxilia*, their weapons poised and shields to the fore, pace by pace, in a stealthy, disciplined wall of shields descending into the treacherous wet terrain.

The soldiers were up to their calves in muck. If nothing interfered, Severus could bring his forces around the forested slope and circle on the barbarians from the rear. But first they had to clear the empty reeds or find themselves stuck and helpless.

Then the reeds began to quiver and shimmer in the afternoon's stubborn rays. My heart soared as if an invisible anvil had fallen off my chest. From the murky thickness, thousands of crouching Alemanni savages slithered out up from the aqueduct's mud like reptiles from a swamp and retreated from our advancing wall for the safety of the wooded slope. They had not been sitting or crouching as we imagined, but lying full flat on their stomachs, heads and shoulders sunk into the mud—invisible even to the birds passing overhead.

They had hoped to catch us unprepared, but they could do nothing against Severus' indomitable troops more than ready for their assault.

The general gave a second signal. His flank advanced faster, flushing the choking enemy away from the forest and toward the bloody plain. The Alemanni's weapons and clothing were soaked, made clumsy by hours caked in the drying slime. Ever steady, Severus' forced mowed the fleeing barbarians like so many sheaves of wheat in the afternoon sun, leaving a harvest of moaning, twitching bodies.

From the catastrophe of the right wing, Julian lifted himself out of his saddle to survey what had befallen his lagging left wing. He saw a sturdy block of Roman troops descending on the unsuspecting *Germani*'s right rear with Severus leading the way.

Gunda had not lied. Old Severus had believed me, even if Hariobaudes and the others did not. Patient Severus had sprung the trap.

In the midst of all that carnage and wailing, I exulted. Gunda had been true to me, to her father, and to his ally, the Empire. Even if our cavalry had broken and fled over a single commander's tumble and even if the battle for Argentoratum had just been lost, the *agentes* were vindicated.

I glanced through the mayhem to witness Julian's wild expression as he saw the swamp disgorge its mud-covered cohort. I saw trust and reputation restored in his eyes.

I rode back towards the imperial escort with pride and relief for the *schola* surging in my breast.

—THE DEADLY CAESAR—

But would I survive today to share it with the woman who had kept her honor and her word?

Would she?

Chapter 21, More Than a King

—Argentoratum, Late Afternoon—

Dust-blown and red-faced, the Caesar had not recovered yet from our shocking setback on the right flank. His prized heavy cavalry had scattered, turning their mounts to flee the barbarians' advance. Their commander had disappeared underfoot, one hand clutching in vain at the passing boot of an enemy swordsman before it was slashed off at the wrist, fingers still closing over the churned-up earth.

Before any guard or fellow officer could rein him in, Julian raced with shoulders rounded over his pommels toward the slaughterers of his men. We followed on his heels at a desperate clip, hearing his thin voice screeching itself hoarse as he led his guard party straight into the fray. He yelled at his panicked horsemen that they would have to kill him first before he would let them flee any farther. But it was a futile threat to make to any frozen metal mask and mail-covered horse racing in the wrong direction past him.

Was Julian not as daring as the legendary Alexander facing Darius? Was he not as determined as Sulla, Roma's forefather, standing his ground alone against the forces of Archelaus, the leading general of King Mithridates?

Julian's fiery expression burned through gusts of hot, swirling dust. His was the bravado of inexperience, not bravery. Pride of such imperial proportions would not permit Roma's 'invincibles' to fail *Flavius Claudius Julianus*. As his cavalry struggled to recover their defensive formation, even as the relentless Alemanni moved harder and harder in on them, I grieved where the Caesar's imagination had led us all.

Before smarting eyes blinded with grit, Julian was acting out legends. He railed at his confused riders as if the lethal missiles singing past our ears were the harmless imaginings of a lonely schoolboy curled up in the Caesarean fortress of his childhood.

The rippling purple *draco* led us directly into the womb of the fighting. Within seconds I was deep in the chaos, kicking away for my life against two towering Alemanni infantrymen. Flinging guttural obscenities at my horse's left flank only inches from my flailing boot, they lifted their lances to bring down my terrified horse and finish me off.

I had done this before. I could do this. I returned to the familiar nightmare of Mursa. I brought my *spatha* down on the attacker on my right. His left ear flew off, leaving a spurting black hole of gushing blood. I kicked my horse to twist away as the second's knife grazed his flank, giving me seconds to save us both. I plunged my sword into the man's exposed and heaving chest, leaving him dropping his knife with a curse into the tumble of fallen limbs.

Had the Caesar's threats turned the *clibinarii* back to their task? I could not see. There was something worse at hand. Instead of randomly chasing down our panicking cavalry—the natural course of barbarian fighters through history—they had regrouped. What few cavalry Chnodomarius still had wheeled around as neatly as the best-trained Sagittarii. Like veteran Romans, they made straight for our infantry center.

The legions saw them coming. They tightened their shield formations, but would they hold?

I heard a familiar, if petrifying sound cut through the pandemonium.

The tribune Bainobaudes had signaled his Cornuti to regroup. Beginning low and rumbling, their voices started rising, rising, rising as one until their war cry broke over the confused heads of the enemy like a crashing cymbal. As if hearing an unworldly melody of their own Frankish legend, the block of infantrymen gave throat to their infamous *barritus* cry and swayed forward in an eerie two-step-forward, one-step-back dance of destruction.

The Bracchiati joined in the song, advancing right behind the Cornuti in step. It was as if a regiment of implacable ghost-warriors had risen up from the ground. Unnerved by the confident music of Bainobaudes' seamless formation, the barbarians took to hurling javelins and axes at our *auxilia* in wild and wasteful fury.

There was no longer any way to know what was happening in the impenetrable storm of flying dirt and severed bodies. It was all I could do to keep my frightened mount under control behind Julian's purple *draco* and his guards' more powerful horses. The infernal creature bucked and twisted, as if he perceived even more danger than I but his terrified dance kept us safe from the aim of short German knives.

For the *Germani* seemed to inhale murderous energy in a single breath. They had not fled at our first sign of determination. They still fought like one man with many thousands of heads. Now they surged at our stalwart Primani who were braced to hold our rear position as fast as an imperial wall of stone.

No longer waiting for an order from the frenzied Julian still rallying the heavy cavalry, the commanders of the Batavi and Regii turned their *testudo* formations toward the center of the battlefield where Gallia's fate now hung in the balance.

Let the center hold, I prayed. The center must hold.

Julian knew it as well as anyone. The Primani were the last bulwark of our defense. Through hellish shrieks of pain and horror, the horns blasted for all imperial fighters to reposition and support this formidable legion of brawn and fearlessness as they advanced, like *murmillones* in the great Arena, foot by foot forward, slashing off limbs and cleaving necks like so many Roman butchers doing a day's work in the shadow of the Monte Testaccio. Only here the body parts flew not into the Tiberis, but blanketed the slippery ground with the red, white, and greenish filth of unleashed sewage.

Romans who had been winded with the weight of their weapons or knocked senseless by an Alemannus' blow to the head, fell into the muck only to rise up again, to the astonishment of their taller, bigger foes.

But even unwounded Alemanni stumbled to their deaths, simply by slipping in the gore and smothering to death under the weight of wounded comrades.

Julian pulled his guard party back to make way as our right and left flanks converged toward the hottest point of the battle, a hellhole of screaming *Germani* hacking and pounding at an impenetrable knot of Romans under overlapping shields, thrusting their blades into thighs and ribs.

Still the maddened Alemanni poured forth, drawing on some furious, inner wildness only they could tap in this abattoir. Even wounded and falling to one knee, a barbarian kept on thrusting at Roman legs and horses—whatever was exposed to his disorganized valor.

My horse's growing panic forced me, gagging on the dust, trotting to the rear of Julian's praetorian center. From there I could see past the clouds of brown mist up to our medical tents.

From under the tent flaps, three dozen *medici* watched us with an ominous calm, waiting for casualties on litters to arrive up the slope. They wore light armor under aprons stained by their gruesome duties. Inside those tents there might be hundreds of wounded by now—the luckier ones still able to crawl or stumble uphill for care.

From behind the surgeons and slaves, a column of light-armed, bareheaded men suddenly crested that low slope. Brandishing common knives and even a whip, they thundered down the hill, shouting at the top of their lungs. These were the *immunes* of our baggage convoy—neither trained nor summoned! Fools to a man, they'd seen the core of our army under the assault of thousands of Alemanni. Overcome with fury, they rushed past my horse to mount a last-gasp rescue.

A little figure trailed after them, waving a *pugio* as long as his forearm. His face contorted with concentration. His mouth with its missing tooth yelled wide as he fought to hold his footing in his headlong rush downhill after the grown men.

I galloped after him, but already the child had thrown himself into the fight. He was stabbing like a maddened sprite from the gods' own nightmares into the calves of an Alemannus aiming his giant lance at a Roman cavalry archer within reach. The barbarian had just realized he'd been slashed in the leg and was slamming his elbow down into the groom's spine.

—THE DEADLY CAESAR—

'Leo! Stop! LEO!' I yelled. The raging battle drowned me out. Even if he had heard me, he was the stable boy Tonantius, not my son.

I slammed my boots into the horse's sides. As if wakened from a tortured dream, the animal galloped straight into a second Alemannus nobleman hacking deep into the flanks of archer's horse. I kicked the man away and wheeled into the lancer, knocking the weapon from his fingers.

Tonantius was within my reach. I leaned down and swooped him up onto my horse, but not before the lancer had swung his vicious *seaxe* down into the boy's rump. Tonantius squealed. I pulled away, swinging my *spatha* in a last effort to rid us of the gigantic man leering at my waist.

His weapon fell away from the boy's body. I dashed as fast as I could , heading for the safety of the slope, my left arm pressing the dangling, white-faced boy as tight as possible against the horse to get him to an orderly.

Then I felt something give way underneath me. We sank down, my boots into the mess and my horse backwards onto his hocks. A helmet rolled under my elbow. The horse reeled over slowly onto his side . . .

※※※

I was staring up at the dusky sky. The battle sounded somewhere out of reach, but shouts closer by startled me out of a faint-headed nausea.

My helmet lay at my side. I shut my eyes to the slanting sunlight, then squinted.

'How long have I been here?' I muttered.

'Half an hour. You kept calling out for Leo.'

I looked up into the eyes of the junior *capsarius* I'd hired in vain to heal Gunda's wound.

'I'm wounded?' I felt no pain.

'You're in one piece.'

'The boy?'

'In the seventh tent.'

'What happened?'

'Someone pulled you out from under a dead horse. You got a blow to your head, we reckon.'

I rose on unsteady boots and pulled my helmet back on. There was a swelling lump over my right ear. Ludovicus steadied me and asked, 'You never showed up. Was your mission called off?'

'No. And we'll go get her as soon as that's over.'

I pointed at the startling change of scene below. The Primani's hard-pressed central position, defended against all odds not long ago, stood wide open and abandoned—nothing more than a field of corpses. The bulk of our army was still fighting, but far off, alongside the Rhenus. They must have battled steadily until they had crossed deep into the Alemanni army's initial position.

Other slaves were carrying litters of wounded Romans to the staff working behind us.

'The boy went to which tent, you said?'

'That one. Are you all right? You look dizzy.'

'I'm all right.'

I braced myself before ducking under the open flap door. No triage tent in warfare is anything but a charnel house under discerning care. I found the boy, eyes closed, half-slumped against the back wall of the seventh tent. His right hip and buttock were wrapped in bandages.

He breathed. Perhaps he slept. I didn't want to disturb him. He looked too drained to be aware of the horrors on all sides.

'Will he be all right?' I asked an orderly emptying a basin of blood. I had to shout over the racket all around us.

'That one? He'll limp if he's lucky and the wound stays clean.'

'See that he gets the best care.' I yelled my name to the orderly and asked that the boy's progress be reported back to me at the Caesar's headquarters.

I felt a hand grasp my wrist—hard.

'Numidianus?' a voice rasped.

I turned to see who held me fast. I looked down at the litter on which a soldier lay. No one attended him. The medical team had left this man to his death. They took hard decisions to save their efforts for men with lighter wounds—no matter rank or family.

—THE DEADLY CAESAR—

The soldier's insignia was that of a tribune, the emblem on his tunic, the Cornuti. But his head was gashed and his tunic lay ripped wide open to expose a festering liver in a swollen belly wound streaked with purple and yellowish green.

I knew his voice, as he had known mine.

'Bainobaudes?'

A scrap of loose linen lay over the throbbing skull, more out of decency than anything else. What was left of his eyes from a savage slash deep into his brow would not focus on me or anything else, ever again. It was a wonder he had survived as far as the tent.

'Numidianus, that is you?'

'Yes?'

'Are the surgeons coming soon?'

'They're ... very busy.'

'Have we lost?'

'No, the tide has turned in our favor.'

He wheezed in agony. 'Am I going to die?'

I squeezed his right hand in answer with both of mine, hard and firm. He knew it was a wordless farewell.

'You will tell my family?'

'Anything, Tribune. Speak.'

'I will be buried with my sword—' he hissed in pain, 'Hercules—!'

His sword lay lost out in the field somewhere. An orderly had detached its empty, fur-lined scabbard from his belt ring and laid it at his feet.

'Numidianus,' he whispered. 'Take my buckle and ring to Agrippina. Tell Clothild and her mother I died reinstated ... in full command.'

'Yes, yes.'

'I rode *facing* the enemy ... leading five hundred men in *barritus*—?'

'I will tell them.'

I yelled for water. No one came. The medics labored with their scalpels and needles on men with a hope of life. The stink of blood and bowels could have felled a Persian elephant. I grabbed a pitcher from a young slave squeezing past.

Bainobaudes swallowed little. His mouth was full of blood that spattered me.

'Don't let that bastard Barbatio slander me. My family keeps my funeral savings.'

'No one casts a slur on your service. Cella will back me up.'

'Don't trust . . . Promise . . . ?'

The great Franco-Roman warrior was gone. The island slaughterer had met his inevitable end. I finished off the entire pitcher of water and went outside the tent.

Then I vomited up all the water along with the stench of what I'd seen.

Horses ran free everywhere now, panting and tired but unburdened at last. I commandeered a magnificent steed that had lost its Sagittarian. Feeling lighter and clearer, I rode down the slope to report to Prefect Florentius and the imperial guard.

Julian and his protectors had halted a few hundred feet from the riverbank. He signaled his troops, poised to plunge after the Alemanni, to hold back. His tribunes and other officers relayed the Caesar's warning down a line of Roman soldiers forming up and down the right bank.

Thirty feet ahead, thousands of frantic Alemanni stumbled and pushed their way to the river. Sinking and sliding down the muddy bank, they shoved each other aside in desperation to enter the current.

The river flowed red with fresh blood. Some of the *Germani* still had shields to float on. Some were kicking, paddling, or drifting, nearly senseless, in a diagonal direction toward the opposite bank.

But others were helpless and hanging on to stronger swimmers with no shields for floats. They were sinking together under eddies rippling with the weight of their armor and weapons.

The river was clogging up with drowning *Germani* as surely as it had jammed with the logs for Barbatio's bridge. The mass of torn flesh and dulled weapons started collecting into a half-submerged island of death. Our soldiers would have been fools to give chase into that.

Instead, they sent up a hail of iron-tipped arrows, twirling *franciscae*, and weighted darts to pin down the fleeing Alemanni.

—THE DEADLY CAESAR—

Some of our men had lost their own weapons and were plunging Alemanni javelins into retreating enemy backs.

The horns signaled our army to regroup in the open field. But the field was no longer open to any passage. Julian's horse picked its way over the bodies and we traced his path, two by two. Some of the men under our hooves still breathed and fought for their last glimpse of Apollo's light. The counting would last through tomorrow, at least. The tally of Mursa had taken a week.

A *cornicen* blared a fresh signal. All eyes followed the sound to the forested slope above Severus' original position.

A squadron of horsemen had chased some Alemanni survivors to the very edge of the dark woods, but there our men halted. The setting sun's rays inflamed the color of the dying leaves, making it look like a fiery fortress no one dared enter.

'The squadron is waiting for your order, Caesar,' Florentius shouted over his shoulder.

'Where is their tribune?'

'Laipso fell today,' Hariobaudes yelled.

'Surround the trees from the north to south,' Julian ordered.

A cohort, muddy and haggard, broke off from our main body and headed toward the slope. Their *optio tribuni* picked out a path over the corpses and around medics still sifting through the barbarian dead for Roman casualties.

An urgent summons blew again. Julian waited no longer. Lifting himself in the saddle, he waved his guard to follow. Our horses stepped along the same ghastly route over piles of weapons, limbs, heads and entrails.

"We have the giant cornered. He was trying to cross the river,' the *optio* shouted over his shoulder.

Another squadron rounded the base of the slope, its leader leading by the ornate reins the magnificent pale stallion on which Chnodomarius had dashed back and forth in front of his massing army. It was an unworldly beast of mythic proportions, unscathed by the day's ordeal and dwarfing its equine escorts. It outshone them all, tossing its fantastic golden harness wrought with gems, champrons painted in colorful Germanic patterns, and a silver lance holder fitted to a leather-covered saddle thick enough to support the Colossus of Rhodes.

Its mud-crusted flanks betrayed its futile foray into the river shallows.

The stallion lifted its muzzle and, peeling back its lips, neighed a salute. His enormous owner emerged from the forest with his helmet tucked under his left arm, his armor in disarray, his trousers soaked. Up close he was jowly, unkempt, and heavy-footed. His boots were soaked through and flecked with broken reeds from an attempt to reach those hidden escape boats.

Behind him appeared the dejected hundreds of his *comitatus*, all wearing costly armor, jeweled helmets, and strutted *cinguli*. These noblemen had followed him into his last redoubt. Honor now demanded they surrender behind their supreme *rex*. There were at least three high-ranking noblemen trailing at his shoulder. One of them might be Mederichus.

I searched for Serapio—for surely Gunda's husband would be next to his uncle until the bitter end? Barbarian after barbarian stepped out of the shadow of the trees and ranked himself in a miserable phalanx around Chnodomarius.

Serapio did not appear. Gunda was free.

Julian ordered Hariobaudes, 'Accompany these guards and take the entire *comitatus* prisoner.

Hariobaudes grinned and jerked the reins of his horse to head uphill, but Julian held up a palm to add, 'Tribune, bring Chnodomarius himself to me. Leave the fetters off for now. Leave his armor on. Tell him, in his tongue, that I will hear him before my entire army before the night is out.'

'He's a barbarian—no more than that, Caesar,' Florentius muttered from his position just in front of me.

'You are wrong, *Praefecte*. I have defeated the barbarians' king today and I have defeated more than a mere king. The Empire has defeated the Alemanni people. Gallia is Roman once again.'

Julian urged his animal to return to the opposite slope behind us where the medical tents, baggage train, and his private attendants still sheltered with Eutherius, his chief chamberlain.

It was over—at least for the legionaries and auxiliaries. The officers had much to do—supervise the body count of both sides, requisition more supplies for the new camp, write reports, and counsel Julian on his next move.

The troops fell to rejoicing with what drink and food they could muster. The surveying team had moved down the rear slope. They started directing the pitching of a fresh camp near those banks of the Rhenus not clogged with corpses. The men had palisaded themselves with rows upon rows of their battered shields. Between the rising boasts and shouts of joy, I heard some of them hailing survivors and others calling the names of *contubernales* lost among the thousands now spreading out across the new encampment.

Julian acknowledged their rising cheers as he rose past their busy heads.

'*Auguste! Auguste!*' cried a voice in a thick band of Petulantes.

Quaestor Salutius, riding at Julian's side, jerked his head in alarm. Julian had heard it too and reined in hard. Lifting his right arm, he halted the imperial cortege.

'Who cried out?' he asked Salutius in a low voice.

It was too late. Other fighters had heard the acclamation and they took it up. A carousing unit of Petulantes some fifty feet away shouted the loudest. The echoes of 'Augustus! Augustus!' caught like a fire rolling through the parched September grass underfoot.

After a day in which I had seen excitement, dismay, determination, and triumph all cross the unlined features of the young Caesar, I now read a new emotion—genuine fear.

'Stop them,' he railed at Hariobaudes. 'Stop them! Find their officers! Stop up their mouths!' but this was drowned out by a group of Celtae taking up the shout.

'*Auguste! Auguste!*' They hailed him and banged their weapons against the double-headed yellow dragons on their upturned red shields. The acclamation spread across the entire camp as their pent-up shame at Barbatio's retreat and other setbacks burst forth. These men who had campaigned all summer with little to show for their patience, hunger, and labor, had just soared to heroic heights under their 'chattering mole' of a caesar.

'I do not expect nor desire to attain that honor,' Julian bleated through the roar. But we all knew that, where the command of Ursicinus and Marcellus had left these men idle and directionless, the ambitious young Constantine had restored their self-esteem as Roma's defenders.

'Stop them! Make them be quiet!' Julian begged. The tribunes sped word through the camp, silencing the most boisterous and disciplining any who argued back.

The sun finally set. The count of dead Alemanni recessed until dawn. Our Roman losses totaled a miraculous few—only two hundred and forty-three soldiers, including the tribunes Bainobaudes, Laipso, Innocentius and one other whose name I did not recognize.

Only two hundred and forty-three? It seemed that the gods had sided with Julian.

I trembled to think Mars, Bellona, and Mercury were so easily bribed by a crude army basin of animal tripe to bend the Fates against the awful odds we'd faced. The day had been won by men—not gods—by the service of furious Bainobaudes, the steadfastness of the legions to the last, and even the foolhardiness of *immunes* like little Tonantius, all fighting as Romans together.

The new Roman camp blazed with lamps and torches as orderly as if there were no mountains of flyblown barbarian flesh piled less than a thousand yards away. When the songs and snacking had settled into an exhausted lull, Julian and his senior officers mounted a platform to read out praise for reports to be relayed to Constantius. Proud tribunes read citations. Heroes of the day heard their names championed for special awards—neck torcs, armbands or *phalerae*, carved parade disks hammered from bronze, silver, or gold.

Only a single thread of foreboding dampened their general cheer. A terrible punishment hung over the heavy cavalry unit that in their panic had nearly handed a murderous victory to Chnodomarius over our thirteen thousand. They could not celebrate tonight. They'd pitched their tents and lifted off their fierce masks, shining mail, and oversized weapons, but shame and fear weighed down their spirits.

At the close of the commendations, a hush spread over the sea of waiting faces. Words like 'flogging,' and even 'decimation' traveled through the ranks. I had obtained permission from Florentius to return to the medical tents and was striding up that way now. I wanted to see how little Tonantius was faring. As I crested the slope, the *medici* listening to the distant speechifying jeered with relief mixed with scorn.

A surgeon took a swig of watered wine before returning to his horrors. 'They are to parade in women's clothes tomorrow at dawn!'

Julian had accomplished a final masterstroke. He had turned his truculent army of cynical centurions and hungry recruits into a fighting force Roma could be proud of. He could not afford to lose their love minutes after he'd earned it. So he'd punished his panicking 'oven men' with a roasting of a different kind—one no soldier would forget but that cost him not a single blooded fighter.

I imagined Constantius II at his court in Sirmium as he read the official reports of this battle. The Emperor would claim all the credit—custom and the man dictated no other outcome. And Julian knew the rules of *Imperium*. He must hand all the fruits of this day to his superior, just as Achilles had handed his trophies of war to Agamemnon.

But Constantius would see the staggering death toll of barbarians feeding the acclaim of his beloved cousin with private discomfort.

I watched the scene far down the slope with the estranged objectivity of the slave boy I once was, sneaking off for an afternoon to sit in the cheapest, highest bleachers of Flavian's amphitheater, the very roof of the civilized world.

Under the light of dozens of torches, Julian strutted far below, a tiny figure in formal costume—his imperial cloak spattered with blood and mud, his scholar's shoulders slumped with fatigue, and his thin voice answering the adoration of his assembled soldiers. The giant Chnodomarius was dragged on to the platform where the Caesar and his staff waited. The army's roar fell away.

Julian greeted the leader with respect and even admiration for his courage. Chnodomarius boomed at him back with the names of the kings who had followed him and their claims to land they'd just lost. But at a word from Hariobaudes, this great opponent abruptly remembered his defeat and dropped to his knees. The tribune prompted the hoary barbarian king into full prostration at Julian's cloak hem where he lay face down, jabbering pleas for his life in gutturals too thick to separate one word from the next.

This was the man who'd gathered a great army and waged an historic challenge to our empire.

But Gunda was right in the end. "Gigas" had collapsed into a heap of bluster and bluff, gilt and plumes. In defeat, he conducted himself like a pathetic windbag punctured by a Roman spear.

Julian turned away, visibly disgusted by his 'epic foe.' His mythical creation, his own personal Vercingetorix to Julian's Julius Caesar, sprawled deflated—a schoolboy's illusion—before the eyes of thousands of soldiers.

The weeping Alemannus was bound and led away. No one cared what fate awaited him. His legend had just died under him.

Inside the medical tent, Bainobaudes' body was gone. The bloodsoaked litter stained by his foul wounds lay stacked with all the others on an ox-drawn cart.

The last Roman casualties, some with weapons still hanging out of their flesh, waited in agony for the surgeons' attention. This was not a place I wanted to linger.

'Where is the stable boy?'

'What boy?' an orderly asked me. He lugged a bucket of *acetum*.

'The horse groom wounded in the buttock. He was lying bandaged over there, out of the way.'

'You sure you have the right tent? People get confused all the time.'

I rounded the tent, got my bearings, and returned. 'Yes, this is the right tent, number seven. You tended the fallen tribune of the Cornuti, did you not?'

'Laid him outside hours ago.'

'Where is the boy I left here? I was brought in with him myself. Has he gone?' I imagined the doughty stable boy limping back to his duties, pricked by the deep stitches holding his poor little bottom together.

'Numidianus?' It was Ludovicus again.

'Yes. The presentation is finished. The Prefect's adjutant sent for you. The Caesar wants you in the praetorian area.'

'Where is the young boy I was carrying on my back while the battle raged?'

—THE DEADLY CAESAR—

An orderly took my elbow and led me away from the wounded men grimacing through the torments of the doctor's swabs and forceps in a fight for their lives.

'Follow me, *Biarchus*.'

Covered head to toe with blood, he walked me farther up the shadowed slope where the edge of the forest faced away from the bloodshed and toward peaceful fields. The tumult and light of the new camp faded away. Some two hundred Roman bodies lay stretched out in neat files, an echo of the busy alleys where officers and their aides worked under torchlight to register units, insignia, and ranks.

The orderly lifted his torch. And there, his bare toes barely reaching the knees of the disemboweled Iovianus next to him, lay young Tonantius. His short leather trousers were stiffened to a reddish brown beneath the makeshift bandage. The boy had bled to death, unnoticed and unmourned.

Silent tears coursed my cheeks. I stroked his curls. 'Oh, Tonantius, you lost more than a tooth today,' I whispered.

I removed the boy's narrow belt and placed it rolled up inside my breast padding next to Bainobaudes' buckle and ring. The boy, too, had died facing the enemy for Roma.

I would show the humble leather strip to Leo and tell him of the bravery of this little Gallo-Roman, so eager to fight for the return of his enslaved parents and the restoration of his land.

I felt less pity for the Cornuti tribune. Seneca teaches us that the Fates ensure that no man dies a day too early.

But boys? Tonight I defied even the greatest Stoic not to grieve over the child spread out on the dry grass at my feet.

※※※

I stood before Julian and his immediate staff half an hour later.

The Caesar looked a man transformed, not only shaved, washed, and refreshed by food and drink spread out on a table nearby, but flushed with his dreams of glory realized.

I knelt as was expected by all the officers looking on.

'Congratulations, Caesar.'

'General Severus reminds me we owe you thanks, *Agens Numidianus*, for the warning of barbarians hidden in the swamp.'

'It is my duty to seek out any information of use to the Empire,' I said.

'Yes.'

For once, Julian was strangely untalkative. Had he counted so hard on my failure? Had he hoped so keenly to use my mistake to discredit our service?'

'How many were lying in the reeds, Caesar?'

'Some two thousand,' Severus grunted from his chair behind a platter of cold roasted meat. 'Well-buried under the reeds and mud like the scum they are.'

'I ask for no reward,' I said.

'I'm not offering one,' Julian replied. 'Accept my thanks. As you say, the *agentes* are there to serve.'

He might well have added 'not execute Caesars,' but his audience might have taken any reference to the late Gallus as ill-timed petulance.

'Your service has other responsibilities under law,' he said. 'You are to escort Chnodomarius with a select guard to wait on the Emperor's pleasure.'

'Yes, Caesar.'

'You were trained for this, were you not?'

'Yes, Caesar. The Castra Peregrina schools us in all legal procedures for the arrest, detention, and escort of the highest senators to the lowliest murderers.'

'There are procedures, then? Special protocols?' Julian looked uncertain.

'Yes, although none I recall applying to gigantic Alemanni in scarlet plumes.'

This brought me a few snickers from those listening and broke the tension that hung like a dark curtain between Julian and myself.

'You will also carry my full report of our victory for the Emperor.'

'I am honored beyond all expectation.'

'Well, as you are no doubt writing your own scurrilous little account, there's no reason not to deliver both versions at the same time.'

Julian got his own round of appreciative laughs. I sighed with relief. Constantines must always have the last laugh.

'May I ask one favor, Caesar?'

'What is it?' He had already turned his back to resume his celebratory chat with Pentadius, standing in full armor and unscratched glory next to Florentius.

'I request permission to retrieve the Alemanna who provided the valuable intelligence used by General Severus. The daughter of Roma's ally, Gundomadus, lies wounded across the Rhenus. She should accompany me to Roma as part of our *schola*'s final record.'

'Yes, of course, Numidianus.' Julian had finished with barbarian allies. 'She goes to Roma, if you wish. She has no future left here. No Alemannus has.'

Julian's quip drew more chortles from his officers.

'In that case, Caesar,' I concluded, 'You will not object if I ask that my escorts into the enemy's territory be the detained envoys, Gribuld and Makrian. Their mission is over, as is mine.'

Chapter 22, The Glint of a Blade

—THE RHENUS CROSSING—

Gibuld and Makrian arrived within hours for the crossing back into barbarian territory. They looked haunted, hungry, and homesick as they galloped into sight down the *Cursus*. They must have ridden for the border as if an entire legion were snapping at their heels.

They gazed across the fallen army of their Alemanni brethren. Makrian retched uncontrollably over his horse's shoulder into the earth below his saddle. Even the hardened Gibuld turned pale. The scar across his cheek twisted into a knot and he swore under his breath.

All their lives these men had warred among themselves or nipped at the fringes of Roman territory, more for sport than for political gain. Such men were used to skirmishing and raiding in a group of a hundred, no more, and suffering few losses for their loot. Today they witnessed the irrevocable cost of Chnodomarius' daring gamble.

I still suffered from the specters of Mursa. Five years ago, I'd watched a rising dawn end a nightmarish blackness of blind fighting to unveil nearly ten times this number of corpses strewn across the horizon. Today there were 'only' six thousand dead Alemanni, but Makrian was right when he cursed under his breath, 'Romans, you have destroyed our people.'

They had not only lost a generation of noblemen and kinsfolk, they had lost their bid to join the Empire. Generations ago, the Toxandrian Franks had been settled inside our borders in peace. The Alemanni stood distrusted, de-peopled, and forever barred.

'Chnodomarius led you to destruction.' I was short on patience. Gunda was waiting for me somewhere in that wilderness Makrian called home.

Gibuld scowled and took out the thick vellum signed by Constantius. Sticking his short blade into its folds, he pulled and yanked until he had cut the treaty in two.

'Keep the pieces,' I said. 'History will listen, even if Julian did not.'

'Get us out of here,' choked young Makrian. 'I cannot breathe.'

Their dead blanketed the field. Our army slaves were busy pulling bodies off pikes and unthreading them from javelins, sorting the valuables, and shoveling the bodies into flyblown trenches full of heads, limbs, and torsos cleaved in two. Only the unlucky men who'd been smothered underfoot had escaped mutilation. Their eyes stared up from fresh graves as if still watching the living at work. Nearby wagons waited to carry away the enemy's weapons, from the crudest knives of unforged iron to fantastic swords with curving narrow blades.

I assumed custody of the two shocked envoys from their fortress guards. A slave ran off to summon Ludovicus. He arrived lugging a leather *capsa* borrowed from his senior *medicus*. He unbuckled it to let me check his supplies: glass vials of tonics and acetum, needles, scissors, and scalpel, rolls of bandages, and two thick tablets of purified clay for sealing Gunda's wound.

The other *medici* were loading the seriously wounded onto supply wagons for the trip back to Tres Tabernae. The remaining casualties, washed and drugged, waited in the tents. The work of the surgeons was slowing down now, but Ludovicus had had to argue hard for release from his duties. We had to be quick.

I led our exit past the palisade of pickets and pitched shields, along new pathways from the upper slope of the medical tents near the forest lining the road down to the river's edge.

There was no need to ride north for the raft crossing— thousands of Chnodomarius' men had tried to flee across the Rhenus and failed. Their corpses dammed up the current near a bend, funneling the water into a natural waterfall at one side and leaving a shallow crossing washing around our horses' knees for most of the breadth of the mucky channel.

—THE DEADLY CAESAR—

We rode to the trampled bank opposite the blackened islands and then the copse of young oaks where I had last seen Gunda. Brown patches of dried blood matted the flattened grass.

From there it was easy to follow the tracks and runnels of the oxcarts and litters that had dragged away the dead and wounded settlers.

Broken weeds and animal droppings led us upland until the trail met an unpaved road wide enough for a wagon. From here, it would be harder to guess Gunda's route.

'The first *vicus* that way,' Gibuld said, 'was the settlement that sent the rescuers.'

My hopes soared and our pace quickened. But when we reached the miserable hamlet of sunken houses and broken fences, we saw everyone had fled farther into the interior. The wind had blown the ashes of their cooking fires hither and thither. The unlit shelters of thatch and mud stood open to any passerby.

'This place is deserted,' I said.

'No, look—' Makrian pointed down an alley strewn with broken potsherds and debris.

An old man sat on the sunken steps of his hovel, petting a mongrel. He scraped a last bit of gruel from the bottom of a clay pot and lifted his head, blinking at the padding of our hooves passing slowly from house to house.

Makrian dismounted and walked up to the edge of the first step, inches from the man's hunched back.

The Alemannus turned whitened, sightless orbs in the young envoy's direction.

'Come to kill me too, Romans?' he asked the open sky.

Makrian answered in guttural dialect. They exchanged a few sentences, the rider using kindlier tones when he saw the panicked old man clutch his emptied pot to his bony chest.

'He says that the villagers feared Julian would cross the river and recapture their Roman slaves.'

'Why did they leave him here, alone and helpless? They had carts he could ride.'

'He refused to leave his plot. He has his dog, a bag of grain, and his knife, he says. He's laid traps and nets all around here.'

'So he thinks. Nothing tripped us up. Old fool. Where are the others?'

'On their way to Serapio's fortress.'

'Serapio can't protect them now. He must be lying dead on the battlefield or he would have surrendered with his uncle.'

'These people cannot know that, *Agens*,' Gibuld said.

'Does this old man know whether Gunda, daughter of *Gundomad*, was with the families who retreated?'

Even if he could not speak fluent Latin, the old man would take note of Gundomadus' name. He turned his empty gaze in my direction and muttered in broken Latin: 'A wounded noblewoman was carried away.'

'They saved her?'

'They stopped her bleeding. I heard her cries. She had fever.'

We persisted, but of course a blind man could not have seen Gunda for himself. He could not be sure the cries were Gunda's. There had been too many wounded men and women struggling up the steep riverbank to be certain. I could only hope.

Ludovicus shook his head, discouraged by this report of her condition.

'They will have taken Gunda to Serapio's people—even against her will.' Gibuld said. 'With no father left to protect her, there is no other place for Serapio's consort.'

'You mean his widow. So we keep going to Serapio's stronghold.'

'It is too dangerous for you, *Agens*. Your commander has just killed all their finest warriors.'

'That leaves no one to fear.' A stronghold emptied of fighters posed no threat to me.

'I'd sooner face a Persian siege than an cohort of bitter widows,' Makrian said.

'How far is this stronghold?'

'One more day's ride, if the weather remains fair.'

The morning was only too fair. The cool breezes were gone. The September day had turned as hot as a *taberna*'s charcoal grill.

We four rode out of the *vicus* in two pairs, the *capsarius* at my side and the two Alemanni murmuring in dialect ahead of us. By late afternoon, I was so tired I drew on old mental tricks from my days as an eager *circitor* delivering mail between Sirmium and Mediolanum just to stay awake in the saddle.

Ludovicus rode slumped over his pommels. He had worked through the night, assisting one gruesome operation after another. I told Gibuld that, for the medic's sake, we had to rest. When we reached Gunda, his stamina would be as essential as his skills.

A strange formation of regular stones appeared in the distance—the ruins of a proper roof. I pointed at a dilapidated Roman trail, half-paved, half-rubble, leading away from our road to the south. A stream of clear water ran toward some exposed plumbing beyond.

'An ancient bathhouse,' Makrian said. 'This land used to be yours, Roman—rich villas and busy markets.'

'We'll shelter there,' I told them. The afternoon was fading. No matter how desperate my desire to reach Gunda, Ludovicus could stay upright in his saddle no longer.

The Roman ruin was a sorry sight. Its main pool area was an echoing hall of cracked mosaics, broken stumps of stone benches, and a deep elongated basin full of dead branches. A mural of dolphins gamboled across the remains of its walls. Perhaps they had warmed the nostalgic memories of Napoli or Ostia for Roman veterans settled in this dark forest. Some fool had scraped off the silvery blue paint from the dolphins' backs curving over the waves. A painted Apollo had once radiated yellow rays from the ceiling center to the octagonal walls. But with only part of the roof still intact, the rays broke off. Above our heads, we saw only the overhang of heavy trees and fading dusk.

'Shhh,' Ludovicus warned. 'I heard something.'

We waited, swords drawn, but no one appeared. We made a quick tour of the building—its dilapidated *caldarium* and *frigidarium*—modest cubicles by Roma's standards. A pair of *strigiles* attached by two chains to a small pot for body oil, all green and eaten away with rust, dangled from a ring on the wall.

There was even a separate entrance at the back. A blushing, half-naked lady wrapped in towels of *tesserae* stones marked the women's entry.

'I was sure I heard a sound,' the youth said. He was nervous. He had never left Roman territory before in his life.

'An animal,' Gibuld said. 'We'll make a fire to keep away the boars.'

I said nothing, but I feared wolves far more than big pigs. I knew what those intelligent canine hunters could do once they smelled prey. Two years ago, I had fought off a pack of them and watched in horror as they devoured my wounded horse.

We tethered our animals in a wide *gymnasium* that had resounded over a century ago with the grunts and laughs of exercising Romans. The autumn evening brought a metallic chill. Makrian lifted his face to the refreshing breeze wafting through the stony rooms and said he 'smelled' early snows for October.

We built a fire and washed down our dried food with watered wine. I left it to our Alemanni companions to bemoan the lack of beer.

I felt a quiet elation. Was it my exhaustion, the light alcohol, or an intimation that the end of this awful mission was in sight? Only one more day or even less remained until I was at Gunda's side. I would hold her in my arms and nurse her until she could travel.

We could argue later over our future together, but her father no longer needed an earthly counselor. When she had healed, I'd reassure her of a safe and happy life under the protection of the Empire.

Wrapping my *sagum* tight around my shoulders, I laid my head down on my travel sack and turned my back on the others. I left my boots on with the hidden knife ready in my cuff. I had not forgotten that my guides were barbarians, whatever the code of our shared vocation.

I cleared my mind of screams and war cries and concentrated on Gunda—her soft skin, glistening hair, and sweet smell. Her magical song drifted back to me. The memory of her voice was lulling me to sleep. I would live with her somewhere not far from Leo and Kahina on the Esquiline Hill or perhaps settle on one of the Manlius estates for which I still held trusteeship.

I made one resolution. Gunda's arrival back in Roma must begin with the court acknowledging in writing her loyalty to Constantius and her father's allegiance to the Empire... I felt Gunda's presence. She was just within reach...

—THE DEADLY CAESAR—

₽₽₽

'They've left us.'

A gentle hand nudged my shoulder. I rolled over. Our campfire had died out. Beyond the half-wall ruin of the bathhouse, gray morning had broken cold and empty.

'They left in the night,' Ludovicus said.

'I'm not surprised.' I bolted upright. 'They left our horses?'

'Yes.'

I fell back on the sack. 'I saw their expressions. They warned us in all but words. They did not want to arrive in the next village escorting two Romans. We're the enemy.'

The slender orderly sat back on his haunches and exhaled. 'I suppose we're lucky they didn't kill us while we slept.'

'We may be enemies but I am a brother envoy. Julian should not have detained them. We are the men who carry messages safely from friend to friend and foe to foe, even if our words fall on deaf ears.'

'Like priests, who listen to everyone's secrets and remain apart from the rest of society?'

'*Agentes* don't pretend to judge—or absolve.'

Ludovicus turned. 'Did you hear that? Someone's coming down the road.'

This time I heard something too. We pulled our horses out of sight behind the highest part of the undamaged wall and scuttled to the rear of the bathhouse. If these were Alemanni mercenaries from a distant territory answering Chnodomarius' call to battle too late, we must not be seen. Voices and footsteps passed down the main road but no horse hooves. We scurried down our rutted lane to spy on these passers-by.

Some two dozen men and women in Alemannic rags moved slowly through a stand of high weeds poking through the rubble of the old *Cursus*. They stumbled and supported each other as if they'd been walking all night and were close to collapse.

'They're Romans,' Ludovicus whispered. 'Fettered Romans.'

We ran to the middle of the road and hailed them back. Hearing Latin, they shuffled and stumbled back in our direction, their leader with his arm around the waist of a frail young woman, urging the stragglers behind him to keep pace.

'Please help us. We have escaped. We need sanctuary,' their leader said, panting up to me. His name was Aegidius. His face was young but his black hair was streaked with strands as iron-colored as the chains his companions dragged across the broken paving stones.

'Shelter in the old bathhouse down this path here,' I said. 'My companion is an army orderly. He can treat your wounds.'

An older woman burst into grateful sobs. She fell to her knees in the very clods of earth churned up by Gibuld's horse a few hours before. They had trudged all night without stopping for fear of recapture.

'How can we be safe there?' asked their leader. 'We must reach the river and cross the border without delay.'

I handed him my bladder of *posca*. One by one, his companions took a sip until it was empty.

'The Alemanni are defeated. They're in retreat,' I told them. 'I seek the whereabouts of the wounded daughter of their king, Gundomadus. Have you heard of her? Have you seen her among your captors?'

Aegidius said, 'If a noblewoman had been wounded before the retreat, our women might have been ordered to tend to her.'

The women shook their heads, no.

Aegidius added, 'We only managed to escape because the settlers were inundated by the sudden arrival of hundreds upon hundreds of wounded warriors. But we were lucky. We left behind many captive Romans, perhaps thousands, spread across this *pagus*.'

We lost a precious hour as Ludovicus examined the children first, cleaning their oozing eyes and washing out sores. The women were full of neglected complaints but Ludovicus begged off. 'I am not trained in female troubles,' he protested as they pressed around him. 'I can only treat fevers and close wounds.'

'We must go on,' I muttered, but seeing what comfort he brought to the mothers of these scrawny, swollen-bellied youngsters, I relented.

'I can guide you directly to the Caesar myself,' I told Aegidius, 'but you must wait for my return. First I must locate the Alemanna noblewoman.'

I did not know if they would wait for us. Ludovicus had done all he could. With sad resignation, I noticed that his medical supplies had dwindled to nearly nothing. Where rolls of useful bandages had bulged, his metal instruments poked through the bottom of the leather bag dropping like an emptied udder.

We remounted and left the prisoners resting in the shade of the bathhouse or washing in fresh water gushing from the broken plumbing.

We rode into the rising sun, following Gibuld and Makrian's fresh tracks toward Serapio's fortress. After six hours, we found shade by the roadside. Romans built comfortable layover stations along the *Cursus*, with baths, dining rooms, and soft beds for state travelers. A miserable slope-roofed shed was the barbarians' answer—a few rough planks laid across forked struts.

Our horses discovered a trickling brook, one of hundreds that slipped away from the great Rhenus like slender tendrils reaching for the endless trees. I spotted a cluster of huts where the water had been channeled to irrigate vegetables.

'I'm going over there to scrounge something to eat,' I told Ludovicus, pressing my hand on his shoulder as he staggered to his feet. 'You've worked all morning. Rest here.'

Hand on sword, I slipped toward the huts and crouched forward into the first yard, on the hunt for the most likely place to store food. The kitchen garden beckoned, but on closer inspection, had been dug up to the very last turnip frond.

'Looking for food, Roman?' cracked a voice behind me. I whipped around. A wrinkled, sunburnt matron watched me from the sunken doorway of her thatched hut.

'Yes. My companion and I can pay you for anything you have to eat or drink,' I said.

She laughed at me. 'I thought you Romans never left the cities without entire kitchens rolling behind you on heavy ox carts.'

'You're alone here?'

'My husband is buried with others beyond those fields you're thinking of robbing. I'll be buried with him soon enough.'

She jerked her head at a fenced-in pasture. Man-sized mounds studded a gentle slope. Some were covered with wildflowers, but others were still raw brown earth waiting for their first snow cover.

'My daughter and son are still alive. We live in peace, Roman. This is our land.'

She offered me a bowlful of stew thick with small bones and thin strips of meat buried under fibrous yellow squash. I ate half and carried the rest back to Ludovicus. He was deep asleep, leaning against the back planks of the shelter. The noises of the forest must have given him a restless night in the bathhouse. I left the bowl at his side.

From her doorway, the woman watched me with a wary expression, still clutching the small deer horn knife she had used to hack off a piece of coarse bread to go with her tasteless mush.

'I must pay you for your kindness,' I said, returning to her steps. Before I could pick out a few bronze *nummi*, she shook her head.

'I have no use for Roman coins,' she said. 'There is no market here for trading. I need useful things for barter—fish hooks, horse tackle, farm tools, or jewelry.'

Her Latin was good enough for business matters. I nodded and returned to my horse, determined to find some small thing of value to her.

Standing full in the beating sun, I felt a sudden chill run down my bones. I returned to the woman, my folded army *susurna* in my arms.

'It is a good, thick blanket,' she said, suspicion creasing her brow. 'Far too good for a bowl of stew and a hunk of bread.'

'Yes, I know. I offer it in exchange for that knife you hold.'

'This?' she said, holding out the sharp blade so it glinted in the sunlight. 'You have a knife better than this *Germani* thing already swinging off your sword belt, Roman.'

I was almost sure. I laid the blanket at her feet and with shaking hands returned to my horse. Without waking Ludovicus, I unbuckled the straps and lifted off the saddle. Hoisting it in my arms, I carried it back to her steps.

'Our bargain is not complete. I offer you my saddle and the blanket in return for the food, that knife, and a golden hair ornament—but nothing tawdry. I want the kind that only the noblest of your women wear.'

She frowned and shook her head in disbelief. Thank the gods, I must be mistaken. But I had to be sure and did not want her to guess the true value of our barter.

'I seek a memento of my travels through your country,' I explained.

The woman reached out and touched the sturdy saddle, still warm from the sun. Its leather padding was thick and the four pommels covered with gilded green leather. Any young Alemannus raider—had any survived Julian's battle—would fight over such a seat.

'Wait here,' she said.

I wanted nothing more than to see her come back empty-handed. As I heard her rustling among her treasures hidden in crude hand-molded pots on her shelves, I prayed to the gods that she would try to fob me off with some cheap silver-plated *fibula*.

She came back to the sunken step, and shading her eyes from the glare, held up her humble cache.

'Take what you like,' she said, 'for the saddle and the blanket. I'm too old for such finery, what with my man dead.'

'I take this,' I said, my eyes welling with tears. I lifted the familiar fox pin to the light. Its two garnet eyes glinted up at me.

'Where did the previous owner go?'

'She lies in the cemetery back there with the others,' the woman said, indifferent to my mounting grief. 'Buried with the islanders who fled your swords.'

'She was wounded in the arm? A noblewoman with silvery-gold hair?'

Her brisk nod cut like a blade through my heart.

I dropped the saddle and ran across the gutted fields to the fresh burial mounds. I fell on my knees and laid my shaking hands on the upturned dirt, but then dropped my head and fell back on my heels. I had no strength to dig up these unhappy souls' remains for confirmation.

The woman had Gunda's knife. She offered Gunda's jewel.

She told the horrible truth.

As I claimed the knife and fox pin from the woman, I gagged on my thanks and even fought off an urge to rob her, right now, in full sight of the gods. I suspected she had dishonored Gunda's last wish to be buried wearing her father's gift.

Then I stopped myself. For all I knew, this precious jewel was Gunda's desperate payment for some simple favor—a sip of beer or crust of bread—or merely the service of a burial.

I honored my trade and handed over my blanket and saddle to the crone.

I woke Ludovicus from his nap. Our search was over. We were too late.

I would give the knife to Hermund in Roma, but he would have no use for the precious fox. I clutched it tight in my fist because if Gunda had left anyone bereaved and bitter, it was myself.

My streaming tears confused young Ludovicus. 'Surely returning to the Caesar with dozens of liberated Roman citizens is more to your credit that the rescue of one female ally?'

It was an innocent observation, the judgment to expect from my *schola* and the Empire. It was the natural comment of all Roma. But it was the last thing he should have said to me then.

⚔⚔⚔

The prisoners had decided to risk waiting for me to escort them back to the river. I spied Aegidius and the two younger men chained to him sitting watch at the junction that led off the main road to the bathhouse.

After bathing, the rest of the escapees had rinsed the lice and fleas from their clothing and hung those pitiable shreds of coarse hemp on branches to dry. Nearly naked, these Romans protected their modesty with shameful scraps of cloaks and borrowed tunics.

I could do nothing to remove their shackles. But bandaged and refreshed, they rallied their courage and resumed trudging behind our horses with backs more erect and hope restored. I led them to the abandoned *vicus*. Over the old blind man's protests, they scavenged whatever remains of the harvest lay in the bottom of barrels and *amphorae*. They found the tools they needed to crack open their chains and bracelets in an abandoned smithy's workshop.

Moving faster now, we passed the copse of young oaks. The Rhenus flowed free of blood, its clear water washing the last of the bodies, robbed of their armor and helmets and stuck defenseless in the silt.

I had not returned with Gunda in triumph. I returned instead with the first band of Romans to be rescued from the defeated Alemanni. It was a victory of sorts, though my heart felt as hard and dry as the gourds of late harvest scattered around the brown fields.

I would soon lead a squadron of guards with the prisoner Chnodomarius riding, bound and gagged, to Roma. It was the only comfort I could squeeze out of my desolation. This was the fate Gunda herself would have decreed for her father's most hated rival.

CHAPTER 23, *AGENTES IN PERICULUM*

—APODEMIUS' STUDY, CASTRA PEREGRINA, ROMA—

'The Caesar writes that the Alemanna's information on the placement of hidden barbarian troops saved Severus' division from being swamped . . .' Apodemius chuckled.

'I am complimented, *Magister*.'

I was also desperate for sleep. Though we had galloped south at full speed, the days spent escorting Chnodomarius and his guards to Roma had dragged. I was tired of the too-familiar irregularities of the *Cursus Publicus* connecting the northern Rhenus with Italia. I'd have welcomed nothing more than a quiet stint in my native Numidia, auditing oil shipments to Ostia or indoctrinating wild Berbers in the civilizing delights of morning mail service.

'. . . solo foray into enemy lands brought fresh information about the whereabouts of hundreds more Roman citizens enslaved in the territories of the *regi* Hortarius and Suomarius . . . Oh, he is pleased indeed, Numidianus. He recommends you for promotion to *centenarius*. What could be next? You replace me as head of our *schola*?'

The *Magister* of the *Agentes in Rebus* wagged an arthritic hand at me.

'Sit down, Numidianus. Enough of the Caesar's encomiums to your brilliance.'

He tossed aside the heavy vellum letter with its elaborate gold seal cracked in two. 'What did the Caesar do when you delivered up your live booty?'

I took the beaten stool in hand and shifted it nearer to Apodemius' cluttered desk.

'He questioned them over three days about other missing citizens. There are thousands still alive out there. As I was leaving Tres Tabernae with Chnodomarius, he was sending the rest of his Alemanni prisoners to detention in Divodurum. Meanwhile, he's building a bridge at Moguntiacum to advance his entire army into Alemanni territory.'

'So little Julian will have his bridge at last.'

'He intends to liberate every Roman captive for the honor of the Empire and to wipe out any lingering resistance among the chieftains who escaped him at Argentoratum.'

'The gods help him,' Apodemius sighed. 'The campaign season is over. He has secured stability in Gallia. In a few weeks, he'll be waist-deep in cold snow and hungry bears.'

The *Magister* shook his weathered head and an aureole of wispy white hair waved in the soft circle of lamplight. It was about an hour after midnight, early in his working shift. His mice lay sleeping in a furry heap in the corner of their cage.

Outside the closed door, the *Magister*'s deaf masseur and his clerk moved about their business on soft sandals. While the Empire slept, they sorted, collated, and filed away the *schola*'s vast accumulation of Rome's crimes, ambitions, and secrets for Apodemius' use.

'I certainly could not endorse your promotion on the basis of your recent communications with us,' Apodemius said blowing his nose into a worn linen handkerchief. 'You sent only one report.'

His knobby fingers flicked the spare impressions of Barbatio's court I'd managed to dispatch the night before fleeing Augusta Raurica for Tres Tabernae.

'I've made a note of Tribune Cella's reactions. He may prove a useful witness later if Tribune Valentinian challenges his dismissal. And he should. He was a coming man, Valentinian.'

'A fair officer, strong and intelligent.'

'But your account of the *laeti* raiders' getaway told me nothing about the depths of General Barbatio's stupidity that I did not already witness in the fortress at Pula.'

'Barbatio's ambition to claim all the credit for the campaign tripped him up at every turn—from thwarting the *laeti*'s arrest to the rush to build the bridge with no coordination with Julian on the opposite bank.'

'That man is a calamity, yet he remains *magister peditum*. Why? We must assume the Empire is full of officers who would do anything for General Barbatio's bribes.'

'Will you invite his son to join our training school?'

'I would sooner let these mice manage the Besontio post station. But I may not be in charge much longer.'

So the old man sensed an invisible net closing in around him. His efforts to clean out corruption in the service had cost him support inside our ranks. The illness that sidelined him in Agrippina during the General Silvanus tragedy had weakened confidence in his physical capacities.

Until now, his worst enemies had been the jealous *consistoriani* riding high in Constantius' favor.

Unfortunately I knew someone even more threatening.

'So let us review your assignments, one by one, about which you were so silent.'

'Some things seemed too sensitive—even for code, *Magister*.'

'You reported to Florentius?'

I nodded.

'And you explained to Florentius your "true" assignment of spying on the Alemanni? Did he believe you?'

'Florentius did. Dr Oribasius was suspicious of me from the start.'

'You reported the failure of the imperial pregnancy?'

Apodemius put his signature to a routine report and dropped it onto a growing pile. He took up another, lending me half an ear's worth of attention—or so it seemed. I chose my words carefully.

'—of no import to the Caesar whatsoever. He chided me for suggesting he would indulge in unmanly mourning. He sees himself as a second Alexander expanding boundaries, not a Constantine fertilizing the family tree.'

'He showed no affection for the *Augusta*? No pity for her loss?'

'Respect, the required solicitousness, but no affection. He places more store in his correspondence with missing friends than in his distant consort. He seems physically chaste, yet displays cerebral affection.'

'For—?' He did not look up. I was boring him.

'That doctor Oribasius and his pagan quaestor Saturninius Secundius Salutius. Salutius knows Gallia well, has held many high offices already, and enjoys a good reputation for devotion to duty and justice.'

'Yes, yes, our records show as much.'

'Both Oribasius and Salutius also share the Caesar's love of Eastern philosophies. It is to these two men that Julian confides his obsessions about diet, dreams, theurgy, meditation, and—'

I bit my tongue. Julian's ritual sacrifices bordered on the highest treason against the Christian emperor's rulings and I had no independent witness.

Apodemius sniffed. 'Ever the Athenian student, I see. We knew that Barbatio would regard Julian as an unblooded, overeducated upstart. Marcellus and Ursicinus let envy of the boy's energy paralyze their command. Now that they're gone, who are Julian's enemies?'

'I would say that Florentius is a jealous rival for civil authority over Gallia, but no more. The Prefect hinted that the two men already argue over taxes and the administration of Belgica Secunda—things like that. These tensions may surface when the campaign against the Alemanni ends but Florentius is too ambitious to cause an open rift. In fact, his was the main voice urging the Caesar into the heat of battle.'

'Interesting.' Apodemius' eyes narrowed. He kept on scribbling signatures. 'One would think that would be Severus' cue in the script.'

I smiled at the memory of the doddering old veteran.

'General Severus harbors no more ambition than to bask in a warm villa by the seaside. He keeps ten paces behind the Caesar. I doubt he has no wish to cross the Rhenus for an endless sweep of the wilds of *Germania*, but he bides his time until retirement. You will never see Severus hauled into Constantius' court on charges of treason.'

'So Severus is not another resentful Ursicinus or Marcellus. That is useful to know. And that will be the essence of your cheerful report to the Emperor—especially the part so flattering to

Severus' loyalty. Keep it short. The Emperor's mind is fully occupied with his negotiations with the Persian king.'

I nodded. 'Severus does not dare challenge Julian, not when the Caesar has done so much to win the enthusiasm of his troops.'

'Enthusiasm?'

'Yes.'

'Adulation?'

'Growing. Especially among the Petulantes auxiliaries.'

Apodemius fingered the wiry hairs of a snowy eyebrow. 'Now that I find curious. On no pay and starvation rations? Constantius has made sure Julian cannot buy his soldiers' love.'

'Not a single coin. Yet they openly cheer him.'

One of the *Magister*'s beloved mice scratched and twitched over a dream on his straw bed. Despite the only danger being interruption from two assistants of proven discretion and sobriety, I whispered across the piles of reports: 'You ordered me to help the Caesar. I tried, *Magister*. But only he can save himself from mounting dangers.'

Apodemius' wrinkled eyes blinked.

'The soldiers—I'm sure it was one of the Petulantes—raised up a shout on the battlefield of Argentoratum. Thousands picked it up in turn. They acclaimed him as *Augustus*.'

The old man slowly clasped his hands and pushed them firmly into the folds of his long robe—as if not trusting how they might shake.

'Go on.'

He kept his words as low and soft as mine. Outside the tall, narrow window an *aedile* at the foot of the Caelian Hill sounded the hour and others echoed and reverberated between the hundreds of walls protecting Roman courtyards and *fora*.

'Julian reprimanded them right away, of course.'

'Of course.' Apodemius allowed himself a thin smile.

'He said it was an elevation he neither expected nor desired. He referred to the *auxilium* custom of hoisting their commander up on a shield after such a great victory, but said that a shield would be too slippery for him to ride.'

'That is prudent of Julian, because I have here before me,' Apodemius reached across his long desk for a thick, portentous-looking report, 'the Emperor's account of his personal role in the Battle of Argentoratum.'

My jaw dropped.

'Yes, as I complained just now, Numidianus, your reporting was woefully incomplete. Whether you saw him there or not, our emperor Constantius II himself "drew up the order of battle, took his place between the standards, put the barbarians to flight, and had Chnodomarius dragged before him in chains". Right there, signed, sealed, and witnessed.'

His gnarled forefinger gave the thick document an ironic tap. 'You must have been blind drunk not to have noticed him.'

'Of course the Emperor takes the glory, but he can't claim to have been there!' I bolted off my stool. 'He was at least forty days' march from Argentoratum!'

Apodemius directed me to sit back down. 'Wondrous work, isn't it, from forty days' march? Constantius does all but claim for himself the honorary title of *Germanicus*. Unusual modesty there.'

'He gives no credit whatsoever to his cousin?'

'None, though the *consistoriani* are mocking Julian behind his back for his boasts of defeating the Alemanni. The nicknames this week in Sirmium were—' Apodemius plucked a terse, coded missive from his pile, 'Victorinus, Ape in Purple, and Greek Dilettante.'

'What else should we expect? Envious tongues called Pompey unpatriotic and ambitious. Then it is just as well the courtiers do not know all I know.'

Apodemius stared at me as I rose from my stool. I had misspoken. I picked up my battered riding helmet and thanking him, excused myself. Opening the door to his outer chamber, the familiar face of an *agens* from the East, one Agapitus, looked up from a doze on the bench. He now wore the insignia of *biarchus*, upper class. I gave him a rueful slap of congratulations for his promotion.

Turning back to Apodemius from the doorway, I added: 'You did not ask me the fate of our faithful informant, the Alemanna Gunda. She died at the hands of Tribune Bainobaudes in a raid on the islands. I have a valuable memento to deliver to Hermund.' I said. 'I hope he's in better health than when I left.'

'Sit down, Numidianus. Close that door.'

—THE DEADLY CAESAR—

I obeyed and waited, head bowed. Did he have my next assignment already? I was tired and anxious to see the Manlius townhouse, to embrace my son, and to resume my care of his mother and their estates. There was the troubling matter of this Christian future for Leo and the charitable donations Kahina planned which would whittle away his fortune. No matter how deep her piety and gratitude to 'her Lord,' I was keen to reopen that debate before it was too late.

'I am an old man and short of time, Numidianus.'

I swallowed hard, remembering Julian's bloody hands thrust into that basin of gore.

'You have not reported everything.'

'No, *Magister*.'

'Who are you protecting? Yourself?'

'No, no, *Magister*.'

I took a deep breath. 'The Caesar sacrifices to the gods in the ancient manner. For the moment, his true allegiance to Helios and the ancient gods is curtained off from his men. His pose as a Christian, faithful to the Emperor's Church, still convinces the rank and file. But the longer he indulges in ritual animal slaughter, the likelier the curtain may slip at any moment.'

Apodemius lifted himself out of his chair with difficulty. His shabby leather cushion released tufts of stuffing in his wake. He rounded the end of the desk and laid a hand on my shoulder. 'I worried that the ways of the East might stick to him. But butchering animals! I asked you to protect him from his foolishness.'

'In that, I failed, *Magister*. Julian puts great store in oracles and dreams. He has confessed to me of a recurring dream: of a tall tree planted inside a large room, leaning down to the ground and hanging over a second tree, smaller, younger and flourishing. Julian is anxious for the younger tree, but sees that while the tall tree lies at full length on the ground, the small one stands erect, and even hangs suspended away from the earth. A stranger in his dream assures him the small tree will become established even more securely in the future.' I paused. 'The Caesar claimed he did not know what it portended and asked me what I thought.'

'When did he tell you of this dream?'

'Riding to Argentoratum.'

'What did you think?'

'The symbolism was too obvious and treasonous to utter. I was appalled he would reveal this vision within the earshot of men like Florentius riding only a few yards away.'

'Why did you not tell me straightaway?'

'Because I tried to forget it myself. I can hardly contemplate the consequences.'

'Another civil war between Constantines?'

'Worse. Much worse.'

He gave a start on those swollen feet laced in worn goatskin. He hunched toward me as if he would butt the truth out of my chest with his bony forehead.

'What could be worse after Mursa? Speak up, Numidianus, speak up!'

'Can you not guess, *Magister*? If Julian should rule unchecked—'

He clutched my shoulder. I felt him leaning on me, as his spirits sunk under the import of my unspoken words.

'The end of our service?'

I nodded.

'That is why you do not mention Pentadius, the *magister officiorum*? It is connected with our execution of Caesar Gallus?'

'Yes, *Magister*. Julian harbors a deep hatred for everyone he blames for Gallus' death. He catalogues them all as his enemies, no matter their true character—Barbatio, Eusebius, Pentadius who served as scribe that night, and—' I broke off. I felt as if I were condemning the head of my service to the agonies of torture and death right there, in his comfortable sanctuary in the silence of the deepest night.

'And myself.'

'*Magister*, please believe me. I did everything during my mission to prove the worth of the *agentes in rebus* to Julian. I labored at every turn to demonstrate how wrong he was to lump us together with that army of cooks and eunuchs and intrigants preying on Constantius. I was even indiscreet. I disclosed you were no friend of the Lord Chamberlain or the *consistoriani*. It went without saying how you hold Barbatio in contempt. Everyone does.'

—THE DEADLY CAESAR—

'And yet the Caesar sends me these instructions to promote *you*.'

Apodemius stared at Julian's letter with fresh understanding. His voice grew hoarse with indignation. 'He decrees your promotion as if the usual chain of authority from the *Magister Officiorum* to this office no longer pertains.'

'Knowing the *Magister Officiorum* Pentadius to be a *consistorium* spy, Julian kept that sinister man at a safe distance—as did I. Julian knew me to be a spy, but he embraced me as an older brother because I shared his secret faith in the ancient gods.'

'You are saying he may become my most powerful enemy of all. And I ordered you to help him.'

'Yes. You ordered me to protect him from his enemies and to guide him from folly—so that one day he can close the Castra, disperse our service, and charge you with foul crimes? *You ordered me to help him destroy you.*'

Apodemius' bleary eyes searched the corners of his room—from the wide map of the Empire on its corkboard mounting to the safe box in the far corner housing copies of the Empire's most sensitive documents.

'It seems I sent you on a mission that had as many facets as a barbarian gemstone.'

'How could I report this in writing? Any warning of the Castra's closure might fall into the hands of your enemies—possibly within this very service. Julian's ambition is the greatest danger to us since Diocletian condemned his *frumentarii* and bolted the Castra gates.'

Apodemius paused a long moment. Then he roused himself and clapped me on the shoulder with a jovial dismissal.

'Is that it, Numidianus?'

'That is what I know, *Magister*. That is everything. I found favor with the Caesar, but it was not put to the credit of our service just when the service needs it most. I have failed and I accept the consequences.'

'These are modern times, Numidianus, not a page out of Plutarch's *Life of Lucullus*. I do not decapitate *agentes* who deliver unwelcome news.'

'Thank you, *Magister*.'

'Go, get some rest, *Centenarius*,' he said with a forced heartiness. 'When dawn breaks, take your memento to Hermund in his cell and warn him he will soon have extraordinary company.'

※※※

Centenarius Marcus Gregorianus Numidianus, at last.

I ate a light breakfast in the Castra *triclinium*, although to call that echoing hall more than a rough canteen was too generous. For hundreds of years, this stony rugged room with its flaking plaster murals had welcomed the *peregrini*, provincial soldiers visiting Roma. Then it had fed the *frumentarii*, agents so corrupt and abusive, they were disbanded in shame for good.

Our service rose up from the ashes of Diocletian's purge and was still there, despite my nightmarish warning to Apodemius.

On this crisp morning, it was as energetic and brotherly as ever. Hundreds of hungry officers milled around me, gossiping about Roman politics, regional economies, and distant municipal governments. Hundreds more boys from the cadet school ate and returned to their exercises, studies, and the typical pranks youngsters play on poisons masters and language tutors.

It was good to see so many familiar faces again and to acknowledge men in all styles of dress and armor visiting from our stations in the far corners of the civilized world. I knew some as hardy riders or discreet postal inspectors, wending their way up the ladders of provincial governments or the different imperial courts. But I wondered about others, comfortable in distant customs or road inspection posts that probably brought them no reputation or glory—only healthy profits.

Why was I, Marcus Gregorianus Numidianus, always the one who found his career singed on the flames of imperial danger and ambition? Well, I had my promotion at last, thanks to the Caesar.

I could postpone my sad visit to Hermund no longer. Wiping away the last crumbs of bread and preserved figs, I emptied my beaker of diluted wine. I headed across the Castra yard to the detention cells tucked into the far corner of the walls under the shadowy arches of the Aqua Claudia. The empty window where

Gunda had serenaded our headquarters with her lonely song sat empty this morning.

I found Hermund's quarters, a single bolted room with few amenities and a single high window, guarded by a service veteran dozing off.

'Do you remember me?' I asked the boy. 'Numidianus. I found you in the camp.'

'That was months ago. Why do you show up now?' he grumbled, scarcely turning from his pallet to look at me.

'I bring you something that belonged to your sister. I'm very sorry to tell you, Gunda's dead. She died up north during a Roman assault on Alemanni settlers.'

'What do I want with the bitch's knife?' he said, after twisting around to see the sharp blade lying in my outstretched palm.

'Surely you will treasure it out of memory of your sister.'

Hermund turned his eyes up at me. By the faint glow of morning, his pupils were nearly as red as the garnet eyes of the fox pin hidden in my purse. He'd been weeping through his breakfast. Or he was drunk. Perhaps both.

'She was not my sister.' He spit some greenish phlegm onto the floor only inches from my boots.

My fingers closed tight round the deer horn handle.

'What do you mean?' I felt like kicking sense back into him.

'Go away,' he said. 'She was not my sister. My true sisters, all four of them, are alive and well, I should expect, nice and comfortable with my uncle Vadomar in the Agri Decumantes. Not that he lifts a finger for me.'

'Of course she was your sister! You're drunk.' I grabbed him by the collar of his sweat-soaked tunic. He looked sallow. 'Gunda knew everything about your father, his alliance, and his loyalty to Roma.'

'Of course she did! Because she's my father's bastard by a Roman cow he took in a raid decades ago. Put her to work in the kitchens. That's where Gunda grew up.'

A bastard by a Roman captive? Her proud carriage, her taunts, and her fears—they all became clear to me. She was no thoroughbred Alemanna—just half-nobility, like me. And half a Roman, like me. I had stumbled on the last and the deepest of Gunda's lies, but it was the lie that explained everything about her—her fluent Latin, her troubled silences, and her insistent love of the word, 'Roman.'

Hermund's rasping voice pierced my thoughts. 'And ever since, Gunda has been trying to get attention for herself, with her airs and her songs and her vulgar hairdos. My sister? My sisters would not admit her to their chambers, much less include her in their rank. Do you want hear the grief that girl caused my mother, Gundomad's true queen? Do you know how long we all put up with the arguing, the recriminations, the jealousies—until we could stand her claims to our pure bloodline not one minute longer?'

'So your father gave her to Serapio?'

'Yes.' Hermund grunted his satisfaction at Gunda's disgrace. 'To use for his pleasure, if that poor prince could find any joy in her haughty ways. How could he touch her, when he found out her mother was the slave who ran our kitchen staff? So Gunda ran away. We were all glad to hear the last of her.'

'But that wasn't the last of her,' I said, my mind racing to comb through Gunda's stories, including her peculiar boast that *her mother never touched a cooking pot.*

'Why did she follow you, Hermund? Why did she come to the prison camp here in Roma? Why did she defend you if you hated her so much?'

Hermund shrugged. 'Who knows? To win over my mother by saving me? To display herself in this foul city as the loyal daughter of Roma's great ally Gundomad? Her real name wasn't even Gunda. Her mother called her Verita.'

'After *veritas* for truth.'

'She was nothing but a liar from top to bottom. I didn't ask for her help, but she even stole my father's name, she was so desperate to belong to our family.'

'Desperate enough to sacrifice herself as an assassin of Constantius to prove herself a true Alemanna?'

'I told you, she was a desperate cunt. But on second thought, I'll take her knife.'

The young man gave a sly smile and stretched out his hand. The cell reeked of wine and vomit. His water basin stood, stagnant and untouched. I told the guard to unlock the door.

—THE DEADLY CAESAR—

'I knew Gunda to be a loyal daughter of Gundomadus,' I said, slipping her knife back under my belt, 'and a loyal daughter of the Empire as well. I am proud to have ridden at her side. I am glad to have known her affection. You're right, Hermund. Do not call her your sister. You are not worthy.'

Chapter 24, A Secret Throne

—THE PRISON CAMP OUTSIDE ROMA—

Nothing at the prisoners' camp had improved since my visit with Ahenobarbus the previous April. No one had repaired the women's toilets. Fetid sewage coursed into the common gutter through a leaking hole in the stone enclosure. The same sentries sat at the guard post outside the camp perimeter. They still played dice and they still let the prisoners rot inside the secured barricade while slave traders culled the best from the lost.

If anything, the camp was more crowded than six months ago. But how could that be? Constantius was based in the East, trying to negotiate peace with the Persians. All the recent victories were Julian's and he'd stopped trying to impress Constantius with prisoner convoys months ago.

Except for one prize.

I was sent here today to claim him. I pushed my way through the idle, querulous hordes in search of his towering figure.

I found Chnodomarius sitting in the open space around the fountain where Hermund's attackers had congregated last spring. The giant been stripped of his fantastic gold battle mask and the helmet with its flaming plume. His uncombed moustache and beard covered half his face. But no humiliation at the hands of his Roman jailers could diminish that massive bulk of muscle, lard, and bone dwarfing the chipped stone bench.

He nodded when he saw me emerge from the babble and racket. 'It is my travel companion, Numidianus. He comes to gloat over an abandoned king.'

'I've come to take you to the Castra Peregrina.'

His long red plaits glinted in the sunshine but the undyed roots had grown out like uncombed iron wires.

'For interrogation?'

'Discussions with our *schola*.'

'Oh, I've heard of your Roman "discussions".' He jerked up the strutted belt that dammed in his enormous beer belly.

'Even in the wilds of our forests, mothers threaten their disobedient little boys with tales of your "discussions." *If you don't behave,*' he wagged an enormous scarred finger up at me, and said in falsetto, '*I'll give you to that Roman, Paul the Chain. If you don't eat, the Chain will shred you with his iron claws. He will turn you on his greased wheels until your little bones snap in two.*'

He squinted up at me against the sunshine of a Roman noon. 'Are I going to a discussion with your Paul the Chain?'

'His fame has penetrated even your black woodlands?'

'Oh, yes. Paul the Chain is a renowned example of your great civilization, your *Romanitas*.' The barbarian spat with contempt on the wet stones.

'The notary Paulus Catena is far away, investigating religious heretics in Egypt.'

'Notary, you call him? Notorious is more like it. Egypt is too close for my peace of mind,' he grunted. 'I stay here.'

Chnodomarius splayed out his trunk-like legs across the bleached and broken paving. Prisoners' children splashed and played around his battered boots. He still wore his fighting trousers and stained armor under-padding over a dirty tunic whose pine-colored wool hemmed with fraying gold and silver falcons had once dazzled the eye.

'Come on.'

'I stay here, Numidianus.'

I enlisted four of the guards. Chnodomarius saw them coming and heaved a great sigh. They lifted the heavy man to his feet. He acted like a weary bull that puts up a token struggle but, once the harness and yoke are laid across its mammoth shoulders, plods into the waiting fields with resignation.

I'd brought a powerful horse to carry him out of the gates, past the rubbled camp walls, down the Via Nomentana to the great city's Porta Collina.

—THE DEADLY CAESAR—

'You think I'm brave enough for your torments, Numidianus? I tell you, I am not.'

He pounded a thick fist on his sagging chest. 'This old carcass was born for raiding and running back into the trees. Do not expect great courage from an old fighter who knows when the legend of Gigas is ended.'

'Apodemius seeks your wisdom,' I called to him from my saddle. 'You may be the Empire's prisoner, but you will be our *schola*'s guest.'

The great warrior's weathered face broke into disbelief mingled with disdain. Over our long journey from the Argentoratum battleground covered with his dead to the crumbling prison outside Roma, he had grown to trust me a little. As our ancient capital's walls hove into view, Chnodomarius lifted himself taller in the saddle and straightened those anvil-like shoulders.

'So you propose to set me up in comfort on a secret throne in a walled prison? For what purpose?'

'Don't set yourself so high, old man. A few centuries ago, Roma's emperor would have dragged you for miles at the head of his prisoners in a great Triumph. He would have paraded you to cheering thousands as the defeated king of your people before executing you.'

'Your empire is not what it was,' he answered. 'Do you call that a victory? Butchering helpless, unarmed settlers on those islands? Breaking treaties signed by your own sovereign?'

'Julius Caesar slaughtered a million Gauls to conquer Gallia,' I said, 'and enslaved two million more.'

Chnodomarius sneered. 'Your history always bleaches the victor white, but our legends paint the true hero.'

I was happy to hand him over at the Castra gates. I was told that the chieftain would be shaved, plucked, and scraped clean in our baths before spending a long night under Apodemius' questioning. My informant was Childeric Merovianus, a young recruit who could not disguise his personal curiosity in the hoary new detainee. Merovianus was none other than Junius, the son of the failed usurper, General Silvanus. He was closely tied by birth to the fate of the Franco-Roman settlements bordering the Alemanni holdings along the Rhenus.

While hiding away from the lingering suspicions and plots of his father's enemies at court, Junius was training to be an *agens*. But I suspected that his ambition to return someday to his people up north was not fading under the Castra's tutelage.

Junius congratulated me on my promotion.

I congratulated him on growing taller by the span of my hand in one summer.

'Are you staying to hear the results of tonight's talk, *Centenarius*?'

'No, Junius. The "political vision" of a barbarian even this supreme is bound to disappoint the *Magister*. Chnodomarius is an empty beer-sack, all bluff and bluster. He managed to rally his fellow kings, but once in the field, they broke up into tribes and clans, each clinging to the banner of his region.'

I was, however, wrong about one thing. As the moon sank below the Castra walls, I saw Hermund, tottering with fever but dressed in fresh clothes, transferred to the custody of *agentes* about to travel north. He would cross the bridge at Augusta Raurica into the care of his uncle, our erstwhile ally Vadomarius.

It seems that Hermund's departure from the Castra was Chnodomarius' first demand in exchange for his cooperation.

As far as we *agentes* were concerned, it was a more than welcome trade.

Hermund started coughing in the middle of the courtyard. He bent over, wracked with spasms. He spattered the pavement with blood. His new tunic sleeve was already stained—this was not his first coughing fit of the morning.

His *agentes* companions signaled it was time to set off for the city gates to de-register their presence in the capital and collect the first set of relay horses.

Hermund threw back his pale face, searching in vain for the first crack of rays from the sun. Gunda's wish for his release had come. But he was not destined for elevation in our ranks—or among his own people, for that matter.

Whatever we had to fear from the Alemanni tribes in future, it would not come from Hermund. He would be lucky to reach the hearth of his noble uncle's stronghold alive.

—THE DEADLY CAESAR—

I finished my report to Constantius after a long morning of diplomatic rewriting. I bolted the door of my Castra room and set off for the Esquiline Hill. Within fifteen minutes I arrived in high spirits under the ancient fig tree. The Manlius entry gate was open and the vestibule empty. Even the domestics' quarters were silent. A few pieces of dried fruit lay on the *lararium* and the wax *imagines* of the Manlius stared past me, their painted orbs trained as always on the trickling fountain in the center of the atrium.

Only Verus was home, left to his reminiscences by the others gone off to the markets and other errands.

With visible difficulty, he limped over to embrace me His eyes were still good, his wits even sharper, but his muscles hung looser than ever on his bent frame and his once-manly profile had turned birdlike, with wattles of loose skin hanging in two folds underneath his chin. His gait had worsened over the summer.

'My old hip, that's all,' Verus said.

'Where is your mistress?'

'Over at the Basilica of St Peter.'

'That's more than an hour each way in those crowds. Did she take the litter? Why not attend the local church?'

He sniffed at Kahina's resuming her public devotions so soon on her return from Ostia. 'Because that's where the fine ladies from the whole city go, ain't it? And she went on foot, of course, getting herself all mucky and worn out for the sheer humbling pleasure of it. What's the point of being a devout, self-effacing Christian if the whole world ain't noticing?'

'She is sincere, Verus. You mustn't mock her beliefs.'

He heaved a sigh. 'It's almost time for me to start off to collect her.'

'Let me go for you,' I said, laying a hand on his withered shoulder. 'And the boy?'

'Oh, last time I saw him he was in the Senator's study,' Verus said with an indulgent smile. 'Go softly, through. If I know him, he's sleeping off his enormous lunch. Eats like an infantryman on campaign, he does. After that, he reads all night. Next day, can't stay awake to do his lessons like he should.'

'Where's Antonius Drusus?'

'Gone for the day. Back tomorrow morning for lessons. He's found that the best way to teach Leo his calculations is to let him do the estate accounts. Our boy's shaping up into a nice little landlord, he is, but he can't sign nothing without your say-so, as he's only nine.'

I tiptoed up to the study. The padlocks Verus snapped shut whenever we feared for the valuable library hung loose from their hinges on the open door.

I peered inside. My son lay sprawled out on a low couch, face down, his limp hand still marking the page of a heavy *codex* that had slipped off a stool at his knees. There wasn't much to see from the doorway—a tumble of dark brown curly hair sunk into the familiar cushions with their threadbare corners and, at the other end, two skinny legs. His tunic was slipping off his narrow brown shoulders.

A high window just below the expensive carved ceiling caught the sun's rays streaming into the beloved sanctuary of my childhood. Dust motes danced in the beams. The air was close. The afternoon warmth drew out beads of innocent sweat on the boy's brow. There was a tiny pimple at the corner of his hairless lip. His mother was allowing him too many sweet cakes.

I remembered that age well, divided between hours of reading to the blind Senator, eating as much as I could in the kitchen while serving the Commander and Lady Laetitia's guests, and playing pranks with other slave boys on the older servants. With the cruelty of boisterous youth, I had ignored my poor mother, the discarded seamstress who slaved away her life to make sure my place as the aristocrat's bastard was protected.

I'd grown tall, but stayed—as slaves must—watchful and wary.

Leo would not have that childhood. But he was going to be as tall as I was and the Commander before me. I peered again at the tanned leg hanging off the far end of the couch. Had he grown *that* many inches in one short summer?

And what was he was reading? If I recognized any of the well-thumbed Senator's scrolls and *codices* as well as I should, I would say our little bookworm had been indulging in the ribald Catullus behind his chaste mother's back.

My darling, my charmer,
Bid me come and rest with you
And doing so, grant me a favor or two:
No locked doors with nobody answering or
'Sorry, Milady is not at home'.
But stay at home and 'prepare' for us
nine non-stop bouts of fucking.
Now if you are busy, let me know right away,
because I am lying down after lunch on my back with a stiff one
boring a hole through my tunic and underwear.

Leo would not like me to discover his nose stuck into those verses. I gently closed the study door behind me as I went back to the public rooms.

'I'll go to the Basilica to surprise Kahina and escort her home,' I told Verus. 'You rest your bones.'

Not being a Christian, I'd avoided the great new church of Constantine, begun around the time I was born, but always under repairs of some kind. It took me a long half hour to cross the city and river to reach the courtyard fronting its facade. I fell back for a moment at the crush of beggars and penitents filling every square foot. These filthy wretches were 'the poor' the Church attracted with their systematic alms giving. The beggars had set up permanent camp outside great basilica. They sent up a noise and a stench that must suffocate the ceremonies inside that imposing carved entrance.

As I worked my way toward the church, its tall doors flew open to release a stream of 'catechists'—trainee Christians, if I understood it right—dismissed from the Eucharist service restricted to the baptized. I pushed my unbaptized self right through the crush and before the doors slammed shut, forced myself through the vestibule to the back of the nave, alongside hundreds of eager Romans anticipating the 'miracle' to come.

I was safe from detection. All faces strained forward to the altar in the far distance, eager for a glance of blessing from the bishop. I was astonished to discover a patrician neighbor from a venerable Roman family standing a few feet away. I would have expected him to protect his bald scalp from sunburn with a clean felt hat and to cloak himself against the street's depredations with an embroidered cloak.

But no, he wore a shabby, loose tunic with no *orbiculi* or other signs of his status. Even more surprising, he was barefoot and dressed in this drab and humiliating fashion as part of some public penance. He was waiting for a sign from the bishop that, despite some awful sins for which he'd no doubt already paid dearly in confession and coin, he was 'reconciled' back to the bosom of this devout fellowship.

In the old days, this scion of an ancient line would have made up for his social shortcomings by building some fine theater or donating to the repair of municipal baths. Instead, here he was, a noble citizen mingled in with all manner of scruffy, nameless people, as if our ancient distinctions of citizen, freedman, and slave no longer mattered.

I felt sickened and slipped back outside, preferring the stinking rabble of the greedy poor to the incense-laden piety of the guilt-loving faces within.

Kahina beamed with pleasure at finding me waiting for her out on the street. She had recovered more animation in her eyes since this time last year. She no longer glanced up and down the street for fear that someone might apprehend her as an escaped war prisoner. She'd resumed most of her responsibilities around the house, keeping the staff fed and nursed. But she had discarded all feminine vanity since her enslavement.

She wore a simple green tunic under a flowing russet *stola* embroidered with gold autumn leaves and a *palla* of beige wool. Her hairpins were unobtrusive and her *fibulae* two small and modest gold circles. As her intimacy with Roman society matrons aspiring to Christian salvation grew, she eschewed the vulgar baubles and lacquered bleached hairstyle of her pre-war days as an arriviste colonial wife of Commander Gregorius.

At least she looked healthy. Her Numidian complexion had bronzed over the Ostian summer and like her son, she'd been eating a fair amount of cake. But she still limped badly, the legacy of her years in shackles in Hispania.

As always, I felt awash with love for her, but carnal desire had vanished years ago.

'You look all brown and fat and happy,' I said. 'Ostia suits you, as always.'

'The apartment is convenient. I look out on the sea each morning and feast on the fresh catch for lunch. It reminds me of home.'

'You miss Africa?'

'Of course. Rome is so crowded... and lonely.' She smiled, but whether it was from pleasure at seeing me or basking in what she and her fellow devotees called their 'state of grace,' who could say?

Her expression brightened, 'Did you see Melania at the celebration?'

'Now who is Melania?'

'The wife of Valerius Maximus Basilius! Everyone knows *him*.'

'Ah, yes. The rumor around the Castra is that he'll be the Roma's next *Praefectus Urbi*.'

'Melania is one of the richest women in the entire empire and only sixteen years old! They have a villa in the suburbs where she meets with other ladies to discuss our faith... I wish she would invite me.'

'Perhaps she will, Kahina.'

It was unlikely, but not impossible. These highborn converts excelled themselves in humility by reaching down into all corners of the Christian community. I pitied Kahina her longing. Her fervor to donate Leo's inheritance to the Church had a lot to do with washing away the last 'rebel' stain from her name and making a life for herself in this new Roman world of public sins and even more public penances.

I was still only a freedman and one of the despised *curiosi* until the day I retired to something more respectable. The freed slaves of emperors might amass great fortunes and lord it over honest citizens. But even if I had wanted to borrow Manlius treasure to raise myself in society, my career at the *schola* dragged me away from the old capital to the powerful Constantinian courts and dangerous, disputed borders.

I could not help Kahina find her place in society.

I took her arm. We two fell into a thoughtful silence as we navigated the narrow walkways. We crossed the river and made our way eastward toward the Esquiline Hill. When we passed through the old Forum—now in broad daylight and engorged with the cries, shoves, and greetings of the tumultuous city—I remembered my midnight vigil with Verus watching its very soul smuggled away in stealth.

The doors of the Senate House were bolted shut. The ancient altar still stood empty. Where had the great statue that had guarded us for so long been closeted away? Had it been shattered by hammers? Dropped in the Tiberis? Was it safe and only waiting for a rebirth of pagan faith?

A memory of the Caesar's hands plunged into the animal blood of ritual sacrifice came back to me.

'What's wrong, Marcus?'

'Oh, nothing, Kahina. An unpleasant memory from the field.'

'Of blood and death, again?'

'Of blood and death, yes.'

She reached up and laid a soft palm on my brow. 'You will forget all that, dear Marcus, with time. You must come with me to church. Christ will bring you peace.'

We continued through the Subura slums to the foot of the hill and started up the long street to the house.

It was easier to let Kahina think I had been revisited by the horrors of Mursa. How could I describe these fresh forebodings? An inexplicable horror chilled me—a horror of unreason masquerading as tradition and of deadly ambition bribing our honest gods with the slippery entrails of some hare or piglet.

The crude vulgarity of such primitive bloodletting disgusted me. We lived in modern times. We left polite offerings with indulgence and affection to the gods who shared our world. We no longer butchered whole animals and waited for painted statues to spring alive in answer. The longer I speculated on Julian's singular obsessions and meditations for the Empire's future, the more my unease grew.

If I fought the idea that Leo would be educated into the ranks of unvirile, sanctimonious Christians, was there anything left of the ancient dignities to offer as an alternative? I didn't look

—THE DEADLY CAESAR—

forward to our return home any longer. The discussion about Leo's education might turn bitter and hurtful.

'Marcus, there's no need to walk that slowly,' Kahina chided. 'My ankles are healed now. Come on!'

When we reached the townhouse, we settled side by side in the garden, enjoying the last blooms of summer and listening to the pleasant gurgle of the fountain. Kahina knew better than to ask for details of my mission. I told her that the battle had devastated the Alemannic resistance and that Roma had won another great victory to seal its borders against the barbarians' depredations. After six years of warfare, Gallia might breathe in peace again.

The cook would soon be setting our meal out on small tables in the *triclinium* and Leo would join us.

'I know you want Leo to enroll in the *agentes*' school,' Kahina said after a long pause.

'Just because the Commander spent his entire life in the army, doesn't mean the old rules must apply. Imagine Leo caught in the kind of slaughter I just witnessed, as honorable as such a career might be.'

'And you refuse to consider sending him for religious training?'

'Of course, Kahina! I object to sacrificing that healthy boy to a life of nothing but prayer and poverty! The Fates have set Leo on a noble path—to rebuild the Manlius *gens*, to seed many sons carrying on the Manlius name, and to preserve the wisdom and wealth of their nobility at the center of this city's history.'

Kahina gave an irreverent laugh. 'Oh Marcus, you don't spend enough time here anymore. You look at all those wax images on our walls and you are blinded by faded glory, when all I see is that the dusting needs doing again. All you can offer Leo is an introduction to your Castra but such an openhearted, proud-spirited boy can never be happy as a *curiosus*.'

'My *schola* is sought out by the highest commanders in the land for their sons.' I dared not name Barbatio for whom Kahina had as much contempt as I. My point was made. 'Retirement at the top of my profession can lead to a good appointment in a provincial administration.'

'Everyone hates the *agentes*,' Kahina said. 'I don't want my son to be an outcast in good society all his life.'

She had never insulted my calling before. It was the first time I felt disrespect from her and I could not think how to answer. We looked up at the sound of soft footsteps entering the leafy space. I expected to see the slave summoning us to eat but it was Leo himself, tousled and smiling.

He embraced me and nestled for a moment in my arms, then lifted his head and retreated a few steps to take us both in.

'You are arguing, *Mater*? Marcus has only just come home.'

'We're not arguing, my son, only discussing your future.'

'My future is decided.'

The child's face assumed an expression very familiar to me and, at the same time, long forgotten. I had been waiting for years for some telltale resemblance to myself to betray our long-buried secret—that while the world thought he was the son of the Commander Gregorius, it was I who was the bastard offspring of the great officer. Leo was not his son, but thanks to an innocent night before I knew of Kahina's betrothal to my own father, Leo was my son. This secret was kept well to protect Leo's standing in the world, his estates, and his future.

But someday the true nature of our shared blood might surface.

Instead, it was not a mirror of my youthful Numidian self that I perceived. Nor was it the once-handsome visage of the Commander, who had set hearts sighing across the city before his cruel disfigurement on the battlefield.

No, Leo assumed a comically stern expression as he prepared to interrupt this debate over his future career. With jaw thrust forward, brow furrowed, and one hand on hip, he was the shrimp-sized incarnation of the beloved old Senator readying himself to declaim on hefty state affairs before the Senate.

'You should help me prepare for a career in the public eye,' he said as pompously as a nine-year-old can sound when he makes a real effort. 'I have discussed it with Antonius Drusus. He is preparing me to study family and property law in Mediolanum when I am ready to leave home.'

'The *law*?'

'An *assessor*?' Kahina turned to me. 'A legal expert?'

'Why not a *quaestor* someday, *Mater*?'

'But Leo—!' I wanted to warn him that legal advocates were often talkative charlatans and smooth-tongued opportunists.

Leo held up his little palm and artfully turned it in a slow and authoritative motion, as if we were already in a tribunal. It was a trick I hadn't seen a Manlius make in twenty years. How had Leo acquired the Senator's favorite rhetorical gesture when the blind old man had died shortly after the boy's birth?

'The Senator was a great man, wasn't he, Marcus?'

'Yes, Leo.'

'I wish to be a great man also. He knew the laws of Roma and he worked to uphold them. Everyone says so in letters filed away in his study.'

Kahina and I exchanged resigned glances. What else could have come of letting the child spend every waking hour among the old man's neglected books?

'But Leo,' Kahina started, 'in the church, you would serve—'

'You're always talking about serving God, but I don't want to be a sniveling priest or desert hermit. It's not my fault I'm not free to serve God. You have no other son. It's my duty to marry and—'

'But priests can marry, Leo,' Kahina said.

'Yes, but I am the last Manlius and I must produce sons. The Synod of Elvira in 306 prescribed in Canon 33 that even married priests should live chaste lives—'

'Oh, Leo, you're too young to even worry about such—'

'My wife will be very beautiful, *Mater*.'

The boy had been reading up on his Church law—and Catullus—very closely indeed.

He dropped his classical pose and put his arms around his startled mother. 'But a successful lawyer or politician—even a married one—can always be appointed a bishop later on, can't he, Marcus?'

'Yes, I know of some but I'm not sure they're encouraged to sleep with their wives after they are ordained—'

'So that settles my future.'

Setting aside a middle-aged wife when she was no longer beautiful was a problem too remote to weaken Leo's argument today.

'Would that make you happy, Mother? To call me bishop someday?'

Kahina embraced her son in answer. And over the bowed head of his tearful mother, Leo smiled at me with triumph glowing on his chubby face.

He had just won his first debate.

The End

Have you read the other *Embers of Empire* books? Read on:

The Veiled Assassin, Embers of Empire, Vol. I
Usurpers, Embers of Empire, Vol. II
The Back Gate to Hell, Embers of Empire, Vol. III
The Wolves of Ambition, Embers of Empire, Vol. IV
The Burning Stakes, Embers of Empires, Vol. VI

Historical Notes

As always with the *Embers of Empire* novels, I've directed the reader's focus on the challenges of the fourth-century Roman Empire through the eyes of a character with official access to state secrets. These secrets pertain to religious dissent, the rise of 'barbarian' military commanders, the power of the eunuch class, the strain of governing the West while fending off the Persian threat, and relations with the border peoples like the Franks and the Alemanni.

One of the arresting aspects of this period is Julian's treatment of the Alemanni in the context of his times. In his enthusiasm for the Caesar, fourth-century historian Ammianus Marcellinus calls Bainobaudes' raid of the islands 'a remarkable feat.' He also passes no negative verdict on Julian's disregard for an imperial treaty shoved right under his nose verifying Constantius' guarantee of land in exchange for the attacks on the failed usurper Magnentius.

More seriously, slaughtering whole settlements of civilian 'allies' would be condemned today as ethnic cleansing. And even in 357 AD, detaining diplomatic envoys during a negotiation was considered an offense against diplomatic practice. But clearly, these were different times. As Chnodomarius reminds Marcus, Roman history sided with the victor.

In clarifying some of the more ambiguous passages of Book 16 by Ammianus, I'm beholden to Prof. John F. Drinkwater's work, especially his lucid and objective summary in *The Alamanni and Rome 213-496 (Caracalla to Clovis)* in which he shines needed light on our original sources (too often colored by prejudice, politics, and cultural custom.) In the University of Nottingham expert's opinion, there was no inevitability about the success of the Franks moving on into later centuries as the heirs of the Romans. The Alemanni were not inherently weaker or less well placed in the Roman military leadership in the middle of the fourth century to prevail.

However, Drinkwater speculates, an important opportunity for Alemanni participation in imperial affairs was squandered in the year 357 through Roman refusal to tolerate the settlements on the left bank of the Rhine.

'A permanent Alemannic community in Gaul would have served the Empire well during the fourth century and might have acted as the kernel of a powerful Germanic successor kingdom in the fifth,' he writes.

I am also thankful for Drinkwater's breakdown of the Alemanni forces against Julian at Strasbourg. Much of Gunda's 'intelligence' for Cella in Chapter 15 is a crude paraphrasing of Drinkwater's careful analysis.

It seems there is still remarkably little from which to judge how the Alemanni saw themselves or even what they called themselves. Like the regional tags Brisigavi and Lentienses, 'Alemanni' is one of the names that Roman army recruiters most likely employed when they gathered up barbarian youths for service.

Drinkwater says that the Alemanni were not necessarily even 'the' Alemanni, but possibly Alemannic groups without the strong single identity of the Franks or Burgundians who bordered their home settlement area along the Rhine. He also suggests that this term, instead of meaning 'All Men' in some inclusive sense, might have meant, 'All these different men,' or more interestingly, 'Men who are All Man,' that is, 'He-Men,' or later, in sarcastic thanks to their behavior, 'those thuggish guys.' Another theory is that the term referred to people devoted to the ancient Germanic god, Mannus.

Drinkwater also considers how very Roman some of the most famous Alemannic officers had become by this time period and how certain observers—including Ammianus Marcellinus—found it convenient to overstress the barbarian or unreliable qualities of Alemannic allies to glorify the actions of his heroes—first his boss General Ursicinus and then Caesar Julian.

This follows a centuries-old tradition of inflating conquered folk into savage hordes to burnish a Roman commander's reputation. Julian had read all of Julius Caesar by the time he reached Reims to start his own military career.

Turning to one of those larger-than-life enemies, it seems almost too poignant that of all places to end his extraordinary career, the Alemannic *uber*-chieftain Chnodomarius resided until his death from peaceful senility (or tuberculosis) in the Castra Peregrina as a guest of the *agentes in rebus*. We do not know what happened to the loyal hundreds of his *comitatus* who surrendered with him as barbarian honor required after their incarceration in Divodurum.

A bigger conundrum of the year 357 is Barbatio's failure to deliver the bridge. Here we enjoy varied opinions, both ancient and modern. Ammianus doesn't even mention a bridge project. Prof. David Woods speculates that Libanius' account blaming barbarian sabotage for loss of the bridge is unreliable.

Woods notes that a bridge was not strictly necessary if Barbatio had already marched up the right bank: 'It is my argument, therefore, that Libanius' description of how the Alemanni used felled trees to destroy Barbatio's bridge constitutes no more than a mistaken inference based on a vague and somewhat misleading source. In brief, he imagined it.'

With all respect to Woods' academic theory that Libanius made it all up, this was rather unwelcome as a plot point—no bridge, no Chapter 16 for this novelist.

To meet the demands of fiction, I turned to John Drinkwater who explores the various bridge theories abroad, including sabotage by the Alemanni versus self-sabotage by one or the other Roman commander out of careerist competition and ill will. He proposes that the most likely explanation is that of an 'industrial accident' involving the preparation of timber for reinforcing the pontoon boats.

I chose to go with Drinkwater, partly for a fresh story. His conjecture diverges dramatically with the fictional vision of the Barbatio Bridge Incident in another novel, *Gods and Romans* by Michael Curtis Ford. Ford opted for the 'sabotage' version in which black-faced Alemanni surface from the river at night like devilish demons from the underworld, slashing away at ropes and boats before floating downriver still flashing their nightmarish white-toothed grins.

In other words, Ford took Libanius' version as inspiration for a scene right out of a D.W. Griffiths' silent film.

David Woods reminds us that in burning his boats, Barbatio was doing nothing different from Julian's actions later when retreating from the Persian front. Boats that speed downriver can become a nuisance returning against the current. Barbatio's action might not be condemned as outright sabotage of Julian, although he did refuse a very specific request to spare seven boats and dispatch the needed food supplies. Considering Barbatio's reputation for rash behavior and dim wits, the fictional version here mixes standard practice with inexplicable vindictiveness.

Woods also presents a convincing argument that the respected eunuch Eutherius, so praised by Ammianus Marcellinus for his honesty and loyalty to Julian, was far more loyal to Constantius II. Woods maintains that, as one of the court officials assigned to accompany Julian into Gaul, Eutherius would be expected to supervise and report back to the supreme sovereign. Woods argues that, far from Julian dispatching Eutherius as his advocate to refute Marcellus' attack in the Milanese hearing, Constantius summoned the Armenian to supply an impartial account of the siege.

As for the Battle of Argentoratum, historians are still undecided as to how many Alemanni challenged Julian's troops. Online war gamer Jonathan Webb neatly summed up authoritative opinions on his web page devoted to the battle thus: 'Numbers as always are controversial and subject to debate. [Hugh] Elton, [*Warfare in Roman Europe AD 350-425*] and [Constance] Head, [*The Emperor Julian*] merely repeat the initial estimates of a vast Alemanni army of 35,000; [John] Warry, [*Warfare in the Classical World*] and [Adrian] Goldsworthy, [*Roman Warfare*] acknowledge this number is speculative; two authors are explicitly critical and offer their own estimates. [Hans]Delbrück, [*History of the Art of War Within the Framework of Political History: The Germans Vol. 1*] estimates only 6-10,000 Alamanni soldiers while [J.F.] Drinkwater, [*The Alamanni and Rome 213-496*] estimates 15,000 based on a core of 9,000, levy of 4,000 and allies of 2,000. The latter estimate is more recent, its author has written more specifically on this time period and region, and is more consistent with the typically meticulous Roman body count of 6-8,000 Alamanni.'

Once again, all roads seem to lead to our helpful authority, John Drinkwater and I have kept the barbarian army to no more than 15,000.

For those who wish to visit the site, the Alemanni position now lies under the Strasbourg rail lines. The Roman position lies in a park on a hill to the west of the city.

Armchair nigglers may complain that I've brought forward certain aspects of Julian's story.

First, the dream of the twig and the tree was reported in a letter to Dr Oribasius only a year or so later, so I've made it a recurring dream.

Second, Julian's private rituals of animal sacrifice were well hidden from the larger public, military and civilian, for some time, so I've underscored how sensitive this discovery would be in the year 357.

A third item is whether there were two Bainobaudes, one a tribune of the Scutarii and the other leading the Cornuti. I've gone with the 'one Bainobaudes' camp to simplify my narrative.

But let no reader quibble with my description of the early 'Swiss army knife' which enables Marcus' rescue from the dilapidated villa *en route* to Tres Tabernae. One of these extraordinary all-purpose tools, complete with hinged spoon, is on display in the Antiquities Wing of Cambridge's Fitzwilliam Museum.

Places and Glossary

acetum—vinegar used for sterilization by army medical officers
adiutor—batman or assistant to camp officer
adventus—emperor's progress into Rome
aedile, aedilis—municipal officials responsible for maintenance of public buildings (*aedēs*) and regulation of public festivals. They also had powers to enforce public order.
agens, agentes in rebus—imperial department in charge of roads, postal services and intelligence gathering in the Late Roman Empire
Agrippina—Cologne, Germany
agalmata, agalmatôn—images, statues (Greek)
agrimensor—military surveyor
angon—Frankish barbed spear
annona—tax or produce
Argentovaria—Colmar, France
armati—warriors
assessor, assessores—legal advisor
asômatoi—without bodies (Greek)
Aventicum—Avenches, Switzerland
Augusta Raurica—Augst, Switzerland
Augustobona Tricassium—Troyes, France
Augustodunum—Autun, France
auxilium palatina, auxilia palatinae—infantry units of the Late Roman army, first raised by Constantine I as part of the new field army he created in about 325. Some of the senior and probably oldest of these units had special names such as Cornuti or Bracchiati; others were named after the tribes from which they were recruited (many of these in eastern Gaul or among the German barbarians)
ballista—catapult
biarchus—a regimental grade between *circitor* and *centenarius*, borrowed from the cavalry by the *schola* of *agentes in*

rebus, who limited themselves to six classes of the cavalry's ten, i.e. *eques, circitor, biarchus, centenarius, ducenarius,* and *princeps*.

Borbetomagus—Worms, Germany

Brotomagus—Brumath, Germany

bucellatum—dried biscuit that was part of a soldier's field rations

buccinator, buccinatores—trumpeter

calceus, calcei—high-cuffed leather boots

capsa—container with bandages and medical implements

capsarius—medic

captatores—legacy hunters

cathedra—wide, low-backed armchair or throne

caupones—unfranchised inns, sometimes brothels, located near state stopovers or along the highway, of generally low quality

centenarius—a regimental grade between *biarchus* and *ducenarius* (see *biarchus*)

cingulum, cinguli—military belt, from word for girdle, with metal plates or buckles riveted to leather. Wearing could be restricted to those in active service

codex, codices—bound books

comitatus—a Germanic friendship structure that compelled kings to rule in consultation with their warriors, forming a warband

Concordia—Wissembourg, France

consistoriani—members of the *consistorium*

consistorium—the Emperor's advisory cabinet

contubernalis, contubernales—tent mate, eight to a *contubernium* in a Roman army tent

cornicen, cornicenes—*aeneator* who signaled army orders on the *cornu*

cultor deorum—worshipper of the gods

cunei—wedges

curiales—members of town councils responsible for the collection of imperial taxes, providing food and board for the army and supporting the imperial post and the Cursus Publicus

curiosus, curiosi—insulting nickname for the *agentes in rebus*

Cursus Publicus—imperial road network

decurio—an officer commanding a turma of thirty-two men in the auxiliary cavalry

delicatus—a spoiled or cherished boy, sometimes a catamite

diploma, diplomata—letter of recommendation or license

discens capsariorum—trainee medic

dispensator—household manager, custodian, majordomo

domesticus—a regimental chief-of-staff or adjutant

domus—household

the Danuvius—the Danube River

draco—windsock attached to wooden, copper or alloy carved animal head, most often a dragon, as a standard for a Late Roman army cohort.

Divodurum Mediomatricum—Metz, France

ducenarius—a regimental grade between centenarius and princeps, borrowed from the cavalry by the schola of agentes in rebus, who limited themselves to six classes of the cavalry's ten, i.e. eques, circitor, biarchus, centenarius, ducenarius, and princeps.

Durocortorum—Reims, France

evectio, evectiones—road warrant for the Cursus Publicus

fabricae—Late Roman state arms factories

fibula, fibulae—pin or brooch fastening a cloak or tunic at the shoulder

follis, folles—like the *nummus,* a mid-4th century silver-coated bronze coin of low value

forum, fora—market or public place

fortiores—leading men

garum—seasoning high in flavor-enhancing glutamate, akin to nam pla or soy sauce, made from salted fermented fish, usually anchovies

Genava—Geneva, Switzerland

gens, gentes—Roman aristocratic clan or tribe

Hel—proto-Germanic person/place meaning grave or underworld

henosis—mystical oneness, union, or unity in classical Greek.

herrschaftszentrum—Germanic term for power center

Hispania—Spain

imagines—wax masks or images in similar media of family ancestors *immunis, immunes*—soldiers exempted from combat duty through performing a more specialist role

insigne, insignia—patch, badge, or emblem

itinerarium pictum—Roman map, such as the surviving Peutinger Table, tended to be elongated illustrations of the state roads, mansiones, and other points of interest along otherwise uncharted territory.

laeta, laetus, laeti—Late Roman term for people from outside the Empire permitted to settle on land granted inside imperial territory on the condition they provide recruits for the Roman military

latrunculi—'capture' board game for two players featuring some dozen 'pawns' and one 'king' for each player moving on a grid of squares

lararium—household shrine for the domestic guardians, the *Lares Familiares*

libertinus—freedman

limitanei—Roman troops assigned to border defense

Lugdunum—Lyons, France

lyra—lyre

magister—head of *schola* in civil service or high-ranking commander in army

manceps—manager of a mansio or statio

mansio, mansiones—state-franchised inn serving travelers on the Cursus Publicus

Mediolanum—Milan, Italy

Mediomatrici—Metz, France

mensor, (metator)—surveyor, architect

Mons Brisiacus—Breisach, Germany, the right bank hill seat of a Celtic prince on which the Romans built a fortress (from the Celtic brisger or waterbreak)

murmillones—very heavily-armed gladiators who depended on strength and endurance to defeat foes more suited to attacking. The tower shield gave them an edge in defense and a *gladius* gave them the ability to thrust and swing at enemies when in close range. The Murmillo were also trained to kick enemies with the thick padding worn around their legs.

mutatio, mutationes—relay station for state riders

—THE DEADLY CAESAR—

Noviomagus—Speyer, Germany
Noviodunum—Nyon, Switzerland
optimates—nobles
optio tribuni—'chosen man of the tribune' i.e. assistant to tribune
orbiculus, orbiculi—ornate rondels commonly embroidered on Late Roman clothing to denote status or wealth
paenula—a commonplace cloak
palla—rectangular woman's shawl
patronus—the head of a clan, responsible for the welfare of family members and clients, freedmen, and slaves
phaulotatous—poorest, shabby, disorganized
plectrum—pick for playing stringed instrument, allegedly invented by the Greek poetess Sappho
plumbata tribolata—short, barbed, and weighted arrow-like dart
posca—a refreshing herb-flavored mix of sour wine or vinegar with water
potestas—the legal authority/responsibility for family members, including married daughters, held by the male head of the family or clan
proskynesis—Eastern protocol of full prostration
protector domestici—imperial bodyguard
pugio—dagger of Late Roman period
puls—lentil stew
quaestor—financial, auditing, or legal counselor
quaestores parricidii—elected Republican officials responsible for investigating homicides and other capital crimes
regalis—prince
rex, reges—king
reguli—sub-kings under the barbarian reges
Rhodanus—the Rhône River
Romanitas—Roman culture, the qualities of being Roman
sagittarius, sagittarii—army archers
sagum—short traveling cloak
Saliso—Seltz, France
schola—a school, association, government department/ professional body
Senonae—Senon, Verdun, France (mistakenly translated by earlier historians as Sens, France)
sômati—with body/embodied (Greek)

spatha—standard issue sword of Late Roman military
stabulensis—a senior officer in charge of stables, particularly imperial stables
stadium, stadia—a furlong, from the Greek *stadion*, Roman measurement approximating 607 feet or 185 meters.
stola—woman's overtunic worn over the *tunica*
stilus, stili—pointed writing tool for etching into a wax tablet
strigilis, strigiles—a strigil or scraper used to clean the skin
supremus—highest, greatest
susurna—coarse blanket made from the fur or hide of an animal
taberna—tavern
taeneotic—poor quality paper sold by weight
Tenedo—Bad Zurzach, Aargau, Switzerland
tesserae—mosaic stones or dice
testudo—nickname for the lyre, often made of tortoiseshell
tiro—army cadet
Taurini—Turin, Italy
Tres Tabernae Cesaris—Saverne, France; 'The Three Shops of Caesar,' sitting at the foot of a pass through the Vosges mountain range in Alsace, France, (not to be confused with the more famous junction, Tres Tabernae, a *mutatio* on the ancient Appian Way, about 18 km from Rome, where St. Paul, was met by a band of Roman Christians (Acts 28:15). The 'shops' refer not to taverns, but to the necessary blacksmith, general store, and refreshment stop.)
Tribunci/Tribuni—Lauterbourg, France; a Roman fortress abandoned in 405 AD, on land occupied during Julius Caesar's time by the 'three-times-terrible-Triboques'
tribunus stablesianus—tribune in charge of army stables
tribunus vacans—an officer without a formal posting
tutela legitimus—trusteeship for financial affairs of an underage heir
tunica—woman's undertunic
tubicen, tubicenes—*aeneator* (horn player) who played the straight-bodied army trumpet, the tuba
Turicum—Zürich, Switzerland
Vosago Mons, Vosego Silva, Vogesus Mons—the Vosges Mountains, France

Acknowledgements

Austin N. J. E., N. B. Rankov, *Exploratio: Military & Political Intelligence in the Roman World from the Second Punic War to the Battle of Adrianople*, Routledge, London and New York, 2002

Ammianus Marcellinus, *The Later Roman Empire (AD 354-378)*, Walter Hamilton, transl. Penguin Books, London, 1986

Barnes, Timothy D., *Ammianus Marcellinus and the Representation of Historical Reality*, (Cornell Studies in Classical Philology) Cornell University Press, Ithaca, New York, 1998

Bury, J.B. *The Cambridge Medieval History*, Vol 1, Cambridge University Press, Cambridge, UK, 1923

Bowerstock, G. W. *Julian the Apostate*, Harvard University Press, Cambridge, Massachusetts, 1978

Bowerstock, G. W. *Late Antiquity: A Guide to the Postclassical World* Harvard University Press Reference Library, Harvard University Press, Harvard, Mass. 1999

Blockley, R. C., 'Constantius Gallus and Julian as Caesars,' *Latomus*, (April-June 1972,) pp. 433-468, The Society of Latin Studies of Brussels

Browning, Robert, *The Emperor Julian*, University of California Press, Berkeley, 1978

Cameron, Averil, ed. *The Cambridge Ancient History*, vol. 13, Cambridge University Press, Cambridge, England,

Clark, Gillian, *Women in Late Antiquity, Pagan and Christian Lifestyles*, Oxford University Press, Oxford, 1993

Derbyshire, David, "Roman PoW camp found at Hadrian's Wall", *The Telegraph*, August 11, 2000

Dixon Suzanne, *The Roman Family*, John Hopkins University Press, Baltimore, 1992

Drijvers, Jan Willem, David Hunt, *The Late Roman World and Its Historian*, Routledge, London and New York, 2012

Drinkwater, John F., *The Alamanni and Rome 213-496 (Caracalla to Clovis)*, Oxford University Press, Oxford, 2007

Faas, Patrick, *Around the Roman Table*, Macmillan, 2003, London

Gibbon, Edward, *The History of the Decline and Fall of the Roman Empire*, in 12 vols, J.B. Bury, ed. with an introduction by W.E.H. Lecky, Fred de Fau and Co., New York 1906, The Online Library of Liberty

Grabar, Oleg, *Late Antiquity: A Guide to the Postclassical World*, Edited by Peter Robert Lamont Brown, Belknap Press/Harvard University Press Reference Library, Cambridge, Massachusetts, 1999

Greenwood, Thomas, *(The First Book of) The History of the Germans*, (*The Barbaric Period*) Longman, Rees, Orme, and Co., Paternoster-Row, London, 1836

Johnston, Sarah Iles, *Animating Statues: A Case Study in Ritual*, Arethusa, 2008 (Project Muse, Scholarly Journals Online)

Jones, Archer, *The Art of War in the Western World*, University of Illinois Press, Urbana and Chicago, Illinois, 2000

Kagan, Kimberly, *The Eye of Command*, the University of Michigan Press, Ann Arbor, 2006

Lee, A.D., *Information and Frontiers: Roman Foreign Relations in Late Antiquity*, Cambridge University Press, Cambridge, UK, 2006

Libanius, *Julian the Emperor, Funeral Oration for Julian*, Roger Pearse, transl., Ipswich, UK, 2003,

Libanius the Sophist, *Orations* Vol. I

MacDowall, Simon, *Germanic Warrior AD 236-568*, Osprey Publishing, Oxford, England, 1996

Mathisen, Ralph W., Danuta Shanzer, *Romans, Barbarians, and the Transformation of the Roman World*, Milman, Ashgate Publishing, Farnham, England, 2011

Milman, Rev. H.H., *The History of Christianity*, John Murray, London, 1840

Potter, David S., *The Roman Empire at Bay, AD 180-395, The Routledge History of the Ancient World*, Routledge, London and New York, 2004

Rike, R.L., *Apex Omnium: Religion in the Res Gestae of Ammianus*, Thompson, E. A., *The Historical Work of Ammianus Marcellinus*, Cambridge University Press, Cambridge, UK, 1947

Todd, Malcolm, *Everyday Life of the Barbarians*, G.B. Putnam and Sons, New York, 1972

Woods, David, 'Ammianus and Eutherius,' *Acta Classica*, XLI (1998) pgs. 105-117

Woods, David, 'Ammianus versus Libanius on Barbatio's Alleged Bridge Across the Rhine' *Mnemosyne* vol. 63 (2010) pgs. 110-116

Zosimus, *New History*, Book 3, Green and Chaplin, London, 1814

Also special thanks to the moderators and community of Romanarmytalk.org, especially moderator/contributors Jasper Oorthuys and Nathan Ross.

About the Author

Q. V. Hunter's interest in classical history began with four years of high school Latin followed by university courses in ancient religions. A fascination with Late Antiquity deepened when Hunter moved to a two-hundred-year-old farmhouse near an ancient Roman colony. The farmhouse is easily reached by modern road, but also by a Roman road running more directly down to the *Colonia Equestris Noviodunum*.

Noviodunum was founded around 50 BCE as a retirement community for Julius Caesar's cavalry veterans. It's listed as the *civitas Equestrium id est Noviodunus* in the *Notitia Galliarum*, (the fourth-century directory listing all seventeen provinces of Roman Gaul.)

Noviodunum became Rome's most important colony along Lake Leman—with a forum, baths, basilica and amphitheater. Potable water came via an aqueduct running all the way from present-day Divonne, France. Noviodunum belonged to a network of settlements radiating out from Lugdunum (Lyon, France) around the Rhône Valley. Roman colonists were encouraged to supervise the Celtic Helvetii who had been transported to the area against their will after their defeat at the Battle of Bibracte in 58 BC.

Much of Roman Noviodunum was razed during Alemanni invasions in 259-260 AD, well before the period of our story, but it flourishes again today as the Swiss town of Nyon.

Hunter is married to a self-proclaimed '*Ur*-Swiss,' a descendant of those very Alemanni barbarians who settled farther north of Nyon in the Alpine lake region that gave birth to the three founding cantons of the Confederation Helvetica, i.e. Switzerland, in 1291 AD.

They have three adult children, all of whom managed to study Latin and Greek in high school before the Swiss cantonal authorities cut Classics from the state curriculum.

Printed in Poland
by Amazon Fulfillment
Poland Sp. z o.o., Wrocław